# STATES OF EMERGENCY

# STATES OF EMERGENCY

British Governments and Strikebreaking since 1919

Keith Jeffery
and
Peter Hennessy

ROUTLEDGE & KEGAN PAUL
London, Boston, Melbourne and Henley

For our parents

First published in 1983
by Routledge & Kegan Paul Ltd
39 Store Street, London WC1E 7DD,
9 Park Street, Boston, Mass. 02108, USA,
296 Beaconsfield Parade, Middle Park,
Melbourne, 3206, Australia, and
Broadway House, Newtown Road,
Henley-on-Thames, Oxon RG9 1EN
Set in 10/12pt Plantin by
Input Typesetting Ltd, London
and printed in Great Britain by
T. J. Press (Padstow) Ltd
Padstow, Cornwall

Library of Congress Cataloging in Publication Data

Jeffery, Keith.
States of emergency.
Bibliography: p.
Includes index.
1. Strikes and lockouts–Great Britain–History.
2. Labor policy–Great Britain–History.   I. Hennessy,
Peter, 1947–    .  II. Title.  III. Title: Strikebreaking
since 1919.
HD5366.J43 1983   331.89'84'0941   82-16606

ISBN 0-7100-9464-7

# Contents

# Preface

THE LITERATURE ON modern British industrial relations is vast, as is that on what has become known as the corporate state. But the greatest single lacuna both in contemporary coverage and more reflective scholarly writing is the vital, concealed area of contingency planning, in which ministers and officials try to calculate the point at which trade union demands will plunge the country into chaos and privation, and how best to mitigate the effects of stoppages in essential industries and services. Whitehall planners engaged in this task are the civilian equivalents of the military strategists who 'war-game' the 'worst case scenarios' that might arise if the country should ever find itself once more involved in a major conflict. The investigation of this hidden factor in the equation of state power versus labour power over the past sixty years is the subject of our book. The issue has rarely lost relevance since the Lloyd George coalition initiated the modern emergency organisation in response to the industrial turmoil which followed the First World War. The dilemmas faced by Lloyd George, his ministers and officials appear very real to their successors in the 1980s. The issue of union power and its naked application in areas affecting the life and limb of the citizen are widely held to have precipitated the defeat of two governments within the last decade: those of Mr Edward Heath in 1974 and Mr James Callaghan in 1979. In addition to being the first full account of this theme, we hope that our book will contribute to the administrative history of this country – a neglected side of the art – as well as adding something to the contemporary debate about the nature and scope of civil-service power in Britain.

In writing the book we have incurred numerous debts. Louis Heren, formerly deputy editor of *The Times,* had the original idea for one of us to investigate just who would 'win' if the country had to go through a re-run of the 1973-4 winter crisis. Howard

Levenson, gave advice on the legal aspects of emergency planning. Paul Arthur, Ken Brown, Tony Morris, Philip Ollerenshaw and Philip Williams read drafts of all or part of the book and offered much useful criticism. David Carlton, Tony Clayton, Geoff Ellen and Major Cyril Wilson also assisted in a variety of ways. Mary McTear gave invaluable help with typing. The bulk of the raw material of our book is drawn from official papers deposited in the Public Record Office – our favourite government department, as it is the only one which gives us files on request – but we are also indebted to those nameless ministers and civil servants in the contemporary civil contingency network without whose clandestine assistance the story could not have been completed. More overt assistance, and indeed much encouragement, came from our wives. The book is dedicated to our parents.

We should like to acknowledge the assistance of the Ulster Polytechnic and the staffs of *The Times* library and the Linen Hall Library, Belfast. Quotation from copyright material is made with the permission of the following: the Controller of Her Majesty's Stationery Office (Crown copyright papers in the Public Record Office); the editor of *The Economist* to reproduce material first published in his newspaper 3 July 1982; the Trustees of the Imperial War Museum (Wilson papers); the Earl Haig (Haig papers); and the Master and Fellows of Churchill College, Cambridge (Hankey papers). Our substantial debt to the other institutions which have kindly granted access to collections of private papers, and to the many authors whose work we have used, is recorded in the references and bibliography. Parts of our book are based on work first published elsewhere: by Keith Jeffery in the *Historical Journal* (Cambridge University Press), vol. 24, no. 2; by Peter Hennessy in *The Times*, especially a series of articles between 13 and 23 November 1979; and by both authors on a number of occasions in *The Times*. We thank the editors concerned for permission to use this material.

Keith Jeffery and Peter Hennessy
Belfast and Walthamstow

# Abbreviations

| | |
|---|---|
| AG | Adjutant-General |
| ASLEF | Amalgamated Society of Locomotive Engineers and Firemen |
| BBC | British Broadcasting Corporation |
| BEA | British European Airways |
| CCR | Civil Constabulary Reserve |
| CCU | Civil Contingencies Unit |
| CEGB | Central Electricity Generating Board |
| CIGS | Chief of the Imperial General Staff |
| COI | Central Office of Information |
| DCO | Defence Council Order |
| DMO | Director of Military Operations |
| DORA | Defence of the Realm Acts |
| EPEA | Electrical Power Engineers' Association |
| GHQ | General Headquarters |
| GOCinC | General Officer Commanding-in-Chief |
| GPO | General Post Office |
| IEC | Industrial Emergencies Committee |
| IUC | Industrial Unrest Committee |
| NUM | National Union of Mineworkers |
| NUR | National Union of Railwaymen |
| NUS | National Union of Seamen |
| OMS | Organisation for the Maintenance of Supplies |
| QMG | Quartermaster-General |
| RAF | Royal Air Force |
| REC | Regional Emergency Committee |
| REME | Royal Electrical and Mechanical Engineers |
| STC | Supply and Transport Committee |
| STO | Supply and Transport Organisation |
| TGWU | Transport and General Workers' Union |
| TUC | Trades Union Congress |
| UWC | Ulster Workers' Council |
| VSC | Volunteer Service Committee |

# I
# War and revolution

CO-ORDINATED GOVERNMENT PLANNING in Britain to counter major strikes in vital industries began during the aftermath of the First World War. Within a year of the Armistice in November 1918 the government had set up the framework of an extensive 'Supply and Transport Organisation' to secure the maintenance of essential supplies and services in the face of industrial stoppages. By 1920 it had been established as a permanent feature of modern British government. The development of this official strikebreaking machine has been conditioned by two principal factors: varying labour militancy and a general expansion of governmental functions in twentieth-century Britain. These two factors also share in its origins. While they began to assume significance before 1914, events during the First World War acted as a powerful catalyst and by 1918 the stage seemed set for major conflict between labour and government, both of which had acquired greater power and authority than ever before.

In the immediate pre-war years there were serious stoppages in the coal mining industry, on the railways and in the docks.[1] In 1911 and 1912 for the first time there were national strikes on the railways and in the mines. During both years a wave of disputes brought docks throughout the country to a standstill, culminating with the bitterly drawn-out strike in the Port of London during the summer of 1912. Mainly prompted by a fall in the value of real wages, the unprecedented scale of this unrest was facilitated by the development of nation-wide unions in each of the industries concerned. In 1908, with the inclusion of miners in north-eastern England, the Miners' Federation of Great Britain effectively became a national body. In 1910, under the leadership of Ben Tillett, twenty-six unions representing seamen, dockers and carters combined in the National Transport Workers' Federation, which became the fully-united Transport and General Workers' Union in 1922. The Amalgamated Society of Railway Servants joined with a number of smaller associations in 1913 to form the National Union of Railwaymen, although in this industry two important groups of workers – the railway clerks and the locomotive engineers and firemen – retained independent unions.

During this period many trade union activists were attracted to syndicalist ideas which began to spread from the continent and the USA in the early years of the century. The syndicalists preached a gospel of revolution through 'direct action'. They argued that only by combining in strikes, and especially a general strike, could workers overthrow the capitalist system and seize power in the state. Although revolutionary syndicalism gained relatively little support among official trade union leaders, committed as they were to constitutional methods and the promotion of labour policies through parliamentary representation, it certainly stimulated rank-and-file militancy and played a part in encouraging union amalgamations. Led by Robert Smillie of the Miners' Federation, some moves were made towards the syndicalist ideal of 'One Big Union'. In June 1914 miners, railwaymen and transport workers agreed in principle to establish a 'Triple Industrial Alliance'. Formally constituted on 9 December 1915, the Triple Alliance was created to co-ordinate industrial action on 'matters of a national character or vitally affecting a principle'. But the Alliance was only ever a loose confederation, united more by rhetoric than anything else. It had no separate organisation or headquarters. Each of the three constituent groups retained full autonomy to act on its own behalf and the Alliance's constitution provided an elaborate series of checks and balances before joint action could be taken.[2] Nevertheless, the Triple Alliance was regarded with suspicion by government and employers, who perceived its potential power more fully than they appreciated its organisational weaknesses. The Triple Alliance, which theoretically could shut down the coal mines and bring the nation's transport services to a standstill – effectively a general strike – embodied the threat of revolutionary syndicalism. The Alliance was not activated during the war, but in the unsettled months which followed the Armistice its existence was a powerful stimulant to the development of a countervailing force in the form of the Supply and Transport Organisation.

The Triple Alliance was not the only factor underlying the

creation of an official strikebreaking machine. The wave of strikes between 1910 and 1914 stimulated an increasing amount of government intervention in industrial disputes. At one end of the spectrum was the use of troops and police to escort blacklegs and to keep order, especially during the Cambrian Combine strike of 1910 in the south Wales coalfield and the railway strike of 1911. At the other end was the spread of officially encouraged 'Joint Boards' in a number of industries and the work of the Chief Industrial Conciliation Officer, Sir George Askwith. But the government had no 'labour policy' as such, neither was there any suggestion of an organised scheme to mitigate the effects of serious disputes. Indeed, the basic administrative framework enabling such a scheme did not exist until the First World War. The demands of 'total' war precipitated an administrative revolution in Britain and central government assumed wide powers of supervision and control over many, if not most, areas of national life.[3] New departments of state were set up. The first of these was the Ministry of Munitions in May 1915. Under Lloyd George's vigorous command the Ministry recruited 'experts', mostly businessmen, from outside the civil service, assumed responsibility for the supply of the finished product, and established an extensive regional network of Area Offices and management boards throughout the whole country. Other new departments followed, particularly after Lloyd George became Prime Minister in December 1916: shipping, labour, food and national service. Along with existing ministries, such as the Board of Trade, they achieved almost total control of the domestic sinews of war. Through the creation of a central apparatus to secure the supply of essential goods and services in wartime, a precedent was established for the provision of a similar function in peacetime, albeit in a less highly developed form. Accompanying his administrative reforms, Lloyd George also brought 'new men' into government at the highest level. One of the most able of these was Sir Eric Geddes, who had been general manager of the North Eastern Railway before the war. Recruited by Lloyd George to the Ministry of Munitions, Geddes later successively became First Lord of the Admiralty and a member of the Imperial War Cabinet. He was a man of exceptional power and administrative ability with the make, as Lloyd George remarked, of a powerful railway locomotive.[4] Following the war, as Minister of Transport, he was to be the guiding force behind the Supply and Transport Organisation.

The general increase of central authority during the war had an effect on both sides of industry. While the government took direct control of some sectors, such as coal-mining, the railways and munitions production, it also sought general co-operation from the labour movement as a whole in order to provide for the central and ordered mobilisation of the domestic labour force behind the national war effort. Not only were parliamentary Labour leaders brought into the government itself for the first time – Arthur Henderson, for example, became President of the Board of Education in Asquith's coalition Cabinet in May 1915 – but trade union officials, both national and local, were drawn into negotiations and agreements concerning the most efficient production and distribution of essential wartime supplies. The government tackled the problem of industrial disputes with the 1915 Munitions of War Act, which established compulsory arbitration procedures and effectively made strikes illegal in war industries. Following the report of the Whitley Committee on Industrial Conciliation in 1917 the contacts between workers and employers in many industries were formalised by the establishment of joint 'Whitley' councils which furnished the opportunity for continuous consultation between both sides. During the latter part of the war and the immediate post-war period some seventy-three councils were set up in various industries and civil departments, some of which still survive today. The wartime partnership between workers, employers and government brought with it an increased status for the trade unions. It also gave a considerable boost to union membership which rose from 3,416,00 in 1913 to 6,533,000 in 1919. Combined no doubt with simple patriotism, it also produced a relative degree of industrial peace. Working days lost from industrial disputes in 1915–18 averaged less than half those lost in 1911–14.[5]

Wartime industrial relations, however, were not all sweetness and light. The 'compact between unions and government'[6] muted the full expression of labour grievances and stimulated the emergence of unofficial union leaders in a widespread shop-stewards' movement. The shop-stewards demonstrated their power in February 1915, when there was a major stoppage of engineers on 'Red Clydeside'. The following July 200,000 miners in south Wales came out on strike. Throughout the war grumbling discontent continued in these areas, both of which had long been notorious as centres of labour militancy with frequent, often violent, outbursts of industrial unrest. More worrying for the government was the wave of disputes which beset the country in the summer of 1918. These were limited by neither industry nor region. Cotton workers in Lancashire, electrical engineers in Birmingham, munitions workers in London and the Midlands, railwaymen in the West Country all came out on strike. Most alarming of all was the London police strike in August when 10,000 of the 19,000 Metropolitan Police failed to report for duty. The government acted swiftly. The Commissioner of the Metropolitan Police was sacked and replaced by Sir Nevil Macready, then Adjutant-General in the War Office.[7] Although the right to form a union, upon which the policemen had struck, was not conceded, the police were granted an immediate pay rise and persuaded to return to work within a very few days. Lloyd George remarked afterwards that the country 'was nearer to Bolshevism that day than at any other time since'.[8] Official reaction to the other strikes was equally emphatic. The dispute in the munitions industry was broken by threatening the strikers with military service, and when in September railwaymen on the Great Western and sections of the London North Western Railways stopped work, troops were at once sent in to run the trains. Sir Henry Wilson, Chief of the Imperial General Staff (CIGS), thought that such an unequivocal response was absolutely necessary, since the strike was 'really a challenge to the Government of the country'.[9]

Perhaps the most influential factor in the official reaction to strikes, both during the war and in the years which followed, was the lurking fear that industrial unrest was simply the precursor of political revolution. Events on the continent, and especially in Russia, gave little cause for comfort. The Russian revolutions of 1917 presented a frightening example of what could happen to a great empire if matters got out of control. The February Revolution had been sufficient to trouble Lord Milner. 'I fear', he wrote to Lloyd George, 'the time is very near at hand, when we shall have to take some strong steps to stop the "rot" in this country, unless we wish to "follow Russia" into impotence & dissolution.'[10] By 1918 and 1919 the spread of revolutionary feeling and social unrest throughout Europe raised the unpleasant possibility that Britain itself might suffer violent revolution. This threat was taken seriously in some quarters of the government. One rough index of official concern lies in the work of Sir Basil Thomson and his successors. Thomson was Assistant Commissioner (CID) of the Metropolitan Police from 1913 to 1919, when he was in charge of the Special Branch, and 'Director of Intelligence' from 1919 to 1921. Early in 1918 he began to issue a fortnightly report to the Cabinet on 'pacificism and revolutionary organisations in the United Kingdom and morale abroad'. When Thomson moved to the newly established Home Office Directorate of Intelligence in April 1919, this was changed into a weekly 'report on revolutionary organisations in the United Kingdom'. Sometimes of considerable length, these reports contained details of numerous apparently seditious organisations and persons. Responsibility for the reports reverted to the Special Branch after Thomson's dismissal in November 1921, but they continued to be issued weekly at least until October 1924.[11] Sometime in the late 1920s the reports appear to have been replaced by a 'Civil Security Intelligence Summary'. Reflecting by this time the almost total absence of fears of imminent revolution, this summary was circulated much less frequently. By 1933 it had become a quarterly production.[12]

But the possibility of revolution in Britain following the First World War lay not so much in the likelihood of armed insurrection or a workers' *coup* of some sort, but in the more subtle, and to some more insidious, challenge posed to the state by an extra-governmental power-centre – the trade unions. The unprecedented strength of trade unionism after the war revived pre-war syndicalist ideas, and in particular the notion of concerted nation-wide action in a general strike. Since the development of wartime collectivism had to a very great extent placed the government, rather than the owners, in control of industry, labour ambitions readily resolved into direct confrontation between unions and government. In these circumstances the line between industrial and political power was fine indeed. It seemed that the labour movement might acquire extensive political power, not in the formal electoral sense, but from simple *force majeure*. Problems were posed, therefore, concerning the ultimate legitimacy of the state to rule.

This issue was sharply perceived by Lloyd George during an interview with the leaders of the Triple Alliance in 1919:

'Gentlemen, [said the Prime Minister] you have fashioned, in the Triple Alliance of the unions represented by you, a most powerful instrument. I feel bound to tell you that in our opinion we are at your mercy. The Army is disaffected and cannot be relied upon. Trouble has occurred already in a number of camps. We have just emerged from a great war and the people are eager for the reward of their sacrifices, and we are in no position to satisfy them. In these circumstances, if you carry out your threat and strike, then you will defeat us.'

'But if you do so,' went on Mr. Lloyd George, 'have you weighed the consequences? The strike will be in defiance of the Government of this country and by its very success will precipitate a constitutional crisis of the first importance. For, if a force arises in the State which is stronger than the State itself, then it must be ready to take on the functions of the State itself, or withdraw and accept the authority of the State. Gentlemen,' asked the Prime Minister quietly, 'have you considered, and if you have, are you ready?'

Robert Smillie, who related this incident to Aneurin Bevan, commented: 'From that moment on we were beaten and we knew we were.'[13] Perhaps so, but what emerges most significantly from the meeting is not so much the rout of the unions as the Welsh Wizard's brilliant negotiating power. Lloyd George's opinion, as presented to the Triple Alliance, was that a co-ordinated large-scale strike posed a direct challenge to the traditional foundations of political power in Britain. It is questionable, however, whether the post-war industrial unrest was in any real sense 'revolutionary'. It is certainly evident from Smillie's reaction that he and his colleagues had hitherto been blissfully unaware of the revolutionary implications of their threatened action. Subsequent prime ministers have made assertions similar to those of Lloyd George that particular industrial stoppages have constituted an attack on the established authority of the state: Baldwin in 1926, Attlee in 1948, Wilson in 1966, Heath in 1974. Subsequent trade union leaders, too, have been taken aback to discover that what they have regarded merely as trade disputes have had such serious implications. But ignorance does not necessarily infer innocence, and it could be argued that once the Triple Alliance leaders, vividly prompted by Lloyd George, realised the full impact of 'direct action', they drew back from the brink. From Smillie's account this seems to have been the case. In the aftermath of the First World War trade unions and Labour Party alike certainly sought radical change in the political, social and economic fabric of the country. But *revolution* implies particular characteristics of pace and procedure. In the political context the phenomenon is commonly both sudden and violent. These two factors are, of course, related. The rate of change is inevitably affected by the means employed. The chief catalyst in the revolutionary's armoury is violent force, and this is the one most frequently applied to greatest effect. Yet the 'revolution', if it can be called that, which the British labour leaders desired was to be neither violent nor particularly speedy. Not only were they for the most part gradualist in their approach, but they also unequivocally rejected violence as a legitimate tool of political expression.

The fact that the established labour leadership was itself not revolutionary does not entirely preclude the possibility that Britain as a whole may have been in a 'revolutionary condition'. Revolutions require comrades as well as commissars. It has been argued that such revolutionaries as there were failed miserably to take advantage of Britain's post-war weakness: 'confronted with the greatest revolutionary opportunity in generations, the socialist movement showed itself largely unaware of its existence.'[14] Even so, it remains debatable whether this 'revolutionary opportunity' existed in any appreciable sense at all. One political scientist has suggested that the society ripe for revolution is characterised by four main features: social and political decay; the alienation of public feeling from the state; general social frustration or 'cramp'; and the failure of pre-revolutionary conservative reformers.[15] Post-war Britain met none of these criteria to any significant extent. Although the Puritan might find ample evidence of social decay in the 'Gay Twenties', the sociologist may be less convinced. Social expectations and mobility were progressively improved both by a series of domestic reforms which presaged the advances following the Second World War and the development of new economic opportunities. While Britain's traditional staple industries – textiles, coal-mining, heavy engineering – declined between the wars, the effect of this was to some degree balanced by expansion in other sectors of the economy, such as electrical engineering, motor car manufacturing and service industries. On the political side Britain's much-vaunted constitutional flexibility went a long way towards accommodating the effects of universal suffrage. The 1920s and 1930s saw no massive alienation of public feelings from the state. Turn-out at general elections, for example, although less than 60 per cent in 1918, did not fall below 70 per cent at any succeeding election. The rise of the Labour Party and the two inter-war Labour governments (albeit minority) did much to relieve such political 'cramp' as existed. Finally, if there was a failure of conservative reformers – and conservative in this context would include Liberals as well as Tories – it was not perceived by the electorate. At no election between the wars was the combined Conservative and Liberal vote less than sixty per cent. At the other end of the political spectrum, the Communist vote never exceeded 0.3 per cent of the United Kingdom total. Revolution, perhaps, is not to the British taste.

To assert that there was no great likelihood of a British revolution in the years after the First World War, or at any time since, is not to suggest that there were no revolutionaries, or that some politicians and officials did not believe revolution to be imminent. Indeed, members of successive governments seem at times to have taken the threat of violent revolution more seriously than the potential revolutionaries themselves. But even Sir Basil Thomson, a man not generally noted for sanguine opinions, had to admit in January 1920 that: 'the minority who would like to see a sudden and violent revolution is ridiculously small.'[16] Yet during what one historian has called 'the 1911–21 crisis of the state'[17] an underlying fear of revolution sharpened the official response to strikes. One modern legacy of this period is the government's strikebreaking machine. Originally established as the Supply and Transport Organisation, after the Second World War it became known as the Emergencies Organisation, and today it exists as the Civil Contingencies Unit. Throughout its life this organisation has, on the one hand, demonstrated the growing power and responsibility of central government in Britain and its assumption of an obligation to secure the nation's 'essentials of life'. On the other, with varying force and by no means always explicitly, it has illustrated the concern of successive governments that industrial unrest might be the tip of a revolutionary iceberg.

## 2
# Establishing the Supply and Transport Organisation January 1919 – March 1920

AS IN THE first year of war, so in the first year of peace Red Clydeside was in the van of 'direct action'. Faced with the problem of absorbing demobilised soldiers into the Glasgow workforce, the Clyde Workers' Committee demanded a 40-hour week. On 27 January their call for a general strike met with almost complete success in Glasgow. Mass demonstrations spilled over into street violence. 'The King', Bonar Law told Lloyd George in Paris, 'is in a funk about the labour situation and is talking about the . . . danger of a revolution.' Law's own reaction was less extreme and he thought the position was 'much exaggerated by the press'.[1] Nevertheless, infantry and tanks were rushed in and machine-gun posts set up in the City Chambers. A dozen of the strike leaders were arrested, and two, Willie Gallacher and Emanuel Shinwell, were subsequently convicted of 'inciting to riot'. The strikers, though shaken by the government's tough policy, held out for a fortnight before returning to work in mid-February, the prospect of a 40-hour week as remote as ever. The government had good cause to feel satisfied at their handling of the strike. It seemed thereafter that the heart had been knocked out of militant Glasgow trade unionism.

Events in Scotland illustrated the negative and coercive aspects of the official response to industrial unrest, but a dispute closer to the centre of power promoted the establishment of a central organisation to deal with strikes. On 4 February 1919 the War Cabinet,[2] faced with a tube and omnibus strike in London and the prospect of an electricians' stoppage, appointed an Industrial Unrest Committee (IUC) 'to make the necessary arrangements for dealing with any situation that might arise from industrial unrest both at the present moment and in the future.' It had 'power to give decisions which did not involve important questions of principle.'[3] Chaired by the Home Secretary, Edward Shortt, the committee comprised the President of the Board of Trade, Sir Albert Stanley, the Minister of Labour, Sir Robert Horne, the Secretary for Scotland, Robert Munro, together with 'representatives of the Admiralty and War Office'. The departmental composition of the committee is understandable enough, but in terms of personnel it was quite undistinguished. Shortt, a competent routine administrator, had been moved from the Irish to the Home Office because he was unable to co-operate with the Viceroy, Lord French. Perhaps his main value to the government was his skill as a parliamentary performer. Faced by domestic unrest he tended to be alarmist. Stanley, one of Lloyd George's 'business' appointments in December 1916, was by the beginning of 1919 'much too weak and flabby a man for the difficult task which confronts a President of the Board of Trade under present conditions'.[4] He resigned in May 1919. Horne was a more distinguished, if docile, character. As Minister of Labour between January 1919 and March 1920 he also showed a tendency to be alarmist. He was later promoted to the Board of Trade and the Exchequer. As Chancellor, in the Bank of England's opinion, he acted most suitably as nothing more than Montagu Norman's parliamentary mouthpiece. Munro seems to have earned employment principally from the happy coincidence that he was both Scottish and a loyal Coalition Liberal.

Despite these weaknesses, the IUC quickly set to work and appointed five sub-committees to deal with public utility services, transport, 'protection', communications and electric works. Interdepartmental arrangements were made with the Ministry of Food and the Coal Control Department to ensure the maintenance of essential services. In consultation with the aptly-named Mr Sparkes, representing the electrical industry employers, the IUC also planned to enlist volunteers to run power stations, the Admiralty agreeing to provide 650 naval ratings as stokers.[5] Although the London transport strike soon ended and the electricians' stoppage never materialised, the government was almost immediately faced with the much more serious possibility of a Triple Alliance stoppage. In February 1919 the pre-war alliance was re-formed and demands were presented for higher wages and shorter working hours. The chief fear in the government's mind was that concerted Triple Alliance action would have the effect, if not the nature, of a general strike. The main impetus behind labour militancy lay in the coal mines. In order to defuse the mining dispute, Lloyd George appointed Sir John Sankey to head a Royal Commission of trade unionists and mine owners to inquire into the industry.

In the meantime the IUC continued conscientiously to perfect its organisation. An order of priority for coal distribution was worked out with the requirements of the food industry at the top and household needs at the bottom. The protection sub-committee drew up a scheme for the military to guard essential services and the Food Controller was instructed to prepare for a return to wartime rationing.[6] Although the government had extensive emergency powers under various wartime Defence of the Realm Acts (DORA), which would not lapse at least until the 'official' end of the war, in March 1919 the cabinet considered further Draconian measures to defeat the Triple Alliance. Had it passed into law, the Strikes (Exceptional Measures) Bill would have given the government power to close public houses, control banks to prevent payment of strike pay, confiscate trade union funds and make it illegal to take part in a Triple Alliance strike.[7] The immediate emergency passed, however, and the question of replacing DORA with permanent peacetime legislation did not arise until the following spring.

When Sankey reported in June it was apparent that the Commission had divided on predictable lines. There was no common ground between the mine owners and the unions. Sankey himself tipped the balance marginally in the unions' favour by recommending, with them, state ownership. But because of the lack of unanimity Lloyd George rejected nationalisation. The only gain for the miners was a decrease in the working day from eight to seven hours. Government control of the mines was to continue. The effect of this on the miners was hardly dramatic. They seemed resigned to accept what was in effect a victory for the employers and their militancy of the spring had certainly ebbed away by the late summer. The outcome of the Sankey Commission left the miners both exhausted and dispirited. Only in Yorkshire was there a spark of defiance. In July-August they struck for over a month. In order to maintain the pit-head pumps, the IUC drafted some 900 naval ratings to Yorkshire. But within three days Lloyd George, evidently unconvinced of the committee's capabilities, sent Sir Eric Geddes north to take charge.[8] However successful the IUC was at administration and planning, clearly an essential component of strikebreaking was the ability to take swift and effective executive action. This was amply illustrated during the police strike of August 1919. Although the strike was more widely spread throughout the country than in the 1918 stoppage, support for the action was much less. The pay rise of the previous year, coupled with the government's adamantine refusal to consider unionisation – a policy implacably enforced by Sir Nevil Macready in London – had the desired effect of undermining police passions. The 2,364 police strikers were dismissed immediately and never re-instated. In London barely a tenth of the number who had struck in 1918 did so again the following year, but in Liverpool 50 per cent of the force came out. This, asserted Macready, was 'due to the presence of many Irishmen in the force, a class of men who are always apt to be carried away by any wave of enthusiasm'.[9] When serious rioting broke out the army were sent in with bayonets fixed to keep the peace and a battleship was posted to the Mersey, no doubt to cow the masses. The show of force succeeded. Order was restored and the police thereafter stayed loyal, even in 1926.

For the greater part of 1919 the army played a major role in contingency planning. This was co-ordinated by GHQ Great Britain, which had been established early in the war to direct military organisation at home. Gradually it had increased its functions to include general responsibility for action 'in aid of the civil power' and it supplemented the civil authorities in certain areas, notably that of intelligence-gathering. It had also developed an independent wireless communications system and acquired extensive control over domestic transport, both civil and military. The command, therefore, was well placed almost alone to meet three of the IUC's five main needs: transport, protection and communications. Early in 1919 the Commander-in-Chief, Great Britain, had been ordered, on Cabinet instructions, to prepare his troops to assist the civil power 'in the event of a national strike of a revolutionary character' and it soon seemed that GHQ Great Britain's principal peacetime function was simply to be an appendage to the government's embryonic strikebreaking organisation. When Sir Douglas Haig took over the command from Sir William Robertson in April 1919 he found that his predecessor's chief anxiety was 'labour trouble'[10]

This had unattractive implications for the army. As Lord Ironside put it, 'for a soldier there is no more distasteful duty than that of aiding the Civil Power.'[11] Both GHQ Great Britain and the War Office were somewhat reluctant partners in the official preparations to meet industrial unrest. Apart from including 'distasteful' duties, the development of a strikebreaking apparatus cut across the War

Office's own plans for the post-war organisation and training of the army. But the army could not entirely resist pressures from civil departments. At the beginning of March 1919 the existing intelligence personnel in the United Kingdom, who during the war had been primarily concerned with assessing military morale, were instructed to gather information about labour disputes, with the condition that 'no form of Military espionage should be carried on in any civilian matters.' Material was to be obtained from, 'and a liaison established with, Chief Constables, large employers of labour, Branches of the Labour Ministry, and any other well-informed sources approachable without giving rise to any unwarranted suspicion or misunderstanding'. There was to be a full interchange of information with other government departments, especially the Home Office and Scotland Yard.[12] Sir Basil Thomson was delighted to acquire an additional source of information, but when he went to see Haig in June 1919 the Field Marshal put the army's point of view most clearly: 'I said that I would not authorise any men being used as spies. Officers must act straightforwardly & as Englishmen.' Haig would have no truck with 'hateful' espionage and he was determined that Thomson's intelligence machinery must work 'independently of the Army and its leaders'.[13]

Contingency plans, nevertheless, had to be prepared in less delicate spheres of activity. At the beginning of September Haig called a high-level meeting of the seven GOCinCs of the army home commands 'to discuss our plans for dealing with a General Strike'. These were 'very complete' and the generals assured Haig that their plans were 'quite ready to put into force at any moment'. Naturally the main emphasis was on protection. Arrangements had been made to guard railways, petrol depots and other 'essential stores'. There was also a programme for assisting the Food Ministry with lorries, drivers and supply officers to organise convoy services. Haig impressed upon the meeting that in any industrial disturbance troops must be used with discretion. He wisely insisted that they 'should only appear when the civil authorities required their help. As soon as the necessity for action was over the troops must at once be withdrawn out of sight.' Haig finally stressed that troops must be armed and 'act as soldiers. It is not their duty to act as policemen as they did in the police strike recently in Liverpool.'[14]

GHQ Great Britain's extensive emergency plans did not meet with wholehearted approval in the War Office. In August 1919 the

Quarter-Master-General (QMG), Sir Travers Clarke, drew attention to the unsatisfactorily wide distribution of Home Service troops in Great Britain. He desired a more economical concentration of forces, but noted that any such move was deprecated by GHQ Home Forces 'on the grounds that present distribution is necessary to assist in suppressing civil disorder'. On 24 September Clarke warmed to his subject: 'It seems to me', he wrote, 'that we shall not arrive at a definite solution of this matter . . . until the policy with regard to strikes is settled.' He argued that the army was in the absurd position of maintaining troops in particular locations simply in order to afford rapid assistance to the civil power in the event of serious unrest. 'The whole situation', he declared, was dominated by 'preparation for a possible civil disturbance.' He believed that the question should be brought before the Cabinet in the hope that the army could be relieved of these onerous duties and settle down in its 'peace stations' and revert to 'normal' functions and training. He thought that the special provision currently being made for aiding the civil power should cease forthwith: 'We are maintaining a staff at G.H.Q., Great Britain, to deal with nothing but civil disturbances, and so long as this staff is in existence so long will the position of the soldier remain that of an immediate reinforcement to the civil power in these areas of unrest.'[15] But any hope of a quick return to pre-war conditions was dashed by the railway strike which broke out suddenly at the end of September 1919.

Angered by a threatened reduction in wages, the railwaymen struck at midnight on Friday 26 September. Since the Cabinet at first thought that the rest of the Triple Alliance would also come out, preparations were made with a general strike in mind. The IUC was disbanded and replaced by a stronger 'Strike Committee' with extensive executive powers.[16] Sir Eric Geddes, with a growing reputation as a successful 'trouble-shooter', was unhesitatingly appointed by Lloyd George to chair the committee. The services' representation was upgraded to include Walter Long, First Lord of the Admiralty, and Winston Churchill, Secretary for War and Air. Only Edward Shortt survived from the IUC. Sir Eric Geddes's brother – Sir Auckland – had replaced Stanley at the Board of Trade. Included also were the Food Controller, George Roberts, and the Minister of Shipping, Sir John Maclay. It is clear that from the start Geddes and Churchill dominated the committee. Haig noted in his diary that Geddes made 'a most business-like Chairman' and that Churchill was 'most energetic & talked more than anyone'.[17]

The Strike Committee met for the first time just seven hours before the stoppage was due to begin. It continued to meet daily until 7 October, two days after the railwaymen had resumed work. The two main priorities were the maintenance of food supplies and 'protection'. To meet the former the Food Controller was instructed to activate at once his comprehensive scheme of food distribution. Rationing was re-introduced and the Food Department was given power (under DORA) to commandeer lorries and issue an appeal for volunteer drivers. For the latter the committee turned to the War Office. Churchill blandly assured his colleagues that the troops in Great Britain were of excellent quality and 'very well distributed'. The arrangement, he asserted, which had been in force since the beginning of the year (to the QMG's dismay) was that 'a certain number of troops were kept at particular centres so that they could be easily moved to points where they were most needed in an emergency.'[18] On the afternoon of 27 September the protection sub-committee ordered the army to secure 'all the important Railways, Power Stations, etc.' against 'destruction or violence'. Fearing that he might not have sufficient men to meet all possible contingencies, Haig urged that companies of Special Constables be formed to relieve the army. But his request was not immediately taken up and in any case the strike passed off peacefully. Although 23,000 troops were deployed on protection duties, a further 30,000, held back as a mobile reserve, remained in barracks.[19]

The Strike Committee held high hopes that the emergency organisation would be widely reinforced by civilian volunteers. An important aspect of the government's strikebreaking strategy – and one which was to become increasingly so – was the attempt to win over public opinion on the side of order and stability. Behind this lay the strong implication that all 'loyal' citizens should close ranks in the face of industrial blackmail. 'National starvation and the ruin of industry', affirmed a proposed hand-bill, 'can only be averted if every citizen does his part,' and volunteers were to be enlisted to assist on the railways, drive motor lorries, save petrol, become Special Constables, help with wireless communications and work in civil aviation.[20] Superficially such a policy held evident attractions since an appeal for patriotic volunteers would at the same time both emphasise publicly the gravity of industrial unrest – the underlying threat of revolution – and also serve to undermine working class solidarity by subordinating sectional loyalties to that of the state. But a dramatic call for the nation to rally round might have quite the opposite effect. Four years of war had blunted the emotional effectiveness of patriotic rhetoric. A call to 'King and Country', moreover, could be interpreted by the revolutionary-minded as a last desperate attempt by the ruling class to underpin their power and a sure sign that revolution was possible. Besides, an endeavour to mobilise national sentiment against the unions could have a polarising effect and, far from fragmenting the working class, might indeed consolidate it. This would be rendered all the more likely if the government made extensive and overt use of servicemen to bolster up its emergency organisation.

It is evident that ministers and officials were aware of this dilemma. When considering assistance from the armed services, for example, the Strike Committee agreed that only volunteers should be employed 'in any work that might be regarded as strike breaking', such as the driving of trains or the care of signal boxes. These men were to be provided where possible 'with plain clothes by the agency employing them'. In the event, the total numbers involved were relatively small. Only 4,000 men out of some 6,000 volunteers were actually used.[21] Another sensitive question concerned the preservation of law and order. Although the Strike Committee instinctively relied on the army to provide adequate protection, there were obvious objections to a general dependence on military manpower. Not only, as Haig had made clear, did soldiers dislike acting in aid of the civil power, but politicians also feared that the widespread use of troops might well inflame passions. The most acceptable solution to the problem (if not, however, the most immediately practicable) was to strengthen the civil police, primarily through the enlistment of additional Special Constables.

Historically the enrolment of Special Constables had been a quick and convenient means of augmenting the forces of law and order. Under the Special Constables Act of 1831 local JPs had been empowered to swear in temporary officers to meet specific threats of public disorder. In 1914 this procedure had been systematised to permit the recruitment of constables to serve for the duration of the war. The experiment proved such a success that in 1919 the Home Office urged local police forces to reconstitute and strengthen the Special Constabulary with a view to maintaining it as a permanent reserve, 'available for emergency duty when the need arises'. A point in the Specials' favour was their relative reliability. Recruited mostly from the middle class, they could largely be depended upon to remain loyal at times of serious unrest.[22] Certainly their use greatly mitigated the worst effects of the police strikes in 1918 and 1919. On the outbreak of the railway strike, therefore, the government saw considerable advantage in reinforcing the police with Special Constables. On Monday 29 September, two days after the strike had begun, an official appeal was published in the press inviting volunteers for the Special Constabulary. But the response was disappointing. As Edward Shortt explained later there was no great public enthusiasm due 'to the absence of any disorder at this stage'.[23] Paradoxically this very factor increased the pressure on the police since the protection sub-committee was readily persuaded that it would be more politic to replace military guards with civilian. In any case GHQ Great Britain were unhappy with their forces being widely scattered in small units guarding vulnerable points and railways throughout the country.

On Thursday 2 October the protection sub-committee decided on further action. Telegrams were sent out that evening to all Chief Constables instructing them 'to take active steps for the increase of the Special Constabulary'. But the following day, before the instruction can have had much effect, the whole question of protection came before the full Strike Committee. The committee were told the military objections to furnishing detached guards and the consequent 'urgent necessity' for expanding the Special Constabulary. 'In view of the possibility of a general strike of all Trade Unions in the immediate future', the committee then agreed 'that it was essential to set up at once a new organisation, to be entitled "The Citizen Guard", to meet all contingencies and to relieve the military forces as far as possible.' To expedite the formation of this new body the committee accepted an offer from Churchill to supply experienced naval and military personnel to act as recruiting officers. Within twenty-four hours they had begun work and by Sunday 5 October progress reports were coming in from a number of counties and boroughs where local recruiting committees had been formed. In some areas, however, including Norfolk, Durham and the City of London, the authorities objected to the new scheme and preferred to continue to concentrate their efforts on the existing Special Constabulary. This attitude seems to have stemmed from an understandable confusion as to the precise nature and function of the Citizen Guard. When the protection sub-committee came to discuss this matter, it appeared that no one had given this much thought. Since the Citizen Guards were to be sworn in as Special Constables and placed under the control of Chief Constables, there was in fact no appreciable difference between them and the existing organisation. The new title, it seemed, had simply been chosen 'as it was believed that this name would prove a stimulus to recruiting'.[24]

But this notion was never put to the test. On 5 October the government settled the strike on the railwaymen's terms and the formation of the Citizen Guard was indefinitely suspended. The future of the organisation was examined by the Strike Committee on 6 October. After considerable discussion it was generally agreed that the scheme should be placed 'on a permanent and comprehensive basis'.[25] The committee's proposal, however, did not go up to the Cabinet until the end of the month, by which time the Home Secretary had considered the matter more carefully. In a Cabinet memorandum he noted that the new force was viewed with some suspicion, especially in 'industrial districts' where 'it is supposed that the Guard will be of a semi-military description and will be armed, and it is useless to attempt to explain that it is merely another form of Special Constabulary and intended for purely police duties.' Virtually every local authority had reported that the desired objects could be best obtained simply by expanding and strengthening the Special Constabulary. Shortt then went on to examine the crucial question of recruitment and laid down guide-lines which would have to be met if an emergency force was to be in any way broadly based within the community:

If men – many of whom are Trades Unionists – are to be induced to give their services for the purpose of protection of life and property in time of emergency – which of course means in time of labour trouble – it is absolutely necessary that four principles should be made clear beyond the possibility of any misunderstanding: – *Firstly*, that the organisation is purely a civil and not in any sense a military one;

*Secondly*, that the main object of having such an organisation is to avoid the necessity of calling in the military to preserve order and to protect life and property;

*Thirdly*, that the organisation is entirely local and is under the direction and control of the local police authorities;

*Fourthly*, that it is in no sense an organisation for strike breaking.[26]

Shortt undoubtedly reflected Home Office and police thinking when he stressed the difficulties of creating what would today be called a 'third force' – however limited in function – to fill the gap between police and army in times of civil disorder. The formation of such a body certainly ran directly counter to the strong tradition of British common-law policing. Shortt chose to remain within that tradition. He recommended that the Cabinet drop the idea of a Citizen Guard and concentrate instead on reinforcing the existing Special Constabulary. This the Cabinet did, not so much from a thoughtful appreciation of the nature of British policing, as from simple pragmatism. For sound political reasons the Cabinet were reluctant to indulge publicly in contingency preparations. In any case there had been little disorder during the railway strike and absolutely none immediately in prospect. The establishment of a new force, moreover, would undoubtedly cost money and, as is evident from the continually gloomy meetings of the Cabinet Finance Committee, the whole thrust of governmental activity at the time was towards retrenchment.[27] Indeed, national economy was to become an increasingly important factor dominating Cabinet discussions and influencing decisions on all manner of subjects.

In the immediate aftermath of the railway strike, however, ministers and officials were too busy congratulating each other to worry overmuch about economy. 'The Government's organisation', enthused Sir Maurice Hankey, 'fairly knocked the strikers endways.'[28] The day before the stoppage ended Haig recorded that food reserves had hardly been reduced and the only worry was a shortage of coal.[29] But the strike had lasted for only eight days and Geddes believed that an extended stoppage would have posed serious problems. On 6 October he proposed that some nucleus of the existing emergency organisation should be continued, 'in order that the machinery constructed for the purpose of grappling with the emergency might again be set in motion in the event of similar, or more serious, industrial crises arising in the future.' He also urged that a record should be compiled of the work done during the railway strike, 'specifying the defects brought to light and embodying the recommendations of the committee with a view to remedying those defects.' The Strike Committee agreed and on 7 October empowered Geddes to recommend that the War Cabinet establish a new 'National Emergency Committee'. It was the last time the Strike Committee met, and was something of a family occasion with only the Geddes brothers and the Food Controller present. A week later the War Cabinet set up a new Cabinet committee to 'take over the functions of the Industrial Unrest Committee and . . . entrusted with the executive powers of the War Cabinet Strike Committee'. The new body was instructed to perfect the machinery for meeting emergencies and prepare a critical report of the Strike Committee's work. It was called 'The Supply and Transport Committee' and comprised the Minister of Transport (Sir Eric Geddes) in the chair, along with the Home Secretary, the President of the Board of Trade, the Food Controller, the Minister of Labour and the Shipping Controller.[30] The service ministers were not included, probably because of their extreme reluctance to take on duties in aid of the civil power. But when Churchill and Long later protested to the Cabinet how little assistance they could offer, Lloyd George neatly invited them 'to associate themselves personally in the work of the Supply and Transport Committee'.[31] Paradoxically they were thus better placed to defend their departmental interests and resist attempts to increase the services' share in the emergency organisation.

The military lessons of the railway strike were initially made clear in a number of reports submitted to the War Office from GHQ Great Britain. In his overall assessment, Sir Douglas Haig emphasised the importance of comprehensive forward planning. At the onset of the strike his troops had been in a 'condition of organised readiness' and it was thought that this had 'an important influence in the quiet attitude of the strikers'. His main concern, however, lay with the future and in particular the general principles underlying military aid to the civil power and the relative functions of police and army. It had hitherto been laid down, observed Haig, that it was the primary duty of the *police* 'to maintain the King's Peace' but that this principle had been 'departed from in many instances in the several strikes that have taken place this year'. Both naval and military personnel had been used 'to carry out duties which do not correctly appertain to those services'. 'The real reason', explained Haig, 'underlying this departure from accustomed practice was doubtless the consideration that, with the exception of

London, the Police Forces throughout the country were insufficient
to cope with a new condition of things.' Haig's solution was to
supplement the police immediately with a Citizen Guard. He concluded his report with a warning as to the future weakness of the
army at home. Assuming that post-war demobilisation would continue as planned, home forces would shortly be reduced to 82
battalions which, 'in the event of serious industrial unrest developing . . . would be inadequate to meet all the demands likely to be
made on it.'[32] Haig firmly put his finger on the two great problems
of 'internal protection' which more than any others exercised the
War Office in the immediate aftermath of the Great War: the actual
responsibilities of the army during periods of industrial unrest and
the prevailing shortage of troops which gravely curtailed the ability
to meet any domestic responsibilities whatsoever.

The specific topics of military communications and intelligence
were dealt with in separate reports. The communications report
emphasised the theme of military insufficiency. During the strike
there was a shortage of signals personnel and the army had been
obliged to recruit civilian volunteers. The wireless stations themselves had been found wanting both in numbers and power. To
meet civil unrest in the future it was proposed that preparations
should be made to cope with severe rioting and sabotage. Among
the expedients suggested to meet this were cars manned by armed
parties and an extension of the existing Air Ministry and Home
Office aerial post system. It was considered that 'private owners of
Pigeons should be approached throughout the country, and a
scheme prepared to utilise their services if necessary'. There was
also a plaintive request that in an emergency officers 'should have
the right to use public call telephones without payment'. On a more
mundane level the report recommended that wireless stations be
retained at all Commands on a 'care and maintenance' basis. It was
calculated that the cadres required for this would include 58 wireless
operators, 39 fitters and 12 electricians. But here demobilisation cut
hard. In November GHQ Great Britain informed the War Office
that if all those eligible were demobilised forthwith, 'the whole of
the Forces in Great Britain' would be left with just one operator,
three fitters and no electricians.[33]

The report on intelligence presented a much happier picture.
During the railway strike the organisation set up in the spring of
1919 'proved itself to be of the utmost value'. Intelligence officers

throughout the country, especially in the chief industrial centres, submitted reports twice daily which 'resulted in first-hand early information being obtained from sources other than those at the disposal of Government offices concerned.' The system as a whole had displayed only some slight defects and delays, but Major Torr, the staff officer who prepared the report, assured the War Office that steps had already been taken to remedy these. Torr's evident enthusiasm for intelligence work was not widely shared in the army. Haig's opinion was already well known and was echoed in the War Office when Colonel Braine, head of the General Staff home defence section, forwarded Torr's report to the Director of Military Operations (DMO). 'The policy of the Army having an Intelligence organisation to deal with industrial unrest is not one that any soldier desires,' wrote Braine, possibly with more assurance than was absolutely justified. He explained, however, that 'these very objectionable duties' had been forced upon GHQ Great Britain early in 1919 when the command had been made primarily responsible for internal security.[34] This was precisely the responsibility which the War Office sought to avoid and during the last quarter of 1919 they largely succeeded in this aim.

Even though Sir Eric Geddes and the new Supply and Transport Committee (STC) had been deputed to examine the whole question of emergency planning, there was much that the War Office could do before the committee reported back to the Cabinet. Indeed there was a lot to recommend a policy of unilateral action to pre-empt any demands which Geddes might make on the army. A few days after the railway strike had ended, the QMG re-circulated his memorandum of August on the unsatisfactory distribution of home service troops. The Adjutant-General (Sir George Macdonogh), who was formally responsible for internal security, responded with a significant re-statement of basic principles:

> It seems to me that we have been attempting to perform duties which appertain to the civil power, & that in so doing we have not merely greatly strained the military machine but the British Constitution as well. We should insist on the Home Office doing its own work, i.e. preserving public order. It is only when the civil power has been proved powerless to carry out this work that the military should be called in. Nothing could be worse both for the Army & for the State than that it should be supposed that the

former is being maintained for the purpose of coercing the latter. I am of the opinion that we ought not to keep up large forces in the U.K. for the purpose of dealing with civil disturbance. Let the Home, Scottish & Irish Offices provide whatever may be considered necessary for that purpose. If in any district the civil forces should prove insufficient, such troops as are available should reinforce them, but it will be a bad day for the Empire if the Government of this country had to look to the bayonets of its troops for its support.[35]

In this cogent minute Macdonogh certainly reflected the views of his colleagues, displaying, moreover, a facility for shrewd and subtle argument not often apparent in War Office memoranda. The appeal to the constitution is especially persuasive and one which the War Office were subsequently to employ in resisting any extension of their 'traditional' responsibilities. It added weight to an attitude which cynics might simply have regarded as being military self-interest and an anxiety to be shot of inconvenient and unpalatable duties. That it reflected in part an unusual view of the British constitution as a static and inflexible creation seems not to have troubled the military mind.

Within ten days of Macdonogh's memorandum the Army Council agreed to the return of all troops in Great Britain to their peacetime stations. The Secretary of State also approved decisions to break up the civil disturbance staff at GHQ Great Britain and to inform the War Cabinet that 'next time we shall have practically no Army or lorries and that the Home Office had better prepare accordingly'.[36] These points, although somewhat less pithily, were reported to the Cabinet when Churchill circulated Haig's official report on the railway strike. In a covering note Sir Henry Wilson observed that 'if all the protection duties anticipated by the various Civil Government Departments, in certain eventualities, had been demanded', Haig would have needed over two and a half times the 100,000 troops actually at his disposal. But post-war demobilisation was soon to reduce the numbers of infantry in Great Britain to a meagre 40,000 troops, 'which will consist of 12,000 conscripts temporarily retained during the period of reorganisation of the Regular Army, and 28,000 Regulars, mostly recruits with young and inexperienced non-commissioned officers, and weak in training and discipline.' Bearing in mind that British garrisons in Ireland and overseas might need reinforcement, it was 'of paramount importance' that this force 'should not be used, except as a last resource, in any future industrial disturbances, but be allowed to prepare itself for its legitimate duties in the defence of the Empire.' Wilson finally put four proposals before the Cabinet: that the existing military guards on 'warlike stores' and munition factories be replaced by civil watchmen; that, in the case of industrial trouble, the police, backed up by Special Constables or Citizen Guards, should do most of the emergency work; that the army be relieved of any responsibility for communications by the General Post Office; and that if the army *had* to be used, the Ministry of Transport would provide the vehicles required for moving troops. On 18 November this paper, along with other aspects of the emergency organisation, was considered by a conference of ministers. Almost without question Wilson's four proposals were approved, although because of great objection 'in certain quarters' the decision on wireless communication was later modified and sent for re-examination to the STC which deputed a committee under the Chief of the Air Staff, Sir Hugh Trenchard, to investigate the problem.[37] The War Office, nevertheless, believed it had won an important point: a re-affirmation of the pre-war principle that the army should only be employed in aid to the civil power strictly as a last resort.

Acting on this assumption, the War Office set about dismantling the wartime structure of military command and in particular decided to push ahead with the abolition of GHQ Great Britain. This was duly set for 1 February 1920. The only problem which remained was whether the War Office should take over any part of Haig's civil disturbance organisation. In the case of intelligence the decision was plain. 'When G.H.Q. Great Britain disappears', wrote Colonel Braine, 'it is not considered desirable or necessary to set up any similar machinery at the War Office to deal with Industrial Intelligence, as this work can be carried out, as at present, by Scotland House and Home Office.' The Home Office readily agreed that such duties could be left to Sir Basil Thomson's Special Branch, but they also enquired as to what arrangements were to be made in the War Office 'to take over the duties hitherto delegated to General Headquarters, Great Britain'.[38] This administrative problem had already exercised the Army Council. Before the war overall responsibility for aid to the civil power in peacetime had rested with the Adjutant-General. During the war, however, this became an operational function and passed to the Directorate of Military Operations,[39] where it was managed by Colonel Braine's branch (MO4). Detailed arrangements had in turn been delegated to GHQ Great Britain. With the abolition of that command this responsibility should have reverted automatically to the Adjutant-General, but this was strongly opposed by MO4.

In November 1919, prompted by Colonel Braine, the DMO, Sir Percy Radcliffe, circulated a minute to his colleagues arguing that, if and when troops intervened in aid of the civil power, 'it will be more in the nature of operations than of police work & that in consequence all arrangements should be made by Military Operations on that basis from the start.' Considering the bleak prospect on the industrial scene, Radcliffe thought it 'essential that a senior officer and staff should be earmarked to take over executive command of all troops in Great Britain in the event of a serious internal upheaval'. He also had someone in mind for the job: Major-General C. F. Romer,[40] Haig's chief of Staff at GHQ Great Britain, who had been extensively occupied in duties connected with industrial unrest and thus was a suitable officer to superintend these matters at the War Office. The CIGS's department approved Radcliffe's proposal, but neither the Adjutant-General nor the QMG agreed. They both argued that the likelihood of serious civil disturbance – and hence extensive active operations – was much over-rated and that there was no need to deviate from pre-war practice. If the CIGS wished some special arrangements to be made, the formation of a small co-ordinating committee would fully meet this need. Although Wilson earnestly declared that 'no such awful thing as a Revolution is going to take place', he thought 'it would indeed be madness' not to prepare plans against the possibility. With Churchill's consent, therefore, he approved the formation, in the deputy CIGS's words, of a 'Silent Section' to study the subject of internal security and liaise with civil departments on matters of organisation and intelligence. Entitled MO4(x), it was to comprise Romer and two other General Staff Officers, one of whom was Major Torr, all transferred from the disbanding GHQ Great Britain on 1 February 1920.[41] The DMO, as no doubt the Adjutant-General had feared, thereafter took a major share in the co-ordination of duties in aid of the civil power, but since the Adjutant-General officially retained ultimate responsibility, the precise division of powers within the War Office remained confused for the next few years. The issue was finally resolved in the DMO's favour following the General Strike in 1926.

While the War Office were reorganising for peace and striving to limit their potential domestic liabilities, Sir Eric Geddes pushed ahead with the tasks delegated to him and the STC by the Cabinet on 14 October. Even before the full STC met for the first time, Geddes instructed his Parliamentary Secretary to gather a committee of civil servants to collect departmental reports on the railway strike and begin preparing a scheme for future industrial emergencies. This sub-committee itself spawned further committees to consider specific aspects of the problem and these official bodies together provided the administrative impetus of the Supply and Transport Organisation (STO). In fact, the Cabinet committee was left with very little to do apart from making the occasional decision of principle and considering what matters should be forwarded to the Cabinet. Between its first meeting in late October 1919 and the end of January 1920, the STC met only three times. Over the same period the sub-committee met fifteen times. Inevitably the official committee made policy decisions. Although individually these may not have been of especial importance, in sum they very largely defined the nature and style of the government's emergency organisation. The STC was less a decision-making body than a convenient mechanism for civil servants collectively to brief their political masters on aspects of civil contingency planning. This early pattern continued throughout the inter-war years. While the Cabinet committee only met intermittently, usually arising from a ministerial panic about industrial unrest, the official sub-committee met on a much more regular basis, continually adjusting and refining the emergency organisation. The smooth administrative machine periodically interrupted by political alarums, it was, in a nutshell, modern British government.

The administrative process, indeed, had already provided a framework for the nascent STO. During the war, both the Ministry of Food and the Board of Trade had developed regional organisations to provide for the supply and distribution of foodstuffs. In the summer of 1919 these functions were combined and the Road Transport Board was amalgamated into the Food Ministry's network of twelve divisional and eighty-five local area offices in Great Britain. Throughout 1919 and early 1920 civil servants also reviewed plans for recruiting volunteer labour. The makeshift arrangements adopted in February 1919 to keep power stations working were refined and developed into the 'London Electric Power Scheme'. Various technical and learned societies, including the Institution of Electrical Engineers and the Institution of Civil Engineers, were approached privately and agreed 'to invite their members by circular to volunteer for service during a strike'. A register was then prepared to ensure that each volunteer was 'allocated in advance to the job for which his experience best fits him and also for work as near as possible to his home'. Where necessary, the Admiralty agreed to continue to provide skilled stokers. An official committee also considered the general question of voluntary work during strikes, and in February 1920 presented a scheme, later approved by both the STC and the Cabinet, for the recruitment and distribution of volunteer labour. The provision of labour for 'local' operations, such as tramway, gas and electric services, would be undertaken primarily by local authorities, while 'national' services – food, transport, shipping – would be handled by some eighty recruiting centres staffed by government officials and superintended by 'a person of considerable local standing'. These local offices were to be co-ordinated within twelve divisions corresponding to the Food Ministry's national organisation.[42]

The effectiveness of the Cabinet committee as a body was undermined by the fact that Geddes was emphatically not a 'committee man'. After testing the general opinions of his colleagues at an initial 'full dress' meeting on 31 October, Geddes prepared a Cabinet paper outlining a 'suggested permanent organisation for meeting strikes'. Although the paper ostensibly came from the STC as a whole, the committee had no opportunity to see it in draft since Geddes did not convene a second meeting until 8 December. The paper was not a detailed blueprint, but simply raised a number of general considerations upon which decisions were needed before such a plan could finally be made. To begin with there was the thorny issue of strikebreaking. Geddes asserted that the proposed organisation might have to enlist, and possibly train, large numbers of volunteers, particularly to provide transport services. But it was widely believed that 'the enrolment of volunteers would at once lead to trouble with Labour'. The second problem was legal. When peace was officially declared, the Defence of the Realm Regulations would lapse and with them the power of government departments to commandeer buildings and goods. Since this had proved vital during the railway strike, Geddes, having consulted the Attorney-General, suggested that a draft bill be prepared to provide the necessary emergency powers. A third problem was one of finance. The establishment of a permanent organisation would entail sizeable expense and to provide this openly out of public funds 'would be sure to raise a storm of protest from certain sections in Parliament and the Press'. Geddes argued, therefore, that 'the only way whereby criticism and opposition might be obviated would be to include such expenditure in the Secret Service Vote'. He was concerned that the whole matter should be treated with the utmost urgency and secrecy, and he asked Sir Maurice Hankey to inform ministers that all copies distributed should be returned to him as soon as a decision had been reached on the subject.[43]

Hankey was less exercised by the importance of the matter than Geddes. In reply to an enquiry as to when the paper might be discussed by the Cabinet, he contended that there were more urgent topics awaiting consideration. He proposed that the paper could be brought up at a Cabinet conference on 17 November, but later telephoned to explain that the Prime Minister would be unavailable that day and that the matter would have to be held over indefinitely.[44] When it became apparent that Lloyd George would be available on 18 November, Hankey still refused to put the subject on the agenda on the grounds that the Treasury, who required a week's notice on questions of expenditure, had not yet been consulted about the emergency scheme. Geddes was infuriated. He was probably not the first, and most certainly not the last, minister to be riled by a Cabinet Secretary's calm and superior management of the Cabinet agenda. In the event, he simply ignored Hankey's secretarial formalities. On 18 November, as Hankey explained apologetically to Austen Chamberlain (Chancellor of the Exchequer), while the meeting was 'waiting for the Ministers concerned in another question', Geddes insisted on discussing his memorandum. Hankey was powerless to intervene, but when he came to draft the minutes he 'was very careful to reserve all financial aspects and all that the Supply and Transport Committee are empowered to do is to go on working out their scheme which will come before the Cabinet before any money can be spent.'[45]

Geddes was not displeased by the outcome of his irregular action. Although the question of expenditure remained outstanding, he gained formal agreement in principle that some nucleus organisation should be kept in being for future emergencies. He also found that ministers were alive to possible accusations of strikebreaking.

> It was pointed out [recorded the Cabinet minutes] that there was an essential difference between a Railway or a Miners' Strike, which threatened to paralyse the life of the nation, and an ordinary industrial and sectional strike, as, for example, in the cotton trade. There was no intention of interfering with the latter, but only of coming to the rescue of the community when confronted with the disasters which would arise under the former.

Finally, the question of special legislation was referred back to the STC for definite recommendations.[46] But Geddes soon ran into a combination of general departmental inertia and War Office reluctance to share in the emergency organisation. On 9 December he informed Lloyd George that it was proving difficult, 'with the great demands for Ministers' time, to get some of my colleagues to fully share [sic] the responsibility for the initiation and perfection of the organisation'. The following day he was told that while the STC sub-committees were generally making good progress, the Adjutant-General's 'Assistance from Fighting Services Sub-committee' was dragging its feet. Geddes's reaction was to instruct Macdonogh to summon his committee and advise what assistance the services could provide in a future emergency. On 18 December the committee reported that troops could not be used for 'other than military duties'. The navy could do no more than find personnel to man electric power stations, pit-head pumps and dock installations. All three services combined to affirm that 'in existing circumstances it was not practicable to offer any assistance . . . in the way of volunteers for civilian work during a Strike' and they stressed in particular the bizarre fact that men would not be available to 'carry on, if necessary, the distilleries in Ireland, upon which this Country is largely dependent for a supply of Yeast'.[47]

Macdonogh was somewhat agitated by Geddes's summons to re-assemble the sub-committee he had chaired during the railway strike. It was all too evident that, despite the Cabinet decision of 18 November, Sir Eric Geddes still expected assistance from the services. Macdonogh told the CIGS that Air-Marshal Trenchard shared his concern, and he wondered if the Cabinet should once more be approached in order to clarify the position. Wilson took the matter to Churchill, who instructed him to prepare another memorandum. By 3 January 1920 the memorandum, which was actually furnished by MO4, was ready for the CIGS to sign. The problem of industrial unrest clearly weighed heavily on Wilson's mind, for he discussed the topic that day both with Sir Henry Rawlinson (GOCinC Aldershot) and, at length, with the QMG, who, recorded Wilson in his diary, 'is in complete agreement with me in cursing the criminal folly of the Government for having *no* plan and for making none & indeed for refusing to realise the position.'[48] This was less than fair. When Wilson became excited (which was frequently), he tended to overdramatise matters in his diary and, indeed, at times displayed an astonishing capacity for self-deception. At best his remarks illustrate part of his desire both to have his military cake and eat it. Wilson knew very well that Geddes was preparing an emergency organisation. He himself had been at the STC meeting on 8 December which had discussed the matter. But he was also in the van of the War Office campaign to restrict the army's domestic responsibilities. Naturally Wilson sought to mitigate the onerous worldwide burden carried by his youthful, partially-trained and undermanned post-war army. But to complain bitterly about the woeful inadequacy of the government's emergency preparations and maintain a resolutely *non possumus* stance at one and the same time was, to say the least, a trifle unfastidious.

The memorandum which Wilson signed on 3 January demonstrated elements of this species of double-think. It confirmed that, following the Cabinet decision of 18 November, the War Office had taken action to limit its internal obligations,

> but it has since become apparent to the Army Council that the Civil Departments concerned have not yet appreciated the extent of the responsibilities placed upon them, and continue to look to the Army for assistance which it is quite beyond its power to afford.
>
> In view of the above, the whole question of the use to be made of the Army in any future internal trouble gives grave cause for anxiety. Not only will the Army be unable to find the guards for which it has up to now been responsible, but also it will be far too weak to give the full measure of assistance to the police necessitated by disturbances on a large scale. Apart from this it is lacking in the necessary technical services for its own mainte-

nance, and must rely on Civil Departments to assist it in carrying out even the limited duties of which it is capable. If it is called upon at an early stage to assist the Civil Authorities, it will be dispersed, and thus the last reserve in the hands of the Government will be dissipated.

In an appendix a more detailed summary was given of the army's capacity (or, rather, *in*capacity) 'to carry out general protection duties, and afford aid to the Civil Power'. It was observed that, after the last of the wartime conscript battalions had been demobilised in March 1920, the army in Great Britain would be severely under strength. This was all the more serious considering that 'an adequate Police Force does not apparently exist'. The units in Ireland, where the army was inescapably committed against increasing nationalist unrest, were also under strength. The appendix concluded, with unconscious irony, by noting that the intelligence section of GHQ Great Britain would disappear when that command was disbanded at the end of January. It warned that there was 'no machinery available at the War Office to carry on this work, and the Army will have to rely for such information on the Home Office and its Intelligence Branch at Scotland Yard'.[49] To ensure that this unaccommodating restatement of the military stance was broadcast as widely as possible, Churchill also circulated it as an STC paper, to come up for discussion at the next committee meeting.

On 14 January, the day before the STC were due to meet, Wilson called in his senior commanders to discuss strikes. 'We have no troops,' noted Rawlinson laconically.[50] At the STC meeting the following afternoon the services were well represented. Winston Churchill and Walter Long joined the committee for the first time. All three service chiefs attended as advisers. Wilson also brought with him Romer and Brigadier-General Ross of GHQ Great Britain. The committee had before it (doubtless to Wilson's astonishment) several papers concerning the proposed emergency organisation. Finance was discussed first. Although it was thought that the introduction in parliament of a specific vote for the emergency organisation 'might be regarded as a challenge by all disaffected parties', surprisingly no one believed that the proposed arrangements could be concealed by providing for them under separate votes. 'The Government', they decided, 'should say quite openly that they were introducing [a] special vote, not for the purposes of "Strike breaking", but simply in order to make reasonable provision for preventing the starvation of the country and maintaining orderly government.' This approach would be facilitated by giving responsibility for the vote to the Treasury, 'which would be regarded as a more neutral Department than any of the Departments actually responsible for the administration of the proposed organisation'.

This evidently tranquil and uncharacteristic acceptance of the fact that the existence, if not the precise details, of the emergency organisation would be made public contrasted vividly with the opinions expressed when the committee moved on to the vexed topic of protection. Churchill introduced Wilson's memorandum and described to the committee the prevailing weakness of the army. He did not get an altogether satisfactory response. While it was agreed that 'the Army should not be dissipated for ordinary protection duties, but should be held as a central reserve ready to deal with any revolutionary attempt', the committee felt that this 'should not . . . preclude the Army from providing guards for certain important strategic points, such as power stations and dock gates, and for the protection of naval ratings employed in power stations.' The War Office were additionally to remain liable for the care of 'all arms, explosives, and lethal weapons generally'. The Home Office added their opinion that, in the event of a large-scale strike, it would 'not be possible to depend for effective protection on the police aided by special constables'. It was resolved, therefore, to refer the whole question of protection to the Cabinet.

The committee's insistent concern with domestic security was fuelled by the extraordinarily pessimistic views put forward when they looked into the immediate future. Literally, they let their imaginations run riot. 'Fears were expressed', the secretary recorded dryly, 'that the country would have to face in the near future an organised attempt at seizing the reins of Government in some of the large cities, such as Glasgow, London and Liverpool.' Careful preparations, moreover, based on the experience of the railway strike, were being made for a coal strike. 'It was not unlikely', continued the minutes, 'that the next strike would commence with sabotage on an extensive scale, directed towards the destruction of means of communication and transport.'[51] Wilson, naturally, painted a more dramatic picture:

An amazing meeting. One after another got up & said that we

were going to have the Triple Red Revolution strike. One after another said there was nothing to be done, that the police were powerless, that the Citizen Guard had been forbidden by the Unions & that now the Unions would not allow Special Constables to be sworn & treated them as blacklegs . . . It is truly a terrifying state of affairs & not one of them except Walter & Winston were [*sic*] prepared to put up a fight. Troup [permanent under-secretary] of the Home Office is hopeless. Shortt was not present. Beatty & I were terrified at the incompetence & cowardice revealed.[52]

Faced with irresolution – and near-hysteria – in the STC, the CIGS was hoist with his own petard. The civil authorities were clearly powerless to pursue the stern Draconian policies he believed would extirpate imminent domestic revolution. Although he had continually asserted military weakness, Wilson was now driven to the conclusion that the 'last resort', when the army would be *obliged* to assist the civil power, was close indeed. He began, therefore, to make counter-revolutionary plans and was even perforce to accept for the army a larger share of 'internal protection' than he had hitherto been prepared to do.

Churchill, Long, Wilson and Beatty had been summoned by Lloyd George in Paris to a conference on various aspects of the peace settlement. That night they travelled over together on the ferry. Before the conference on the following afternoon, Wilson arranged with Hankey that the state of unrest at home was placed first on the agenda. Duly the travellers reported the 'very grave statements' which had been made at the STC meeting. But no decision was taken. Two days later, on Sunday 18 January, they returned to the topic, this time joined by Sir Robert Horne who declared that the miners planned 'to take the country when it was at its weakest, that is to say, in March'. Wilson waxed lyrical about the lack of troops, but again Lloyd George temporised and requested detailed statistics before any decision could be made.[53] The truth of the matter was that the men in Paris did not believe the position at home was as serious as the STC imagined. Bonar Law had the greatest reason to be unsympathetic. At nine o'clock on the Monday morning, while he was still in bed, Wilson turned up and harangued him at length on the perilous state of England. 'Bonar said he did not believe in a Revolution,' noted Wilson. Hankey privately thought that Wilson and his colleagues simply had the 'wind up', and he told Lloyd George that it was 'difficult to understand the reason for the very obvious preoccupation of the First Lord and the C.I.G.S. as to the future'. On the contrary, so far as he could judge, though there were 'many clouds on the horizon, the sky seemed to be getting clearer'. Lloyd George, too, had a wider perception of the problem than Sir Henry Wilson. The Prime Minister was fully aware that social unrest could not simply be met with force. Although the phrase 'a fit country for heroes to live in' soon rang hollow, the coalition government was making some progress towards that end. There were significant advances particularly in the fields of unemployment insurance and public housing. There was much to be said, indeed, for attempting to treat the cause of the illness rather than trying just to stifle the symptoms. As Thomas Jones, Assistant Secretary to the Cabinet, put it: 'What Churchill and co. forget is that there are other ways of averting discontent than with civil guards and the military.'[54]

Frustrated by his reception in Paris, Sir Henry Wilson returned to London on 21 January. His only consolation lay in having persuaded Lloyd George to let him temporarily hold back eight battalions of infantry which had been earmarked to supervise a League of Nations' plebiscite in Silesia. But he was determined to do more. On the morning of 22 January he held a long meeting with the military members of the Army Council on what was to be done 'in the case of industrial unrest & revolution. No one knew,' he noted. That afternoon he got out Haig's civil emergency plans and went over them with the deputy CIGS (Harington), the DMO and Brigadier-General Ross. During the next fortnight, assisted by Harington and Romer, Wilson worked out the details of his strategy to meet revolution. Since he believed that a railway strike would inevitably paralyse military transport, he aimed to hold the bulk of his forces south-east of a line drawn from Colchester to Plymouth and 'near the salt water', convenient to sea-transport. There is no evidence to suggest, however, that he anticipated having to make amphibious landings in the north of England or Scotland. In any case this arrangement made sense, as there was a high concentration of barracks in southern Britain. Eighteen infantry battalions (of which ten were Guards), just under half the available force, were to be retained to safeguard London. On 6 February he described his strategy to a meeting of home GOCinCs and instructed them to make plans for specific centres, such as Liverpool, Glasgow and Hull, where serious unrest was likely to occur.[55] Whatever attitude the Cabinet might have, Wilson made sure that the War Office was prepared for the worst.

Sir Eric Geddes was also convinced that he had done all within his power to prepare the government, if not quite for the worst, at least for a major strike. But he was concerned that his own Ministry of Transport was carrying too much of the responsibility for emergency arrangements. This had political implications. 'It was not desirable', he told Arthur Neal, his Parliamentary Secretary, 'that any one Minister should continue to be solely responsible for "strike-breaking" schemes.' Geddes's refreshingly enlightened opinion on the subject of committees also led him to assert that once the STC had fulfilled the brief given by the Cabinet in October 1919, it should cease to function. Neal passed these views on to the STC sub-committee, of which he was *ex officio* chairman, causing considerable alarm among the assembled officials. Abolishing committees struck at the heart of civil service government. It was strongly urged that some means 'for discussion and co-ordination generally' should be retained. Neal took the point and suggested to Geddes that the STC sub-committee continue in some form, possibly under the Cabinet secretariat. He would cease to be chairman and Sir Edward Troup would make a most suitable replacement.[56] This particular hot potato, therefore, would conveniently pass to the Home Office.

As major matters of policy, both the questions of protection and the future of the STC were submitted for Cabinet consideration at a conference arranged on 2 February. Sir Henry Wilson described it with characteristic hyperbole: 'It was one of the worst Cabinets I ever saw. An enormous number present of elderly men (some 20)[57] quite unable to come to a decision. Lloyd George one of the worst.' The most complete account of the meeting comes from Thomas Jones, who took verbatim minutes throughout. Jones observed that the Prime Minister, who did not believe in 'the imminence of the revolution', indulged in 'a lot of unsuspected leg-pulling'. Having ascertained from Trenchard that his pilots had no weapons for ground fighting, Lloyd George presumed that 'they could use machine guns and drop bombs.' He interrogated Generals Macdonogh and Macready, both happily unaware of *reductio ad absurdum,* on the merits of hand grenades. But the Prime Minister also observed that 'an army of a million men would not be able to prevent the great power stations being suddenly put out of gear.' There was much discussion about the possibility of enlisting and arming loyal citizens. Shortt proposed raising a temporary force of 10,000 volunteers, but this was not approved. Macready said that there were some ex-soldiers in his police force who could use rifles, and Auckland Geddes 'pointed to the Universities as full of trained men who could co-operate with clerks and stockbrokers.' This was, perhaps, gratifying to Bonar Law who, in Jones's account, 'so often referred to the stockbrokers as a loyal and fighting class until one felt that potential battalions of stockbrokers were to be found in every town.' In the end the conference delegated both Shortt and Macready to look into the whole question of licensing firearms (to discover who held them) and to make recommendations 'as to the best method for making them available to loyalists in the event of any emergency'.

With all the talk of revolution, Geddes's proposals concerning the emergency organisation were hardly discussed at all. He had circulated a memorandum embodying the financial arrangements approved by the STC on 14 February, which provided for £14,380 initial expenditure and £92,240 recurring. This did not include the Food Ministry's scheme for road transport which was already running at a cost of £52,000 *per annum*. There was also to be added a loss of some £290,000 'accruing to the Government for the retention of certain surplus stores from disposal (e.g. motor lorries, vans, Crossley Tenders, bedsteads, bedding, tents, huts, etc.)'. The conference unanimously accepted the STC proposals and sanctioned the necessary spending. It was decided, however, to give the Home Office, not the Treasury, the privilege of guiding the expenditure through parliament. At the very end of the meeting Geddes voiced his opinion that the STC should be disbanded and requested, at least, that he be relieved from its chairmanship. Neither suggestion found favour. Both the Prime Minister and Bonar Law made flattering references to 'his special qualities for the job', and Lloyd George concluded that, since ministers took so sombre a view of the immediate future, the STC should continue to exist. After much persuasion, Geddes finally agreed to carry on for a couple of months. 'There was a momentary fear', recorded Jones, 'that Churchill would offer himself for the job and perhaps this had some influence with Geddes' holding on to it.'[58]

Geddes, however, remained unhappy as to how exactly the organisation would be run in an emergency and when a miners' strike threatened in March 1920, he proposed to the Prime Minister that a number of junior government ministers be named as Civil Commissioners to superintend it. Without consulting the Cabinet, Lloyd George agreed and decided to appoint eleven Commissioners in England and Wales, corresponding to the regions of the voluntary labour scheme and the emergency food organisation, and two for Scotland, although these were later dropped in favour of the Secretary for Scotland acting as Commissioner alone. Sir Hamar Greenwood, Secretary of Overseas Trade, was invited to be Chief Civil Commissioner and authorised to enlist a personal staff. Greenwood, a conservative-minded Liberal with a reputation for mental inflexibility, accepted the job. Geddes was more than happy to divide his irksome responsibilities, but harboured no illusions that this emotion might be shared. 'I am afraid', he wrote to Greenwood, 'you will not be particularly gratified at the honour which the Prime Minister has done you.' Nevertheless he arranged at once for St Quintin Hill, secretary of the STC, to forward 'all the documents' and offered temporary accommodation at the Ministry of Transport for Greenwood's headquarters staff.[59]

Thus the organisation, which had developed largely on an *ad hoc* basis to meet the strikes of 1919, was established on a systematic footing. It was to underpin the government's policy towards major strikes for the next twenty years. In early 1920, however, the Supply and Transport Organisation still owed much to wartime experience in its wide-ranging scope, its unprecedented degree of inter-departmental co-operation and not least in terms of lavish expenditure. But the lean financial years following the collapse of the post-war boom in the spring of 1920 brought an end to generous government spending. This affected the STC as much as any department, but before the full effects of retrenchment were felt, the organisation had a chance to show its paces during two disputes in the coal industry: in the autumn of 1920 and the spring of 1921. By March 1920, moreover, the principal themes of industrial contingency planning had been laid down: the extent to which the armed services might be called upon to render assistance; which department, if any, took final responsibility for the emergency organisation; how secret the government's plans should be; the role of civil servants in making policy; the employment of 'loyal' volunteers; and who was to foot the bill. Above all was the central problem (most bedevilling for a Labour government) of when did making 'reasonable provision for preventing the starvation of the country and maintaining orderly government' become strikebreaking? The British government's preparations for industrial unrest between the wars, and since 1945, is the history of variations on these themes.

# 3
# The Supply and Transport Organisation in action April 1920 – October 1922

BY 1920 THE British government's emergency organisation had become sufficiently well-established to excite interest abroad. In January the Norwegian Minister in London asked for a copy of the Ministry of Transport scheme 'for co-operation between the railways and motor transport'. This request was passed on to the STC who decided it was 'undesirable that the scheme in question should be communicated in writing', but saw no objection to it being 'explained verbally' to a representative of the Norwegian Legation.[1] This was followed in April by a request from the Chargé d'Affaires at the French Embassy for information about British arrangements 'in the event of a general strike'. This inquiry was apparently not discussed by the STC, yet St Quintin Hill drafted an extensive memorandum on the subject in reply.

Although Hill's memorandum, dated 2 June 1920, was never sent to the French government, it is of particular interest since it describes for the first time in one document the entire emergency organisation. It is clear, moreover, that by describing the Supply and Transport Organisation, Hill also went some way towards defining it, and his original draft memorandum laid down the general limits within which the organisation and its component parts were to operate. Having summarised the establishment and composition of the STC, Hill noted that the 'day to day work' was handled by an official sub-committee, which itself had spawned further sub-committees to operate a number of 'special organisations'. These organisations dealt with finance, communications, fuel, power, transport, protection and publicity. Plans had been prepared to provide, among other things, an internal airmail service, the supply of wood for fuel, restrictions on the use of petrol, the London Electric Power Scheme, road transport, and volunteer labour to work coastal shipping 'in the event of a strike of seamen occurring simultaneously with a strike of transport workers'. There were also some peripheral bodies, such as the Canal Control Committee and the Railway Committee, which had survived from the war. The Railway Committee, consisting of the General Managers of the principal railway companies, represented what was to be an increasingly important aspect of the emergency organisation. As the structure of wartime controls was dismantled and successive governments espoused, with some notable exceptions, the principle of industrial non-intervention, it was hoped that private employers and 'management' generally would play a leading role in mitigating the effects of major strikes.

Although the STC sub-committee's 'special organisations' handled many of the emergency arrangements, the still somewhat makeshift nature of the STO as a whole was illustrated by two important functions being managed separately. The Food Ministry retained its wartime responsibility for the supply and distribution of essential foodstuffs. During a transport strike the Minstry's normal organisation would be complemented by the Road Transport Organisation transferred from the Board of Trade in August 1919. Under the Defence of the Realm Regulations, which still applied in 1920, private owners were compelled to register all goods-carrying vehicles with Area Road Transport Officers and in an emergency the Ministry was empowered to requisition as many of these as were needed. The scheme for recruiting volunteer labour, approved by the Cabinet in February 1920, was also organised individually. By the time Hill had prepared his memorandum in June the plans for national and local recruitment were virtually complete. Ninety-two Volunteer Emergency Committees (later known as Volunteer Service Committees) had been set up in Great Britain to provide for national services, each chaired by a 'prominent local gentleman, unconnected with official life'. At the local level, an instructional memorandum, called the 'Strike Book', had been prepared for distribution to Chairmen and Clerks of local authorities. This posed political problems. The Labour Party had done well in the municipal elections of November 1919, gaining control of a number of boroughs. No one was quite sure how these councils would react to the emergency organisation. Thus, 'in view of the political complexion of certain Local Authorities', it was decided that local authorities generally 'should not be given their instructions until the actual emergency'. Supervising the labour scheme were the newly created Civil Com-

missioners and it was within their organisation that the nucleus of
a central Supply and Transport executive began to emerge. As soon
as he was appointed Chief Civil Commissioner in March 1920,
Greenwood began to collect a staff of his own. By June this had
developed into 'a department, known for purposes of disguise as the
"Supply Department" '.[2]

The Supply Department was Hamar Greenwood's sole contribution to the Supply and Transport Organisation. Within ten days of
becoming Chief Civil Commissioner, he was promoted from the
Department of Overseas Trade to the Chief Secretaryship of Ireland.
With a department divided between London and Dublin, and Ireland itself beset by nationalist unrest, the Irish Office was one of
the most demanding and time-consuming posts in the government.
Geddes appreciated this: 'In view of your new appointment,' he
wrote, 'I do not think that you will wish to continue your work as
Chief Commissioner.' He suggested Sir Laming Worthington-
Evans, recently appointed Minister without Portfolio, as a possible
successor. Greenwood replied that he had spoken to Bonar Law –
temporarily in charge of the government while Lloyd George was
away at the San Remo conference – and resigned from the Commissionership. Law favoured Sir James Craig, Financial Secretary
to the Admiralty, for the job. Craig had regularly represented the
Admiralty at STC meetings and was presumably familiar with the
organisation, but Geddes's advice prevailed and Worthington-Evans
was appointed Chief Civil Commissioner towards the end of April
1920.[3] In any case, Craig was increasingly becoming preoccupied
with Ulster Unionist matters and in June 1921 resigned from his
seat at Westminster to become the first Prime Minister of Northern
Ireland.

As Minister without Portfolio, Worthington-Evans had been deputed to deal as required with outstanding questions of finance and
trade. Before the war he had been a successful commercial solicitor,
but gave up his practice in 1910 when he entered Parliament as
Conservative Member for Colchester. During the war he had held
a number of relatively minor government posts. He picked up the
nascent Supply Department where Hamar Greenwood had left off.
One important decision made in the late spring of 1920 – whether
by Greenwood or Worthington-Evans is not clear – was the appointment of Christopher Roundell from the Ministry of Health to be
Chief of Staff in the Supply Department. He was to remain in this

post for the next twenty years and his long tenure of office at the heart of the emergency organisation serves to emphasise the importance of the official role in contingency planning. Indeed, there was a remarkable continuity of higher civil service personnel in the various departments involved with the STO throughout the interwar years. Sir Maurice Hankey, Sir Warren Fisher and Sir Herbert Creedy headed the Cabinet Office, the Treasury and the War Office respectively for almost the whole of this period. Sir William Robinson was Permanent Under-Secretary at the Ministry of Health for fifteen years from 1920. Thomas Jones was Deputy Secretary to the Cabinet from 1916 to 1930, while Sir John Anderson and Sir Cyril Hurcomb were the senior officials at the Home Office and the Ministry of Transport for a decade between the wars. It has been observed that 'in some respects the period [between 1919 and 1939] is the one in which the higher civil service in Britain probably reached the height of its corporate influence',[4] but it remains difficult to assess the actual effect of this influence on emergency planning. Hankey and Jones seem to have taken little more than a supervisory interest, while Creedy largely – and correctly – left questions of military policy and tactics to the servicemen at the War Office. Sir William Robinson ignored the matter and left all relevant administration to the Chief General Inspector at the Ministry of Health. Anderson and Hurcomb, however, were both regular members of the STC sub-committee. Anderson was certainly influential and unmistakably set his careful stamp on the strikebreaking organisation during the 1920s.

While there is no doubt that individual civil servants were influential in the development of the STO, any attempt to evaluate the official role in policy-making must also take into account the interdepartmental balance of power and function. Strikebreaking plans inevitably involved some departments more closely than others. Thus, Sir John Anderson played a prominent part, not only because of his legendary personal abilities, but also by virtue of being permanent head of the Home Office. Similarly civil servants in the Board of Trade and the Ministry of Transport *ex officio* had an important place in the emergency organisation. The role of the Treasury must also be considered. Under the dynamic guidance of Sir Warren Fisher the Treasury between the wars sought to assert a greater measure of control over departmental policies than had hitherto been the case. This is certainly evident in foreign affairs, imperial policy and defence.[5] There is, moreover, a clear indication from the available documents that from about 1925 Treasury officials began to take a supervisory interest in the STO. Specific departmental proposals for expenditure were examined increasingly closely. So much so that by 1938 there was concern at the Treasury that it had shouldered too much responsibility. The Treasury shared with every other government department a reluctance to be held solely responsible for the STO. 'It seems to me undesirable', wrote one official, 'that the Treasury should concentrate in its own hands too many of these emergency arrangements, although we shall, of course, continue to control the general principle on which they are based.'[6] The fact remains, however, that at no time did the Cabinet delegate to the Treasury control of 'the general principle' on which the emergency arrangements were based. The Treasury arrogated that responsibility to itself.

Christopher Roundell's appointment to the Supply Department demonstrates the importance of Ministry of Health officials in the Civil Commissioners' organisation. For most of his civil service career Roundell was a Health Ministry inspector, holding the post of Chief General Inspector from 1935 until he retired in 1941. In each of the eleven regions established in England and Wales, administrative Chief Assistants and Finance Officers were drawn from the Ministry of Health Inspectorate and Audit Staff respectively.[7] This, in turn, illustrates the extent to which central government sought co-operation from local authorities. The Ministry of Health was effectively a 'Ministry of Local Government'. It was created in 1919 by amalgamating the administration of the National Health Insurance with the Local Government Board, which, since its establishment in 1871, had enabled Whitehall to exercise some central control over local authorities. Roundell and his colleagues, all formerly officials of the Board, were therefore ideally suited to provide local co-ordination and articulation to the national emergency organisation. They were the 'unsung heroes' of the STO. Leopold Amery, Chief Civil Commissioner in 1921, placed in his memoirs a 'belated tribute' to Roundell, since he 'was never able to secure official recognition for services which no individual Government Department was prepared to include in its own list.'[8]

Although ministers and departments were more than happy to co-operate in the emergency organisation during strikes, or when a major industrial dispute seemed imminent, at other times the STO was treated like a species of departmental pariah. Ministers, especially, were reluctant to become closely involved, and risk becoming labelled as 'strikebreakers'. Geddes was no exception. He clearly thought, moreover, that Worthington-Evans's assumption of the Chief Commissionership might enable him to bow gracefully out of the STC. The day after the new appointment was confirmed, Geddes wrote to Hankey to remind him of the Cabinet's decision on 2 February that his chairmanship of the STC would be reconsidered after two months. Hankey duly placed the matter on the Cabinet agenda and it was discussed at a ministerial conference chaired by Bonar Law on 4 May 1920. Worthington-Evans agreed to head the STC 'on the understanding that he would be relieved of some of his present work'. The Minister of Transport, however, was to remain as an ordinary member of the committee. Geddes was delighted and resolved to restrict his Ministry's responsibilities within the STO as much as possible. On 6 May his second-in-command, Arthur Neal, told Worthington-Evans that he would not in the future be able to rely on the Ministry of Transport 'being fully at his disposal'. He also refused to continue as chairman of the STC sub-committee. Neal told him, as he reported later to Geddes, that this would provide 'an official link between this Ministry and the committee which as a mater of policy you thought it undesirable should exist'. Clearly dissatisfied, Worthington-Evans went directly to Geddes who softened sufficiently to permit the use of Transport Ministry staff for a fortnight while a new central organisation was set up.[9]

In his anxiety to be rid entirely of the STC, Sir Eric Geddes overplayed his hand. By denying any real assistance, he put Worthington-Evans in an impossible position. The new chairman and Chief Commissioner soon discovered that, apart from the embryonic Supply Department, the Supply and Transport Organisation was entirely (and not without reason) run by Geddes's own officials at the Ministry of Transport. Since Geddes was prepared only to retain responsibility for railway traffic arrangements, Worthington-Evans was faced with the tedious task of building up a central headquarters almost entirely from scratch. Had Geddes offered to co-operate, it is possible that Worthington-Evans might have carried on, but after just a week as chairman of the STC he had had enough. On 11 May he circulated a memorandum to the Cabinet on the current and future position of the emergency organisation. It was a thinly veiled attack on Geddes's obstinate refusal to help, and Worthington-Evans made it clear that in any case he had no desire to remain in charge. 'There seemed to me two alternatives', he wrote, 'either that Sir Eric Geddes should continue his work with his staff or that the work should be put in charge of the Home Secretary with a small headquarters staff for the purpose.'[10]

There was an immediate reaction from Edward Shortt. He strongly asserted that the Home Office could not take charge. The 'supply of food and other necessaries of life' was not part of his Ministry's functions; Home Office control would identify the emergency organisation too closely with the police; and besides he had no spare staff available. Shortt suggested a compromise. If Geddes could not cope, a Minister without Portfolio should chair the STC and be assisted by a separate Chief Civil Commissioner. Because the Ministry of Transport possessed valuable experience gained during the railway strike, Neal should remain chairman of the sub-committee. All the rest of the work would be 'done by the proper departments'. The Ministries of Transport, Shipping, Food and so on should each make emergency arrangements within their particular competence. The emphasis on departmental responsibility was echoed by the Food Controller, Charles McCurdy. He observed that although it was necessary to have a 'generalissimo' to co-ordinate services, it was 'equally essential, having regard to the technical and diverse nature of many of such services . . . that each of the departments concerned should themselves be responsible for maintaining the several services which come within their normal duties'. During the railway strike the Food Ministry had exclusively arranged the supply and distribution of foodstuffs. It had, moreover, maintained a neutral stance in the dispute, and 'confined itself to being, as it were, a trustee for the community'. Indeed, the Ministry had obtained, 'in a great many instances, the actual assistance of strikers and their sympathisers in the duties it had to perform'.[11] In stressing his anxiety not to become directly embroiled in industrial disputes McCurdy hit on one of the central problems of emergency planning. While in theory the STO might set itself up as 'a trustee for the community', in practice it might go beyond this. The maintenance of food supplies was relatively non-contentious, and the Food Ministry could effectively assert that its emergency duties did not constitute 'strikebreaking'. Other departments were less happily situated, as Edward Shortt and Sir Eric Geddes were only too acutely aware.

Geddes took no part in the exchange of memoranda, but he continued to be unhelpful towards Worthington-Evans. On 31 May he wrote to observe that the fortnight's grace he had allowed on 7 May 'is now 24 days'. Worthington-Evans replied asking for continued use of the Ministry of Transport and said that the whole question would shortly be decided by the Prime Minister. Lloyd George had not so far been involved, but on 14 June 1920 he convened another ministerial conference to examine the matter. It was argued that because the Ministry of Transport would play a central role if there were a strike in the railways, docks or coal mines, 'the obvious course would be to place the Supply and Transport Committee and its Sub-committees once more under the control of the Ministry of Transport'. Geddes, on the other hand, urged that he would be prejudiced 'in the eyes of Labour if he were made responsible for work which was generally regarded as "strikebreaking" work'. But he protested in vain. Since no minister actually wanted the job, the lot fell to the department with the most expertise in the field. 'After considerable discussion', the conference decided that Geddes should resume the chairmanship of the STC and Neal that of the sub-committee. 'The Minister of Transport desired that his dissent from this decision should be recorded.'[12] Geddes's fate was sealed not so much from a consideration of the future as of the immediate past. More than anything else, the accident of the first major post-war strike being in the railways condemned the Ministry of Transport to play a central role in the emergency organisation. Had the strike been in the gas or electricity industries, or even the coal mines, perhaps then the mantle might have fallen on the Board of Trade.

The Cabinet conference made no decision as to the Chief Commissionership. Geddes seized upon this lacuna in an attempt to salvage something from his defeat. On 15 June he wrote to Worthington-Evans: 'As you are apparently no longer Chairman of the Supply and Transport Committee, will you now revert to your old position as Chief Civil Commissioner because I should like to know very much how that organisation has progressed.' Geddes noted that Hamar Greenwood had housed some staff in offices belonging to the Ministry of Transport. These were now urgently required by the Ministry, and Geddes asked Worthington-Evans as Chief Commissioner (if that were the case) to find other accommodation as soon as possible. Worthington-Evans replied by return of

post. 'I thought it clear', he wrote, 'that the Cabinet decision concerned the chief Commship [*sic*].' He observed, no doubt with some
pleasure, that Arthur Neal was the only man who knew 'the details'
and *he* should be Chief Commissioner 'as your staff will be acting
as headquarters staff'. On 7 July Geddes took the matter to Bonar
Law and pressed strongly for 'the additional assistance of a Chief
Civil Commissioner'. Two days later Law and Neal interviewed
Frederick Kellaway, Greenwood's successor as Secretary of the Department of Overseas Trade, and asked him to take the job. Kellaway accepted and set to work at once. Roundell was confirmed as
Chief of Staff and arrangements were made to issue invitations to
potential Civil Commissioners. 'It is a great relief to me', confided
Geddes to Kellaway on 26 July, 'to know that at last a Minister has
been found who is prepared to take the thing up and share in the
general responsibility.'[13]

During the spring and summer of 1920, while ministers squabbled
among themselves over the executive control of the STO, a number
of outstanding military and legal problems were also considered. At
the ministerial conference on 2 February, Sir Nevil Macready had
been delegated to examine the question of firearms licensing and the
possible distribution of arms to loyal citizens. Macready gathered a
committee from the service departments – Romer represented the
War Office – and the Ministry of Munitions. He submitted his
report in the last week of February. The committee advised changes
in the law. The 1903 Pistols Act required licences to be held for
weapons with barrels not exceeding nine inches in length. Macready
recommended that this be extended to cover all firearms. As to the
more contentious part of their brief, the committee argued that in
the event of serious civil disorder, it would be necessary 'to organise
loyalists into cadres and units before any distribution of arms is
made to them'. They concluded that this could be done most effectively through the Special Constabulary organisation, with the War
Office and Admiralty assisting local Police Authorities to make 'a
selection from volunteers of those who had been accustomed to the
use of arms'. The committee also suggested that the War Office
hold at each regimental depot '1,000 stand of arms, together with
an adequate amount of small arm ammunition' for distribution when
required by the GOCinCs of each Army Command.[14]

Macready's legal recommendations were embodied in the Firearms Bill which was introduced into Parliament at the end of March.

The measure proposed, for the first time in the United Kingdom, a comprehensive system of gun licensing and control. In keeping with prevailing fears of possible civil disorder, it empowered the Army Council, the Air Council and the Admiralty to issue unlicensed firearms to civilians. The Bill passed through its successive stages in both Houses with relatively little comment, although Captain Wedgwood Benn, Liberal Member for Leith, expressed some concern with the powers given to the service departments. 'It would be interesting to know', he observed, 'how they intend to exercise that power and what their policy is with regard to such weapons.'[15] But there was no serious opposition, and in August the Bill passed its Third Reading in the Commons without a division. It took effect from 1 September 1920.

The Macready Committee report had less public consequences. The Home Office once more looked into the problem of reinforcing the police. In December 1919 Sir Edward Troup had written to Chief Constables encouraging them to develop a reserve force of Special Constables. He repeated his call in March 1920 and re-emphasised 'the fact that special constables will not be employed as strike breakers'. Within the Home Office there was concern about 'the reluctance of men of the middle class (who are specially interested in the maintenance of good order and ought to be the mainstay of the police reserve) to offer their services'. This was put down to a general uncertainty as to what liability Special Constables would incur and a strong plea was entered for new legislation to make the position quite clear. There was no immediate action on this and in the meantime Special Constables continued to be sworn in under the temporary legislation introduced at the beginning of the war. But despite departmental worries, Troup was able to tell the STC protection sub-committee towards the end of March that full-time police numbers had reached 54,000 in England and Wales. The men, he added, were 'quite contented and may be fully relied on'. In case of an emergency, about 91,000 Specials were available for immediate service, and it was thought that an additional 60,000 might be recruited in a few days.[16]

From the War Office Sir Henry Wilson kept on stressing the weakness of the forces in Great Britain. In March 1920 he sent a secret memorandum to Lloyd George outlining how few troops would be immediately available to meet any trouble in 'the colliery districts' and particularly drew attention to deficiencies in the transport and signals branches. The army, however, could not escape all responsibility for internal security. Eight hundred officers and men were earmarked to protect electric power stations and the principal railway termini in London. The Navy, too, provisionally agreed to assist in guarding various dock and port areas, but 'for extreme emergency only when police and military protection is not available'. In August the protection sub-committee, noting that there were then only 38 infantry battalions in Great Britain, as against 128 in September 1919, accepted the general principle that 'in any future emergency the reinforcement of the Regular Police should be effected by the enrolment of able bodied men in the Special Constabulary'. Wilson was quite prepared, as the Macready Committee had recommended, to hold weapons for their use. After the Firearms Act had received the Royal Assent on 16 August Wilson held a meeting at the War Office which agreed to stockpile rifles, machine guns and other equipment throughout the country in order, as Wilson put it in his diary, 'to start off Loyalists when they join up'.[17]

The question of special peacetime emergency legislation also exercised ministers and officials throughout much of 1920. The matter had received desultory attention during the winter months. In January the STC asked the Home and Scottish Offices, in consultation with other departments, to draft a Bill which would give the government full powers during an industrial emergency. On 23 March the Home Office presented a broadly drafted Bill to the committee. After a lengthy discussion it was agreed that no action should be taken until each department had decided what precise powers they would require under the following conditions:

(I)   At the outbreak of a strike and up to, say, the end of the first four days.

(II)  After the first four days when the struggle was becoming intense and was similar in gravity to the last railway strike.

(III) When the struggle involved serious civil disturbances amounting to attempts at revolution.

The committee added a specific wish 'that one of the powers should be authority to use armed forces of the Crown for non-military service during a strike.' But as was so often the case with planning for a hypothetical emergency, long-term preparations were upset by an actual crisis. In the last week of March 1920 there was a sudden threat of a national miners' strike, led by men in the South Wales pits, who demanded an increase in pay. On 25 March the STC met to consider the position. They redrew their three stages of emergency to include successively a coal strike in South Wales only, a national coal strike and a Triple Alliance strike. Departments were instructed to prepare accordingly. On 27 March they decided to postpone all work on the projected Emergency Powers Bill since the Defence of the Realm Regulations still applied, and 'the Government still possessed all the powers they had used during the last strike.'[18] At the beginning of April, however, the miners' immediate demands were met and the possibility of a strike receded.

The question of a permanent emergency legislation had still to be settled. As Arthur Neal remarked, sooner or later the wartime regulations would lapse and in default of any positive action, the government could easily be left with no emergency powers at all. The most pressing difficulty concerned the possible employment of servicemen. On 16 April Churchill circulated an important opinion which Sir Felix Cassel, the Judge Advocate-General, had prepared at the beginning of the year. He addressed himself to the problem of 'whether an order to soldiers or airmen to carry on vital services in the event of a strike is a lawful command.' He concluded that in general it was not and that a soldier could only be commanded 'to perform vital services' either if 'some military object, purpose or proceeding' was affected, or if 'the safety of the realm and the existence of the King's Government and authority' were so endangered that His Majesty had decided to hand over vital services to military administration or control. In his only Cabinet memorandum as chairman of the STC, Sir Laming Worthington-Evans urged that an Emergency Powers Bill be introduced without delay especially in order to give the administration power to employ servicemen on civilian duties. No one doubted that permanent legislation was necessary, but the question now arose as to how best it should be presented and when it would be most expedient to introduce it into Parliament. On 14 June the Cabinet Home Affairs Committee were deputed to examine the matter 'more particularly from a political point of view'.[19]

When the committee met on 12 July, Sir Eric Geddes noted that a draft Bill had been prepared by the Home Office, along with a summary of the powers desired by individual departments for the three stages laid down by the STC on 23 March. But the idea of a progressive increase in emergency powers had found little favour. Most of the powers requested fell into Class (I), including extensive authority for the control, rationing and requisitioning of vital supplies, and power to require servicemen to perform 'essential work'. In Class (II) the Home Office placed a number of more contentious items, such as 'extended power of police control', the prohibition of meetings, processions, picketing and 'loitering near railways with intent to injure', restrictions on the supply of alcohol and the power to sequester strike funds. They added that it would have been preferable to place these under Class (I), but, 'in view of Parliamentary considerations', this had not been suggested. Class (III) was left blank since no department was 'prepared to defer action until revolutionary disturbances arise'. Faced with so considerable a catalogue of emergency powers and a Bill which Geddes described as 'of a very drastic character', the committee were sharply divided on whether or not to recommend its immediate introduction into Parliament. If so, would it then be less provocative to labour opinion than if it was introduced when a major strike seemed imminent? On the one hand it was argued that 'if the Government were ever to legislate they should choose a time of industrial peace and not wait until a crisis.' On the other, it was asserted that 'a Measure of this sort would certainly raise highly contentious questions and might precipitate the crisis which it is desired to avoid.' Although Geddes and Shortt favoured immediate introduction, Herbert Fisher, the cautious chairman of the committee, preferred to play safe and not to risk stirring up labour passions. His views swayed the Cabinet and on 4 August they decided 'to hold the proposed Bill in abeyance until the autumn session'.[20] It was characteristic of successive British governments between the wars – and since – to adopt a circumspect approach to contingency planning. Ministers and officials were tremendously wary about revealing to Parliament or the general public the nature or extent of their emergency arrangements. Partly, no doubt, this stemmed from the inherent secrecy of British administration. But it also arose from quite genuine, although largely unfounded, fears that the Labour movement would vigorously, if not violently, resist any schemes which might be interpreted as 'strikebreaking'. The result of this was that when any element of emergency planning was made public, it was generally at the height of an industrial crisis, at precisely the time when Parliamentary and public opinion was least able dispassionately to weigh up either its short-term merits or long-term consequences. Such was the case with the Emergency Powers Bill.

Throughout the late summer of 1920 tension rose in the mines. In April Lloyd George had instructed the mine owners to pay additional wages for increased production, but negotiations between employers and miners on the details of a productivity agreement began to falter in August and September. It seemed certain that a strike must come sooner or later. On 12 August the STC was convened for the first time since May to prepare for a full-scale mobilisation of the STO. So seriously did Geddes consider the position that he rushed with Shortt from the STC to a meeting of the Cabinet Finance Committee to urge Lloyd George both that the organisation be activated and that the Emergency Powers Bill be introduced at once. The STC, he claimed, 'could do nothing further until open action could be taken', and he stressed the over-riding need for legislation enabling servicemen to perform civilian duties. It had already been pointed out to the Cabinet that, although there was provision for this in the Defence of the Realm Regulations, because active hostilities were at an end and the war continued only in a technical sense, to use servicemen for pumping the mines or maintaining electric power stations would be of doubtful legality. But ministers still hesitated to introduce the Bill and they decided 'it would be better to rely on the inherent powers of the Crown and obtain indemnity from Parliament afterwards.'[21] It was more expedient to break, rather than make, law.

The government's worries were also increased by a general upsurge in labour militancy. Since early in the year it had seemed possible that Britain and France might intervene on the side of the Poles in their war against Soviet Russia. This was solidly opposed by the Labour movement. 'Councils of Action' sprang up throughout the country and plans were made for a general strike. 'Though the threatened strike of the miners looms so large,' reported the Special Branch, 'it is probably not really the most dangerous factor in the present situation. The real danger is the very rapid growth of revolutionary feeling that has followed the establishment of the "Councils of Action".' The STC proposed a sustained propaganda campaign 'showing the suffering that would arise from revolutionary movements' and urged the Home Secretary to press on with the recruitment of Special Constables, confidently assuming that this 'could not be described as provocative action nor could it possibly result in irritation of the public.' The seriousness with which some officials viewed the position is illustrated by the suggestion made to the STC in late September that British workers might follow the example of Italian extremists by commandeering factories and means of transport. But this was going too far. 'Even in South Wales', the secretary minuted, 'the spirit of the workers was quite different from that of the Italian workmen.'[22]

Although the threat of war passed – the Poles managed to defeat the Russians without assistance – that of a miners' strike did not. Despite being hampered by the government's insistence on secrecy, the STC continued to tune up the emergency organisation. Sub-committees were instructed to review their strike arrangements and 'Zero Lists' were prepared of the action required both in the event of a coal strike and a full-scale Triple Alliance stoppage. The Supply Department, adopting a pseudonymous telegraphic address – 'Seaweed Cent London' – devised a simple code to inform chairmen of Voluntary Service Committees when the enrolment of volunteers should begin. The STC determined the powers and duties of the regional Civil Commissioners, all of whom were junior members of the government. These extended even to dealing with general questions of policy 'in the event of all communication with the Central Government breaking down'. Tentative and confidential contacts were made with the Federation of British Industries who had offered assistance in maintaining essential services.[23] While Lloyd George left detailed planning to the STC, he was not himself entirely free from the prevailing concern for internal security. On 15 September he asked Sir Henry Wilson if the army was 'sound'. Wilson assured him that it was and described the precautionary measures he had already taken. All drafts of troops abroad had been suspended and infantry battalions were being brought back from the Rhine and Constantinople. Wilson also increased the reserve stores at each infantry depot to 10,000 sets of rifles and equipment.[24]

After a breakdown in negotiations, the miners decided to strike on 16 October. At once the tempo of government action quickened, but it was still characterised by an element of indecision. While civil servants were inclined to take a hard line towards the strike, ministers, presumably more aware of the political implications of over-hasty action, hesitated to adopt a full-blooded approach. On 14 October the STC agreed that the Civil Commissioners should leave for their districts not later than 16 October. The following day they reversed this decision since the Commissioners themselves strongly believed that no overt move should be made until it was 'imperatively necessary'. In the meantime the Cabinet returned to the question of the Emergency Powers Bill. At a meeting on 15 October the First Lord of the Admiralty observed that naval ratings could not legally be used for civilian duties. 'The men', he continued ominously, 'knew their legal position, and had been urged by Bolshevik agents to refuse to obey orders in the event of a strike.' This was precisely the difficulty the Bill had been drafted to meet, but the Cabinet generally thought that unless the railwaymen (as seemed possible) also came out on strike, it would be better not to rush the measure through Parliament. At the War Office Sir Henry Wilson swung into action. All leave was cancelled, two battalions of Guards were moved from Aldershot to London and armoured car companies were sent to 'Scotland, York & Worcester'. Wilson additionally wanted to send tanks north, but Bonar Law asked him to wait until it became clear whether or not there would be a railway stoppage.[25] In this respect, as in others, the government were anxious not to do anything which might provoke further labour unrest.

On Thursday 21 October the railwaymen announced that they would come out on strike if negotiations with the miners were not resumed within three days. The government reacted with a mixture of coercion and conciliation. Late that evening Sir Henry Wilson obtained Lloyd George's permission to move two battalions of infantry by rail to Liverpool and tanks to the North. Next morning the STC discussed the possibility of railwaymen refusing to work troop trains. It was suggested that the Ministry of Shipping could provide for their transport by sea, but this was opposed 'on the ground that it would probably antagonise the Seamen's Union and might result in a Seamen's strike'. In the end it was left to the Ministry of Shipping and Admiralty together to arrange transport. The STC decided that the Civil Commissioners should immediately go to their districts and 'make all necessary preparations which could not be considered provocative'. It also instructed the Admiralty to dispatch a battleship to Liverpool 'for purposes of protection, if required'. Since it was widely believed that a railway strike would inevitably presage a more general stoppage, the Cabinet agreed that naval ratings would have to be used for running power stations, even if it were not possible to obtain the passage of the Emergency Powers Bill beforehand.²⁶ The Prime Minister decided that the Bill must be introduced at once. On the afternoon of Friday 22 October it was presented to the Commons by the Home Secretary. Although the government had intended to ask Parliament to suspend standing orders and pass the Bill in one sitting, there was such strong opposition to this – not only from Labour members – that the second reading debate was held over until Monday 25 October. During the weekend the railwaymen's action had a more direct effect on the coal dispute itself. Lloyd George invited the miners to renewed negotiations. The railwaymen withdrew their strike notices and within a few days the government had agreed to pay an interim rise in wages, leaving a more permanent settlement to be made in 1921, when the pits were to be handed back to their private owners. The Cabinet, nevertheless, pressed on with the Emergency Powers Bill. In Parliament Bonar Law denied that the Bill was provocative, observed that it had been prepared for months, and disingenuously implied that the present time was as good as any for its passage. Although there was a general feeling on both sides of the House regretting the timing of the measures, the strongest criticism naturally came from the Labour benches. It was led by two miners' union leaders, William Adamson and Stephen Walsh, who characterised the Bill as an attack on the working class and the trade union movement. 'I do not think', commented Adamson, 'that panic legislation of this kind can be good legislation.' J. M. Hogge, an Asquithian Liberal, tried to frighten the House with the spectre of a socialist administration employing emergency powers. 'The Bill', he observed, 'confers a dictatorship upon the Executive of the Government – not only this Government, but a Labour Government which may happen to be in power.' Members, however, were doubtless reassured by J. R. Clynes, the cautious, conservative vice-chairman of the Parliamentary Labour Party, who approved the Bill in principle. 'Provisions must be made in an exceptional way', he asserted, 'to meet the life needs of the nation. I do not regard steps of that kind as breaking a strike.'²⁷ Many Labour politicians – as would be demonstrated by both MacDonald and Attlee – shared with their Conservative and Liberal colleagues a determination to resist the apparently increasing power and willingness of the unions to bring the country to a standstill. After twenty hours' debate, the

Bill was passed by 238 votes to 58.[28] It received the Royal Assent on Friday 29 October 1920.

The Emergency Powers Act[29] is a statute of only three clauses. It provides for the declaration of a state of emergency – to last for one month – at any time when the action or threatened action of 'any persons or body of persons' interferes with the community's 'essentials of life'. It specifically lists disruption of the supply and distribution of 'food, water, fuel, . . . light, or . . . the means of locomotion'. Under a state of emergency the executive is empowered to make any regulations necessary to secure the supply of essential services, 'for the preservation of the peace' and 'for any other purposes essential to the public safety and the life of the community'. In order to meet some of the criticisms voiced during the Second Reading debate, government amendments were added in committee to prohibit the making of regulations either 'imposing any form of compulsory military service or industrial conscription', or limiting the existing right to strike or to picket. Emergency regulations were specifically excluded from the normal procedure for making statutory rules, which required that proposed rules be published at least forty days before being implemented. Although no provision is made for Parliament actually to revoke a declaration of emergency, the Act requires that Parliament should meet within five days of such a declaration, and also that any regulations will lapse unless confirmed by parliamentary resolution within seven days of being made. The Act finally released the government from the unsatisfactory necessity of having to rely on wartime legislation for emergency powers in peacetime, and in particular provided the means by which servicemen might be employed on non-military duties. Since 1920 states of emergency have been declared on twelve occasions – three times between the wars and nine since.[30] Although the majority of declarations have been made by Conservative governments, Labour administrations have done so on four occasions (1924, 1948, 1949, and 1966). In this respect, at least, Mr Hogge was proved right.

The events of October 1920 aptly demonstrate Lloyd George's consummate ability to run with the hare and hunt with the hounds. By compromising with the miners he defused a tense industrial crisis and neatly avoided the possibility of a Triple Alliance stoppage. At the same time he took the opportunity to establish the legal basis for the government's strikebreaking organisation. The

Emergency Powers Act, moreover, was couched in such broad terms as to give the executive almost complete freedom to introduce what regulations it chose. Since the miners returned to work on 3 November there was no need to declare a state of emergency and the Supply and Transport Organisation, which had spent nearly £70,000 preparing for a major strike, was swiftly run down. Over the winter months Geddes busied himself with putting the whole organisation on a sound permanent footing. He had the backing of the Cabinet who agreed in January 1921 that 'the greatest danger in front of any Government in the next two years would be the danger of a great strike.' In March £64,000 was allotted to be spent on a 'skeleton' organisation in the following financial year. Mainly for reasons of economy a general principle was established that civil servants should not work exclusively on emergency planning. The Supply Department, for example, with an annual budget of just £1,000, was staffed entirely by Ministry of Health officials. Christopher Roundell combined a Ministry inspectorship with being 'chief of staff', although he was later given a generous allowance of £150 per annum for these additional duties – thus increasing his salary by almost one-fifth. The winding-down of wartime government departments brought some changes in the emergency organisation. Preparations were made to transfer emergency functions from the disbanding Ministries of Food and Shipping to the Board of Trade. Since the Emergency Powers Act potentially secured wide powers of requisition, the STC were able to dispose of nearly half a million pounds' worth of retained stores and vehicles.[31]

Peacetime 'decontrol' in the mines had a more dramatic effect. With the collapse of the post-war boom and the recovery of the French and German coal industry, at the beginning of 1921 the government found itself losing money in the mines. It was decided to bring forward their transfer back to the private owners from 31 August to 31 March. On 1 April the owners, whose proposals for wage-cuts had been rejected by the miners, began a lock-out. In return the miners appealed to the Triple Alliance to come out in sympathy. The government's reaction was swift. On 31 March a series of high-level meetings set the Supply and Transport Organisation in action. At midday the STC met. It noted that 'the Miners' strike might develop into something much wider', and the secretary sombrely recorded that 'although the Railwaymen were understood to be averse to a strike they might go so far as to declare coal

"Black".' The committee authorised the Home Secretary to make an immediate proclamation under the Emergency Powers Act, halted all exports of coal and activated the finance and publicity sub-committees. That afternoon another sub-committee prepared 'Zero' lists – now to be called 'action lists' – both for a coal stoppage only and a full Triple Alliance strike. Representatives of the Home Office and the service ministries met to discuss the available military and naval resources along with the possibility of moving troops to potential trouble-spots. At the War Office Wilson, although noting in his diary that he did not fully believe the Triple Alliance would strike, still thought 'we should prepare for & consider the worst'. His principal concern was a shortage of troops and, not being a man to do things by half measures, he drew up plans to bring units back to Great Britain from Ireland, the Rhine, Malta, Egypt, Palestine and Constantinople.[32] On 1 April the 'coal only' list was activated, although this included little more than a series of measures to conserve fuel, along with instructing police forces to enrol Special Constables. Among the former, the STC decided that horse racing should be suspended 'both in order to save coal and petrol and in order to bring home to the public the seriousness of the situation'.[33]

On the first day of the stoppage the government also issued the first set of regulations promulgated under the Emergency Powers Act. It contained most of the powers requested by departments the previous summer. Any 'approved' government office was authorised to take possession 'where it appears necessary to do so' of 'land, . . . food, forage, material and stores'. The Board of Trade was given extensive powers 'for the purpose of securing or regulating the supply and distribution of food'. The Ministry of Transport received similar authority with regard to road, rail and canal transport. Specific regulations dealt with the control of all firearms, public meetings, processions and acts 'likely to cause mutiny, sedition or disaffection among any of His Majesty's forces, or among members of any police force, or any fire brigade, or among the civilian population'. Under this last heading, however, it was provided that no one would be guilty of an offence 'by reason only of his taking part in a strike or peacefully persuading any other person to take part in a strike'. The most contentious regulation was No. 22 which laid down that members of the armed forces had to perform any service which a Secretary of State 'by order' had declared to be 'of vital importance to the community'. The regulations were debated in the House of Commons on 5 and 6 April. Edward Shortt told members that the government was simply 'carrying out a duty which we owe to the community'. There was, however, considerable opposition from both Labour and Asquithian Liberal MPs. Josiah Wedgwood – who was, ironically, to be appointed Chief Civil Commissioner by Ramsay MacDonald in 1924 – described the regulations as 'autocracy', while Wedgwood Benn declared that the Prime Minister was 'arming himself with the necessary powers to carry out . . . class war'. The most strenuous objections were levelled at Regulation 22. Lieutenant-Commander Kenworthy called it 'forced labour' and J. R. Clynes asserted that servicemen 'did not join up to become blacklegs upon compulsion'. But their protests were in vain. The regulations were passed with a very comfortable government majority.[34]

With the introduction of the emergency regulations and the 'tuning-up' of the Supply and Transport Organisation, the government had begun to withdraw an iron hand from what was in any case a somewhat threadbare velvet glove. Yet there was more to come. On Monday 4 April the Cabinet met to consider the coal crisis for the first time. Nearly all ministers came, with the most notable exception of Churchill who was at the time returning home from a conference in Cairo. Significantly Sir Henry Wilson was invited to attend. Although Lloyd George announced that the government's policy ought to be moderate and conciliatory, he also reported J. H. Thomas's[35] opinion that 'Jesus Christ couldn't prevent the railwaymen coming in'. The meeting began optimistically enough, but ministers progressively became more gloomy. Edward Shortt thought there would be bloodshed. Birkenhead and Austen Chamberlain took a similarly bleak view, while Sir Eric Geddes, who had begun the meeting in a comparatively sanguine frame of mind, had become convinced by the end that a Triple Alliance strike was a near-certainty. Sir Maurice Hankey blamed Wilson for the Cabinet's alarm. Apparently Wilson had travelled up from the country with Chamberlain and had infected him with his own panic. Chamberlain, in turn, had influenced his colleagues and even, by the end of the meeting, the Prime Minister himself. Whatever doubts he may have confided to his diary, in Cabinet Wilson pursued his point with ruthless logic. If, he argued, the government *was* up against 'the big thing', then serious action had to be taken. It should scrape up troops from every command, mobilise the Army Reserve, embody the Territorial Force and 'call upon all loyal citizens to enrol'. Almost nothing pleased Wilson more than 'frightening the Frocks'. On this occasion his words struck home and the Cabinet approved most of what he wanted. Later that day Wilson ordered infantry units back from Ireland, Malta and the Rhine. Tanks and armoured cars were concentrated at London, Glasgow, York and Worcester. He also instructed three cavalry regiments and eleven infantry battalions to move to London, where a special camp was established in Kensington Gardens. The question of organising loyal citizens was delegated to a committee chaired by Birkenhead. 'I wish Winston were here for this,' remarked Lloyd George. 'He would be useful.'[36]

Lloyd George was clearly concerned with the possibility of troops being brought in to keep order on the streets. Alarmed, perhaps, by military attitudes as expressed by Wilson, on the evening of 5 April he interviewed General Jeffreys, GOC London District. The meeting was deeply unsatisfactory for both men. Jeffreys struck the Prime Minister as 'bumptious and half insolent', lacking 'the judgement, the calm, and the commonsense' required for the defence of London. Lloyd George asked Worthington-Evans, the Secretary for War, to replace him. 'Premature and unwise action', he wrote, 'by a light-headed officer with great notions of showing himself to be a strong man may well precipitate a terrible catastrophe.' For his part the General took equal umbrage with Lloyd George and went to see the CIGS. 'Jeffreys described to me his interview last night . . .', noted Wilson, '& the d – silly questions L.G. asked him about the danger of Red Trench Mortars on the roof of the Ritz, of crowds collecting in 2s and 3s, of guarding Whitehall, etc.' Wilson was outraged that on a matter of military policy Lloyd George had gone behind his back. He assured Worthington-Evans that he had complete confidence in Jeffreys and that, in his opinion, 'to put it bluntly, the P.M. was in a funk'. In the end Wilson settled for a compromise. Jeffreys remained at his Command but the Earl of Cavan – generally accepted to be a 'steadier' officer – was brought in over him with the special temporary appointment of GOCinC, Metropolitan Police Area.[37]

While the government geared itself up for a Triple Alliance strike, so too did the railwaymen and transport workers.[38] On 9 April the executives of the National Union of Railwaymen and the Transport Workers' Federation threatened a joint strike if the government had not begun negotiations with the miners within three days. Henry Wilson interpreted the period of grace as faint-heartedness on the part of the unions. 'One quick movement of troops', he concluded crudely, 'has given the brutes cold feet.'[39] But this was too simple a view, particularly since naked force was as likely to inflame labour feeling as to disarm it. The principal points at issue were the miners' insistence that wages should not be cut and their demand that a 'national pool' be established to equalise wages throughout the industry. Funded by a levy on every ton of coal produced, the pool would make up the shortfall between production costs and revenue in the poorer pits. For the miners' allies, although they generally approved the principle of national wage rates, their chief interest lay in resisting the massive wage cuts threatened by the pit owners, which would inevitably have an effect on the whole labour market. The government, however, believed that since the pool could only work through state regulation, it was tantamount to nationalisation. On 11 April Lloyd George secured a postponement of the 'Triple' strike by agreeing to chair a conference of miners and mine owners, but the following day negotiations broke down when the Prime Minister, while prepared to offer a temporary government subsidy to take the sting out of wage cuts, absolutely refused to consider the pool. The transport and rail leaders, despite growing irritation among their union members with the miners' apparent intransigence, responded by announcing that they would come out at 10.00 p.m. on Friday 15 April.

With the emergency machine already on 'stand-by', the STC considered what further action could be taken. They discussed sending government propaganda personally to the wives of miners, denying subsidised school meals to their children and sequestering trade union bank accounts. But common sense prevailed and these suggestions were not taken up. On 14 April, after a final appeal to the transport and railway unions had been rejected, the Cabinet gave Sir Eric Geddes authority to activate the full STO. The STC met hurriedly to make the necessary arrangements. That evening, however, there was a dramatic turn in events. At a meeting in the House of Commons, Frank Hodges, Secretary of the Miners' Federation, said that he believed his executive would be prepared to accept a satisfactory pay settlement pending an agreement on the national pool. At once Lloyd George offered to convene talks on wages alone. On the Friday morning there was great confusion. The press asserted that the crisis was over and the Triple Alliance strike off. The railwaymen and transport workers urged the miners to resume negotiations. But the miners' executive, declining to discuss their position even with the other members of the Alliance, refused to back Hodges and stood firm on their demand that wages and the pool must be considered jointly. This was too much for their allies for whom the wages question was paramount. That afternoon – 'Black Friday' as it became known – they decided not to strike. Ironically the news was formally conveyed to the Prime Minister by J. H. Thomas. Next day the STC, who had already begun to wind down their machine, was officially instructed 'to demobilise that portion of its organisation which had been put into force to meet the Transport Strike'. Thus they were denied the opportunity fully to test the emergency organisation. 'Judging by what happened in those districts which could not be reached by cancelling telegrams during the night', recalled Leo Amery, who had taken over as Chief Civil Commissioner from Kellaway at the beginning of April, 'the mobilization would have gone like clockwork.' Tom Jones took a typically disrespectful view:

> The Strike Committee very sick. They had been waiting for two years to press the button. They had pressed it. . . . But Jim Thomas upset it all and despoiled Sir Hindenburg Geddes of the fruits of victory and was being damned as a traitor by the miners and was hardly being thanked as Saviour by the Cabinet, so hard is it even for Welshmen to please everybody.

Following Black Friday the Cabinet concluded that 'the readiness of the Supply and Transport arrangements had been an important factor in avoiding an extension of the Coal Strike.'[40] There was some truth in this. The government could hardly 'break' a coal strike, merely mitigate its effects. Against transport workers, however, the STO was a much more formidable weapon. While no one considered enlisting volunteers to dig coal, there was no shortage whatever of men willing to drive buses, lorries and, perhaps especially, trains. The real power of the railway and transport unions lay not so much in actually striking but in *threatening* to strike. This tactic worked successfully in October 1920, but six months later Lloyd George called their bluff. 'I do not mind their coming out,' he had told the Cabinet on 12 April. 'I believe you can prick the bubble.'[41] The miners, not unnaturally, were less concerned with the pragmatic difficulties of a transport strike than with their allies' apparent promise of support. Betrayed on Black Friday, they bitterly held out alone until the beginning of July when they were forced to accept the owners' terms.

Although the government's action during the first fortnight of April was superficially resolute, it stemmed more from panic than confidence. At times ministers and officials seem to have been unsure as to whether they were facing a strike or nascent revolution. Birkenhead's committee on military resources viewed the position so seriously that they advised the Cabinet both to mobilise the service reserves and also to set up a 'Defence Force' in which ex-servicemen and Territorial soldiers would be specially invited to enlist. On 8 April this was done. The Defence Force was not a revival of the Citizen Guard raised in October 1919, but a specifically military force, armed, and enlisted under the Army Act for a limited period of ninety days. Although some 80,000 men joined the force, only a small fraction of this number was ever employed on protection duties. The establishment of the Defence Force raised a number of largely unforeseen difficulties. On 13 April the Cabinet was told of reports that 'Sinn Feiners, strikers and Communists were enlisting with a view to levanting with their arms'. Shockingly, 'the Recruiting Officers had no means of distinguishing Sinn Feiners or Communists'. Ministers, however, were doubtless reassured to learn that 'a careful watch was being kept' and they somewhat superfluously agreed 'that it was inadvisable at present to enlist strikers'. Another problem lay in the attitude of local authorities, who had been specifically requested by the Prime Minister to encourage recruitment for the Defence Force. The Lord Mayor of Birmingham, as a Quaker, personally refused to co-operate in raising a 'military force'. In Nottingham there was general hesitation concerning the scheme, while in south Wales, where Labour was well represented on the local councils, doubts were raised as to the value of the force at all. 'Against whom', telegraphed one council chairman, 'in this area do you presume it is necessary to use proposed Defence Force?'[42]

The mobilisation of military reserves was symptomatic of the government's trepidation. It also demonstrated the dangers of over-hasty action. Since it was believed that the army could not cope alone, royal navy and air force reservists were collected into units for general protection duties throughout the country. The naval contribution alone was equivalent to twenty-five battalions of infantry. But the Cabinet's action caught the services somewhat unprepared. Units were hurriedly mustered and given no clear idea of their exact function. Many of the naval battalions were billeted in sub-standard temporary accommodation. The result – particularly after Black Friday, when the steam had been taken out of the emergency – was a grumbling discontent which even reached the Admiralty. Late in April two companies of a Royal Fleet Reserve battalion stationed at Newport, Monmouthshire, refused to parade. Although their principal grievance concerned living conditions, the men also pointed out that nearly all of them were trade unionists and 'would lay down their arms if called to use them upon their fellow workmen'. There was some unrest too among the army reserves. Early in May Sir Henry Wilson spent two days among the troops in Dover, investigating complaints and giving morale-boosting talks to the officers. Some time later all three service departments urged the Cabinet not to call up the reserves except in times of the gravest crisis. The men, maintained the Admiralty, had been very much disturbed by the mobilisation since 'they never contemplated the possibility of this happening in any emergency other than actual war'.[43] But the mobilisation also had its lighter side. Reservists of the Lancaster Regiment had sufficient free time to play football with the strikers. Edward Russell (later Lord Russell of Liverpool) found himself posted as adjutant to a reserve battalion composed almost entirely of Yorkshire miners. 'They gave us no trouble', he recalled, 'and appeared to enjoy the change, and they saw the funny side of striking and then being called back to the Army to keep order if necessary.'[44] Doubtless, under the circumstances, they also appreciated even army rates of pay. Perhaps this is some evidence to suggest the inherent improbability of a British revolution; the lack of a 'revolutionary condition'. Nevertheless, the mistake of calling up the service reserves was not repeated in 1926.

Throughout the 1921 coal crisis the Cabinet were keenly aware of the power of propaganda and the need to turn public opinion against the unions. A particular point was made of stressing the 'neutrality' of the government. When announcing the creation of the Defence Force, Lloyd George declared that it was being recruited, 'not for the purpose of interfering in any wage dispute, but solely to support the Police in the fulfilment of their duties to the community'. Volunteers for the emergency organisation were en-

couraged to join up by advertisements in the national press headed
'How can I help the Nation?' The STC publicity sub-committee
under Sir Philip Lloyd-Greame (later Cunliffe-Lister) pursued its
task with devious sophistication. Pamphlets, press releases, 'cinema
propaganda' and posters were produced. As Lloyd-Greame told the
Cabinet, 'the art of propaganda was to conceal it.' Briefs for speakers
and writers, 'bearing no indication of their official origin, were
issued two or three times a week during the critical period' and
distributed through various political and semi-political organisations
such as the Central Unionist Association, the Middle Class Union
and the Women's Guild of Empire, who were afterwards singled
out for their 'very capable and effective service . . . in house to
house visiting, speaking and distribution of literature'. A special
effort was made to circulate a pamphlet entitled 'Save the Mines' in
Scotland, which was particularly thought to be the 'danger zone'.
The publicity committee operated throughout the coal strike and in
July Leopold Amery, who succeeded Lloyd-Greame as chairman,
reported that in three months over £55,000 had been spent on
government propaganda.[45]

After Black Friday the STC continued to deal with the problems
of the continuing coal stoppage. The state of emergency was extended three times – until 26 July – but the emergency regulations
were allowed to lapse after the miners had returned to work. During
the early summer, however, the Supply and Transport Organisation
was gradually demobilised, principally, as Geddes observed, in order
to save money. Horse racing was again permitted. Although the
Defence Force was retained for its full ninety days, the service
reserves were demobilised with a gratuity of £5 each at the very
beginning of June.[46] There was also a widespread decline in industrial unrest, so much so that in August the Special Branch assured
the Cabinet: 'the general aspect of labour is more peaceful than it
has been for several years.' More than anything else, this change
was due to the deepening economic depression. In mid-1921 unemployment passed two million.[47] Industrial wages fell. Trade union
membership dropped. This was not the time for labour militancy.

It was equally not the time to be spending large sums on a
strikebreaking organisation. Faced with mounting public criticism
of the high level of government expenditure, Lloyd George em-
barked on a policy of strict retrenchment. Every department was
instructed to economise and Sir Eric Geddes was appointed in

August 1921 to chair a committee of businessmen with a brief to examine national expenditure. Although the committee did not specifically consider the STO, on 15 September Geddes himself circulated a Cabinet paper on the subject. He proposed that, with the exception of the Supply Department, which had valuable expertise for recruiting volunteers, the STO should be disbanded. Even to retain a skeleton organisation would cost over £50,000 a year:

This machinery has been in existence for two years and has, I think, served its purpose well. It was essential that for the maintenance of order and decent living the Government should take upon itself during the period of unrest which followed the war, the duty of protecting the community from the irresponsible attacks of extremists. The war had created in the people a habit of looking to the Government for direction and initiative in almost every department of life, and the Government was the only body which possessed sufficient strength to oppose the great industrial organisations. This state of things has now passed. Private initiative has once more reasserted itself. The power of the Trade Unions has visibly diminished, principally from economic causes, and the general strike has failed. I do not think it will be tried again in the immediate future.

Geddes's paper prompted Leopold Amery and Stanley Baldwin to add their opinions. Amery supported the view that the Supply Department should be retained along with the local organisation of Voluntary Service Committees. The cost, he remarked, would be negligible. Baldwin, who as President of the Board of Trade was responsible for the food scheme, agreed that the time had come for disbandment and echoed Geddes's *laissez-faire* sentiments. The government's change of policy, he argued, should be announced publicly since 'traders and consumers alike have become so accustomed during the last two years to regard the maintenance of food and other essential services as a normal function of government, that private enterprise can hardly be expected to reassert itself adequately unless the necessity is made absolutely clear.'[48]

The matter was referred to the Home Affairs Committee for a final decision. It accepted Geddes's proposals and instructed the STC sub-committee to prepare a nucleus scheme costing not more than £2,000 a year. Arthur Neal told the meeting that Sir Eric

Geddes was shortly to resign from the Cabinet and resume his business career. It was decided, therefore, that the Home Secretary should be appointed in his place 'with the special duty of watching the industrial situation and with power to call together the Supply and Transport Committee should occasion arise'. The sub-committee re-affirmed the policy that the main burden of responsibility for emergency planning should be shifted from the government to industry and local councils. It is always a convenient means of cutting public expenditure to switch the onus from the Treasury either to the private sector or to local authorities, or, as in this case, both. In order to restrict central expenditure as much as possible, it was also laid down that 'any necessary work on emergency questions should be recognised as part of the ordinary duties of a Government Department' and should not require any increase in the normal staff. They recommended a scheme costing £1,750 a year and suggested that the sub-committee itself should continue in existence, meeting to review the organisation at least every six months during times of industrial peace. These proposals were approved by the Home Affairs Committee in March 1922. Although the committee did not take up Baldwin's suggestion of a public announcement, in May local authority clerks were informed that in future they would have to make their own emergency arrangements.[49] Thus the STO was reduced to little more than the Supply Department – now re-named the Civil Commissioners' Department. St Quintin Hill, however, conscientiously prepared a detailed memorandum describing the organisation 'as it existed during the Coal Strike of 1921, at which time . . . [it] . . . had reached its highest stage of development'. This was in case, 'at some future date, His Majesty's Government may desire to reconstruct a similar organisation.'[50]

# 4
# Conservative concern and Labour caution
# Late 1922 – February 1926

IN OCTOBER 1922 Lloyd George's coalition government was brought down by a revolt of Conservative backbenchers. On 23 October Bonar Law, who had resigned from the Cabinet through ill health in March 1921, formed the first Conservative government for sixteen years and immediately called a general election. It resulted in an unexpectedly decisive victory for the Conservatives, who won 345 seats and gained an absolute Parliamentary majority of 75. The Liberals, split between Lloyd George and Asquith factions, won only 116 seats. The election marked a significant rise in the fortunes of the Labour Party who received nearly 30 per cent of the popular vote and increased their representation from 87 MPs at the time Parliament was dissolved, to 142.[1] Their newly elected leader, Ramsay MacDonald, became Leader of the Opposition and thus raised the possibility, unattractive to some, that he might one day head a Labour administration. The opportunity was to come sooner than anyone expected.

In the meantime Bonar Law had to form a government of his own. With the notable exceptions of Lord Curzon and Stanley Baldwin, who became Foreign Secretary and Chancellor of the Exchequer respectively, most of the leading coalition Conservative ministers refused to serve under Bonar Law and his eventual team was marked by a combination of land-owning gentility and political obscurity. Of the 16 members in the Cabinet, 7 were peers and 8 had no previous ministerial experience. The new Home Secretary, William Bridgeman, was dismissed by Churchill as 'a man hitherto utterly unknown'.[2] But it was not perhaps a great disadvantage that the Cabinet was largely composed of undistinguished and unexciting men, since the new Prime Minister, in marked contrast to his restless predecessor, cultivated a deliberate policy of dullness. In his election mainfesto Bonar Law promised 'tranquillity and stability', and declared that the nation's 'first need' was 'to get on with its own work, with the minimum of interference at home and of disturbance abroad'.[3] He firmly set himself against any dramatic change and, in so far as he offered any positive policies at all, these were restricted to dismantling what he saw as the worst excesses of the Lloyd George administration.

One such was the Cabinet Secretariat, which had effectively included Lloyd George's substantial retinue of personal advisers. Housed in temporary huts behind No. 10, it was popularly known as the 'Garden Suburb'. During the election campaign Bonar Law promised to 'bring the Cabinet Secretariat in its present form to an end'. In the interests of efficiency and economy it would in future be amalgamated with the Treasury. This was the signal for some sharp Whitehall infighting. Sir Warren Fisher, who as Permanent Secretary to the Treasury resented the Secretariat's influential position, immediately, in Hankey's words, launched a 'long prepared attack with the whole strength of the Civil Service Rifles'. Hankey, Cabinet Secretary since the office had been established in 1916, was appalled and dismayed by the Prime Minister's attitude. But he was well able to defend himself. After strong representations to Bonar Law and arduous negotiations with Fisher, he succeeded in retaining his department's independence. He could not, however, save the Garden Suburb and the size of the Secretariat was drastically cut from 144 to 28. One victim of the purge was St Quintin Hill, who was transferred to the Board of Trade. Secretary of the STC subcommittee since 1919, Hill, according to Hankey, probably knew 'more than anyone else of the dormant arrangements as a whole for maintaining the essential services of the nation during great strikes'.[4]

By the time Bonar Law assumed power the economy had begun to recover from the 1920–1 depression. During 1922 industrial production (with some exceptions such as building and shipbuilding), exports and consumer expenditure all showed signs of improvement. Although the numbers of unemployed fell to 1.4 million in October 1922, there was widespread concern that this figure was altogether too large. Unemployment was a constant worry in the inter-war years. Between 1921 and 1939 it never fell below 1 million and was frequently very much higher. Bonar Law's attitude was one of orthodox economics. In contrast to the unprecedented and aberrant level of state intervention during the war, the government clearly saw its role as simply one of providing for the efficient operation of a free market economy. This meant little more than balancing the budget irrespective of the state of the economy, reducing taxation and pursuing a policy of industrial non-intervention. This did not preclude the government offering advice and encouragement to industry. Early in December 1922 Bonar Law urged the railway owners to undertake 'works which might set the wheels of industry turning'. But he refused to intervene in wage negotiations between miners and employers, and rejected a call from the TUC in January 1923 that Parliament should be specially summoned to debate the unemployment problem. He was, however, attracted to the idea that tariff reform might protect some sectors of industry from cheap foreign imports, but, knowing that to abandon the traditional British policy of free trade might again split the Conservative Party as it had done in 1906, he pledged that he would not introduce protective tariffs without first calling a general election.[5]

There was markedly less industrial unrest in 1923 than in any of the years since the war. In 1921, for example, 86 million working days were lost through industrial disputes; in 1923 the figure was 10.6 million. In the spring of that year, however, there were serious disputes in the building trade, on the railways and among agricultural workers in Norfolk. This seems to have persuaded Bonar Law that the time had come to review the government's strikebreaking organisation. On 21 March, two days after the builders had threatened a nationwide stoppage, Sir Maurice Hankey, at the direction of the Prime Minister, circulated to the Cabinet a memorandum describing the STO as it had existed under the previous government: the Cabinet committee, the system of Civil Commissioners and the Standing sub-committee. 'As the result of measures taken to secure economy', he continued, 'many of the Supply and Transport arrangements have been allowed to fall into abeyance, and it follows that, while it is necessary to retain the organisation in some form, modifications of the machinery hitherto existing are entailed.' Hankey suggested that the two committees be retained as before, although the sub-committee should be no longer chaired by a junior minister, but by a civil servant – the Permanent Under-Secretary to the Home Office. As a result of the Cabinet Office's contraction he also recommended that overall responsibility for the STO should be transferred to the Home Office, 'as the Department charged ultimately with securing the internal safety of the subject and of the community'. Finally it was proposed that, if no ministers objected, the STC sub-committee would be reconvened, under the chairmanship of Sir John Anderson, to investigate the whole existing organisation and report 'at an early date as to the best machinery and its method of control'.[6]

The review of the STO, however, was delayed by the illness of Bonar Law, who since late 1922 had been plagued with a troublesome throat. His health deteriorated, and on 20 May he resigned the Premiership. The disease – cancer – killed him within five months. He was succeeded by the hitherto largely unremarked Stanley Baldwin, whose only rival for office was the intensely ambitious Lord Curzon. But Curzon was not well liked on the Conservative back-benches, and the fact of his being a peer proved a major handicap. Baldwin's government did not differ greatly from Bonar Law's. He combined the offices of Prime Minister and Chancellor of the Exchequer himself until August 1923, when he promoted Neville Chamberlain from the Health Ministry to the Chancellorship. The new Prime Minister was anxious to reunite the Conservative Party, but tentative approaches to Austen Chamberlain came to nothing. One prominent Coalitionist only was included in his Cabinet, Sir Laming Worthington-Evans, a former Secretary of War, appointed to the relatively minor position of Postmaster-General. Although Baldwin was known to be in favour of tariff reform, his succession to power was not initially marked by any significant changes in policy. Temperamentally he shared with Bonar Law a taste for undramatic administration, clearly preferring reaction to action. Progress on the STO enquiry, for example, was stimulated more by sporadic industrial unrest than any enthusiasm evinced by Baldwin or the Cabinet to perfect and refine the emergency machine. Some ministers, indeed, were against formally resurrecting any part of the STO, even to conduct Hankey's proposed review. To meet their objections, Sir Warren Fisher, perhaps eager to assume Hankey's effective status as chief official adviser to the government, suggested that the inquiry be conducted, not by the STC sub-committee, but by an '*ad hoc* interdepartmental committee' chaired by Sir John Anderson.[7] This was accepted and the committee set to work at once.

Anderson submitted his report on 5 July. The committee unequivocally agreed that 'if only as a preventative measure, the Government should have ready prepared plans for dealing with emergencies.' Its conclusions generally reflected both Hankey's views and the recommendations made by the STC sub-committee itself to the Home Affairs Committee in March 1922. The direction of emergency arrangements should be entrusted to an *ad hoc* Cabinet committee, preferably chaired by the Home Secretary. This would be supported by a standing sub-committee, chaired by the Chief Civil Commissioner, ideally a Cabinet minister with relatively light departmental duties. Clearly bearing Christopher Roundell in mind, they added that his chief staff officer should be a General Inspector of the Ministry of Health. The committee laid down that the executive direction of the STO should be decentralised as much as possible, both within Whitehall and throughout the country. They re-affirmed the 'underlying principle' that the ordinary responsibilities of government departments should include emergency planning, but added specifically that the Ministry of Labour should *not* be responsible for the recruitment and allocation of labour. Since that department was 'concerned with conciliation and negotiation with the strikers', it seemed better that it should 'be as far as possible dissociated from activities which might be regarded as strikebreak-ing'. The co-ordination of local services should continue, as before, to be controlled by Civil Commissioners, and the existing Volunteer Service Committees (VSCs) should be retained. The committee also considered the problem of secrecy. Their general view was 'that while there is something to be said for allowing the existence of a Government plan to become known, disclosure of details should be avoided as far as possible.' It was recognised, nevertheless, that since many local schemes, particularly in the haulage, food, shipping and coal trades, would in future depend largely on committees of businessmen, 'preliminary meetings . . . would probably involve risk of leakage of the Government plans.' The committee decided that individual departments should decide for themselves 'how far the appointment of any particular bodies (or the issue of instructions to particular classes of persons) in advance should be carried in the interests of efficiency despite risk of leakage'.[8]

A wave of unofficial dock strikes, which eventually involved some 40,000 men throughout England and Wales, animated the question of reviving the STO. On 11 July the Cabinet re-established a 'Supply and Transport Committee' to examine Anderson's report and select Civil Commissioners. The committee met twice during July and accepted all Anderson's recommendations without amendment. Curiously, there was already a Chief Civil Commissioner, Leo

Amery, appointed in April 1921 by Lloyd George, when Amery had
been a junior minister to the Admiralty. In default of any specific
decision to the contrary, he had technically retained the post even
after his appointment as First Lord under both Bonar Law and
Baldwin. Since it now seemed likely that the post would become
active, Amery asked to be relieved, and the STC appointed in his
place J. C. C. Davidson, Chancellor of the Duchy of Lancaster.
Davidson had some experience of the emergency organisation.
When Baldwin was President of the Board of Trade in 1921, Davidson, as his Parliamentary Private Secretary, had attended meetings
of the STC.[9] He remained exceptionally close to Baldwin throughout
his life and in 1923 his office at the Duchy of Lancaster has been
described as 'very much Baldwin's own Garden Suburb'.[10]

On 31 July the Cabinet formally approved the implementation of
the Anderson committee proposals and authorised the STC 'to take
such further action . . . as the industrial situation might require'.
Although the STC had learned in the middle of July that there was
'barely a week's supply of flour left in the country', by the end of
the month dockers had begun to drift back to work and the immediate threat of food shortages was lifted.[11] Nevertheless, Davidson, who after all had very little else to do, spent the rest of the
year 'unremittingly' (his own word) building up the STO with the
particular assistance of Sir John Anderson. There is very little evidence to suggest that this amounted to much more than a detailed
examination of the various emergency schemes 'mothballed' by departments in the spring of 1922.[12] The army and air force took the
opportunity afforded by relative industrial peace to review their
emergency arrangements. At the STC meeting of 17 July Lord
Derby, Secretary for War, was assured by Anderson that the police
'did not contemplate the assistance of troops being required at
present'. This was welcome news for the War Office, but in November they took the precaution of instructing all Home Commands to
draw up new lists of 'officers suitable for employment to augment
the staff should troops be called out in aid of the civil power'.
Towards the end of the year they issued a revised edition of a
pamphlet entitled *Duties in aid of the Civil Power*, which covered
both the principles and tactics of operations at times of civil and
industrial unrest. Under the heading 'Blackleg Labour', it reiterated
that 'troops should not be employed in any form of manual assistance without reference to the War Office, except when the Emer-

gency Powers Act is in operation.' In January 1924 a copy of the pamphlet was sent for information to the Admiralty, who were so impressed that they requested seventy additional copies for distribution to home units. A copy was also sent to the Air Ministry, who were less admiring, having issued their own 'Orders for the R.A.F. (Home) in the event of Industrial Unrest' at the beginning of November 1923. This laid down that the three primary duties of the RAF would be to maintain communications, protect RAF and other government property, and to provide air assistance to the military authorities, with the strict provision that 'under no circumstances . . . will offensive action be taken from the Air'. Armed guards were to be provided for protection since it was 'thought possible that attempts will be made on government property by local hooligans at the instigation of extremists or on their own initiative'. The use of firearms was covered in particular detail. 'In no case is fire to be opened until the crowd or mob has been properly warned. . . . When fire is opened, the number of rounds per man to be fired must be specified. Machine guns should only be used as a last resort.' The RAF instructions usefully added that, 'Bandsmen below the rank of Sergeant may be issued with rifles and used for guards during the emergency.'[13]

One aspect of 'protection' which was dealt with during 1923 was the question of Special Constables. Since 1919 the Home Office had been pressing for permanent legislation to provide for their appointment in peacetime. This wish was met in the Special Constables Act which received the Royal Assent in June. The Act made 'perpetual' the 1914 wartime law which enabled Special Constables to be sworn in 'apart from any immediately apprehended disturbance'. Clearly this provided the police with a quick and convenient source of reinforcement at times when public disorder might seem imminent. Although the Bill was presented by Walter Bridgeman as little more than a 'tidying-up' exercise, during the committee stage it came in for strong criticism from Emanuel Shinwell, Labour member for Linlithgow. He complained that the object of the Bill was 'to provoke disorder, in order to suit the employer class', and he accused the Home Secretary of 'seeking to create a fascisti movement in this country'. He asserted that the Bill would be used to create 'an auxiliary force' which would be used 'not merely when the constabulary itself is busily engaged for ordinary purposes, but . . . for the purpose of preventing disorder, which the authorities believed is likely to arise from strikes'.[14] As events during the General Strike were to demonstrate, Shinwell was exactly right.

During the summer and autumn of 1923 the government became increasingly preoccupied with the problem of unemployment. In July a Cabinet committee bleakly concluded that they could foresee no immediate reduction of the numbers out of work. For Baldwin the answer was tariff reform. Unemployment, he declared in October, was 'the crucial problem of our country', and 'the only way of fighting this subject' was 'by protecting the home market'.[15] Honouring Bonar Law's pledge, he called a general election for 6 December. While the votes gained by the three major parties – the Liberal factions had reunited in defence of free trade – were substantially the same as in November 1922, the share of seats was different. The final result was: Conservative 258, Liberal 159, Labour 191.[16] Since no party had an absolute majority, there was some uncertainty as to who would form the next administration. On 18 December, however, Asquith, unshakeably opposed to tariff reform and no doubt confident that Labour would make a mess of government, announced that the Liberals would neither keep the Conservatives in office nor join in any combination to keep Labour out.[17] Although Baldwin temporarily remained in office, and even proposed a full legislative programme when Parliament assembled in January 1924, Asquith was true to his word. On 21 January Labour and Liberals united to defeat the government. Baldwin resigned. The following day MacDonald took office as the first Labour Prime Minister.

The arrival of a Labour government had more symbolic significance than practical effect. As leader of a minority administration MacDonald was hardly in a position to do anything other than demonstrate his party's 'fitness to govern'. In February 1924 he assured Parliament that his first priority was simply to carry on the administration of the country and he offered the unexciting motto of 'security and confidence based on goodwill'.[18] It could as easily have been tendered by Bonar Law or Baldwin. Indeed, apart from the inherent novelty of Labour assuming power, MacDonald's government had much in common with its Conservative predecessor. Like Bonar Law and Baldwin (apart from his injudicious espousal of protection), MacDonald, in his anxiety to be 'statesmanlike', had no desire to excite the nation. Depending on Liberal support in Parliament, moreover, he could only hope to retain power by eschewing socialist policies. Thus he came up against the problem which bedevils all Labour governments: that of accommodating the party's left wing. Both within Parliament and throughout the trade union movement many were disappointed that the government were not more 'revolutionary'. From the opposition benches Leo Amery wryly observed Labour back-benchers 'discovering that their Ministers take, in office, practically the same view of things as the late capitalist Government'.[19] But left-wingers were in the minority. The Cabinet and the bulk of the Parliamentary Labour Party were happy to accept MacDonald's cautious objectives and where it was politically feasible ministers did attempt, not always with success, to apply at least a small measure of socialism to the solution of administrative problems.

In common with Bonar Law's government, MacDonald's was sadly short of ministerial experience. Of 20 Cabinet ministers, 5 had served in previous governments, but only 2 at Cabinet level: Haldane, Secretary of War and Lord Chancellor in successive Liberal governments, 1905–15, and Arthur Henderson, who had been President of the Board of Education under Asquith and a member of Lloyd George's War Cabinet between 1916 and 1917. MacDonald's Cabinet was an unlikely mixture of veteran Labour MPs, trade union leaders-turned-parliamentarians, recruits from other parties, and one life-long Conservative, Lord Chelmsford, a former Viceroy of India, whom Haldane enlisted – 'much to the recruit's surprise' – as First Lord of the Admiralty.[20] From the unions came moderates such as J. H. Thomas (railwaymen), J. R. Clynes (general workers) and Tom Shaw (textile workers), whose places on the TUC General Council were taken by militant left-wingers like Ben Tillett of the transport workers. A number of miners' leaders also joined the government and their departure from the union hierarchy also provided an opportunity for left-wingers to advance. Frank Hodges, for example, who resigned as secretary of the Miners' Federation of Great Britain to enter Parliament in December 1923, was appointed Civil Lord of the Admiralty. His union successor was the uncompromisingly militant A. J. Cook. An unexpected consequence of the 1924 Labour government, therefore, was a leftward swing in trade union leadership during 1924–5.[21]

These inexperienced ministers treated their departmental officials with respect and caution. According to Josiah Wedgwood – Chancellor of the Duchy of Lancaster with a seat in the Cabinet – the

government's slogan was 'We must not annoy the Civil Service.'
For their part civil servants carried on as normal. 'I begin to see',
wrote MacDonald in his diary, 'how officials dominate Ministers.
Details are overwhelming & Ministers have no time to work out
policy with officials as servants; they are immersed in passing business with officials as masters.'[22] One of MacDonald's odder appointments was that of the Lancastrian miners' agent, Stephen Walsh,
to the War Office, probably on the strength of Walsh's three months
as Parliamentary Secretary to the Ministry of National Service in
1917. Haldane told Tom Jones that he had given Walsh 'a little
book on War and the War Office' and instructed him 'that when he
meets the generals he is to say "We are out for efficiency!"'
Whether or not Walsh took the advice, he seems to have won over
Sir Herbert Creedy and the CIGS, Lord Cavan, by inviting them to
lunch at his home in Wigan. Cavan, considerably less politically
minded than Sir Henry Wilson whom he succeeded in February
1922, afterwards maintained of Walsh that 'a more loyal and
straightforward little man never existed.' It may, however, be an
indication of War Office concern for the immediate future that just
four days after MacDonald took office, Creedy signed a letter to all
home GOCinCs requesting them to bring up to date their lists of
officers and *private individuals* available for army intelligence work
during an emergency.[23] There were worries in other quarters too.
Shortly after the election in December 1923, Lancelot Storr, one of
J. C. C. Davidson's aides, wrote him an alarmist memorandum on
the subject of the STO, which raised the possibility under a Labour
administration of the organisation being continued and 'a prominent
trade unionist' being appointed Chief Civil Commissioner.

> In this event, whoever was appointed would at once become
> acquainted with all the machinery for quelling that very crisis
> which he himself, when in opposition, may have done his best to
> foment. In these circumstances, it is for consideration whether
> the organisation had not better be wrapped in temporary obscurity
> and silence, and the various papers handed over – not to your
> successor – but to Sir John Anderson or Mr Roundell. Probably
> the best thing to do would be for you to hand over your papers
> to Roundell for safe custody: and leave it to Hankey to raise the
> question of your successor, if any, with the Home Secretary of
> the new government.[24]

This was no idle concern. A modest improvement in the economy towards the end of 1923 encouraged union leaders to act against the steady fall in wages which had occurred since the end of the post-war boom and the new year saw a resurgence of labour militancy. On 20 January 1924 69,000 train drivers and firemen went on strike against a wage settlement to which their own representatives had agreed. The STO immediately prepared for action, and continued to do so after MacDonald formed his government on 22 January. Davidson wisely ignored Storr's injudicious advice, although he recalled later urging 'Josh' Wedgwood, who took over the organisation, that 'whoever was in power, it was his duty to protect the Constitution against a Bolshevik-inspired General Strike'. Davidson also begged Wedgwood 'not to destroy all I had done and not to inform his Cabinet of it . . . Josh said that he could not continue to build my organisation, but he promised not to interfere with the work we had done.'[25] In any case, even had he so desired, it would have been quite impossible for Davidson to prevent the new government finding out about the STO. Apart from anything else the organisation had been created specifically to meet the sorts of strikes which broke out in the first three months of 1924. In addition, higher civil servants were on the whole too scrupulous, and Sir John Anderson in particular too principled, to engage in large-scale deceit. It is possible, nevertheless, that some aspects of emergency planning may have been less emphasised than others and it seems clear that, under the Labour government, the War Office rather 'soft-pedalled' the use of soldiers as strikebreakers or to maintain public order. At the Admiralty, however, both Frank Hodges and the former civil service union leader Charles Ammon (Parliamentary and Financial Secretary) received copies of naval emergency instructions.[26] Equally, there was no question of Wedgwood keeping the existence of the STO from his ministerial colleagues. At MacDonald's very first Cabinet meeting, on 23 January 1924, ministers discussed the problem of food, milk and coal supplies arising from the railway strike. The Home Secretary, Arthur Henderson, was instructed to keep the Cabinet informed of future developments, and not to introduce a declaration of emergency without specific Cabinet approval. Far from being 'wrapped in temporary obscurity and silence', on the same day the STO began circulating bulletins, prominently marked 'S. and T. Committee', containing lengthy reports from the Ministries of Transport and Labour, the Home

Office, the Scottish Office and the Board of Trade on the effects of the strike. But the government did not have to act. The TUC General Council intervened and the railwaymen returned to work on 29 January.[27]

A much more serious dispute occurred the following month. On the day the railway workers went back to work, a dockers' conference agreed to begin a national strike on 16 February if their demand for a wage increase of 2 shillings per day was not met. The employers offered 1 shilling, but the dockers were adamant, and despite intervention from the Ministry of Labour, negotiations broke down on 12 February. At noon the Cabinet met and appointed a committee 'for the purpose of enquiring into the emergency organisation in the event of a strike'. The composition of the committee reflected the government's perception of the emergency organisation. It was chaired by Henderson and had five other members. Two were leading trade unionists: J. H. Thomas, the Colonial Secretary, who had been Secretary of the NUR and was perhaps closest of all ministers to MacDonald, and Harry Gosling, the Minister of Transport, who was President of the Transport and General Workers' Union – ironically enough the dockers' union. There were also all three service ministers: Walsh, Chelmsford and Lord Thomson, the Secretary for Air. Henderson's committee met at 6.00 p.m. that evening. Among the officials present were Sir John Anderson, Christopher Roundell and H. A. Payne of the Board of Trade, who had been involved in emergency planning since 1919. They considered the Anderson committee report of July 1923 and decided to adopt it in full. They also appointed Wedgwood as Chief Civil Commissioner. Cabinet approval was given the following day and the 'general direction of special Government arrangements' was delegated to what was officially described as the 'Supply and Transport Organisation Emergency Committee'. Two additional ministers – Sidney Webb, President of the Board of Trade, and Wedgwood – were formally added to the STC.[28]

Henderson and Wedgwood, briefed by Anderson and Roundell, immediately began activating parts of the STO. Since Henderson, who had lost his seat in the general election, was occupied with a by-election campaign in Burnley – he won the seat in March – Wedgwood did most of the work. It perhaps reflects ministers' uneasiness with the STO that the actual direction of the emergency machine was largely shouldered by the official sub-committee, chaired by Anderson, which met regularly during the strike. In contrast, neither the Cabinet nor the STC itself met between 13 and 18 February. One of Wedgwood's first actions was to appoint ten junior Ministers as Civil Commissioners to take charge of the regional organisation. On 14 February the sub-committee learned that departmental preparations were in a high state of readiness and could be put into operation as soon as a state of emergency was declared. Considering the nature of the strike, the operation of many schemes clearly depended for success on the navy. Admiralty plans, which like those of the army and air force had continuously been refined since the end of the war, were collectively known as 'U[nrest]. C[ivil]. Scheme "P" ', and embraced some thirteen individual schemes. Among these were 'U.C. 4', which provided for the supply of yeast from Irish distilleries, 'U.C. 12', the operation of food docks, and 'U.C. 13', the London Electric Power Scheme. On 13 February lists of ratings were prepared available for despatch to food docks. In the event they were not sent. The strike lasted for only ten days and food never became really scarce. Just before the strike began the Board of Trade had estimated that with 'informal rationing' there was enough meat to feed London for two weeks, and the capital's millers had four to five weeks' supply of wheat and flour. On 16 February Arthur Henderson instructed the Admiralty to prepare 'U.C. 4' and on the following day destroyers were sent to Greenore and Belfast ready to begin carrying yeast to Great Britain. But only one delivery of yeast was required before the supply scheme was stood down on 25 February.[29]

Josiah Wedgwood did not entirely approve of the organisation bequeathed him by Davidson. Shortly after taking charge he argued that 'it would be well, now that a Labour Government is in power, if the whole system of dealing with emergencies could be recast.' There had in the past, he observed, been 'an almost melodramatic air of secrecy about the whole business, as though a revolution were being combated, rather than a straight forward effort made to keep the essential services going.' He noted that, while the chairmen of the Volunteer Service Committees 'may be admirable', the only three he knew were 'prominent Conservatives unconnected with the local authorities'. His hope was that more reliance could be placed on the elected local councils and he made a plea for the whole organisation to be treated less secretively:

A great deal of the hostility to the work which has to be done comes from suspicion created by the secrecy with which the organisation is carried on. If there is in this country a body of citizens who are opposed to the steps which any Government would have to take under these circumstances, it is better to face them openly. If that policy were carried out the response to the demand for recruits for the essential services would bring forward better and more numerous material, while the Fascisti atmosphere would be effectively dispelled.

Wedgwood, therefore, intended to work out 'a plan more appropriate to a Labour Government and the real needs of whatever situation may arise'.[30] Wedgwood's call for more 'open government' made admirable good sense, but was destined, like similar calls in later years, to fall upon deaf ears in Whitehall.

One innovation under the Labour government was an attempt to involve trade unions themselves in the emergency organisation. At the STC's second meeting, on 18 February, it was agreed 'to seek the co-operation with the Government of the parties concerned in the Strike for the transport and distribution of essential foods and fuel'. Making the most of their union contacts, Thomas was to see the railwaymen and Gosling the TGWU, which included the striking dockers. The Cabinet were reluctantly prepared to declare an emergency but postponed any action until it was known whether the unions would co-operate. Thomas quickly secured agreement with the NUR, but Gosling had less success with the TGWU. It was arranged, however, that a delegation from the union, led by the General Secretary, Ernest Bevin, should meet the whole STC at 6.00 p.m. on 20 February. At the meeting it was explained to the union leaders that 'the Government were under an obligation to secure the food of the people, but that they would prefer to do it with the assistance of the Union now on strike.' Bevin and his colleagues, who wanted time to consider the request, refused to reply immediately. At 9.00 p.m. that evening the STC reported progress to the Cabinet, who were also informed that pressure was being exerted on the dock employers to come to a settlement. Nevertheless, the Cabinet decided that, 'in the event of an unsatisfactory answer from the Union', a state of emergency would be declared and the government would not 'hesitate to use the powers which this will confer'. They instructed that a code of emergency regulations be drawn up, 'but that the Law Officers should have full discretion to delete from them all objectionable, vindictive or inapplicable clauses'. Thus they salved their socialist consciences. An abbreviated code, based on the 1921 regulations, was prepared, notably omitting provision for the employment of servicemen in duties 'of vital importance to the community'. Even so, Wedgwood apparently warned Bevin in private that, should the dispute continue, troops would be used to move food supplies. But the strike ended before there was any need to declare an emergency. Government pressure brought both sides back to the negotiating table, where the employers conceded defeat. The men returned to work on 27 February.[31]

The government's respite from industrial unrest did not last long. Within a month they faced another stoppage led by Ernest Bevin. This time it was the London tramway workers, striking for increased wages, and supported by a sympathetic stoppage of London busmen. The strikes began at midnight on 21 March. The government reacted by appointing a court of inquiry. An interim report issued on 24 March accepted that the wage claim was just, but indicated that the only long-term solution of the problem lay in the co-ordination of London's transport services under a single authority. So long as motor buses successfully competed with a variety of public and private tram services, the tramway employers were in no position to pay increased wages.[32] At this stage there was no suggestion that the emergency organisation might become involved. Indeed, when the STC met on 24 March to discuss a paper by Wedgwood on the future organisation of the STO, the transport strike was apparently not discussed at all. Wedgwood's memorandum stemmed from his belief that the existing organisation could be improved. He again criticised the practice of secrecy and asserted that there was 'nothing to be ashamed of in action which will tend to preserve the essential services and the life of the people'. He proposed that the only matters which should remain secret were Cabinet papers and proceedings of committees dealing with emergency matters, along with details of communications schemes. The latter, he argued, 'presuppose a condition of dislocation, with possible sabotage by irresponsible members of the community'. Wedgwood then turned to the question of VSC chairmen. In the past the idea of using independent chairmen arose from 'the certainty of loyal co-operation', as there had been doubts regarding the attitude of 'some local authorities'. Wedgwood believed that these doubts had probably been unfounded and suggested that in future, when the chairmanship of a VSC fell vacant, a direct representative of the relevant local authority should be appointed. Finally he submitted to the committee a new recruiting poster for volunteer labour, which prominently included the reassuring message: 'No Blacklegging Involved'. These proposals met with general approval and the STC sent them on for the Cabinet to consider.[33]

But the Cabinet had other fish to fry. On Wednesday 26 March, determined to secure the wage increase, Bevin announced that the railway unions were to close the Underground from midnight on 28 March. Workers at the Lots Road power station in Chelsea also came out in sympathy, raising the unpleasant prospect of a general electrical power stoppage in London. This was too much for Mac-Donald. He told Bevin that, if the strike were extended, 'the Government could not stand aside any longer'. The STC was rapidly convened and agreed that if the stoppage went ahead a state of emergency should be declared on 28 March. A full set of emergency regulations – virtually the same as those used in 1921 – was prepared. This time they included the employment of service labour. But when it came to specific emergency schemes, the committee were understandably equivocal. To take the overmighty Bevin down a peg or two was one thing; actual strikebreaking quite another. Thus they were driven into semantic arguments about which services could be regarded as 'essential'. After a long discussion, for example, they agreed that transport should only be provided for *government* employees and that a Ministry of Transport scheme for the use of omnibuses should be replaced by one using charabancs instead, presumably because these would seem less provocative. Regarding the threat to electricity supplies, they also decided that preparations should be made for activating the London Electric Power Scheme. At Plymouth, Portsmouth and Chatham, parties of ratings were placed on eighteen hours' notice to go into the London power stations.[34]

The following morning Henderson presented these decisions to the Cabinet whose conclusions, reached 'after considerable discussion', reflected the difficulties felt by the STC. The declaration of emergency and the draft regulations were approved. On the matter of transport, 'hospital patients' were added to government employees. While they rejected an STC proposal to make a general appeal for assistance to the 'motor-owning public', they decided that 'in any public announcement it should be intimated that all vehicles might be found necessary to be employed'. The proposed use of charabancs was not to be announced. 'Adequate protection' would be offered to 'any omnibus, Tube or tram services that found themselves able to run', and it was agreed to enlist additional Special Constables. Finally the Cabinet agreed that no emergency action was to be taken by the Admiralty until after the emergency proclamation had been issued. The Cabinet meeting was interrupted by one welcome piece of news. Representatives of the Electrical Trades Union called at No. 10 to tell the Prime Minister that they were 'anxious to avoid being drawn into the strike', but they also warned that they would have difficulty controlling their members if naval ratings were put into Lots Road. Late that evening MacDonald told Parliament that while a proclamation of emergency would be made, the government would 'not act merely as a strike-breaking organisation'. He added that negotiations were nevertheless continuing, and announced that the government intended to introduce a Bill to reorganise London transport.[35]

Friday 28 March was a busy day. Throughout the morning and afternoon, meetings were held between government, unions and employers. At 1.00 p.m. the Privy Council met at Knowsley, Lord Derby's house in Lancashire where the King was staying. It confirmed the proclamation of emergency. At 2.30 p.m. the STC, clearly anxious even at this late stage to avoid a full-scale confrontation, met at the House of Commons. The news was good. Because of the 'resumption of negotiations on a new basis', they gratefully decided neither to publish the Proclamation nor to take any emergency action so long as the negotiations continued. Even so, at 3.00 p.m. the parties of naval ratings were put on four hours' notice. But the government's promise to reform London transport was enough to enable employers and the TGWU to compromise. The employers offered an interim rise in wages, the Underground strike was called off, and at midnight on 31 March the tramwaymen and busmen went back to work. Next day the proclamation of emergency was revoked.[36]

MacDonald may have employed 'brinkmanship' to bring the dispute to an end, but, while it is clear that the Cabinet were reluctant to activate the STO, there is no evidence to suggest that they did not intend to use it if really necessary. Yet even the threat of

emergency action had stimulated bitter opposition within the Labour movement. At the height of the transport dispute the TUC
General Council and the national executive of the Labour Party
issued a joint resolution deploring the government's intention to
invoke the Emergency Powers Act.[37] It is not altogether surprising,
therefore, that after the strike ministers dropped all discussion of
the emergency organisation. For the rest of MacDonald's time in
office (to November 1924), there were no more STC meetings.
Wedgwood seems to have lost interest – he had never been very
keen on the job anyway – and there was no further consideration of
his proposals. There was, however, no pause in civil service activity.
The Home Office, ever anxious to learn from experience, prepared
a 'consolidated draft' of emergency regulations and in August circulated it to other departments for comment. Their intention was
that the draft 'should be kept ready, with type standing, for use
when occasion arises – not necessarily for issue as it stands, but
rather as a collection of regulations from which a selection may be
made to suit the particular exigencies of the moment.'[38]

The original emergency regulations in 1921 had been drawn up
to meet a coal strike, one dispute MacDonald's government was
spared. Although the British coal industry, hit particularly hard by
depressed export markets and a switch to alternative sources of
energy, was in almost constant decline between the wars, special
conditions made 1923–4 unusually profitable. The French occupation of the Ruhr in January 1923, which temporarily closed the
German coal mines, and miners' strikes in the United States limited
world supplies of coal, encouraged British exports and stimulated
an artificial boom in the British industry. In these circumstances,
and under threat from the government that they would raise miners'
wages by Act of Parliament, the owners agreed in May 1924 to a
substantial pay rise.[39] For the moment this defused the mine union's
militancy.

'For the life of me', MacDonald had written in December 1923,
'I cannot see this Parliament lasting any time.'[40] He was right. With
neither an absolute majority nor any guarantee of consistent Liberal
support in Parliament, his government lived a somewhat insecure
existence. In the end it was brought down by a relatively trivial
incident. During August, John Campbell, temporary editor of the
Communist paper the *Workers' Weekly*, was charged under the In-
citement to Mutiny Act for publishing an article which called on

soldiers 'to let it be known that neither in the class war nor in a military war, will you turn your guns on your fellow workers'.[41] The Attorney-General decided to drop the prosecution both on the grounds that Campbell, who had an excellent war record, was prepared to write what amounted to an apology, and also because the prosecution itself looked uncomfortably like an interference with the right of free speech. But the Conservatives chose to regard this as political interference in the judicial process and on 1 October tabled a motion of censure in the House of Commons. The Liberals proposed that a select committee should be set up to inquire into the case, but MacDonald declared that 'the only select committee whose judgement he would accept was the twenty million electors of Great Britain.'[42] On 8 October the Liberal proposal was carried in the Commons by 364 votes to 198. MacDonald immediately asked for a dissolution and a general election followed on 29 October. The election was effectively a straight fight between Conservative and Labour. Four days before the election, a letter was published allegedly written by Gregori Zinoviev of the Third Communist International. It called on British Communists to promote revolution and may well have persuaded many Liberals to vote Conservative. Although the total Labour vote increased, the party lost 40 seats. The Liberals lost 118 and were reduced to 40 MPs. The Conservatives won 419 seats and emerged from the election with a Parliamentary majority of over 200. There was some approval for the result in Whitehall. 'As you know the civil service has no politics,' wrote one official to Lord Derby, 'but I fancy they would contribute heavily to a statue to Zinovieff & Mr. Campbell, for the effect they had on the election.'[43]

Baldwin's new government took office on 4 November 1924. The arrival of Labour into power had done much to reunite the Conservative Party and Baldwin's Cabinet included both Austen Chamberlain at the Foreign Office and Lord Birkenhead at the India Office. Worthington-Evans was promoted to his old post at the War Office. By the autumn of 1924 Baldwin had dropped the idea of protection. He had learned his lesson from the 1923 election and was never again to promote a dramatic change in policy. The abandonment of tariff reform also enabled Churchill to rejoin the Conservative Party. To the surprise of many, Baldwin appointed him Chancellor of the Exchequer. The Prime Minister appointed a less notorious politician to the Home Office: Sir William Joynson-Hicks, who had first gained office under Bonar Law in 1922. 'Jix' was a puritan, diehard Tory, with a keen interest in philanthropic and charitable work. He was also rabidly anti-Bolshevik. Within a fortnight of taking office, he circulated the Anderson report of July 1923 and asked his colleagues for a decision on the future of the STO. On 26 November the Cabinet appointed a new STC, chaired by the Home Secretary, and formally re-established the STO. J. C. C. Davidson, who resumed his post as Chief Civil Commissioner, was reassured by Wedgwood, 'I haven't destroyed your plans. In fact, I haven't done a bloody thing about them.' In November 1924 Davidson was appointed Parliamentary Secretary to the Admiralty and he was unable to continue the Commissionership. On 3 December he was replaced by the Postmaster-General, Sir William Mitchell Thomson, who had been Civil Commissioner for the South Wales division during the 1921 coal dispute.[44]

Over the next six months the STC encouraged government departments to prepare a comprehensive series of emergency plans – commonly known to those involved as 'Emergencies Made Easy or Strikes Without Tears'. The work which Davidson had done in 1923 provided, in his own words, the 'broad outlines' for coping with any serious emergency. In order to prepare more detailed arrangements, what was required now was the collection of information about 'the bulk requirement of food for each area, the normal channels of supply, and the road transport position'.[45] Some departmental plans were already well advanced. In the War Office, for example, work had quietly continued under the Labour government on a detailed composite memorandum concerning duties in aid of the civil power. First circulated to the military members of the Army Council just three days after Baldwin returned to power, the paper was intended to assist Commands to prepare schemes for use in 'the type of civil emergency in which strikes, industrial unrest, or other civil disturbances have gravely affected or are likely to affect the national life'. It was also very secret. When it was duplicated in June 1925, only twenty copies were made. Of these just eight were distributed (to home GOCinCs) outside the War Office.[46]

Drawing on the army's experience of 1919–21, the memorandum described the intelligence organisation, the protection of vulnerable points, communications and the appointment of special emergency staff. The 'intelligence organisation for emergency home defence', originally drafted in June 1921, is especially interesting. Commands were instructed to prepare nominal rolls of officers to fill intelligence appointments during a crisis and to divide them between what were called 'Intelligence (A)' and 'Intelligence (B)' duties. The former included information generally received from service sources, while the latter was to be obtained both from the police and also 'by cultivating the interest of well-informed civilians of all classes'. Further particulars concerning the duties of these officers were given in an appendix. 'The army', it read, 'take no part whatever in any industrial dispute' and might have to act against anyone who advocated violence, whether against or in support of Crown forces. There was also the familiar rubric that 'the army in suppressing civil violence acts only as a second line to the police'. A strict prohibition was imposed on employing 'agents paid to spy upon . . . fellow British citizens', although in language worthy of *Iolanthe* it added:

> Due allowance must be made however for prejudice and tradition, and there are many people, especially in the hereditary criminal classes, who respect and would die for the old flag but would not on any account give information on any subject to the police. Many of these men, especially if ex-soldiers, would give infor- mation freely to the army, and it might be permissible under certain circumstances for them to receive their out-of-pocket and loss of time expenses from army funds.

Intelligence officers were also advised that

> Trade Unions have a definite, legal, valuable and responsible position in the country. The army must not make the mistake of approaching the officials of a Union or Federation of Unions as though their existence was illegal or even antagonistic to the national welfare. When they are directly or indirectly involved in the apparent cause of violence and disorder, it will nearly always be found that their own authority has been usurped by irrespon- sible communists, anarchists or local hot-heads out for personal advantage or plunder only. . . . Intelligence officers must beware of prying into bona-fide Trade Union organisation work and mem- bership, as though they were exploring a conspiracy.

That armies must take into account the 'battle for hearts and minds' was also recognised. 'The military security branch in each Command', declared the instructions, 'must make itself popular with all classes, official and private. Avoid all arbitrary and jack-boot methods and statements and sabre rattling.' Other appendixes provided detailed lists of 'vulnerable points', including railway goods yards, chemical works, civil munitions factories and bulk petrol depots. There was also an emergency communications plan comprising air mail services and a wireless telegraphy scheme for which ciphers were provided.[47] This memorandum provided the basis for military action during the General Strike in May 1926.

Other departments were also polishing up their plans. On 12 February 1925 the STC met to review progress. If there was a coal strike, though this was thought unlikely in the 'next few months', plans 'similar to those that worked successfully in 1921' were ready to be put into operation. The recruiting organisation of VSCs under the Chief Civil Commissioner's department was ready to function, as was the London Electric Power Scheme. The food supplies scheme was progressing satisfactorily, although it was observed that 'no hard and fast plans for the maintenance of food supplies can be concerted beforehand with the various trades unless the Government is in a position to guarantee transport, protection and probably also drivers.' The local organisation of the Ministry of Transport scheme was in the hands of Divisional Road Engineers, who had been furnished with 'information as to the principal owners of fleets of lorries in their areas'. But again there was a problem of securing drivers. Here, it seems, the Home Secretary was able to offer a suggestion. Before joining the government in 1922 Joynson-Hicks had been President of the Automobile Association and he now assured the committee they could count upon co-operation from this quarter. It was proposed that the Ministry of Transport should obtain regional lists of volunteer drivers from the various motoring organisations. One other problem was considered: sewage disposal and water supply. The committee decided that the probability of a strike in this industry was 'remote', but if it occurred, a stoppage would raise serious difficulties. The War Office, therefore, was asked to inquire into 'the possibility of supplying volunteers from the Royal Engineers'.[48]

During May the STC spent a series of meetings examining the Ministry of Transport scheme. On 4 May the Minister of Transport,

Wilfrid Ashley, asserted that 'no effective transport organisation could be established without either publicity or appointing additional whole-time staff to supervise it.' These were both sensitive points. No one on the committee echoed Josiah Wedgwood's pious faith in the desirability of openness. On the contrary, the STC was most reluctant to court any sort of publicity, asserting that much could yet be done 'discreetly'. Equally there was no enthusiasm to go beyond the principle of ordinary departmental responsibility laid down in the Anderson report. It was proposed instead that the transport schemes might be improved by setting up local 'haulage committees' at each emergency centre. By the end of the month these had been established in each of the eleven regions. They were all chaired by 'local men of standing'. In Newcastle-upon-Tyne, for example, the chairman was head of the Newcastle Cartage and Motor Haulage Association; in Nottingham there was a 'prominent lace manufacturer'; in Cambridge 'Mr John B. Walford, Managing Director of the Ortona Motor Company'. 'Mr Walford', noted the Minister of Transport, 'personally is the right type of man to take the lead in Cambridge.' Ashley, however, continued to maintain that he could not make further progress until the question of full-time staff was settled.[49]

In the summer of 1925 the STC's somewhat leisurely progress was interrupted abruptly by a crisis in the coal industry.[50] By the beginning of the year, competition from the United States, Polish Silesia and the revived Ruhr coalfields was cutting deeply into British export markets. The return to the Gold Standard in April 1925 revalued the pound and made it harder for British industry generally to export at competitive prices. This was especially true of the fragmented, under-mechanised and inefficient coal industry. By mid-1925 the mines were losing a million pounds a month. In June the owners reacted by cancelling the 1924 agreement and they gave a month's notice from 30 June of reductions in wages and a lengthening of the working day from seven to eight hours. This was contemptuously rejected by the miners who turned for support to the TUC. Since the collapse of the Triple Alliance after Black Friday in April 1921, the General Council of the TUC had begun to assert itself as leader of the trade union movement, especially encouraged by A. A. Purcell and A. J. Swales, the left-wing chairmen of the council in 1923-5. On 10 July the council assured the miners of their backing. The railway, transport and seamen's unions offered practical assistance and ordered their members to place a complete embargo on the movement of coal from midnight 31 July. From the government's point of view, the coal dispute was beginning to take on the appearance of a general strike. Various attempts to promote a settlement all broke down because of the owners' constant assertion that they simply could not afford to continue paying wages at the 1924 levels. One possible option, an interim government subsidy, was strongly opposed in the Cabinet, especially by right-wingers such as Bridgeman and Joynson-Hicks. Baldwin told the miners on 29 July that there could be no subsidy and that the 'industry must stand on its own economic foundations'. With neither unions, employers, nor the government apparently prepared to compromise, the stage seemed set for a major industrial battle.

Meanwhile, the government were making their own preparations. During July the Home Office brought the emergency regulations up to date. On 15 July the STC considered a draft code. The same day they decided to 'triple the number of existing centres for Haulage Committees'. The Minister of Transport agreed to send a list of principal electric power stations to the Home Office 'so that protection requirements could be reviewed'. The food and transport organisations were almost fully staffed and the communications schemes were ready to go. J. C. C. Davidson was brought back to the committee as assistant Chief Civil Commissioner with special responsibility for publicity. Joynson-Hicks summarised the position in a Cabinet paper. He reported that the coal scheme was ready for action and described the additional measures which had been prepared 'in the event of complications with the railway and transport workers'. He added, however, that owing to 'the disappearance of all the special war-time organisation, material and personnel', it was 'no longer possible to make detailed arrangements and to maintain a complete and elaborate organisation which would be ready to function immediately an emergency arises.' What the committee had aimed at, he said, was 'to provide a nucleus organisation which can be expanded to meet the needs of the situation'. Individual departments were also finalising arrangements, although curiously the problem exercising them most was the possible stoppage of public transport in London. Plans were made for the transport of essential government employees and the provision of sleeping accommodation in ministry buildings.[51]

On 30 July Baldwin told the Cabinet that if there was a coal stoppage, it would very probably be accompanied by both a railway and a transport strike. The emergency preparations were reviewed and pronounced 'ready and complete so far as circumstances permitted'. As Joynson-Hicks had observed, the organisation was 'only a skeleton', which could not be activated until volunteers had come forward. But the recruitment of volunteers could not begin until an emergency was proclaimed. This was not a legal requirement, merely political expediency. The Cabinet were assured, however, that the arrangements for a Proclamation were 'in readiness'. Nevertheless it would take a few days to enrol and sort volunteers before the organisation could begin to function properly. Ministers were informed that there were plenty of available troops in the country. The position, indeed, was better than it had been in 1921, when two divisions had been stationed in Ireland. There were no great fears of immediate civil disorder and it was thought unnecessary 'for some time, at any rate' to call up reservists, 'much less to enrol a Defence Force for support of the civil power'. An encouraging feature was that 'all the public services, and most of the railways, had comparatively large supplies of coal, and there was an unprecedentedly large amount of oil fuel available'. The Cabinet's chief concern was with the wider impact of the stoppage. There was no comfort here, but 'general agreement that . . . the effect on the financial position of the country and on the trade and industry of the country must be very serious.' By this time Baldwin had changed his mind about a subsidy and now felt that one spread over nine months could be used 'to fill such gap as would remain between the terms offered by the owners and the terms which the men were willing to accept'. He suggested that it be coupled with a major inquiry into the problems of the coal industry. He persuaded the Cabinet to agree. But they also decided that 'unostentatious preparations should continue for maintaining public services in the event of a strike.' That evening the miners' executive and the TUC accepted Baldwin's compromise. The owners, who saw no point in either a subsidy or yet another inquiry, at first refused. The next day, Friday 31 July, with the lock-out imminent, but negotiations continuing, the STC gathered, ready to mobilise the emergency machine. At 4.00 p.m. they learned that the owners had lifted their notices.[52] This day – 'Red Friday' – was hailed as a great victory for the trade unions.

In attempting to explain why Baldwin changed his mind, much

has been made of the fact that both he and Cunliffe-Lister claimed afterwards: 'We were not ready.'[53] So far as the STO is concerned, this was not strictly true. The coal emergency scheme had been ready since February and the nucleus of the full machine was well prepared at the end of July. It is possible that ministers were concerned about the predicted delay in recruiting volunteers, but a Proclamation could have been made as soon as the lock-out began and it was not expected that the railwaymen and transport workers would strike immediately. Wilfrid Ashley asserted that 'within two days' the government could have had 'the machine in working order because the goodwill evoked by an Emergency enables things to be done rapidly'. Perhaps a more important consideration was that a strong current of public opinion was running in favour of the miners. Amery believed that Baldwin wanted delay because the *country* was not 'ready for a total conflict on an issue which had not yet been subjected to nationwide debate'.[54] In any case Baldwin was by temperament a conciliator and reluctant to force the issue between miners and owners until every possible avenue had been explored. On the other hand, as he demonstrated in the spring of 1926, once he believed that had been done, he could become as obdurate as the most hawkish member of the Cabinet.

'Red Friday' stimulated the Cabinet to take a direct interest in the STO. On 5 August they asked the Home Secretary to circulate a paper for their next meeting (on 7 August) on the recruitment of volunteers and the question of publicity. It was also agreed that the Prime Minister should 'have discretion to give a hint or otherwise, according as he might think fit, as to the intention of the Government to make more elaborate arrangements than at present exist for maintaining essential national services during a strike.'[55] The next day Joynson-Hicks, rather exceeding his brief, circulated a lengthy and very detailed report 'on the present position of the Emergency Organisation'. After a general survey of the STC and STO, the report dealt with a series of 'particular arrangements'. On the recruitment of labour, it confirmed that there had been no change in the VSCs under Wedgwood's management. Each chairman was 'a gentleman of local influence'. It was expected that the VSCs could start work within twelve hours of receiving an 'action' telegram. Under 'protection', the report observed that the police 'are not, and cannot be, maintained at a strength sufficient to enable the Chief Constable to afford specific protection at any large number of points.' There were currently about 100,000 Special Constables in England and Wales, but 'generally very few are in the industrial districts.' Regular police and Special Constables, 'though they may be usefully employed for watching purposes, may be regarded as of doubtful value where there is any probability of any determined attack being made.' In that case, military protection would be required. The reports on the supply schemes well illustrate two important features of the STO: co-operation with private industry and secrecy. 'Coal Emergency Officers' were 'merchants or factors of standing', appointed to supervise the distribution of coal in their local areas. Ministry of Transport schemes had been drawn up in consultation with the Railway General Managers' Committee, and representatives of harbour authorities and ship owners. The Board of Trade's food organisation reported that United Dairies had their own private emergency plan for the supply of milk to London. There was considerable emphasis on secrecy. To that end a number of emergency committees were not to be appointed until after a proclamation of emergency. Divisional Coal Officers, it was darkly recorded, had specifically been 'pledged to secrecy'. Since the secretary of the National Council of the Port Labour Employers had advised that 'if the Association were approached officially the fact would immediately become public property', the Board of Trade was privately approaching individual local secretaries of the Council.

The STO had made plans for nearly every possible contingency. A mercantile marine scheme was ready to organise 'the movement of foodstuffs coastwise' and arrangements had been made to recruit seamen for essential shipping services. 'There has, however,' added the report, 'never been any occasion for this part of the organisation actually to function.' There was an extraordinarily comprehensive series of communications plans, ranging from despatch riders to air mail services, and a wireless scheme 'in the event of sabotage on a large scale'. In the seemingly unlikely event of a strike in the BBC, 'Senior Officers in the telegraph service would be available.'[56]

On the morning of 7 August the STC approved the Home Secretary's report. They decided that the Cabinet should be asked to sanction the establishment of a 'permanent standing organisation' at the headquarters of each region. It was also agreed that the VSCs should continue to be kept secret. In the afternoon the Cabinet had a long discussion on the STO. Some ministers were now in favour of bringing the organisation out into the open. Indeed Churchill apparently wanted to bring Sir Eric Geddes back and place him at the head of a widely publicised body. The Cabinet did not go this far, but they allowed that 'the time had come when it was necessary to risk a certain amount of publicity.' They also made a number of decisions which amplified the STO's functions and laid the basis for the emergency organisation as it operated during the General Strike. Ministers knew that the coal subsidy would cease on 1 May 1926, and past experience of the mining industry's appalling labour relations suggested that renewed unrest then was more than probable. Equally, the official inquiry – it was to be a Royal Commission chaired by Sir Herbert Samuel – was unlikely to 'solve' the industry's problems. The Cabinet accepted the STC's proposals. It permitted the regional headquarters 'to place themselves in touch as necessary with Local Authorities, notwithstanding that a certain amount of publicity would be involved'. £10,000 was set aside for the new standing organisation. The Home Secretary was authorised 'to make a gradual increase in the number of Special Constables'. A week later the Cabinet returned to the subject of the STO. 'Great stress', record the minutes, 'was laid on the importance of utilising the next few months to bring this organisation up to the highest possible point of efficiency.'[57]

From the summer of 1925 to the spring of 1926 the STO put flesh on the skeleton which had existed at the end of July. Most of this work was done at an inter-departmental level. After 7 August the STC met just once (in October) before 27 April 1926. The sub-committee met only three times between October and February. During the late summer Joynson-Hicks busied himself with the emergency organisation. In August he authorised the Special Constabulary 'quietly to recruit', and warned Baldwin that he would shortly request greater powers for the STC, 'as the time has come to really have [*sic*] the buttons not only there but with the names of individuals attached to each button.'[58] Jix's efforts had some odd effects. At the beginning of September, for example, a Colchester man with a distinguished military record, who had noticed in the *Daily Mail* that the Home Secretary intended to 'elect' Special Constables, offered his services. 'May I respectfully request', he wrote, 'that you appoint me a Secret Service agent to your office. I feel I would be very useful. I would only require a small salary – say 45/- weekly to cover out-of-pocket expenses.' The Home Office replied advising him to approach his local Chief Constable.[59]

Offers of assistance also came on a somewhat grander scale. In October Joynson-Hicks reported to the Cabinet that while no public arrangements had yet been made for recruiting volunteers, various unofficial organisations had been formed for the purpose. These included 'the O.M.S., the Chambers of Commerce, the Fascisti and the Crusaders'. The most important of these was the Organisation for the Maintenance of Supplies (OMS) which was established in September 1925 as 'an association of loyal citizens organised in the public interest to provide the Government in times of emergency with classified lists of those who will assist in maintaining essential public services'. Among its leaders were Lord Hardinge, who had been Viceroy of India, 1910–16, and ambassador to Paris, 1920–23, and Admiral of the Fleet Earl Jellicoe. Similar 'citizens' unions' had been set up in a number of European countries, notably the 'Technische Nothilfe' ('Technical Emergency Corps') in Germany, which between 1919 and 1924 organised voluntary labour during some 3,900 disputes. In November 1925, however, the Ministry of Labour noted that the Corps was regarded by most German trade unions as a 'mere strike-breaking agency'. The government did not wholly disapprove of this private enterprise, but Joynson-Hicks explained to the STC that he anticipated the OMS only to function in 'normal times'. As soon as the government machinery for recruiting volunteers was put into operation, the OMS 'would be expected to hand over to the Government representatives any list of volunteers prepared by them.' In November, Sir Arthur Steel-Maitland, who in common with other Ministers of Labour regarded the STO with some circumspection, warned that 'no step should be taken which would mark it [the OMS] out as under the patronage of the Government, or in other words, Government enrolment by alias.' Relations between the STO and the OMS in the months leading up to the General Strike were both confused and intermittent. Although Mitchell-Thomson told OMS representatives in December 1925 that there could be no further formal contacts between members of the government and the OMS, he allowed consultations to continue with civil servants. In the absence of any explicit government dissociation from the OMS, the Organisation became identified closely with the official emergency machine. As Steel-Maitland had feared, this devalued the Home Secretary's bland assertions in Parliament that the government's preparations were merely to secure essential services and not to break strikes.[60]

In the autumn of 1925 ministers remained preoccupied with the problem of publicity. In order particularly to complete the government's own scheme for raising volunteers – the VSCs – it was necessary to secure the co-operation of local authorities. This meant formally telling them about the STO. No one doubted that they would have to be told sooner or later, but the question was one of timing. It was eventually agreed that information should not go out until after the municipal elections in November. In October 1925 the STC sub-committee approved a draft Ministry of Health circular giving details of the emergency organisation to local government. It went through the STC and was finally approved by the Cabinet on 18 November. Two days later it was issued by the Ministry of Health as 'Circular 636'. It described the division of England and Wales into ten regions (there was a separate organisation for Scotland) and their sub-division into 'suitable areas' for the administration of national services and the recruitment of labour. The Ministry 'earnestly hoped' that 'in any town in which the Chairman of the [Recruiting] Committee considered it necessary to open a recruiting centre . . . it would be found practicable for the Local Authority concerned to combine with him in making the centre available for recruiting both for national and for local purposes.' It was suggested that local authorities might co-operate 'in securing able-bodied citizens of good character to serve as Special Constables'. Although it was 'impossible to draw a hard and fast line of demarcation between national and local services', there was a broad definition of the position. Local authorities were expected 'to undertake responsibility for the maintenance of local public utility services' and to co-operate with the national organisation regarding local transport and the distribution of coal. It perhaps reflected some hesitation in Whitehall to take local government fully into their confidence that 'in the absence of further directions' the councils were not expected to undertake any responsibility for food distribution. Shipping, railways and communications remained a central responsibility. Not the least important point made in the circular was the observation that 'no responsibility could be accepted by the Government for expenditure incurred by Local Authorities in meeting local needs'. The circular was generally well received. Joynson-Hicks was pleased to report in February 1926 that the reaction in Wales had been 'not unfriendly'. The only resistance was in London, where 'the municipalities abutting on both sides of the River, east of the City', had 'shown no desire to co-operate'. But, added Jix reassuringly, 'when an emergency is imminent they will probably agree to assist.'[61]

Progress on the STO over the winter of 1925–6 was mostly confined to the establishment of full-time Divisional Headquarters, the appointment of local officers and the general co-ordination of the organisation as a whole. From November 1925 informal inter-departmental meetings (not the STC sub-committee) were held in Whitehall every fortnight. Conferences were organised for the Civil Commissioners' Chief Assistants, each of whom was a local Ministry of Health Inspector. In November the Commissioners themselves met.[62] As the Anderson Committee had advised, these men were all junior members of the government, and mostly attached to departments involved in the STO.[63] As early as October four-fifths of sub-area officers had been appointed. All this cost money. Food Officers, District Haulage Committee chairmen, Police Liaison Officers were each paid expenses and some also received honorariums. The Treasury were determined to maintain tight control over expenditure. In October, when the Board of Trade requested £2,000 for emergency food arrangements, the Treasury trusted 'that it may be possible to keep expenditure well below this limit'. They also wanted it 'clearly understood' that the expenditure was only sanctioned as a specific result of the Cabinet decision of 7 August. It was intended to meet 'a particular situation' and was not 'of an annual character'. In order to keep a check on spending, departments were requested to furnish a statement at the end of each quarter of their 'actual additional expenditure'. Nevertheless expenditure grew and by the end of October the Treasury itself had approved spending amounting to £10,200. By earmarking £10,000 on 7 August, the Cabinet had let in the thin end of what the Treasury feared would be a very expensive wedge. Try as they might the Treasury seemed unable to control spending. Towards the end of the year, for example, there was a lengthy correspondence with the Office of Works who had been requested by the Ministry of Health to provide 'burglar-proof safes', costing some £30 each, for the provincial Civil Commissioners. Treasury suggestions that steel cupboards at £10 be used were not well received, and it was eventually decided that 'ordinary' safes at £23 could be purchased. In the Treasury, J. B. Beresford, who had the unenviable task of monitoring emergency expenditure, minuted 'from experience' that the STC was 'almost invariably against the Treasury when it comes to the point'.[64]

Reports from all parts of the STO were gathered by Sir John Anderson at the Home Office. In February 1926 the Cabinet were told that detailed returns of food stocks, as on 30 January, were being prepared for each division. These returns would include wheat, flour, meat, bacon and ham, butter, cheese, canned foods, canned milk, jam, sugar and tea. Some reports demonstrated a little over-enthusiasm. On 12 February the Civil Commissioner's Department forwarded a progress report from the Chief Assistants in the south-western division which mentioned that Colonel Metcalfe, the Chief Constable of Somerset, had proposed that volunteer lorry drivers be sworn in as Special Constables. The Home Office were not pleased, especially since Bridgeman had specifically assured Parliament in 1923 that the Special Constabulary would not be used as strikebreakers. 'The proposal', they wrote to Metcalfe, 'is one which we could not for a moment entertain.' For one thing, it was very important 'to keep the Special Constabulary clear of schemes for the running of transport or other services'. For another, 'you surely would not want to be saddled with the responsibility for having in your Special Constabulary, even on a nominal footing, a promiscuous crowd of lorry drivers who, for all you know, may be drunken ruffians or thieves or anything else.'[65]

The government's improvement of the STO during the winter months was almost too successful. In December 1925, faced with a strike of sewage pumping staff, the London County Council turned immediately to the government and asked that the emergency machinery be set in motion. The government naturally refused. As Anderson explained to the STC sub-committee, the organisation was 'not intended to be used for the purpose of a sectional dispute not amounting to a national emergency'. It was important, he emphasised, 'that any misapprehension on this point should be corrected wherever it arose in order to avoid the danger of creating an impression that the Government Organisation was a strike-breaking machine'.[66] But it was inevitable that the STO would popularly been seen thus. In any case, the distinction between 'strike-breaking' and 'the provision of essential services' was a fine one. Where a trade unionist saw simply a trade dispute or a wages claim, a government minister might see a national industrial emergency. In addition, when a number of unions combined to strike in sympathy with a particular demand in one industry, the government might regard it, not just as an 'industrial' matter, but as a direct threat to the constitution. So it was in the general strike. In these circumstances, and in the minds of ministers, the STO became even more than a strikebreaking machine: it became the principal national bulwark against revolution and anarchy. However the STO was viewed, by February 1926, two months before the coal subsidy was due to end, it was almost fully prepared for action. 'There is', wrote Joynson-Hicks, 'now very little remaining to be done before the actual occurrence of any emergency.'[67]

# 5
# The general strike and after
# March 1926–1939

THE REPORT OF the Royal Commission on the Coal Industry – the Samuel Commission – was published on 10 March 1926. It identified a manifest 'need for change' and made a number of detailed recommendations for reforming the inefficient organisation of the industry, promoting the 'scientific' use of coal, developing marketing and improving labour relations. While the Commission rejected the miners' long-standing demand for nationalisation, it proposed that the state should acquire the mineral itself and hence mining royalties. Most of the recommendations were long-term, which it was recognised might take years to implement fully. In the meantime the Commission noted – ominously for the miners – that 'the hard economic conditions of the moment remain to be faced'. The continuance of a government subsidy was flatly rejected. It was uneconomic and an experiment which 'should never be repeated'. In order to secure an essential immediate reduction of working costs the Commission recommended a 'revision' of the current wage-rates, 'fixed in 1924 at a time of temporary prosperity'. 'Should the miners', they added helpfully, 'freely prefer some extension of hours with a less reduction of wages, Parliament would no doubt be prepared to authorise it.'[1]

Although the government particularly disliked the proposal for nationalising mining royalties, Baldwin announced that they would accept the report provided the other parties did so as well. Hopes for any such happy settlement were soon dashed. The owners largely ignored the proposals for reorganisation and gave notice that substantial wage-cuts would apply from 1 May. But this was precisely the point the miners refused to concede and they took an uncompromising stand summed up in A. J. Cook's graphic phrase, 'Not a penny off the pay, not a second on the day.' Throughout April, government, owners and unions engaged in a series of inconclusive negotiations, resulting in little more than a general hardening of attitudes.[2]

A notable feature of the weeks leading up to the general strike was the increasingly central role played by the TUC – a development actively encouraged by both miners and government. The TUC's part in the victory of Red Friday in July 1925 did much to secure a place for the General Council as the co-ordinating central leadership for united union action. In 1925–6 such action in effect meant support for the miners. Although the events of July 1925 began to make amends for Black Friday in 1921, many trade unionists still felt morally in debt to their comrades in the pits. Perhaps more importantly, by the mid-1920s the unions were very much on the defensive. Between 1924 and 1926 unemployment rose by 350,000 and there were widespread fears that the successful imposition of wage cuts on the miners might precede equally severe cuts in other industries. The miners themselves were glad to tap the fears and emotions of fellow unionists. Apart from anything else, the lesson of Red Friday had been that swift and effective pressure could only be brought to bear on government and owners by controlling the movement and use of coal. This required union co-operation, especially from transport and railway workers, and raised the possibility – which the government perceived as a threat – of very widespread industrial action indeed, if not a full–scale general strike.

But for all their sympathy with the miners, the TUC in the spring of 1926 were neither particularly enamoured with nor prepared for a general strike. The annual conference in September 1925 had refused to vote on a motion empowering the TUC to call such a strike and had simply referred the matter to the General Council for consideration. The 1925 conference also marked a sharp reduction in left-wing influence. J. H. Thomas returned to the General Council, where he was joined by Ernest Bevin. The moderate Arthur Pugh replaced A. J. Swales as chairman in October; Walter Citrine – a careful union bureaucrat – became general secretary. Between September 1925 and the end of April 1926 the General Council did nothing to prepare action in support of the miners, but left the matter in the hands of its 'special industrial committee'. Early in 1926 Citrine prepared a memorandum for the committee strongly urging that preparations be made to meet the 'reasonably probable' crisis which would occur after 30 April. But at a joint meeting of the committee and the miners' executive on 19 February further discussion of the question was postponed until after the Samuel Commission had reported.[3] Union inaction, as Citrine pointed out, was in sharp contrast to the government's extensive and well-publicised preparations. Nevertheless, at this stage not even the miners were actively spoiling for a fight. Apart from hopes that the Samuel Report might provide a satisfactory basis for agreement, union leaders also appreciated that the STO would be most effective, not against the miners themselves, but against their allies. The immediate brunt of the official strikebreaking organisation would be borne mainly by the railway and transport workers. For both government and unions, therefore, the point of greatest strength was also the point of greatest weakness. The success or failure of a general strike turned on the question of 'supply and transport', which itself largely depended on two factors: efficient organisation and strength of will. The union movement was deficient in both.

By the third week in April negotiations between miners and owners had effectively reached deadlock. On 23 April Sir Alfred Mond, one of the leading owners, wrote privately to Baldwin and suggested that the only way out of the impasse would be an imposed solution. 'If the responsibility was taken off the shoulders of the two contending parties', he wrote, 'they would be pleased.'[4] Although Baldwin was the only person in a position to impose a solution, such action was anathema to his *laissez-faire* principles. Instead he turned to the TUC in the hope that they might act as a moderating force. At the same time the miners also turned to the TUC for support. The TUC's evident enthusiasm for Samuel's proposed reorganisation pleased the government, but the union leaders were at one with the miners in refusing to accept the owners' steadfast demand for wage-cuts. On 27 April the TUC General Council at last turned to the question of 'a possible breakdown in negotiations'[5] and appointed a 'ways and means' committee, including A. A. Purcell and Ernest Bevin, to prepare plans for widespread union action.

On the same day the STC met for the first time since October 1925. With only two vacancies remaining to be filled in the entire emergency organisation, the committee made a long series of decisions preparing the STO for mobilisation in the event of a coal stoppage. Within twelve hours of it beginning a state of emergency was to be proclaimed, the coal organisation and the publicity machine activated, civil commissioners were to go to their district headquarters and local authorities alerted. There was some discussion as to whether only the emergency regulations pertaining to coal should accompany the proclamation. A Ministry of Labour official argued that the inclusion of regulations 'not obviously necessary for dealing with coal' might be regarded as provocative. He observed 'that at present the other Trade Unions are doing their best to avoid a stoppage and are having considerable difficulty with the Miners and that it might be very undesirable to do anything which would make their task more difficult.' But he was over-ruled and it was decided to promulgate all the regulations together. The committee showed more discretion on the subject of military aid to the civil power. No troops were to be moved before a stoppage began, although the War Office had prepared infantry units for immediate despatch to expected trouble spots. The possibility of a railway strike interfering with military transport, which had so concerned Sir Henry Wilson, once again exercised the army. A fortnight earlier, on 14 April, they had gained Cabinet sanction to spend up to £10,000 'to secure the free movement of troops' and they told the STC that secret arrangements had been made to move one battalion by road from Tidworth to south Wales, and three battalions by sea, two from Devonport to Lancashire and one from Dover to Scotland. In the event of these moves being carried out, a special announcement was to be issued to the press 'making clear that the troops were intended for protection purposes only and not for taking sides in the strike'. Despite these military dispositions the STC hoped to rely more on the police than had been the case in 1920–21. A new emergency regulation was prepared authorising the Home Secretary and the Secretary of State for Scotland to move police from one district to another. The mistake made in 1921 of calling up service reservists was not repeated.[6]

Next morning, 28 April, the Cabinet approved the STC decisions and accepted the possibility of 'zero hour' falling at midnight on Friday 30 April. With negotiations still continuing between government and TUC, they determined that preparations should be made discreetly. The emergency should not be proclaimed until after zero hour, no special publication of regulations was to be made, and troops should be moved 'as unobtrusively as possible'. On 29 April the STC met again, although there was little to do now except wait. Worrying perhaps that the police alone might not after all be sufficient, they discussed the possibility of small detachments of troops being armed only with truncheons or sticks. This directly contradicted the army's own instructions in the pamphlet, *Duties in Aid of the Civil Power*. Reflecting Haig's views in 1919, the War Office representatives vehemently objected, especially when it appeared that the only available weapons were chair-legs. Reluctantly, however, they had to accept defeat.[7] Over the next few days the committee's worries concerning the available security forces and their fears of violent unrest revived the idea – rejected in July 1925 – of creating a special body to reinforce the police. Apart from this it seemed that the STO, carefully perfected by men such as Anderson and Roundell, was ready to go as soon as the word was given. But Mitchell-Thomson drew Baldwin's attention to one snag which even Sir John Anderson had overlooked: the absence of a Sunday postal delivery. It was planned to distribute the circulars alerting some two thousand local councils through the normal letter post. Mitchell-Thomson noted that if zero hour was, for example, to be midnight, Saturday 1 May, the latest time the government could decide to activate the STO would be 5.00 p.m. on Friday 30 April. The matter was of some importance, reported the Commissioner alarmingly, since 'Local Authorities must have their circulars on the morning following zero hour, otherwise the whole machine will be thrown out of gear.'[8]

In the event he need not have worried. When the Cabinet met at 4.00 p.m. on 30 April they agreed both that there was no prospect of a coal settlement before the owners' notices expired and that a general strike might very well begin 'the following morning'. Zero hour was set for midnight that evening. A Privy Council meeting was arranged at 5.30 p.m. to proclaim an emergency, although it was thought 'undesirable' to publish the proclamation until after midnight. No one quite knew what was going to happen. There were fears that the emergency arrangements might be dislocated by 'sabotage (e.g. by dropping a spanner or other instrument in some delicate part of machinery) by electrical workers immediately before leaving work'.[9] By deciding to meet the coal stoppage with a proclamation of emergency and partial mobilisation of the STO, the Cabinet appreciably increased the likelihood of a general strike. News of the proclamation leaked out almost as soon as it had been made. The OMS prepared a circular announcing the emergency and appealing for volunteers, but their printers refused to set it up and George Isaacs, general secretary of the printers' union, passed a copy to J. H. Thomas who taxed Baldwin with it at a negotiating session that evening. Thomas described the government's action as 'dangerous' and A. J. Swales thought that perhaps the union leaders should 'not be negotiating but going to their people and telling them to prepare'.[10] Admittedly the government were in a difficult position. Obviously they had to take some steps to counter the practical effects of a coal stoppage. But the machinery available to them had been designed to meet rather more than that. The proclamation of an emergency, with its attendant and comprehensive series of regulations, was a particularly unsubtle weapon. Moreover, the distinction – clear in the government's mind – between 'coal only' action and the full mobilisation of the STO was lost on the TUC.

This soon became apparent. Since 29 April a conference of trade union executives had been meeting in London. On the morning of 1 May, with nearly a million miners locked out, they learnt of the emergency proclamation and the government's warning circular to local authorities. With almost complete unanimity the conference voted to place the conduct of the dispute – including any strike call – entirely in the hands of the General Council. The only group of any size which opposed the motion was the seamen's union, a decision which incidentally vitiated the STO's elaborate plans for volunteer coastal shipping services. Ernest Bevin, who described the government's action as a 'declaration of war', explained to the conference the plans made by the ways and means committee for what was called a 'national', rather than a 'general', strike. The TUC were prepared to continue negotiations for two more days, but if no settlement had been reached by 3 May workers in a 'first line' of industries would be called out. These included transport and railwaymen, printers, workers in heavy industry, building, electric power stations and gas works. Late in the afternoon telegrams were sent out to union branches throughout the country confirming this policy. The General Council were as anxious as the government to maintain essential services. They directed that 'sanitary services' should continue and that there should be no interference with health and food services. Citrine wrote formally to Baldwin offering the TUC's co-operation in the distribution of food. The Council also issued a strong warning against *agents provocateurs*. 'It should be pointed out', they cautioned, 'that the opponents will in all probability employ persons to act as spies and others to use violent language in order to incite the workers to disorder.' Both government and TUC wished to avoid violence. The General Council's specific warning reflected J. H. Thomas's conviction that there would inevitably be serious disorder fomented by fascist extremists.[11]

While the TUC conference was contemplating a strike, the STC met twice to finalise government preparations. In the morning they learnt that the Civil Commissioners were all at their posts and that warning telegrams had been sent to VSC chairmen. Food, fuel and transport, protection and finance sub-committees were set up. The movement of troops approved by the Cabinet had already begun, and, in the event of a railway strike during the weekend, the committee agreed to move four more battalions by road to the north of England to act as a general reserve. In the afternoon the STC took further steps towards full mobilisation of the emergency machine. Hyde Park was to be closed from midnight on 2 May and used as a depot for the London Milk Scheme. Civilian volunteers and naval ratings earmarked for service in the power stations were ordered to stand by. But since it was not yet completely certain that there would be a strike, the committee decided not to begin the general recruitment of volunteers before noon the following day. Citrine's letter offering union help to maintain food supplies received short shrift. 'The Government', they concluded, 'could not delegate their responsibility in this matter.' Two days later Churchill publicly rejected the offer in typically dramatic terms. 'What Government in the world', he asked the House of Commons, 'could enter into partnership with a rival Government, against which it is endeavouring to defend itself, and society, and allow that rival Government to sit in judgment on every train that runs and on every lorry on the road?' Churchill's description of the TUC as an alternative government was at one with the Cabinet's general view of the strike. 'It is not wages that are imperilled', declared Baldwin solemnly, 'it is the freedom of our very Constitution.' Trade union leaders were 'threatening the basis of ordered government, and going nearer to proclaiming civil war than we have been for centuries past'.[12] The fear of political revolution, which had impelled the original creation of the STO in 1919–21, continued to colour government policy during the general strike. Although this fear had lost some of its immediate urgency by 1926, its importance as a major factor influencing the government during the first week of May should not be underestimated.

During the evening of Saturday 1 May discussions continued between the government and the TUC. Shortly after midnight a loose basis for further negotiations was agreed: the TUC thought they could persuade the miners to accept the Samuel recommendations – at least on reorganisation – if the government temporarily extended the subsidy and persuaded the owners to lift their notices. The union team refused to commit themselves to any definite agreement and told Baldwin they would have to consult the miners' Executive before meeting the government again on Sunday. But when the Cabinet gathered at noon on 2 May they learnt that the miners' leaders had gone to the coal fields to rally their locked-out members, and the TUC would be unable to respond until that evening. Cabinet attitudes hardened considerably when the Postmaster-General produced intercepted copies of the TUC telegrams sent out at 6 p.m. on Saturday. These were interpreted as instructions for a general strike and, in the words of the Cabinet minutes, 'constituted a new factor'. The Cabinet met again at 5 p.m., but, having received no reply from the TUC, adjourned until 6.45 p.m. When they re-assembled, they were told that Baldwin would not now meet the TUC until 9 p.m. Clearly exasperated by the continual delays, ministers drafted a statement for use if negotiations finally broke down. Representing the telegrams of 1 May as involving 'a challenge to the Constitutional rights and freedom of the nation', the Cabinet agreed that this threat would have to be withdrawn unconditionally before negotiations could proceed. By this stage the Cabinet seem to have become convinced that a general strike was now inevitable for they also decided to mobilise the full STO.[13]

Joynson-Hicks hurried round from the Cabinet to inform the waiting STC of this decision. The committee agreed at once to send 'action' telegrams out to the 88 VSC chairmen. In keeping with the policy laid down the previous December, the OMS were asked to suspend their activities immediately in favour of the STO. The milk distribution scheme based in Hyde Park was to begin and the London Electric Power Scheme activated. Air mail services were instructed to start at midnight on Monday 3 May, a destroyer was despatched to Belfast for the yeast supply scheme, and divisional road officers were ordered to commence training lorry drivers. J. C. C. Davidson, who had been appointed Assistant Chief Civil Commissioner specially responsible for publicity, told the committee that he was actively endeavouring to requisition a small printing works to produce a government news sheet. Local emergency organisations seem to have responded particularly quickly to the STC's instructions. In Birmingham the city council's 'emergency sub-committee' began calling for volunteers to enlist at a special 'registration centre' in the town hall during the evening of 2 May.[14] So far as STO were concerned the general strike had begun.

For the Cabinet and the TUC, however, the final steps had not yet been taken. At 9.30 p.m. the Cabinet assembled for their third meeting of the day. Meanwhile Baldwin, Birkenhead and Steel-Maitland were meeting the TUC team of Pugh, Thomas and Swales. Still subject to the miners' agreement, the union leaders were prepared to accept the substance of the Samuel Report, understanding that this might involve some reduction in wages. They added that if the government could secure withdrawal of the lock-out notices, the TUC would call off the strike. At about 11 p.m. the miners' leaders arrived and the TUC negotiators withdrew to meet them. Baldwin went to the Cabinet to report progress. By now most of his colleagues were strongly against further negotiations and only the Prime Minister himself, Birkenhead and Amery wanted to continue. Shortly after midnight news arrived that *Daily Mail* compositors had struck rather than set up an editorial strongly hostile to the unions. This incident was enough to unite the Cabinet. The draft statement prepared earlier in the evening was amended to take account of 'overt acts' which had 'already taken place, including gross interference with the freedom of the Press'. At 1.15 a.m. Baldwin presented the statement – now an ultimatum – to the TUC delegation, who had in the meantime been attempting to agree proposals with the miners' leaders. But the government now refused to continue negotiations until the unions unconditionally withdrew their strike notices. This was more than the TUC were prepared to do, and the strike – 'general' or 'national' – beginning at midnight 3/4 May became a certainty.[15]

The general strike lasted for nine days, during which the STO had its first, and only, full-scale trial. Strengthened by the inclusion of Birkenhead and Churchill, the STC met at least once every day during the strike, and assumed effective executive control of the emergency organisation. When the committee met on the morning of 3 May, there was little it needed to do regarding the STO itself, which was apparently working smoothly. There was, however, some concern about the preservation of law and order. Reflecting under-lying fears of violent public unrest, questions of 'protection' re-mained high in the minds of ministers and officials throughout the strike. Sir John Anderson, who was chairman of the protection sub-committee, told the STC that the Special Constabulary through-out the country had been mobilised and an appeal for further vol-unteers was about to be issued. In addition to the troops moved north, during the day two and a half battalions were brought up from Pirbright to reinforce the small London garrison. Churchill was evidently not satisfied that these arrangements would be suf-ficient and he raised the question of forming a defence force as in 1921. But this was opposed by the AG who explained that 'the number of troops in Great Britain was now about five times as large as in 1921'. Since chief officers of police were of the same mind, preferring 'an augmentation of the regular police' to the creation of a new force, the question was deferred.[16]

The general strike, as the Ministry of Labour observed, provided 'an extraordinarily impressive demonstration of working class soli-darity'. It has been estimated that on 4 May, including the miners, over 3 million workers were involved. The most dramatic effect was on the railways where only 850 trains – less than 5 per cent of the normal number – ran throughout the country. There was also an almost complete shutdown in the docks. At the TUC headquarters in Eccleston Square Bevin tried to rationalise the strike's central organisation by persuading the General Council to set up a 'strike organisation committee'. For the most part, however, the actual running of the strike was left in the hands of local strike committees, who improvised detailed arrangements with remarkable speed and efficiency. One immediate problem to be faced was interpreting the General Council's wish to maintain supplies of essential services. In most centres permit systems of one kind or another were devised. In Birmingham, for example, the 'trade union emergency commit-tee' agreed to issue passes 'to trade union labour to load, unload and distribute goods and foodstuffs'. In some areas, especially where there were Labour-controlled local authorities, STO food officers at the beginning of the strike co-operated in the issue of food permits. The Civil Commissioner for the Northern Division, Sir Kingsley Wood, actually met representatives from the Northumberland and Durham joint strike committee to discuss the movement of food in Newcastle docks. But the government's attitude was made clear when the food officer in the North-Western Division was instructed that under no circumstances could he recognise any permit system organised by the local 'provisional council of action'. In fact the issue of permits at all by strike committees – even for food supplies – weakened the effects of the stoppage. The extent to which they were issued varied considerably from centre to centre, as did local judgments of what constituted 'essential' or 'non-essential' supplies. So much so that on 10 May Bevin ordered that permits should only be issued thenceforward to Co-operative employees delivering bread and milk to members.[17]

Other weaknesses soon became apparent. Oil tanker drivers did not strike and petrol remained freely available. This in turn eased the problems facing the STO's local haulage committees who made extensive use of road transport – described by one historian as 'the strikers' Achilles Heel'. Volunteer lorry drivers, indeed, provided the backbone of the STO in 1926. Fuel stocks generally remained high. Over 12 million tons of coal had been stockpiled during the spring, sufficient for eight weeks' supply for power stations and five weeks' for the railways.[18] Stocks were further conserved by the happy accident (from the government's point of view) of the weather remaining fine during the strike.

Another flaw lay in the failure to close down electric power stations. This stemmed from a combination of the TUC's good intentions, the refusal of white-collar workers to participate in the strike and efficient government action. The TUC had intended to cut off the electric power supply to industry, but not to homes or hospitals. This proved to be easier said than done. Apart from the technical difficulties involved, many rank and file workers favoured a complete stoppage. Sixteen of the 79 stations in London came out within the first few hours of 4 May, and 15 more had joined them by the end of the strike. This posed particular problems in Labour-controlled authorities. At Stepney, where Clement Attlee was chairman of the borough electricity committee, the power workers were at first persuaded to stay in. But the maintenance of only a partial supply contravened the statutory requirement to supply power to all consumers and on 5 May the STC noted the 'unsatisfactory position' at power stations run by Stepney and four other Labour boroughs in London. A similar state of affairs obtained at St Helens where the council cavilled at supplying power for pit-head pumps and glass factories. The STO's reaction was to take over the borough power station itself. Right at the end of the strike the government threatened to take legal action against Stepney council if full power was not restored. A more serious factor handicapping any stoppage of electric power was the attitude of the Electrical Power Engineers' Association (EPEA), which was unaffiliated to the TUC. Before the strike began the association had passed resolutions in favour of maintaining electric supplies for 'essential public services' and, while deprecating 'the introduction of volunteer workers', they instructed their members to co-operate in the government emergency scheme. Despite the somewhat lukewarm tone of their resolutions, such co-operation was sometimes quite active. At Pinkston power station in Glasgow, which was protected by electrifying the iron railings and where workers slept in the station itself during the strike, EPEA members persuaded their fellow employees to stay in. The Minister of Transport declared after the strike that without the assistance of EPEA personnel, 'the task of maintaining the stations would have been rendered far more difficult and indeed almost impossible'. The London Electric Power Scheme was one of the STO's greatest successes. It demonstrated the value of detailed and careful forward planning. On the afternoon of 3 May parties of naval stokers arrived in London, and soon after midnight, along with specially designated civilian volunteers, they began moving into affected stations. On 5 May the STC approvingly recorded that every application for assistance from station managers had been met. In addition, 270 naval ratings and 311 civilian volunteers were manning some 30 power stations. This commitment was just a fraction of that prepared for in the London scheme: it involved a third of the available naval personnel and only an eighth of the civilians. The navy also provided notably imaginative assistance in the London docks. On the afternoon of 10 May strikers at West Ham power station cut off the electric supply to pumps, cranes and cold stores. Within twenty minutes substitute power was provided from the batteries of six submarines which had been moored in the docks for this specific purpose. Strikebreaking parties were only used in a handful of places outside London. Naval units were called in to power stations at Gravesend, Ipswich and Holyhead. Portobello station, which supplied electricity to Edinburgh, was operated entirely by managerial staff and civilian volunteers, including some from Heriot-Watt Technical College.[19] Many other parts of the country suffered power cuts and none of the stations manned by naval or civilian parties were fully able to avoid intermittent reductions in supply. Nevertheless, the working of the London scheme particularly demonstrated the feasibility of employing pre-arranged and to some extent skilled voluntary labour as an effective strikebreaking force.

The superabundance of available labour for the London Electric Power Scheme reflected a general and unexpected problem for the STO: an *embarras de richesse* of volunteers. A major flaw in the emergency machine was that, while ample arrangements had been made to enlist volunteers, little detailed planning had been devoted to employing them. In contrast to the London power scheme, local recruiting officers were faced with a mass of largely unskilled labour. As early as 6 May the Chief Civil Commissioner was receiving reports that VSC chairmen were worried because there was hardly any demand for the services of volunteers. The STC's sharp response was that the VSCs 'existed to provide men for jobs and not *vice versa*', although they helpfully added that 'chairmen should instruct all young and active volunteers to enrol as Special Constables'. By 11 May 114,000 volunteers had registered in the London and Home Counties Division, of whom only 9,500 had actually been employed. A similar pattern emerged throughout the country. At Plymouth less than a fifth of the 800 men who volunteered for work on the Great Western Railway were used. In the South Midland Division on the last day of the strike there were 10,000 volunteers who could not be found work. Some categories of volunteer were more extensively employed than others. Two-thirds of the 3,350 undergraduate volunteers from Cambridge University found work 'in various parts of the country from Hull to Dover'; 700 of these were used as Special Constables, most of them, unsuitably, in Whitechapel. Undergraduates, wrote one observer with extraordinary confidence, were especially reliable since 'they have no loyalty which conflicts with their loyalty to the State'.[20] For the government, the recruitment of volunteers in large numbers may well have served the superficially useful purpose of enabling citizens generally to demonstrate their 'loyalty'. Had, however, the strike continued for much longer than it did, the retention of these volunteers, for whom the STO had apparently no use and while transport services and heavy industry were largely at a standstill, might have had an adverse effect on public opinion.

Although naval personnel were used in power stations, and also replaced strikers in a number of other locations, especially docks, the army and navy were mostly employed in 'protection' duties. Once the strike had begun, the preferred technique was to show publicly the government's available forces. The navy took part in a domestic variety of 'gunboat diplomacy'. Battleships were sent to the Clyde, the Mersey and Rosyth; cruisers and destroyers to other harbours. A destroyer was even stationed in the Manchester Ship Canal. The army were similarly employed to demonstrate *force majeure*. From 1 May, although 'care was taken to avoid any military action which might be regarded as provocative, . . . no attempt was made to conceal the movement of troops.' An infantry battalion stationed on the outskirts of Cardiff, while never actively used, made its presence felt by 'marching through the streets daily for exercise'. At Birmingham several thousand troops, gathered for a military tattoo in King's Heath Park from 28 April to 3 May, had their stay prolonged to 10 May, which, claimed one officer, materially helped to preserve 'a peaceful atmosphere' in the area. Both army and navy units – the RAF was exclusively occupied with the emergency communication scheme – were also widely used to guard vulnerable points and parties of volunteer strikebreakers. On the morning of 4 May each detachment of naval ratings going to London power stations was escorted by twelve Guardsmen. The navy landed men to protect volunteers working in a number of docks, including Govan, Rosyth and Hull. The chief burden of protection duties, however, fell on the regular police and Special Constabulary. As with the recruitment of volunteer labour, large numbers enlisted in the Specials. By 11 May 226,000 men had been enrolled in England and Wales, although the distribution of recruits varied considerably from place to place. Only 3,500 men joined in south Wales, as compared to 23,250 in the home counties area (excluding London).[21]

The most intensive use of the army was in London. In addition to the general instructions circulated by the War Office, the staff at London District headquarters had prepared specific emergency schemes for the capital. The two most important of these were the 'civil disturbance scheme' and the 'Whitehall defence scheme'. The former included plans for assisting the police 'at any point at short notice in case of a riot etc.' and also in the protection of 'supplies and communications'. Detailed arrangements had been made to guard both military and civilian vulnerable points. In keeping with War Office orders, these locations had regularly been reconnoitred by London District officers, but after the strike the GOC, Lord

Ruthven, felt that such inspections had been of little practical use.
Not only had offence been given 'on more than one occasion in the
past few years by young officers arriving at Railway Stations and
too ostentatiously reconnoitring the premises', but also when the
time came for troops to move, 'the same officer was seldom available'. Since at the beginning of the strike Ruthven had only four
infantry battalions and one cavalry regiment at his disposal, he
decided not to dissipate all his infantry on guard duties, but to
concentrate them as a mobile reserve at the Tower, Wellington
Barracks on Birdcage Walk and Chelsea Barracks. A number of
guards, nevertheless, were provided for various important locations
such as arms factories, petroleum stores, the Bank of England and
the London General Omnibus Company's main depot at Chiswick.
Ruthven had also to commit a battalion of Guards (with the cavalry
regiment at Knightsbridge Barracks in reserve) to the Whitehall
defence scheme. Based at Wellington Barracks they took up positions behind specially constructed portable barricades on all the
principal approaches to the Whitehall area.

Emergency communications and intelligence schemes were also
implemented successfully. Since the London telephone system remained working throughout the strike, wireless sets, although issued
to troops, were not required. At the London District headquarters
in Horse Guards, the Post Office 'increased the number of women
telephone operators in the building by day and kept a continuous
service at night with men'. Ruthven was most impressed by the
women telephonists who were 'markedly quicker, cleverer and more
polite' than their male colleagues. He was concerned, however, with
the question of secrecy. Although there was no evidence to suggest
telephone-tapping or 'leakage of information through operators',
Ruthven thought it unwise to assume that 'a future strike will be so
inefficiently run'. He proposed, therefore, that a 'simple speaking
code' be devised and employed in future. 'This', he reported afterwards, 'would have been of the greatest assistance both for operations and I[ntelligence] (B) work and is far more important than the
cipher issued, which was never used.' Following the War Office
instructions first prepared in 1921, London District set up a special
intelligence organisation. Because it was realised that 'important
intelligence . . . would be found among the civil population', particular emphasis was placed on intelligence (B) work. With the
agreement of the War Office, MI5 lent London District the services

of twelve trained officers who 'were of the greatest assistance during the emergency'. Although information was received from a variety of civil and military sources, 'the best and quickest information came from the I(B) Officers'. The only difficulty that emerged was 'to arrange to get I(B) Officers into their areas and to pick them up again'. After the strike it was requested that in future six cars should be provided for this purpose.[22]

One of the most prominent features of the emergency machine during the general strike was the government's publicity organisation[23] and especially the publication of the *British Gazette*, whose notoriety stems chiefly from Winston Churchill's editorship. On a logistical level the *Gazette*'s production was a triumph for J. C. C. Davidson, who commandeered the *Morning Post* offices, the Arus Press in Tudor Street, W. H. Smith's despatching warehouse in Carey Street and the Phoenix Wharf for paper storage. Supplies of newsprint were ensured by operating the Bowater paper mill at Northfleet with 200 volunteers, protected by naval picquets and a company of Royal Engineers. The print run for the first issue on 5 May was 230,000 copies. By the final issue on 12 May this had risen to 2½ million. Editorially it was less of a success. Churchill's insistence on censoring any news which he thought might encourage the strikers and his heavy emphasis on the constitutional issue reduced the paper to little more than a propaganda sheet. Its influence is difficult to assess. The only direct effect it had on the strikers was to prompt the TUC to produce a rival *British Worker*, which reached a circulation of some 700,000 copies, printed at the *Daily Herald* and a number of other centres. The *British Gazette* may have had some effect in strengthening middle-class opinion behind the government. But its appeal was socially limited. As Thomas Jones realistically commented, it was 'a paper for suburbia and not for the working man'.[24] Contrary to expectations, many other newspapers continued to publish during the strike, if only in issues of reduced size. Most of them came out strongly in favour of the government. Local strike committees responded with their own lively and often satirical newsletters and bulletins. But on the whole the propagandists on both sides simply preached to the converted. Of more significance, perhaps, was the government's use of radio. While the *British Gazette* echoed Churchill's vigorous pugnacity, the BBC spoke with the calmer voice of Baldwin. This was literally so on 6 May when he broadcast to the nation and quietly called on 'all good

citizens' to trust him and to 'stand behind the Government'.[25]
Although John Reith, the BBC's managing director, retained more
independence than Churchill wished, he was well aware that to
broadcast anything which could be construed as sympathetic to the
strike would jeopardise the little freedom he had. No labour leader
was permitted to broadcast and Reith even vetoed the transmission
of a conciliatory sermon by the Archbishop of Canterbury. The
greatest advantage for the government was the extent to which
wireless broadcasts emphasised the continuance of normal life.
Nevertheless, the BBC's importance can easily be over-estimated.
At the time of the strike less than a quarter of all households had
wireless sets and these were naturally concentrated among the better
off.

Although stressing the seriousness of the challenge to the constitution, the government also made understandable efforts to preserve
a semblance of normality, at least in some areas of life. While horse
racing was banned, cricket was not. The STC decided that 'it was
desirable, but not essential, that cinemas should be kept open'.
Half-way through the strike Churchill told the Cabinet that there
was no case for closing the Stock Exchange. Such a suggestion, he
averred, was 'to be deprecated as calculated to create alarm and to
depress credit'. The army also played their part. Both the mounted
Life Guards in Whitehall and the King's Guard at Buckingham
Palace remained in ceremonial dress. But the Life Guards were
armed only with swords and, in order to provide a proper degree of
protection, they were reinforced by a small detachment in service
dress, armed with rifles and kept out of sight. 'A guard to guard a
guard,' remarked Ruthven in his report. 'This is an absurdity.' He
argued that in a future emergency all such guards should be in
service dress and equipped with firearms. 'I do not believe', he
asserted, 'that the General Public would view the matter in any
other light than that the authorities meant business.'[26]

For the first three days of the strike the government mainly acted
defensively and spent the time taking the measure of the unions.
On 5 May Baldwin told Thomas Jones: 'we must wait for the strike
to wear itself out.' But on Friday, 7 May, the government began to
move to the offensive. At a long meeting that morning the Cabinet
effectively laid down the broad lines of policy for the rest of the
strike. Ministers were influenced by the fact that the TUC, for their
part, had begun to intensify the stoppage. The Cabinet were told

that union permits for the movement of food were being withdrawn and that this meant 'stronger measures would be taken in the direction of picketing the docks and other food supplies'. They were also informed that the TUC were considering extending the strike, possibly to include the Post Office. Although an emergency communications scheme was ready to go into operation, this would certainly have been a serious blow. The Postmaster-General was authorised 'to issue a warning as to the consequences to established Civil Servants who deserted their posts'. It was left to his discretion whether, in addition to raising the possibility of dismissal, 'he should also mention the loss of pension rights.' With the exception of a few naval and RAF technicians, the threatened Post Office strike – which never materialised – was the only instance when the government were faced with the possibility of civil servants striking. In order to forestall trouble the Postmaster-General had taken the unusual step before the strike of assuring the Post Office staff associations that 'Post Office servants will not be required as a condition of service to perform duties previously performed by railway or transport workers in the event of a stoppage.'[27] It was an official assurance that at least some government employees would not be compelled to blackleg.

Another matter which the Cabinet considered was the possibility of taking legal action against the strikers. A number of ministers, notably Sir Douglas Hogg, the Attorney-General, had been pressing Baldwin to introduce legislation declaring a general strike illegal. On 7 May the Prime Minister agreed to set up a small committee of the Lord Chancellor (Viscount Cave), Birkenhead and Hogg to consider the matter. On 8 May they presented their colleagues with a 'most secret' draft 'Illegal Strikes Bill', which prohibited 'any strike which has any other object than the maintenance or improvement of conditions of labour in the industry or the branch of the industry in which the strikers are engaged'. It also made provision for the High Court to 'restrain the application of the funds of any trade union . . . in furtherance or support of any such strike'. It was agreed that, 'subject to the circumstances then existing', the Bill should be introduced into Parliament on Monday 10 May.[28]

The Cabinet were less secretive regarding protection. Worried by reports of intimidation by strikers, they decided that a new 'special paid Civil Force should be raised as part of the Police'. This was exactly what Churchill had been urging. Indeed, his bellicosity had alarmed even Sir John Anderson. When, early in the strike, it had been reported to the STC that pickets were attempting to prevent supplies of paper reaching the *British Gazette*, Churchill had demanded that an armed detachment of Guardsmen be posted to ensure that the paper got through. Anderson sharply quashed the proposal. 'I would beg the Chancellor of the Exchequer to stop talking nonsense.' On 7 May Churchill wrote to Worthington-Evans that he 'must embody the Territorial Army'. He begged him not to 'be misled by silly War Office objections against this necessary measure. The Territorial Army will recover after the conflict is over.' In Cabinet, later that day, however, the Secretary for War successfully resisted attempts either to embody the Territorials or mobilise the service Reserves. But Churchill was not to be thwarted and he ingeniously suggested that the new civil force could most efficiently be formed by inviting complete units of the Territorial Army to volunteer for service. A committee of three, chaired by Churchill, with Joynson-Hicks and Worthington-Evans, was delegated to work out the details.[29]

The committee met at 3 p.m. that afternoon and rapidly drew up a scheme. Named the 'Civil Constabulary Reserve' (CCR), the force was to be recruited and equipped by the army, but under the tactical command of the police. As with its forebear, the 1919 Citizen Guard, the men were to be sworn in as Special Constables. They would be unarmed and provided only with truncheons, armlets and steel helmets. Joynson-Hicks raised the question of finance, asserting that the Home Office had no available funds. Churchill brushed the problem aside. 'The Exchequer will pay,' he declared. 'If we start arguing about petty details, we will have a tired-out police force, a dissipated army and bloody revolution.' Recruiting opened on 10 May, but was suspended only two days later when the strike was called off. Drawing recruits, not only from the Territorials, but also from among reliable ex-servicemen and others recommended by the police, the CCR enlisted 11,000 men in the Metropolitan Police District and some 7,000 more in the provinces. It was never required for 'active intervention' and its duties were confined entirely to patrol work.[30] Although short-lived, the establishment of the CCR was most encouraging for the War Office. Rather than the Cabinet resorting to a para-military organisation such as the Defence Force in 1921, it seemed that the message had finally registered that primary reinforcement for internal security duties should be pro-

vided through the police and not the army. This was the view they
had held since 1919, and they were to continue to press it forward
in the years following the general strike.

The Cabinet meeting on the morning of 7 May also made a
number of decisions regarding the employment of military force.
GOCs were permitted to use tear gas 'in any case where a situation
became so serious as to involve the alternative between that course
and the use of firearms'. This, as it turned out, was not necessary.
They endorsed Worthington-Evans's policy of making available as
many armoured cars as possible. Tacit approval was also given for
the largest single military undertaking of the strike: the occupation
of the London docks. Here the stoppage was complete. Between 4
and 6 May union pickets prevented any food from leaving the docks,
and the authorities soon began to worry about increasing shortages
of flour and meat in the capital. Lord Ruthven's staff decided to
meet this problem with two operations: the first to 'free' the docks,
and the second to cow the local population. Having received reinforcements from a number of camps in the home counties, Ruthven resolved to take over the Victoria and Albert docks 'with as
much show of force as possible'. On the afternoon of 7 May a
battalion of Coldstream Guards marched through the East End 'with
drums beating' and occupied the docks. Later that day they were
joined by the Welsh Guards travelling, more prosaically, by lorry.
Under cover of darkness the navy brought five hundred volunteers
down river by boat. On 8 May the first food convoy left the docks.
Escorted by twenty armoured cars, it consisted of one hundred
lorries, each carrying two armed soldiers. Although great crowds
came out to watch the convoy, no one attempted to stop it. 'There
was', reported London District with satisfaction, 'a considerable
amount of cheering.' Other sources suggest that the reception was
'jeering and booing', although 'quite good humoured'. The police
later broke the crowd up with baton charges. For the remainder of
the strike food convoys moved out of the docks without serious
incident. The second operation was more dramatic. During the
night of 7/8 May the 1st Guards Brigade (comprising four battalions)
were moved up by lorry to a temporary camp in Victoria Park,
Bethnal Green. Since the park had conveniently been provided with
water pipes for a Defence Force camp in 1921, advance parties of
Sappers were not required. The operation was both a surprise and
a complete success. 'The inhabitants', reported Ruthven, 'woke up

on Saturday [8 May] to find a large military camp in being in their midst. There is no doubt that the sudden arrival of so large a force . . . had a profound effect.'[31]

At the start of the strike's second week the STO appeared to be running very smoothly indeed. On the morning of Monday 10 May the President of the Board of Trade told the STC that 'the reports received from Divisional Food Officers for the preceding day had been the best since the beginning of the strike.' Indeed, by this stage the STC seems to have settled down to quite a comfortable routine. But there were still a few black spots. In Hull there was rioting after crowds of strikers had attacked trams driven by volunteers and intimidation was reported from the East End. During the night of 9/10 May 50 volunteers were brought in to load carcases at Poplar Meat Depot, where some maintenance volunteers had stayed at work. But so much intimidation ensued that they all left except one, 'who was informed by the strikers that he would be "done in" '. An infantry company had to be despatched to protect the depot thereafter. On 10 May, too, the TUC called out their 'second line' of engineers, shipyard and textile workers. Throughout the country, indeed, the strike remained remarkably solid until the very end. But by this stage the TUC General Council, who had never fully been committed to the strike, were also looking for a way out of the impasse. Using Sir Herbert Samuel as an intermediary, they began making discreet approaches to the government. There were fears, voiced especially by J. H. Thomas, that the longer the dispute lasted the more likely serious clashes between strikers and police became. There was also some doubt as to exactly how long the strike could be sustained. Bevin, for example, thought that it could not last longer than three weeks. Increasing pressure for a settlement came especially from the railwaymen, who were among the most vulnerable groups on strike. The general strike resolved itself into a battle of wills between the TUC and the government. The TUC's will broke first. Perhaps Thomas Jones's assessment was nearest the truth. 'The General Strike', he thought, 'could not succeed because some of those who led it did not wholly believe in it and because few, if any, were prepared to go through with it to its logical conclusion – violence and revolution.'[32]

Yet there was reluctance on both sides to go to extremes. Within the government senior civil servants sometimes demonstrated more caution than their political masters. Sir John Anderson vetoed a proposal in the STC to use police vans to deliver medical supplies to hospitals in London. Such action, he argued, would contravene the important principle that in a dispute the police did not take either side, and any impairment of police impartiality would undermine their power to keep order. When civilian stokers operating the Admiralty central heating system struck, they were replaced by naval personnel. But the Permanent Secretary to the Admiralty, Sir Oswyn Murray, had these men withdrawn since their use 'was deliberate strike-breaking and really could not be tolerated'.[33] Thus were attempts made to draw the fine line between maintaining essential services and strikebreaking. Moderate counsel also came from higher sources. When Churchill published an announcement in the *British Gazette* advising members of the armed forces that 'any action which they may find it necessary to take in an honest endeavour to aid the Civil Power will receive both now and afterwards the full support of His Majesty's Government', the King himself protested.[34] The King was also worried that the Illegal Strikes Bill would be counter-productive. On Sunday 9 May Thomas Jones learned that the government planned to introduce the Bill the following Tuesday and rush it through Parliament within a day. Jones was well aware of Sir Herbert Samuel's efforts and believed, moreover, that the TUC were already beaten. The Illegal Strikes Bill would inevitably be regarded as provocative by the union leaders and might well frustrate a rapid settlement. On Monday morning he began an intense round of lobbying which took in the Prime Minister, Hankey, Sir Warren Fisher at the Treasury, Sir John Brooke, Permanent Secretary to the Ministry of Transport, and the King's Private Secretary, Lord Stamfordham. When the Cabinet met in the late afternoon, the Chief Whip reported unexpected opposition from Conservative backbenchers, Baldwin persuaded his colleagues to postpone further consideration of the Bill until 12 May, although with only reluctant assent on the part of some ministers, notably, Churchill, Balfour, Neville Chamberlain and Amery.[35]

By the time the Cabinet met on Wednesday 12 May the question of the Illegal Strikes Bill had become irrelevant. At noon the TUC called off the strike. Their discussions with Sir Herbert Samuel had resulted in a memorandum which linked any possible reduction in miners' wages with a guaranteed reorganisation of the coal industry. The miners refused to agree to any wage-cuts. But the General

Council had by now convinced themselves that the strike should end. They broke with the miners and finally surrendered unconditionally to Baldwin. By the weekend of 15/16 May there had been a general resumption of work. As soon as the Cabinet learned of the TUC's action, they agreed to stop recruiting Special Constables and volunteers. By the weekend, too, the STO was being wound down. Food convoys continued until 15 May, but two days later both troops and volunteers were evacuated from the London docks. On 17 May the Civil Commissioners were told to stand down. The CCR was disbanded on 15 May. Strict instructions were issued regarding the return of all equipment, although they included, oddly, that 'truncheons may be retained by members'.[36]

Bitterly intransigent, the miners stayed locked out for another six months until hunger drove them to concede the owners' terms. From the late summer the men began to drift back and by December the dispute was over. Although the state of emergency remained in force until 19 December, the STC played little part in the coal stoppage. The committee met twice in June to discuss importing coal. On 17 June they were told that coal stocks were much higher than at the corresponding stage of the 1921 dispute and that imports would soon reach over a quarter of a million tons per week.[37] These imports, although at considerable cost to the country's balance of payments, mitigated the most immediate effects of the stoppage. After mid-June the problem of coal supplies was handled by the Mines Department in the Board of Trade. The STC did not meet again until March 1927.

On the official level, however, there was a considerable amount of activity assessing the performance of the emergency organisation and planning for the future. An early question to be dealt with was the future of the OMS. On 17 May an OMS representative telephoned Mr Maxwell at the Home Office to inquire if 'they could usefully continue their activities in keeping an up-to-date register of volunteers'. Maxwell's opinion, in a minute to Sir John Anderson, was strongly against the OMS continuing at all. It was, he noted, 'regarded by large sections of the community as a kind of strike breaking organisation financed by employers' associations.' During the strike the OMS had been embarrassingly (though not wholly unjustifiably) linked with the official organisation. Maxwell thought it 'quite clear that the Government will be able to get all the volunteers they want in the first hour or so after the opening of the voluntary recruiting offices.' The 'real difficulty', he observed, was 'to find persons sufficiently skilled to carry on special technical operations and this difficulty cannot, I think, be met by any organisation such as that of the O.M.S.' Anderson agreed. 'The O.M.S. was a useful lightning conductor before the strike', he wrote, 'but apart from the fact that it trained a few drivers its practical utility was almost nil.' The question of the OMS raised the wider problem of enrolling volunteers, which had been a general success only in terms of volume. Maxwell had identified the crucial need for highly selective recruitment of specialised labour, but Mitchell-Thomson, in his report as Chief Civil Commissioner, took an alternative approach. He argued that the unemployment of useful volunteers stemmed from too narrow an interpretation of 'essential services' and that, in a future general strike, volunteers should be used in *all* forms of transport, for whatever purpose. Civil Commissioners, he proposed, 'should not adhere too rigidly to what have previously been considered essential services'. This was dangerous ground indeed and would seriously have undermined the careful limits which the STO bureaucrats had tried to set to the organisation's scope. In the event the Chief Commissioner's proposal was wisely ignored. Regarding the OMS, Mitchell-Thomson was at one with the Home Office and reported that in some cases the organisation 'did positive harm as tending to confuse the Government arrangements with what was considered a "class" organisation'. On 30 June Joynson-Hicks wrote formally and dismissively to Lord Hardinge, president of the OMS. He observed that the only possible function for Hardinge's organisation would be to keep registers of 'key men', such as train drivers, electrical workers and motorists. But the railway companies and the Electricity Commission could cover their own needs. 'The only remaining class of key men are motor drivers, on which the O.M.S. would hardly think it worth while concentrating their attention. If', he concluded, 'you have any further suggestion to make I should be very happy to consider it.' Hardinge did not reply.[38]

Although most of the reports received after the strike stressed the success of the STO, that from Colonel Strange, South Western Divisional Food Officer, sounded a more cautionary note. He recorded that local food stocks ran very low and that the 'huge problem' of replacing rail by road-borne transport was never thoroughly tested. 'Had the General Strike lasted another fortnight or even another week', he warned, 'a very different story would have had to be recorded.' Strange also identified a problem in the STO's co-operation with private industry. The railway representatives had been 'of little use' on the Divisional staff. 'They manoeuvre all the time in the interests of their companies.' He recommended that in future independent Rail Officers be appointed.[39] Most of the strike reports paid little attention to the wider issues raised by the dispute. The Ministry of Labour report was an exception, which addressed itself unusually thoughtfully, although slightly equivocally, to the constitutional question:

> There appears, in fact, to be little in the contention that the General Strike was unconstitutional. The constitutional issue is raised not by the end desired but by the means adopted to secure that end. Under the British Constitution there are constitutional means of attaining any end provided people can be persuaded to adopt those means. And the means known as striking is a well-recognised means. . . . But this does not mean that the General Strike should not have been *resisted* with all the means and powers at the Government's disposal.[40]

This was not quite the line taken by the government during the strike and Baldwin was subsequently pressurised, not only to make future general strikes illegal, but also to reform trade union law generally. In October the Conservative Party Conference told the government to 'get on with it or get out'. Churchill was all for incisive legislation. 'We shd have a real Bill which rallies our own forces for the fight,' he told Baldwin, '& wh when passed will have cut into the vitals of our enemies, & given them something to cry out for.' Resulting from prolonged discussion during the winter of 1926–7, the Trade Disputes and Trade Unions Bill came before Parliament in May 1927. In much the same terms as the still-born Illegal Strikes Bill, it prohibited sympathetic stoppages. To this it added sections which prevented civil servants from joining trade unions affiliated to the TUC, limited unionists' freedom to picket and it laid down that any worker who wished to contribute to his union's political fund would thenceforward have to 'contract in'. Despite strenuous opposition from the Labour benches, the government's comfortable majority – not to mention the determination of Conservative MPs – ensured its passage. The Act was vaguely drafted and the ban on sympathetic strikes was never legally tested.

But it was bitterly resented in the labour movement. Vindictive in conception and repressive in tone, it commemorated the defeat of the general strike. Bevin swore that he would never rest content until it was removed from the statute book.[41]

One aspect of the emergency organisation which caused continued problems was that of finance. In national economic terms the cost was incalculable. 15 million working days (excluding miners) were lost. An additional 145 million resulted from the coal stoppage, which, Churchill told Parliament in April 1927, had cost the taxpayer some £30 million. The Treasury calculated that the specific cost of the STO in 1926 was £740,000. In keeping with the principle first laid down by the STC sub-committee in March 1922, rather more than half this expenditure was charged to individual departmental votes. In some cases expenditure was offset by receipts. By 30 November 1926 the Board of Trade had spent a total of £121,000 on emergency arrangements mostly connected with the food transport organisation. But it had also received £84,000 – £80,000 from the London Milk Scheme alone. The Mines Department's emergency purchases and import of coal actually made a profit of £634,000. At an early stage in the strike the Treasury attempted to keep control of spending by insisting that Accounting Officers should send in reports twice every week. This seemed to work well enough, but the continuation of emergency expenditure at a relatively high level after the strike had ended caused some disquiet. In August the Treasury wrote to the Board of Trade observing that staff for the Food Scheme in England and Wales were still costing approximately £500 per week. This compared unfavourably with 'the economical character of the organisation in Scotland', where the equivalent cost was £6. Indeed, the total weekly expenses of the Scottish emergency organisation were 'now only £21'. The Board of Trade responded by stressing the importance of the scheme, but promised to do what they could. By the beginning of September they had reduced their weekly expenditure to £437. The Treasury's obsessive attention to detail is well illustrated by the financial residuum of the strike. They adopted a characteristically finical attitude to matters of minor expenditure. The North-Eastern Divisional Food Officer claimed £9/10/- for taxi fares incurred during the strike. The Treasury allowed only half the claim. The London Divisional Food Officer had required a carpet for his office. Since the Office of Works had none available, he had bought one himself from the Army and Navy Stores. But he had to wait until April 1927 before the Treasury reluctantly allowed his full claim of 8 guineas.[42]

The question of protection was dealt with in detail by a number of reports. The Metropolitan Police generally welcomed the large numbers of Special Constables who had enlisted. Flying squads of Specials were organised, which in some cases comprised up to 60 cars and 160 men. One chief constable regarded them as 'very effective in impressing the strikers with the force available to deal with disorder'. Special Constables on motor cycles were usefully employed to patrol 'disaffected areas' and gather information. A unit of Special Constabulary mounted on polo ponies was formed, mostly from ex-cavalry officers. The superintendent at Hammer-smith thought they 'looked very effective and workmanlike, but had no opportunity of proving their utility'. Problems were recognised in policing working-class areas with the overwhelmingly middle-class Specials. The chief constable based in Hackney noted that volunteers imported from the West End aroused hostility as soon as they arrived. His solution was to use Specials raised, for example, by Buck's Club 'to patrol Bond Street, thus freeing regular police to reinforce in Canning Town'. The CCR was less well received. One officer ominously reported that 'the type of some of the [CCR] men was such as to suggest that they would have been a positive danger had they not been disbanded so quickly'. In general, how-ever, the police were agreed that it would be an advantage to have a large reserve force available for employment in an emergency. This view was echoed by Mitchell-Thomson. Although he saw clear difficulties in maintaining a permanent body 'ready for immediate use', he urged that the question should receive 'renewed consideration'.[43]

Lord Ruthven's report made a number of important general ob-servations arising from London District's experience of the strike. He observed that there had been very little violence and 'no surprises were sprung'. The strike leaders 'in no way carried out a planned campaign against the troops, there were no previously thought out offensives or plans of sabotage' and public opinion was 'undoubtedly on the side of the law and order'. One particular lesson was the value of armoured cars, whose effect 'was always immediate and overwhelming'. Ruthven stressed the potential dangers of employing firearms to control civil disorder and asserted that a platoon of troops 'with bayonets fixed and rifles unloaded is really formidable in appearance and could clear any crowd'. Only in very exceptional cases should machine guns be taken. 'They decrease the bayonet men', he added, 'and are unsuitable for strike work in this country.' The GOC had a very low opinion of both the Special Constabulary and the CCR, who were 'undoubtedly looked on as a species of strike breaker and "black and tan". . . . In attacking them strikers did not feel they were up against the law in the same way as the police.' On the contrary, 'they were quite ready to take on a Harlequin Football team, or a party of medical students.' He offered no solution to this problem, but merely observed that in consequence he had needed to employ troops freely, especially in the East End. On the whole, Ruthven was pleased with the army's performance during the strike. In some respects, indeed, the experience had been positively beneficial. 'Commanding Officers', he wrote, 'are unanimous in stating that the general strike was the best training for war young officers had obtained since the war, at Aldershot or elsewhere.'[44]

Following the general strike the War Office sought to limit the army's responsibilities for internal order and to ensure that in future *civil* security forces should be primarily responsible for the maintenance of public order. There was, wrote the AG in November 1926, a 'clear necessity in times of civil disturbance for the existence of some efficient force of a semi military character intermediate between the regular police forces of the country and the fighting Services'. Echoing Lord Ruthven's reservations regarding supplementary police forces, he remarked that the Special Constabulary, 'composed of patriotic and worthy citizens . . . could hardly be relied upon as a really efficient reinforcement to the regular police.' But the AG did not address himself to the central problem of how exactly force should be employed against civil disorder, and his remarks seem principally to have been stimulated by a desire to relieve the army of unwanted responsibility. Colonel William Dobbie of MO 1 was more to the point when he made the pertinent observation that soldiers sent out 'armed with a deadly weapon' might well appear so menacing as to provoke disturbances themselves. The fact that this did *not* happen during the strike was due to 'the sound commonsense of the average citizen and the absence of bitterness, rather than the correct application of the use of force'.[45] Although Dobbie wisely drew attention to the dangers of employing troops too readily in aid of the civil power, he did not go on to discuss whether a constabulary reserve would itself provide for 'the correct application of the use of force'. No one in the War Office seems to have considered the possibility that utilising a part-time, essentially amateur force, however 'efficient' or 'semi military', during a civil emergency might in the end prove to be counter-productive. Put under stress, such a force would be more likely than the regular police or army to break discipline, over-react and, perhaps, precipitate, rather than prevent, serious violence.

Within the War Office the problem was simply seen as one of reinforcing the police and limiting military obligations. In July 1927 they sent an important letter to the Home Office setting out the army council's opinion of the principles governing military aid to the civil power:

> Troops should not be called out in aid of the civil power unless or until the resources at the disposal of the civil power are unable to maintain law and order; that is to say, until the local police force supplemented by additional police drafted in or by Reserve of Special Constabulary are inadequate. It is not contemplated that troops should be employed in lieu of police or on police duties. . . .
>
> In order . . . that [military] resources may not be called upon prematurely . . . the Army Council urge that every possible step should be taken to provide from civil sources the necessary reserve police forces for the maintenance of law and order.[46]

Having reaffirmed their position, the War Office had now to persuade the Home Office to establish a permanent CCR scheme. Opinion was divided as to how best this might be done. Some officers, including the AG, felt that the War Office might follow the precedent set during the general strike and offer Territorial Army facilities to assist in raising the force. Others, including the CIGS, Lord Milne, believed that the matter should be left entirely in the hands of the Home Office. 'It is not the duty of the Army Council', he wrote, 'to help the Civil Authorities . . . even though the creation of such a force will free the Army from many calls on it in connection with civil unrest.' Milne's view prevailed and the Home Office was informed accordingly. But Sir John Anderson smoothly replied that his department had no organisation to raise a constabulary reserve.

Without being able to rely on the resources of the Territorial Army, the Home Office would be quite unable to enlist a force on the outbreak of an emergency, 'save perhaps with great difficulty and after long delay, involving in the meantime added risk of the Civil Authorities being compelled to have recourse to military aid'. 'This', noted Milne, 'reads to me very much in the nature of blackmail.' So it was. In the absence of any agreement the matter was sent up to the Cabinet where a compromise was worked out in November 1927. The Home Office agreed to undertake the recruitment of the force and its command when raised, while the War Office accepted 'so far as is practicable, responsibility on the equipment side'.[47]

Since this commitment was rather more than the Home Office had wished, Anderson proceeded to do nothing. In February 1928 the War Office wrote inquiring if any progress had been made. There was no reply. In December 1930 they wrote again. Anderson replied that the matter had been put to one side because of more urgent concerns and that he would take up the scheme again 'when circumstances permit'. In the meantime the director of recruiting and organisation at the War Office had actually prepared a complete scheme for raising the CCR. This came to Milne in April 1931 with the suggestion that it be forwarded to the Home Office. But the CIGS put his foot down. 'A hint', he minuted, 'that we were preparing a scheme would only encourage the Home Office in their present attitude.' Not that the Home Office needed any encouragement, for Anderson continued to procrastinate and it was the War Office which finally gave in. The scheme was sent to Anderson, who replied with a charming letter of thanks. 'May I say in conclusion', he wrote, 'how grateful we are to the War Office for having taken up this question in so helpful and practical a way.' After some further, although rather shorter, delays, the two departments worked out the practical details of raising the CCR in a series of meetings during August and September 1932. So anxious were the War Office to have the scheme finally completed that they agreed to go beyond the assistance they had offered in 1927. 'War Office action', recorded the Assistant Adjutant-General, 'is limited [*sic*] to such assistance as can be given in the matter of organising, recruiting and administering the force.' This was approved by the CIGS in November 1932.[48] The scheme had been almost exactly five years in the making, and, as it turned out, was never implemented. The CCR waited for a civil emergency which never came.

Consideration of the STO's future after the general strike was conducted with rather more despatch than the CCR question. On 26 July 1926 the STC standing sub-committee appointed a 'general purposes sub-committee', chaired by Sir John Anderson, to review the STO. Anderson's new committee met for the first time on 23 September, but there was little it could do pending the receipt of several outstanding departmental reports on the strike. It was generally agreed, however, that the emergency organisation for the docks had been notably unsatisfactory. A sub-committee, again chaired by Anderson, was set up to examine the problem. During this period the Treasury began to take a greater interest than hitherto in the STO. Their chief concern was to save money. Early in November J. B. Beresford, a Treasury principal and their 'authority' on emergency arrangements, circulated a long minute discussing the cost of the permanent organisation. He assumed the STO would be continued, 'as I take it no Government will go back on the Report of Sir John Anderson's Committee of July 1923'. Remarking approvingly on the economical nature of the nucleus organisation Anderson had established, which cost 'little more than – if indeed as much as – £1,000 a year', he observed that the present annual cost of the Civil Commissioners' organisation alone was more than £7,000. This had resulted from additional permanent staff appointed to the Ministry of Health in the summer of 1925, along with special allowances paid mostly to local authority officers for Divisional emergency duties. Other parts of the STO brought further expense. The Board of Trade's Food Organisation had an annual cost of £2,000, mostly arising from retaining fees paid to Divisional Food Officers. Beresford believed that the preparation of emergency plans should be treated as part of a department's normal function. 'The most hopeful line for efficiency and economy will be the greater utilisation of Civil Servants *without allowances*.' This was largely the case in Scotland where the emergency organisation cost less than £200 annually. In England and Wales Beresford asserted that 'Area Officers should either be content with their Local Authority salaries, or should be replaced by Civil Servants. During the General Strike', he added, 'it will be remembered numberless Civil Servants were pining for something to do.'[49]

Beresford's minute met with the wholehearted approval of his colleagues. The Treasury establishment officer declared that 'there are Civil Servants galore who would like to form part of the Emergency Organisation.' A. E. Watson went further: 'I have had personally numerous requests from individual civil servants to find them a job of any description so long as it's strike breaking.' Watson also thought that 'with reasonable handling' Town Clerks 'might be induced to make free offer of their services.' He did not think that it would be difficult, moreover, to get local authority staff to volunteer as Food Officers, since 'these staffs are not, in my experience, greatly different from civil servants in mental outlook.'[50]

On 1 December 1926 the general purposes committee met to consider the future of the STO. They agreed that a permanent Divisional organisation should be retained, with Ministry of Health staff ensuring that any vacancies among VSC chairmen were filled and liaising generally with local authorities. Anderson argued that 'it would be preferable to keep the organisation in a state of continuous preparedness', since it would be difficult to build on a 'paper' scheme without 'incurring the accusation of being provocative'. Sir Russell Scott strongly put the Treasury view that the work of chief and deputy chief assistants to the Civil Commissioners should be combined with the ordinary duties of the Ministry of Health Inspectorate. This opinion received some support from J. A. N. Barlow, head of the industrial relations department in the Ministry of Labour, who argued that it would be best if the STO relied as far as possible on the services of government officials only. He thought that 'the open maintenance of the organisation would make it very difficult for the country to settle down to industrial peace'. 'If it were known', he continued, 'that expenditure was to be incurred on preparations for dealing with strikes, it would tend to embitter the relations between the Government and organised labour.' Objections to the STO being run entirely by civil servants came both from the Scottish Office, who stated that their organisation could not operate without outside assistance, and A. E. Faulkner of the Board of Trade, who maintained that it was 'essential' to select independent persons to act as Divisional Food Officers. The Treasury, nevertheless, had some success in reducing expenditure. On 22 December Beresford noted that the Ministry of Health had 'practically retreated all along the line' regarding the Civil Commissioners' staff. But the Board of Trade stood their ground and persuaded the STC itself to authorise the permanent appointment of ten Divisional Food Officers, each with an annual retaining fee of one hundred guineas. Some savings, however, were made and in the financial year 1927–8 the Board of Trade spent only £1,150 on emergency arrangements. By contrast, over the same period, Ministry of Health expenditure fell to £283.[51]

The 'first interim report' of the general purposes committee dealt mostly with the need for improved arrangements in the London docks and at other principal ports. One difficulty lay in the stabilisation of food prices. Inevitably the emergency operation of the docks would cost more than normal and the committee feared that this might push food prices up to an unacceptable level. They suggested that the government could either take upon itself the responsibility for maintaining stable prices, or simply leave prices to be adjusted by market forces 'in the expectation that they will not rise to a level which will create serious dissatisfaction'. This was considered by the STC in March 1927 when the question provoked some debate. Cunliffe-Lister, who as President of the Board of Trade was responsible for the food organisation, agreed in principle to 'the policy of passing on the costs of emergency services to the consumer wherever possible'. But he considered food price controls to be 'of vital importance'. It was necessary to bear in mind, he argued, not only Parliamentary criticism but also that 'the effect of inflation of prices would be to inflame public opinion not only against the persons responsible for the emergency but also against retail traders, whose zeal in carrying out their normal functions . . . would thereby be seriously weakened.' Anderson outlined the objections. Government intervention would contravene the limited scope of the STO. It might prove expensive and, besides, price controls were not necessary to ensure the *supply* of the nation's food. The Treasury voiced strong opposition on the grounds that it would set a bad precedent. Cunliffe-Lister agreed to re-examine the question.[52] When the STC met again in July the Board of Trade accepted a compromise. In the event of an emergency they would negotiate with food traders 'with a view to agreeing maximum increases in the wholesale prices of the principal commodities'. This arrangment was to be incorporated in a comprehensive scheme for the London docks which was currently being prepared. To accommodate this scheme the STC made some adjustments in the STO's regional organisation and appointed a Civil Commissioner specially responsible for the London docks. A new South-Eastern Division was established, comprising the home counties, while London was henceforward to be run centrally under the supervision of the deputy Chief Civil Commissioner.[53]

Further work on the STO proceeded at a somewhat leisurely pace and the STC did not meet again during Baldwin's second administration. In May 1929, however, the general purposes committee completed a second interim report in which they reviewed the STO generally. 'We are satisfied from the experience of 1926', they wrote, 'that the organisation requires little or no overhauling.' Included with the report was the new London docks scheme, prepared in consultation with the Port of London Authority and other port employers. Drawing on the 1926 arrangements, it formally incorporated some of the *ad hoc* Admiralty schemes. Six submarines, for example, were to be held ready to supply electric power. It was proposed that, as soon as the stoppage began, the docks would be sealed off and only those entrances 'essential to their working' would be left open. Each would be guarded with a strong force of police. Plans were also made for the army to provide two infantry battalions and armoured cars for escorting convoys. One problem which had arisen in 1926 was that of 'subversive or recalcitrant local authorities'. The committee took a serious view of this and recommended that members of a local authority refusing to operate essential services 'should be subjected to a statutory disqualification for office.'[54]

Baldwin's administration fell before the STC could meet to consider the report. With the government coming towards the end of its term, Baldwin called a general election on 30 May 1929. After a lacklustre campaign, characterised by the Conservative slogan of 'Safety First', the result was inconclusive. No party secured an absolute majority, but for the first time Labour gained the most seats.[55] Baldwin resigned and MacDonald, with Liberal acquiescence, took office for the second time. Although the Labour government, which survived until August 1931, was confronted by a number of major industrial disputes, the Cabinet never considered implementing the STO. Apart from any natural reluctance they may have felt to using the emergency organisation, none of the disputes fully came within the STO's terms of reference. 'Essential services' were not threatened by the lock-outs of cotton operatives in July-August 1929 and January 1931, or the strike of wool textile workers between April and August 1930. There were also stoppages in the coal industry arising from the application of the Coal Mines Act of 1930, which reduced working hours from 8 to 7½ per shift. The most serious dispute occurred in south Wales where 150,000 miners struck on 1 January 1931 against the coal owners' policy of reducing wages in line with working hours. On 5 January a deputation from the South Wales Miners' Federation asked MacDonald to invoke the Emergency Powers Act *against* the owners, but government intervention was limited to the Board of Trade's ultimately successful efforts at conciliation. A compromise agreement was reached and the strike ended on 17 January, long before coal shortages were likely to entail recourse to the STO.[56]

In their general approach to industrial disputes the Labour government, as in 1924, were more willing than their Conservative predecessors to intervene directly in the search for settlements. This they did with some success, but on the wider question of trade union legislation they failed completely to amend the Trade Disputes and Trade Unions Act. The need to retain Liberal Parliamentary support limited the government's freedom of action. MacDonald hoped that the TUC would agree to 'a clause making political and revolutionary strikes illegal, but being so worded as not to interfere with the pursuit of an industrial strike'. But any interference at all with the right to strike was more than the General Council would tolerate and they insisted on complete repeal of the 1927 Act. A Bill was introduced to this effect in October 1930. It was opposed by the Liberals, who carried an amendment 'aiming to make any strike illegal which adversely affected the interests of the community'. Since this was quite unacceptable to the TUC, the government withdrew the Bill in March 1931.[57]

Although the STC itself fell into abeyance during the 1929–31 Labour government, it seems that civil servants continued to make routine adjustments to the STO. When Cunliffe-Lister returned as President of the Board of Trade in August 1931, he found that 'throughout the term of office of the Labour Government the whole of the organisation we had created in the Board of Trade had been maintained at concert pitch,' but only a little documentary evidence survives to confirm this.[58] Both the Admiralty and the War Office continued to refine their emergency arrangements. In 1929 the War Office produced a new edition of the pamphlet *Duties in aid of the Civil Power,* which included for the first time tactical instructions for the use of tanks and armoured cars. 'Armoured fighting vehicles can exert a great moral effect by their formidable appearance,' declared the pamphlet, 'but as this effect is greatly decreased when crews are seen to dismount and attend to engines, vehicles of doubt-ful reliability should never be taken out.' In March 1930 the Direc-torate of Military Operations issued a revised memorandum on civil emergency schemes, which remained in force until 1939. The Admiralty and War Office together made minor adjustments to the London Electric Power Scheme. But in May 1931, with both miners and dockers actively resisting threatened wage-cuts, Sir John An-derson instructed that for the present no further orders for emer-gency schemes should be issued. There was, he maintained, the possibility of information leaking out, and 'any abnormal activity on the part of the Emergency Organisation (the existence of which is now well known to both employers and employed)' might preju-dice current negotiations 'of extreme delicacy'.[59] Anderson's caution was possibly sharpened with Labour in power, but where the STO was concerned, even under Baldwin, the instinct of Whitehall had been for discretion. When in March 1928 it seemed that the Public Accounts Committee might inquire closely into expenditure on emergency services, a meeting at the Treasury agreed that 'Account-ing Officers should refrain from giving details of the technique of their organisation' to MPs.[60] Such an attitude towards a Parliamen-tary select committee is not unknown today.

Between 1929 and 1931 substantial work on the STO ceased. It was ignored, no doubt thankfully enough, by the Labour govern-ment. It is in any case a characteristic of British government that administrative activity is more often stimulated by exigency rather than expediency. Illustrating this is the attention paid by successive governments to the STO which varied in direct proportion to the likelihood – real or apparent – of major industrial unrest. One such crisis occurred in 1931. It was produced by the economic slump which began in the autumn of 1929 and eventually brought down MacDonald's Labour ministry. Throughout the government's life ministers grappled vainly with the problem of unemployment, which rose from almost 1,200,000 in June 1929 to over 2,500,000 in the middle of 1931. Along with this increase went a massive rise in the cost of paying unemployment benefit and government expen-diture began seriously to exceed income. Prevailing economic or-thodoxy, which the government espoused, held that in order to maintain national financial stability the budget should be balanced. The principal means of doing this was to cut government spending. In August 1931 the Cabinet considered a substantial series of proposed economies, but it split on the question of a 10 per cent cut in unemployment benefit. Since 9 out of MacDonald's 20 Cabinet ministers threatened to resign rather than accept the cut, it was clear that the government could not survive. During the crisis informal meetings had taken place between the leaders of all three parties and the notion of a coalition government had gained wide support. Already persuaded that this might be the best course, MacDonald went to the King to offer his Cabinet's resignation and agreed to head what he thought would be a temporary 'National' government.[61]

The Prime Minister quickly formed a small Cabinet comprising 4 Conservatives (Baldwin became Lord President), 4 Labour ministers and 2 Liberals. Parliamentary support came from the Conservatives, most Liberals, but only 14 Labour MPs. The Cabinet had to deal immediately not only with the problem of balancing the national books but also with a serious financial crisis set off by a run on the pound. In September an emergency budget raised income tax and cut the stipends of everyone paid by the state, including the unemployed, by 10 per cent. Since the nation's gold reserves were virtually exhausted, the pound came off the Gold Standard. No one knew quite what effect any of this might have. There were fears that Labour opposition – in and out of Parliament – might precipitate serious industrial action. On 20 September Hankey noted in his diary that he had 'looked into our food supply, which appears satisfactory and the national strike organisation, as we cannot foretell what will happen'. Action had already been taken concerning the STO. On 7 September a meeting of ministers met 'to consider what steps would be required to revivify the Supply and Transport organisation'. Two days later the Cabinet agreed that the STC should be reconstituted, that government departments should bring emergency arrangements up to date, 'but that no action should be taken involving publicity'.[62] Work soon got under way in individual departments,[63] but the feared unrest never materialised. The National government lasted longer than had been anticipated. Having restored a measure of confidence, the government agreed to ask the nation for what MacDonald called a 'Doctor's Mandate'. A general election was held on 27 October. The result was a triumph for the new government, who gained an absolute majority of over 400 seats. Labour, despite winning a third of the votes, were reduced to 52 MPs.[64]

Although a number of former Labour and Liberal ministers remained in the government – MacDonald, for example, stayed on as Prime Minister until June 1935 – its Parliamentary support was overwhelmingly Conservative and for many the National government soon became politically indistinguishable from a Conservative administration. This was especially so after Baldwin succeeded Mac-Donald and won a general election in November 1935.[65] Conservative in all but name, it continued officially as a 'National' government until 1940. After the immediate crisis of September-October 1931 had passed, the STO resumed the intermittent progress it had experienced under previous Conservative governments. The relaxation of fears regarding unrest is illustrated in a memorandum by Sir John Anderson which was circulated early in 1932. 'The situation', he wrote, 'has changed since September and the political considerations which operated against publicity have now receded into the background.' He argued that there was now an admirable opportunity to bring the STO 'into a state of full preparedness', since 'there is no industrial emergency in prospect and therefore no cause to fear an accusation of being provocative'. This was a novel approach to emergency planning. Drawing on his ten years' experience with the STO, Anderson no doubt wished to avoid the hasty preparations with which the organisation had met successive crises. His paper was also a valedictory exercise, and perhaps he wanted to ensure that emergency arrangements would in future be properly maintained without his careful supervision. In November 1931 he had accepted the Governorship of Bengal, which he took up in the spring of 1932. On 15 January the STC, chaired by the Home Secretary, Sir Herbert Samuel, unanimously approved Anderson's proposals and decided to revise the various emergency schemes, appoint Civil Commissioners and fill vacancies among VSC chairmen, district emergency committees and the lists of volunteers for the London Electric Power Scheme. No appointment was to be made to the Chief Civil Commissionership. Responsibility for this was left with the Home Secretary himself. The Cabinet approved this refurbishment, lifted the ban on publicity and accepted the risk that news of their action might 'reach the Press, no doubt in a distorted form, and that this would lead to comment, perhaps of a sensational kind'. Anderson succeeded in his intention. By the autumn of 1932 the STO was automatically being reviewed on a regular basis as a normal departmental function. 'Our instructions

. . .', wrote a Ministry of Transport official, 'are to overhaul all the emergency arrangements as a matter of course, even if such a course would involve consultation with outside persons or organisations.'[66] In December the Prime Minister appointed Commissioners for the 9 Divisions and the 2 'special areas' of London and the London docks. All except one were both junior members of the government and Conservative MPs.[67]

The principle of treating emergency planning as part of a government department's normal functions became well established. One benefit arising from this was economy. Although the Treasury were never able to abolish the retaining fees paid to the Board of Trade Food Officers, they cut back on the allowances hitherto paid to Ministry of Health Officials and in 1934 they finally stopped Christopher Roundell's allowance for his duties as Permanent Assistant to the Chief Commissioner. Between 1932 and 1937 the STC standing sub-committee was revived and met at intervals to check on the organisation, usually when there appeared to be some industrial trouble brewing. There were threatened coal stoppages in October 1935 and January 1936. The sub-committee also met in May 1937 when the possibility of a coal stoppage coincided with a strike of London busmen. But on each occasion departments did little more than review emergency regulations. In 1936 this procedure raised an unforeseen problem. During the preparation of a draft code of emergency regulations, Parliamentary Counsel had raised doubts, later confirmed by the Law Officers, as to the legality of certain regulations previously made under the Emergency Powers Act relating to administrative duties performed by local authorities. Section 2(1) of the Act conferred powers on the government 'or any other persons in His Majesty's service or acting on His Majesty's behalf'. The Law Officers declared that this provision was 'not sufficiently wide to include a statutory local authority', whose employees are not civil servants. Thus those parts of the STO which depended on local authorities, particularly distribution schemes for food and coal, had actually operated illegally in 1926.[68]

At an STC meeting in March 1936 the Home Secretary outlined three possible courses. The STO could carry on as before and 'make Regulations of doubtful legal validity'. They had not been questioned in the past and the risk of challenge, although possibly very embarrassing, was small. Secondly the Emergency Powers Act could be suitably amended, or, thirdly, 'entirely new machinery' could be created. He dismissed the latter two courses as potentially provocative. Differing somewhat from Sir John Anderson's general opinion in 1932, he asserted that it was clearly impossible to introduce amending legislation 'in a clear sky'. He favoured the first course and argued that 'if the Regulations were challenged it would be during an emergency and the challenge would not be well received by the House of Commons so that the conditions for getting amending legislation would be more favourable.' The committee concurred, but also agreed that a draft Bill amending the Emergency Powers Act could be prepared 'for introduction at a suitable opportunity'.[69] Such an opportunity never arose and section 2 (1) of the Act remains unamended.

From 1936 onwards the emergency organisation was affected by the growing possibility of a European war. One casualty was the CCR scheme. Since it had been assumed that most of the force would be composed of Territorial Army men, the War Office began to worry about a possible conflict of interests. By 1937 more than half the Territorial Army establishment in London alone was committed to anti-aircraft defence units. The Home Office was therefore informed that 'in the event of an international crisis', the War Office would find it most difficult to raise and administer the CCR. In the spring of 1939 the whole scheme was put into abeyance.[70] But the chief concern for the STO was to adapt it to possible wartime needs. In November 1936 the Food (Defence Plans) Department was established in the Board of Trade. It took over the existing emergency organisation and began drafting a rationing scheme in consultation with STO Divisional Food Officers. In May 1938 Sir Maurice Hankey and Sir Warren Fisher circulated a major paper to the Cabinet Committee of Imperial Defence (CID) on 'the co-ordination and control of passive defence measures in time of war'. In it they recommended the establishment of a 'Ministry of Home Security' specially responsible for civil defence. They suggested that the new ministry should have an extensive regional organisation. This drew heavily on the STO. The country, for example, was to be divided into the number of Divisions 'on the same lines . . . as has been done in the case of the Civil Emergency Organisation'. Each Division would be put in charge of 'specially selected persons of outstanding ability and experience' who would assume wide executive powers in time of emergency. They added that, if war should break out before their scheme had been completed, 'it would probably be possible and desirable to use the Civil Emergency Organisation'. On 2 June the CID agreed to this proposal. There was only one doubtful voice. Captain Austin Hudson, Parliamentary Secretary to the Ministry of Transport, was worried about how quickly the STO could be brought into action. He told the committee that he was a Civil Commissioner 'under the old scheme', but 'he had heard nothing about it since 1933'. On 26 August a sub-committee reported to the CID the minimum modifications required for the STO 'to function as a piece of emergency wartime machinery'. The report concentrated mostly on the Civil Commissioners' organisation. The Commissioners, 'who in a War Emergency should be called Regional Commissioners', would continue with the local staffs earmarked under the STO. To these would be added officers capable of dealing with such questions as casualties, hospitals and cash relief in cases of distress. It was thought that the VSCs need not be activated in wartime. The next day the CID approved the report, noting that the modifications should not affect 'the existing Civil Emergency Organisation when embodied for a *civil* emergency'.[71] The provisional plan for adapting the STO was not needed. By the time war broke out the Ministry of Home Security scheme was complete. On 3 September 1939 Sir John Anderson,[72] suitably, was appointed Home Secretary and Minister of Home Security.

# 6
# Mr Attlee faces the dilemma
# 1939/45 – April 1947

THE POLITICAL NATION inherited by Mr Clement Attlee and his
ministers in July 1945 was, by historical and subsequent standards,
a highly self-disciplined one. Almost six years of total war had left
no citizen untouched by its rigours, whether in the form of the siege
economy on the Home Front or by military service abroad. The
population was used to receiving orders and to strict regulation in
face of shared dangers. From the government's point of view, the
condition of the people was a policy-maker's boon, all the more so
as such self-restraint and national unity initially took the habitual
pessimists in Whitehall by surprise. 'However ingeniously and wisely the civil and industrial controls and rationing schemes may have
been devised . . .', wrote Sir Richard Hopkins, Head of the Civil
Service and Permanent Secretary to the Treasury 1942–45, 'they
would not have achieved their full success but for the goodwill with
which amid the strain and stress of war they were accepted by
industry and by the community as a whole.' This goodwill, he
added, 'went beyond – in my judgment much beyond – any forecast
which could reasonably have been made before hostilities began.'[1]
After the exigencies of the blitz, the U-boat blockade, the flying
bombs, the progressive transfer of productive resources from consumption to weaponry, and the increasingly efficient network of
civil defence, dislocations caused by strikes during the reconstruction period should, on the face of it, have confronted both government and governed with relatively few problems. This is especially
so since the war also bequeathed to Attlee both a wide range of
general emergency controls and the legal power to break strikes.[2]
  The statutory basis for wartime control was initially contained in
the Emergency Powers (Defence) Act which became law in August
1939. This was purely an enabling measure which empowered the
government to make 'such regulations as appeared necessary or

expedient' for, among other things, 'the maintenance of the supplies and services essential to the life of the community'. Under this Act the 'Defence (Armed Forces) Regulation 6' provided that service personnel could be temporarily employed in 'urgent [civilian] work of national importance'. At first this power only covered agricultural duties, but in 1941 it was extended generally to include 'such other work as may be approved'. It was not expected that this work would arise from industrial disputes, 'but from shortages of civilian labour here and there owing to the war'.[3] This, however, was not always the case. In May 1942, for example, troops were used in the Tyneside docks to replace 158 striking dockers, incidentally provoking a further 150 more men to stop work. Nevertheless, for the most part servicemen were not employed to break strikes during the war. By contrast, after August 1945 Regulation 6 was used on a number of occasions for just this purpose.

The 1939 Defence Regulations made no provision for any alteration in the conduct of industrial relations. Indeed, for the first eight months of the war there were no major strikes or great changes in the number and distribution of industrial workers. But when Winston Churchill's coalition government took office in May 1940 – at a time of extreme national crisis – there was a substantial review of policy. Churchill imaginatively appointed Ernest Bevin, veteran of the general strike and General Secretary of the TGWU, to be Minister of Labour and National Service.[4] Appreciating that the efficient use of labour required the closest possible co-operation between both sides of industry, Bevin set up a Joint Consultative Committee of employers and unions. For the rest of the war this committee played a central role in manpower policy-making and administration. Another innovation was the effective introduction of domestic conscription. Under the Emergency Powers (Defence) Act 1940 – 'the most drastic Act ever passed by a British parliament' – Bevin was armed with 'sweeping powers to order anyone to do anything that he might require'.[5] A third important action was the establishment of a legally enforceable procedure for dealing with trade disputes. This was contained in the 'Conditions of Employment and National Arbitration Order 1305' of July 1940. Part I of the order provided for the establishment of a National Arbitration Tribunal to which trade disputes could be referred by employers, employees or the minister. The Tribunal's decisions would be binding. Part II prohibited strikes and lock-outs, 'unless the Minister had failed within twenty-one days of having the matter reported to him to refer it for settlement to arbitration.'[6]

In the opinion of the official 'manpower' historian, the provisions for compulsory arbitration in part I of Order 1305 were 'at least a contributory cause of industrial peace' during the war.[7] Although there was a higher incidence of stoppages during the Second World War than during the First, they tended both to involve fewer workers and to be of shorter duration. Part II of the Order was less successful. It may be that the declared illegality of strikes had some effect on labour opinion, but from February 1941 there was a trickle of prosecutions under Order 1305. In all 6,300 people were prosecuted, resulting in some 5,100 convictions.[8] The difficulty of using Order 1305 to break a strike is illustrated by the outcome of the largest single prosecution. After the Betteshanger Colliery dispute in January 1942, over a thousand miners were convicted. Most of them were fined £1 each, but only nine men ever paid their fines. Since there was not sufficient prison accommodation to take the defaulters, and it seemed probable that further arrests would only provoke more trouble, court officials were instructed not to pursue the matter. The episode demonstrated that, particularly in a major dispute, Order 1305 was effectively unenforceable.

Two features emerged from wartime experience which were to have continuing importance after 1945: the high incidence of unofficial strikes, and the suspicion, held especially by Bevin, that industrial unrest was increasingly being fomented by political extremists. During the war, trade unions and employers' associations amalgamated with the government into what was virtually a 'corporate state'. This, along with the high-level agreement that the successful prosecution of the war effort over-rode all other considerations, to a certain extent upset the 'normal' balance of industrial relationships. Although Bevin made great efforts to ensure that proper consideration was given to such questions as wage-rates, working conditions and excess profits, in many cases workers came to feel that their union leaders were no longer fully representing the interests of the rank and file. In the autumn of 1943 the Ministry of Labour noted a growing lack of contact between trade union executives, local officials and members:

Compulsory arbitration and prohibition of strikes have made the Trade Union executives themselves both less sensitive to local

> feeling and less free in their handling of a difficult situation. They
> are apt to assume a dictatorial attitude to their branches and
> members and rely upon Government Departments to support
> them with, if necessary, the power of the law. Even when mistakes
> are made or a Union fails to do its obvious duty the Department
> has to support the Executive.[9]

The estrangement of union leaders from their members stimulated
a militant attitude among shop stewards, who frequently arrogated
the role of representing labour opinion which union officials seemed
to have relinquished. The 'corporatism' of wartime administration
also placed Ministry of Labour conciliation officers in a difficult
position. Before the war the ministry had attempted to take the
Baldwinian line that the government should not intervene directly
in industrial disputes but merely act, if at all, as an 'honest broker'.
The wartime combination of responsibility both for the direction of
labour and the settlement of disputes undermined this role.

The problem surfaced in the first month of the war with an
unofficial strike at an iron works in Lanarkshire. Here the matter
was complicated by an alarmist Civil Commissioner who wanted to
send in troops to protect the plant 'as there were fears that owing
to the presence of an Irish element in the district there might be
disturbances'. But the local chief conciliation officer recommended
that the government should not intervene in the dispute at all since
union officials themselves were doing their best to get men back to
work. This policy succeeded and the strike was later used as a 'case
study' for staff training in the ministry. It was emphasised that
officials must be 'very careful to proceed on the principle that in
the case of unofficial stoppages no action of any kind should be
taken that can be construed as intervention'. Such action could
undermine the authority of 'constitutional machinery' and 'minority
movements will be encouraged in further stoppages of a similar
character.' In June 1942 a court of inquiry, set up to investigate
persistent stoppages in the Tyneside docks, identified two 'fundamental causes': an unsatisfactory wage structure and the inability of
local union officials, although 'desirous of adhering to principles to
which they have officially agreed', to 'control their members or
induce them to give effect to their Union's wishes'. The inquiry
recommended some adjustments to wage rates, but also somewhat
lamely called on the union officials to be 'more assertive in upholding

the authority of their organisation'. The chairman of the court suggested privately that one particular troublemaker should be dropped 'by parachute over Germany, having first ascertained that the parachute will refuse to open'.[10]

In 1943 and early 1944 there was a growing inclination on Bevin's part to identify industrial disputes with political extremism. In September 1943 he warned Parliament of the dangers of strikes inspired by Trotskyists and other groups opposed to the war. But there is not much evidence to support his apprehension. MI5 were asked to investigate Communist and Trotskyist involvement in strikes at the Vickers Armstrong shipyard in Barrow, a Rolls Royce works at Hillington near Glasgow and among Clydeside shipyard workers. They reported that where such activity occurred at all, it had not initiated disputes, but had simply aimed to exacerbate existing grievances. At Barrow both MI5 and the local Chief Constable regarded the causes of unrest as 'essentially industrial', rather than political. The Chief Industrial Commissioner at the Ministry of Labour thought that one of the most serious aspects of the Barrow strike had been 'the loss of control by the Trade Union officials as a direct result of absence of proper contact between the Executive and the local officials and members'. Nevertheless Bevin was determined to act against subversion and in April 1944 introduced a new 'Defence Regulation 1AA', laying down heavy penalties on anyone convicted of 'inciting strikes or lock-outs which interfere with essential services'. At the same time Regulation 1A was amended to prohibit peaceful picketing. Neither of these Draconian measures was ever used. Their effect, like that of Order 1305, is debatable. In April 1945 the Chief Industrial Commissioner thought it 'a matter of opinion' whether or not the Regulation had been 'effective in deterring persons from instigating strikes'. He was sure, however, that it could serve no useful purpose after the war had ended. This met with general agreement and on VE Day, 8 May, Regulation 1AA was revoked.[11] For the meantime Order 1305 remained in force.

The coalition government broke up almost as soon as the war in Europe ended. Although some ministers, both Labour and Conservative, felt that the government should continue at least until the end of the war against Japan, the Labour party generally believed strongly that a general election should not be delayed, particularly since Parliament had now lasted ten years. On 23 May 1945 Chur-

chill called an election for 5 July and immediately formed a 'caretaker' government. It was widely assumed not so much that the
Conservatives would win the election, but, with Churchill's im-
mense prestige as national saviour, they could not lose it. Possibly
with this in mind, and certainly remembering the aftermath of the
First World War, the Home Office began thinking about possible
civil emergencies. On 4 June Sir Alexander Maxwell raised the
matter in a letter circulated to a number of Whitehall departmental
heads. Maxwell was a reforming, liberal civil servant who had been
Permanent Under-Secretary to the Home Office since 1938. He had
also been closely involved with Sir John Anderson and emergency
arrangements during the general strike. 'I think that the time has
arrived', he wrote, 'to consider the question of resuscitating the
Supply and Transport Organisation.' He invited representatives to
a meeting for this purpose and, if it was agreed to revive the STO,
to discuss what modifications were required to bring it up to date
and 'to prepare proposals to put before Ministers.' On 15 June the
Home Office circulated a brief account of the STO between 1919
and 1939. It pin-pointed 'the main problem throughout' as having
been 'how to maintain the nucleus of an organisation which would
be ready to function at reasonable notice of large scale industrial
troubles without giving the organisation undesirable publicity.'[12]

Maxwell's meeting was held in the Home Office on 19 June and
comprised 28 people representing 18 departments. Apart from Maxwell himself there were only two old STO hands present. One was
Sir Frank Newsam, Deputy Under-Secretary to the Home Office,
who had been Sir John Anderson's private secretary in the 1920s.
During the general strike and after he had regularly attended meetings of both the STC and its sub-committees. The other was Mr J.
Thomson, the Chief Inspector of Fisheries, who had attended the
last pre-war meeting of the STC in March 1936. Maxwell began by
remarking that 'whether industrial trouble was or was not likely,
one could not rule out the possibility of large-scale industrial disturbances during the next few years, and it was the business of the
Government to be prepared for an emergency of that kind.' This
met with general approval and the meeting quickly moved on to
consider details. It was agreed that the wartime Civil Defence regions could serve as they stood for the Civil Commissioners' scheme.
Every department had its own regional organisation from which
staff could be drawn and the Ministry of Health offered the services

of their Inspectorate as had been the case before the war. There was a lengthy discussion on the recruitment of volunteer labour. Robert Gould, the Chief Industrial Commissioner, asserted that, even armed with the present emergency powers for directing manpower, the Ministry of Labour could not cope with large-scale industrial unrest. It was, he argued, preferable for 'volunteers to be organised under pressure of public opinion'. This raised the question of whether suitable people should be approached to become chairmen of VSCs. Gould thought not 'as it would have the most unfortunate results if there was a leakage'. Newsam suggested that the Women's Voluntary Service might be maintained as the nucleus of an organisation and a civilian representative from the Admiralty approvingly noted that 'there should be many more women available to help in an emergency than there had been in 1926 because of the number of women who would have had experience in the Services'. Maxwell was strongly of the opinion that VSC chairmen should be appointed well in advance of any possible trouble and that this question should be considered by ministers as a matter of some urgency. Towards the end of the meeting when the committee came to discuss protection there was an echo of the early 1920s. They were told 'that for some time to come the police would not be so capable of dealing with an emergency as they were in 1926 because they were so much below strength'. Although the Special Constabulary would be available, it was thought that 'something on the lines of the Civil Constabulary Reserve might have to be considered'. Maxwell concluded by saying that he would write a memorandum summarising the decisions of the meeting. There was no question of the matter being brought before the caretaker Cabinet. His paper would be prepared 'with a view to its submission to Ministers after the General Election'.[13]

Although most constituencies voted on 5 July, the count did not take place until 26 July, by which time the votes of Armed Forces' personnel serving overseas had been brought home. The election result was a triumph for Labour, who emerged with an overall majority of 146 seats.[14] Unlike MacDonald, Attlee was not handicapped by a lack of available ministerial experience. Most of his new Cabinet had served in the wartime coalition or in 1929–31, and five (including himself) survived from the first Labour government. Of these Arthur Greenwood became Lord Privy Seal and Emanuel Shinwell took over Fuel and Power. Attlee appointed Herbert Morrison as Lord President of the Council to act, with Greenwood, as a senior minister co-ordinating domestic policy. Bevin, who had wanted the Exchequer, was sent, somewhat to his own surprise and disappointment, to the Foreign Office. The Treasury went to Hugh Dalton, a gregarious academic economist, who, although he had first been elected an MP in 1924, symbolised the changing nature of the Parliamentary Labour party. Middle class, educated at Eton and Cambridge, he was more a socialist by conviction than experience. In 1945 the party was more 'national' and less specifically working class than it had ever been before. Only two members of the Cabinet took government office for the first time. Both were trade unionists: Aneurin Bevan, a left-wing miner from south Wales, and George Isaacs, a past president of the Society of Operative Printers and Assistants. Bevan became Minister of Health, and Isaacs Minister of Labour. A slightly unexpected appointment was that of James Chuter Ede to the Home Office. Ede was a somewhat withdrawn, didactic nonconformist of the old school, 'an ex-school-master and an ex-infantry sergeant, and looking, to perfection, both these parts'. He had intermittently been an MP between the wars, but his only experience of government had been as Parliamentary Secretary to the Ministry of Education from 1940 to 1945, where R. A. Butler remembered him as being 'consistently loyal and wise'. Attlee told Ede that he was 'the only man . . . who had some knowledge of the work of Justices as well as of Local Govt.'[15]

In the King's Speech to Parliament on 15 August the government set out its legislative programme for the coming session. Nationalisation, specifically of the coal industry and the Bank of England, featured prominently, as did the proposal to establish a national health service. The government announced that the Trade Disputes and Trade Unions Act 1927 would be repealed. Because of the difficulties likely to arise in 'the period of transition from war to peace', it was also proposed to retain 'such powers as are necessary to secure the right use of our commercial and industrial resources and the distribution at fair prices of essential supplies and services'. The matter was discussed in Cabinet the following day, when it was agreed to extend selected emergency powers for a further five years. It was noted that after the First World War, 'the period of industrial and economic difficulty had not begun until 1921; and it was arguable that, if the Government had then enjoyed sufficient powers of economic control, it would have been possible to avoid the industrial crises of 1921, 1924 and 1926.' This decision found effect in the Supplies and Services (Transitional Powers) Act 1945. Although most of the powers retained were economic controls of various sorts, they also included those under Defence Regulation 6 and Order 1305. Isaacs had raised the question of Order 1305 with the Joint Consultative Committee, who had approved its retention until such time as the TUC and the British Employers' Confederation wanted it abolished. Despite reservations regarding the continued illegality of strikes, trade union opinion generally favoured the Order's provisions for arbitration, including the imposition of binding decisions on employers.[16]

The Labour electoral victory seems to have had no effect on the Whitehall plans for reviving the STO which Sir Alexander Maxwell had set moving in June. On 2 August, the day before Chuter Ede was appointed, the Home Office, as promised, circulated a draft paper on the subject, which they were 'anxious to put . . . before the new Home Secretary at an early date'. Maxwell evidently lost little time in briefing Ede. On 22 August Ede, having consulted the Secretary of State for Scotland, wrote to Attlee recommending that the question of reviving the STO be placed before the Cabinet. He felt that since the proposal would involve setting up a ministerial committee and 'the selection of Junior Ministers to be designated as Civil Commissioners for the several regions', he ought to consult the Prime Minister 'beforehand' to give Attlee an opportunity to consider exactly who would be chosen for these posts.[17] Nothing in Ede's note suggested that he thought the matter was anything more than routine. Indeed, the letter carried no secrecy marking. But it was political dynamite. Here was the first ever majority Labour government, engaged upon the priority task of repealing the Trade Disputes and Trade Unions Act – the embodiment of Baldwin's victory over trade union power – being asked by its Home Secretary to consider the reactivation of the sharpest weapon Baldwin had possessed in 1926. Ede's letter was the first link in a long chain of contingency planning which preoccupied the Attlee Cabinet in short bursts throughout its six-year life. Without the stimulus of any serious industrial dispute in August 1945, the initiative faltered a little. A gap of nine days elapsed before anything stirred in No. 10 or the Cabinet Office.

On 31 August Norman Brook, deputy to the Cabinet Secretary, wrote a minute for Attlee in response to Ede's letter. It is a classic example of a modern Whitehall brief from one of the most influential of post-war civil servants. Brook began by summarising the STO and the Emergency Powers Act 1920, 'passed when the country was faced with the prospect of grave industrial unrest after the end of the last war'. He went on to state some general principles:

> It is clearly necessary that plans should be made so that we may be ready, if need arises, to bring such an organisation into operation again – and we should certainly take advantage of the experience gained in the Regional organisation of Civil Defence during the war. It also seems expedient that this planning should be put in hand at once, on the basis of proceeding with these preparations as a matter of course on the termination of the war – rather than waiting until such preparations might appear to be related to some estimate of a forecast of actual industrial unrest.

At this point Brook showed himself to be acutely aware of the political implications of the Ede letter. The matter was so sensitive, he felt, that perhaps it should not be discussed by the full Cabinet, so great was the need for secrecy:

> There is, however, much to be said for handling this as a mere matter of planning, and confining knowledge of the plans within the narrowest possible circle. The Government are proposing to repeal the Trade Disputes Act, which declared a general strike to be illegal: and it might be embarrassing if it became known, and could be alleged in debate, that at the same time the Government were preparing plans for defeating a general strike if one occurred.

He thought that in these circumstances it might be preferable simply to place the matter before a small meeting of directly concerned ministers, which 'could give authority for planning to proceed at a high official level'. A minister could be designated Chief Civil Commissioner, but 'junior Ministers who would act as Commissioners in the Regions would merely be earmarked, and would not at this stage be brought into the discussion of the plans'. Brook concluded with a proper deferral to the Prime Minister's authority:

> It may be that I exaggerate the risks of discussing this matter on the basis of an ordinary Cabinet Paper. You may think it quite

proper to have the matter raised in Cabinet, as the Home Secretary suggests. In case however you should feel any doubts about
this, I thought it right to put before you an alternative course by
which you could meet the essential needs of the present situation,
while confining discussion to those directly concerned with these
plans.[18]

The subject of contingency planning was no stranger to Norman
Brook, who had been moulded by the Home Office, that grimmest
and most conservative of departments. He entered in 1925 and at
a critical time in the late 1930s became Assistant Secretary in charge
of the policy division dealing with civil emergencies, War Book and
Defence Regulations, the work for which he was best remembered
in the Home Office. He was similar in temperament to Sir John
Anderson, his great patron at successive stages of his career. Like
Anderson, he attracted the epithet 'Olympian'. Anderson first came
across Brook when he was Permanent Secretary at the Home Office
and arming Baldwin with a well-oiled emergency machine. When
in 1938 Anderson joined the government as a minister, Brook became first his Principal Private Secretary and later 'Personal Assistant' when Anderson was appointed Lord President in 1940.
Churchill's perfect description of Anderson as 'the automatic pilot'
could just as easily have been applied to the fastidious, ever-reliable
Brook. In 1942 he moved to the Cabinet Office and remained there
until his retirement. From 1947 to 1962 he was Cabinet Secretary,
combining this with being Head of the Home Civil Service from
1956. Brook's service to successive Prime Ministers (in the end he
took care of four) was a model of efficiency, propriety and conserv-
atism. Consistently cautious and almost obsessed with secrecy, he
was neither a radical nor an innovator, but the supreme executor of
Prime Ministerial will. This is not to say he was without influence.
Most of his masters in No. 10 swore by him. In 1959 Macmillan
extravagantly told Lord Moran: 'Norman has most wonderful judgment. He is always right. Pure inborn judgment, because, as I
expect you know, he had no background.'[19]
    Attlee, who regarded the question as 'not very urgent', fell in
with Brook's caution and decided to discuss it in a private meeting
with his closest and most senior colleagues: Bevin, Morrison and
Greenwood. Without an industrial dispute to impart a sense of
urgency nobody gave the matter a high priority. After some delays,

while arrangements for the meeting were made and the Prime Minister took a short holiday at Chequers, it was finally held on 8 October. As no civil servants were present, Attlee wrote up the minutes himself in his neat hand on a tiny slip of paper. They read:

Conclusion of a Meeting of Ministers.
Organisation to be set up on official level.
Cmtee of Ministers under Home Sec to approve scheme and to report to me generally and in particular whether there is need for Junior Ministers in view of the development of regional organisation in the Ministries.

*Cmtee*
Home Sec
Min War Transport
– Food
– Health
Labour
B of T
S of Scotland

*No publicity*
Arrange for me to see Home Sec before any action taken

C.R.A.

On 11 October Attlee gave Ede details of the discussion. He again emphasised the need for secrecy and instructed the Home Secretary personally to arrange a meeting of the new committee.[20]

In October 1945, however, the government faced its first serious strike. Towards the end of September sixty men at Bidston, on the southern shore of the Mersey, had gone on unofficial strike over the rate of pay available for handling pit-props. By 1 October the strike had spread to the Liverpool side. The following day virtually the entire Birkenhead and Liverpool docks were idle, with 13,000 men out. On Tuesday 9 October – the day after Attlee's meeting – the strike surfaced on the Cabinet agenda. Isaacs reported that 'a serious situation was developing as a result of the dockers' strike'. Six ships 'containing cargoes of perishable foodstuffs' were held up in Liverpool. He told his colleagues that 'two of these contained cargoes of bacon; and he was informed that, if these cargoes were lost, an immediate reduction in the bacon ration would be necessary'. The Cabinet quickly approved his recommendation that military labour should be used for unloading food. There it was. Less than three months after taking office for the first time with an overall majority, a Labour government contemplated the use of troops to break a strike, apparently without any dissent from the ministers around the Cabinet table. This was not in fact quite the first such use of troops during the Attlee administration. At the end of July, while the Prime Minister was still selecting his Cabinet, between three and four hundred soldiers were briefly deployed to unload timber and sugar from seven ships held up by a 'go-slow' in the London docks. It is not exactly clear who authorised this, but it seems as if the new government inherited the decision since it was in keeping with a Ministry of Labour announcement, made *before* the general election votes had been counted, that the government would 'take all necessary steps' to ensure 'expeditious handling' of ships carrying essential cargoes.[21]

As the Cabinet was meeting in Downing Street, the strike was spreading rapidly. *The Times* round-up the following day showed 2,000 men out at the Royal docks in London holding up five food ships; Manchester was at a complete standstill and the men passed a motion of no confidence in the leaders of the dockers' section of the TGWU; 500 men were out at Preston; Middlesbrough was completely strikebound; at Hull the lightermen joined in bringing the total to 4,500; at Grimsby and Immingham on the other side of the Humber estuary crane drivers walked out preventing troops from loading ships with vegetables for the British Army of Occupation in Germany.[22] The dispute had come a long way from sixty men and pit-props at Bidston. This explosion of waterfront unrest ostensibly stemmed from a pay dispute, but on a deeper level it expressed the frustration of five years' self-restraint under Order 1305. Since 1940 trade union militancy had been denied an official outlet, a position reasonably easy to hold during time of war, but very trying, perhaps even 'provocative', once peace was restored. Although no action was taken under Order 1305, the government's reaction to the strike in other ways reflected wartime approaches to industrial disputes. The use of troops – on the basis of national needs over-riding sectional interests – was one aspect. Indeed, the government were able to employ substantial numbers of trained stevedores in wartime Royal Engineer Port Labour Battalions. By the weekend of 13/14 October over 6,000 troops were working on Merseyside, Humberside and in London. A second feature was the

high moral tone adopted by government spokesmen. On 8 October
a Ministry of Labour statement noted that the stoppage was likely
to 'inflict serious hardship' on the country generally. 'Prolongation
of the strike', it declared, 'can only result in harm to the country's
food supply, to demobilisation and also to the men's own best
interests.' Thirdly there were suggestions that subversive wreckers
were manipulating the strike. This became a routine feature of
disputes in the 1940s. In October 1945 the theme was played, not
by the government, but by the trade union leadership. On 12 October Arthur Deakin, who succeeded Bevin as General Secretary of
the TGWU in 1940 and a man who was inclined to see 'reds under
the beds', asserted that 'the present stoppage had been seized upon
by people connected with certain political organisations who had
ready-prepared machinery at their disposal for encouraging and
maintaining strike action.' When pressed, he specifically named the
Revolutionary Communist Party. This party was a Trotskyist splin-
ter group which had a five-year life, under that particular name,
from 1944 to 1949. For a brief spell it united virtually all the
fissiparous elements in British Trotskyism. Its greatest recruiting
officer was Order 1305. It stood alone with the Independent Labour
Party in advocating strikes during the wartime coalition period. At
the time of Deakin's attack, its membership numbered around five
hundred, but it went into steep decline in the late 1940s when the
orthodox Communist Party of Great Britain and some trade unions
once more began to recommend strike action. As much a part of
the ritual of these events as Deakin's intervention was the statement
put out on 12 October by the committee of the Revolutionary
Communist Party accusing Deakin of 'miserable falsification'.[23]

Although employing troops in the docks, principally to move
food, the government steadfastly refused to intervene directly in the
search for a settlement since, as Isaacs told the Cabinet on 15
October, this 'would tend to weaken the normal procedure of negotiations between the duly accredited representatives of workers and
employers.'[24] Isaacs rested in the huge shadow of Ernest Bevin who
had persuaded Attlee to put him in the Ministry of Labour. In the
early days of the 1945 Parliament Bevin was constantly on the
telephone from the Foreign Office to St James's Square offering
Isaacs advice he was in no position to refuse. Bevin was not a man
given to self-doubt at the best of times. When dealing with dock
disputes he had no scepticism about the accuracy of his insights.

He knew, or thought he did, those people inside out. But not all of them placed Bevin on a pedestal. Jack Dash, the militant London docker who won national fame in the 1960s, tells a revealing tale to illustrate the mood of the men towards Bevin in the late 1940s. During one of the long winters of austerity and rationing which characterised those years, a large crate arrived in the Royal Docks around Christmas time addressed to 'The Right Hon. Ernest Bevin, PC, MP, The Foreign Office'. The men's curiosity was aroused. The box was 'accidentally' dropped and split wide open. A luscious array of delicate and exotic foods spilled across the quayside. It was a gift to Bevin from some foreign government. The dockers confiscated the lot, carefully repacking the crate with rubble and rubbish from the warehouses. On the top they placed a note which read: 'TO ERNIE. MERRY CHRISTMAS FROM SOME OF YOUR OWN!'[25]

Over the weekend of 20/21 October, with the stoppage moving into its fifth week, the government announced that it was increasing the number of strikebreaking troops from 7,000 to 10,000. The strikers replied by claiming it would take 60,000 troops to do the work dropped by the 40,000 men in dispute. By the end of the week there had been very little visible movement as the strikers continued to ignore union appeals to return to work. By Friday 26 October 46,500 men were out and another 1,000 troops were drafted in to Avonmouth. The Cabinet, however, met on Friday morning. Before them was a memorandum from Alfred Barnes, the Minister of War Transport, as he was still called. Its tone was gloomy, reflecting the dim prospects of a quick settlement. Barnes told his colleagues that 10,500 troops were already involved, only half of whom were skilled stevedores. A maximum of 20,000 would be available if required. He spelled out in detail the number of ships and categories of cargo affected. Some 225 ships in ports throughout the country were now totally immobilised. In the largest single group waiting for unloading were 72 timber ships needed for the housing drive. Fifteen ships held grain and 5 meat. In the circumstances, Barnes felt moved to seek Cabinet approval for an extension to the use of military labour to vessels loading cargo for export and 'sterling ships', irrespective of their contents, whose clearance would aid the 'immediate import programmes of essential food and raw materials' and keep the use of 'dollar tonnage' to a minimum.[26]

The chief worry behind Barnes's Cabinet paper was the country's grave economic position. Lend-lease from the United States had been abruptly ended by President Truman at the end of the Japanese war in August. Lord Keynes and Professor Lionel Robbins were engaged in increasingly difficult negotiations in Washington to secure an American loan on terms that would not cause the British economy to founder in the long-run. Standards of living were low and rationing tight. The public's desire for an easing of conditions was understandably strong after the privations of war. Indeed, Labour's huge majority was, in one sense, a reflection of the revolution of expectations. But economic ministers had to grapple daily with a dollar shortage in determining priorities for imports. An export drive was under way to recapture world markets lost, mostly to the United States, since 1939. For these reasons Sir Stafford Cripps, President of the Board of Trade, was acutely concerned about events on the waterfront. He had warned Barnes that the volume of exports was 'catastrophically below recent experience' and had pointed out that 'we cannot sustain interest in exports if it is known that they cannot be shipped.'[27]

The Cabinet discussion on the dockers' strike on 26 October began with a report from Ness Edwards, a former miner, now George Isaacs's deputy as Parliamentary Secretary to the Ministry of Labour, on the latest prospects. Meetings were to be held that day and over the weekend, but there was no evidence to suggest the strike would collapse during that period. As matters had reached such a critical pass, Winston Churchill, the Leader of the Opposition, had been asked to defer a Parliamentary Question, due to be answered that day, until Monday. Labour Cabinets, recent and past, tend to devote close attention to the political presentation of public statements on strikebreaking. Such matters call for the balm of conciliation and the resolve of statesmanship to be combined in a few carefully phrased sentences. Ministers concurred that the best way to handle Churchill would be to confirm that the government 'did not intend to intervene in any way which would jeopardise the working of the constitutional machinery for the settlement of issues between employers and workers.' At the same time it would be emphasised that 'they could not allow the clearance of ships carrying essential cargoes to be held up by an unofficial strike'. Ministers then turned their attention to Barnes's memorandum. His wish to extend the use of troops to the additional types of strikebound vessels was supported. The Cabinet record bears dry witness to a psychological slide into acceptance of industrial dislocation as a routine fact of life. During discussion it was suggested that 'arrangements should be made to enable the Minister of Labour to obtain advice on the extent to which it would be justifiable to employ military labour in the docks, without having to seek specific authority from the Cabinet on each occasion'. It was also proposed that 'there was need for some standing machinery to review . . . questions of wages policy and other questions arising from industrial disputes'. This proposal posed an unexpected problem arising from the extreme secrecy surrounding Ede's initiative on the STO. It seems probable that the suggestion came from a minister unaware of the Home Secretary's impending review, which was not mentioned at any stage in Cabinet. Attlee instead agreed to set up a Cabinet committee, chaired by the Chancellor of the Exchequer, to examine these problems and 'to authorise such emergency action as may be necessary, by reason of industrial disputes, to maintain supplies and services essential to the life of the community'.[28]

The choice of Dalton as chairman was odd, but is probably explained by the prominent place given to wages policy in the terms of reference and the likelihood of the committee having to take executive action during the dock strike. In the latter case Attlee was no doubt anxious to have a man of more experience than Ede in charge. Following the Cabinet meeting the Prime Minister approved Brook's recommendation that the committee should otherwise contain the same ministers as Ede's *ad hoc* body, but excluding the Minister of Health and the Secretary for Scotland. The Secretary for War was to be co-opted when any question arose of using military labour. Attlee also agreed that the relationship of the new committee to the proposed STO could be decided after Ede had completed his review.[29] Dalton's committee never met. Indeed, the 'Industrial Emergencies Committee', as it came to be known, only met for the first time in January 1947. The dockers' strike began to lose impetus from the weekend of 27/28 October. On 2 November mass meetings up and down the country voted to accept conditions for a return to work drafted by the national strike committee in Liverpool. A ballot in Liverpool showed 70 per cent of the militant Merseyside dockers ready to go back to work with the rest of the nation on Monday 5 November. The strike had lasted 41 days. It involved a total of 43,000 dockers and 21,000 strikebreaking troops. It seems that the government's hard line paid off. No firm pay award was on offer at the time of resumption and the strike committee merely insisted that any award should be backdated to 27 September 1945. Attlee handled the first substantial industrial dispute of his administration by sending in the army of which he was so proud. There was no hesitation about it and no reservations around the Cabinet table. What became clear, however, was that even a nation with an unusually high proportion of its men under arms would find it difficult to replace civilians with military labour and manage to maintain essential services at the normal level.

The restriction of knowledge about Ede's review of the STO to only a small number of specified ministers did not evidently apply in Whitehall. Before convening his ministerial committee, Ede asked for an official group to examine a number of salient questions, particularly the extent to which the STO could function on a purely official level; whether Civil Commissioners need be appointed immediately; and how far arrangements could be made without publicity. Sir Alexander Maxwell called a meeting on 10 November. It was attended by representatives from sixteen departments. Two-thirds of the 26 officials present had also been at the original meeting in June. In contrast to the June meeting, Maxwell began by warning his colleagues that their discussion should be 'treated as highly confidential'. The meeting generally agreed that Civil Commissioners need not be appointed at once, but that they would serve an essential function as co-ordinators during an emergency. It would be 'desirable but not essential' if the Commissioners were junior ministers. There was a 'consensus of opinion . . . that such limited outside contacts as were necessary during the preparatory stage could be established at the official level'. The officials did not commit themselves to make no contacts outside the government. They merely agreed not to involve ministers. It was, however, widely stressed that, in the event of an emergency, extensive liaison with non-official bodies would be required. The Ministry of Transport, for example, 'would need to get in touch in advance with the three Motoring Associations, the Railway Companies and with the Managing Directors of about ten of the principal Dock Authorities'. When the meeting went on to discuss the provision of labour, Maxwell sensibly argued that it was 'politically and socially undesirable' to recruit volunteers through the Employment Exchanges. The 'only alternative was to enlist the help of local people of recognised impartiality'. The Ministry of Labour representative agreed, but thought such people need not be appointed until an emergency was actually approaching. 'Asked whether this was not the time when recruiting would be most provocative, he said that an attempt to recruit volunteer labour would be regarded as provocative whenever it was made.' With little discussion it was agreed that 'the question of the use of military labour should be referred to Ministers'. The thorny problem of publicity was similarly left for the politicians to decide. At the end of the meeting Sir Frank Newsam raised the matter of emergency regulations, observing that before the war it had been the practice to keep two codes ready for use: 'one for a sectional strike (such as a coal, transport or dock strike) the other for an emergency on a large scale'. He also mentioned the dubious legality of emergency powers over local authorities, which the Law Officers had questioned before the war. Maxwell asked departments to consider 'whether their emergency plans would necessitate imposing duties on local authorities' and also 'to inform the Home Office as soon as possible of their own requirements for emergency regulations'.[30]

During the winter of 1945 the problem of maintaining essential services was highlighted by a series of unofficial strikes which seriously disrupted gas supplies in London. Like his father in the aftermath of the First World War, George VI in the aftermath of the Second was worried about industrial unrest. Unlike George V, however, the King was not so much concerned with the immediate likelihood of revolution as with the freedom and welfare of his people. He told Attlee that 'the liberty of the subject was at stake if a strike interfered with home life. Essential services such as gas, electricity and water should never be used for those purposes in an unofficial strike.' George VI then raised the novel possibility of Monarch and Prime Minister themselves taking industrial action. 'He & I could easily go on strike', wrote the King in his diary. 'He would send me no papers and if he did I would not sign them. But we don't!'[31]

Since June 1945 Whitehall, and the Home Office in particular, had clearly been working on the assumption, not only that the STO would be re-established, but that it would be revived very much in its pre-war form. In one respect, however, the Home Office overstepped the mark. Maxwell's request for departments to prepare emergency regulations evidently went too far too soon and the process was soon postponed. Indeed, not all departments were as keen as the Home Office to press on with the STO. The news that detailed emergency arrangements were being made quickly circulated throughout Whitehall and in January 1946 the Electricity Commission, who had not been represented at the Home Office meeting in November, approached the Admiralty requesting a meeting to discuss 'the possibility of the Admiralty rendering assistance in keeping electricity supplies going'. The Admiralty, who were in any case perhaps not very anxious to revive their commitment to the emergency organisation, demurred. They observed that in fact no final Cabinet decision had yet been made on the STO and that 'if the Government should decide to proceed with these arrangements it would be preferable to wait until the official machinery contemplated in Whitehall and in the Provinces had been initiated'.[32]

In most respects, however, Chuter Ede unquestioningly fell in with Whitehall policy. On 22 January 1946 he circulated to his review committee a memorandum embodying the decisions made at Maxwell's meeting and also including some observations drafted separately in the Home Office. Ede confirmed that the STO should be re-established with a ministerial committee 'to decide major questions of policy and priority'. Routine administration would be handled by an official committee on which all the departments concerned would be represented. As had been the case before the war, there would be a number of sub-committees to deal with particular problems 'such as food, fuel, transport, protection, finance, publicity and communications'. Staff in the regions would be supervised by the Ministry of Health in England and Wales, and the Scottish Office in Scotland. Ede added that he would be glad to discuss 'without delay' the question of reviewing the names of possible Civil Commissioners. Regarding the problem of publicity, he observed that the Parliamentary opposition were well aware that the STO had existed before the war and might well inquire about it during the debates on the repeal of the Trade Disputes and Trade Unions Act. In order to avoid the embarrassment of such inconvenient questions, it might be better for the government to make a general statement announcing the existence of the STO. Ede – or, rather, his officials since this part of the memorandum had been drafted in November 1945 – argued that it was 'the elementary duty of the Government to ensure that the community does not suffer as a result of the interruption of essential services', and that the establishment of an emergency organisation was a 'routine precaution, which would . . . be taken by any Government at any time'. In the early 1930s Sir John Anderson had pointed out the expediency of making at least the general idea of the STO public at a time of relative industrial peace. In the mid-1940s his successors at the Home Office perceived positive benefits for this course of action:

> If the public are accustomed in advance to the idea that a Government organisation will operate in an emergency to maintain essential supplies and services, the knowledge is likely to discourage unofficial attempts to bring such an organisation into being, and to facilitate both the preparation of plans and the working of those plans when an emergency occurs.

Ede also followed the November draft when he discussed the possible use of service labour. Noting that 'while it would be wrong for the Government to use troops as strike-breakers' (*sic*), it was legitimate to employ them to maintain the essentials of life. In the present economic circumstances the movement of 'vital export cargoes and the discharge of incoming supplies of important raw materials' might also be regarded as 'essential'. Although the Ministry of Labour felt that 'the unwise use of military labour in connection with export trade might give the impression that troops were being used for strike-breaking and precipitate a serious crisis', Ede suggested that a decision should be made in principle to use service labour when required for essential needs.[33]

The re-establishment of the STO had so far progressed more or less smoothly. But this stopped when Ede's committee met in January 1946. Objections were raised by Aneurin Bevan and Sir Stafford Cripps. Both men were prominent left-wingers. They had been expelled from the party together in March 1939 for advocating a 'Popular Front', including Communists and even Conservatives, to oppose the National Government's policy of appeasement. Although Bevan was readmitted in December 1939, Cripps remained excluded until February 1945. Bevan's characteristically unrestrained opposition to Defence Regulation 1AA – 'the disfranchisement of the individual' – in 1944 briefly threatened him with expulsion for a second time. Neither man was likely to regard the STO as conceived by the Home Office with undiluted approval. At the committee meeting Bevan virtually ignored Ede's carefully prepared paper.

Apart from anything else, the initiative was ill-timed. Six days earlier the Bill to repeal the Trade Disputes and Trade Unions Act had been presented to Parliament. While agreeing that 'it would be generally accepted that it was the Government's duty to ensure that the essential services of the community did not suffer during industrial disputes', Bevan saw 'great political objection' to discussions concerning an emergency organisation continuing while the Trade Disputes Bill was before Parliament. Cripps agreed and said that in any case 'the establishment of an efficient organisation must necessarily involve discussions with a wide range of official and non-official organisations and persons'. This should be done publicly and should involve consulting all sections of the community, including the TUC. 'Only in this way', he declared, 'would it be possible to ensure that the organisation was not represented as a strike breaking body on the lines of the Organisation for the Maintenance of Supplies'. Bevan also believed that the unions should be consulted and he argued, carrying the committee with him, that the first thing to be done was to formulate 'a statement of the broad principles on which the organisation should be based'. The committee also decided that while the Trade Disputes Bill was under consideration no further action regarding the STO should be taken at any official level.[34]

Attlee's position regarding the STO was already quite clear. On 8 October 1945, along with Bevin, Morrison and Greenwood, he had approved the establishment of an emergency organisation, at least on an official level. But when Ede told him about the review committee's discussion, the Prime Minister, no doubt anxious to accommodate Bevan and Cripps, agreed that they should frame a statement of general principles. In February the committee met again to consider a draft statement of three paragraphs prepared by the Home Office. The first paragraph established the 'elementary duty of the Government' in much the same terms as Ede's memorandum of 22 January and followed it with a description of the Emergency Powers Act 1920. The second paragraph, covering the aims of government policy towards serious disputes, was more contentious. 'The object of Government intervention in the circumstances contemplated by the Act', it read, 'would, of course, not be to break a strike or lockout, and it would not be designed to favour one side or another in a legitimate industrial dispute.' Bevan objected to the suggestion that the government intended to *intervene* in disputes. There were also doubts about the apparent implication that the government might take sides if the dispute was *not* legitimate (as, indeed, were the majority of current stoppages). The sentence was accordingly amended as follows: 'the object of Government action . . . would, of course, not be to break a strike or lockout, or to favour one side or another in an industrial dispute.' The final paragraph of the draft, which referred to the possibility of the government co-operating with both employers' organisations and trade unions in the emergency organisation, was passed without comment. Bevan did not stop merely at amending Ede's draft, but went on to question the actual need for a large-scale organisation at all. He felt that each dispute should be dealt with individually as it occurred, 'rather then by attempting to build up an elaborate organisation designed to cater for disputes which might never arise'. The conditions in which the Emergency Powers Act was passed, he argued, 'had long since disappeared and were unlikely to recur in foreseeable time. Moreover,' he continued, 'an announcement of the Government's intention to set up an organisation and formal approaches to the TUC and employers' organisations . . . would give the subject more importance than it warranted.' Bevan received some support from the Parliamentary Secretary to the Board of Trade, who was deputising for Cripps, but neither the Secretary for Scotland nor the Minister of Labour were prepared to abandon the STO. The committee finally agreed only to submit the statement of principle to the Cabinet.[35]

On 7 March Norman Brook briefed the Prime Minister on the STO question for a Cabinet meeting the following day. He noted that there had been a substantial weight of opinion in Ede's committee against creating an official organisation, but a compromise had eventually been reached in the recommendation that, if an organisation were to be established, all sections of the community should be invited to co-operate both in its framing and operation. 'I must confess', remarked Brook, 'that this compromise seems to me to be unpractical.' He could not see how the trade unions might be persuaded 'to agree in advance that their members should help to *operate* such an organisation, when the time came. Nor do I see how in fact men who ex hypothesi would be on strike could, when the time came, be used to run an organisation which would make the strike less effective.' Brook, who expressed no worries that consulting employers might cause difficulties, was so convinced that creating an emergency organisation openly would not work that he preferred 'to take the risk of not making any arrangements at all'. If the worst came to the worst, the accumulated experience of the wartime Regional Organisation put the government in a 'better position now to improvise . . . arrangements at the last moment, if need should arise, than we were after the last war'. Brook concluded with a well-tried Whitehall response to difficult problems: 'I suggest . . . that this is a case in which the best decision might be to postpone a decision.' Nothing should be done at the present time, but the Home Secretary might be asked to bring the matter forward again 'if the industrial situation showed signs of deteriorating'.[36]

In Cabinet Bevan returned to the fray. Despite having been a member of Ede's committee, he declared that he could not support its recommendations. He himself thought that 'the Government should make no such preparations in advance for maintaining essential services in the event of widespread industrial disturbances.' Such action would be highly embarrassing to defend in Parliament and 'he would not himself be prepared to defend the use for these purposes of the regional organisation of the Ministry of Health.' He thought it impractical 'to prepare in advance plans for meeting a purely hypothetical situation' and believed that 'the Government should rely on improvising arrangements at the last moment to meet the particular kind of situation with which they were faced.' But Attlee was not moved by the Minister of Health's vigorous arguments. Nor was he so pusillanimous as Brook. He quietly asserted, taking the perhaps unfortunate analogy of war preparations – 'against hypothetical contingencies' – that effective plans could *only* be made well in advance. Failure to do this, he added, 'would increase the risk that at the last moment undue reliance would be placed on military assistance'. Bevin, among others, endorsed these views and it was stressed that planning should be 'confined to senior officials in the Whitehall Departments mainly concerned'. There were to be no discussions with regional officials and no one outside the government was to be brought into consultation at this stage. Morrison recommended that preliminary work should include the drawing up of draft emergency regulations. The decision, therefore, was made to continue preparing emergency plans, albeit in strict secrecy. The Cabinet proceeded to discuss the suggestion that representatives of employers' organisations and trade unions should be brought into 'confidential consultation'. Here again Bevan was in the minority. With him was Cripps, who put forward the argument for a degree of openness. But Bevin, speaking with all the assurance of thirty-five years' trade union experience, said that it would be 'inexpedient' to consult either employers or unions. Apparently without irony he asserted that if the unions 'were asked in advance to collaborate in devising an organisation for this purpose, they might regard this as an invitation to assist in building up a strike-breaking organisation.' Bevin's opinions won the Cabinet over. Even Isaacs and Westwood (Secretary for Scotland) announced that, 'although they had supported the recommendation made by the Committee, they were now opposed, on further reflection, to any advance consultation with the trade unions'.[37] Thus ministers resisted the temptation to make radical changes in the STO. The trenchant voice of the left wing cut little ice in Attlee's Cabinet. In their approach to emergency planning they showed themselves to be closer to Baldwin than Bevan.

The Cabinet's instruction that planning should be conducted by no more than 'a small number of senior officials' was not slavishly followed in Whitehall. On 17 May, the day after the Trade Disputes and Trade Unions (amendment) Bill passed its Third Reading in the Lords,[38] another Home Office conference met, with twenty-three people representing fifteen departments. Although most of the officials present were of Assistant Secretary rank or above, four principals also attended. The War Office saw fit to send only a Captain – a far cry from the days of General Romer in 1919–20. This time the meeting was chaired by Sir Frank Newsam, who succeeded Maxwell as Permanent Under-Secretary to the Home Office in October 1948. He was a strong-minded individual with a reputation for severity. One colleague who worked with him on emergency arrangments in the late 1940s recalled that Newsam was 'very fierce', and had a habit of calling meetings late on Friday afternoons, when he would have 'no idea who would be coming or how many until they turned up'.[39] Newsam supervised the emergency organisation from 1946 until his retirement in 1957. The conference put Newsam in the chair of a co-ordinating committee, with seven sub-committees, to prepare detailed emergency schemes. They set to work over the summer of 1946. The 'Labour Supply' sub-committee, for example, made inquiries into the exact procedure for the use of service labour in industrial disputes. A Labour Ministry memorandum prepared in September noted that the current arrangements dated from an agreement originally made between the War Office and civil departments in 1942. It was strictly laid down that military labour could only be employed after the personal approval of the Minister of Labour and the minister in charge of the Supply Department concerned had been secured. Departments were also instructed (as always) that 'movements of the Military must be discreet whether before the strike or lock-out begins or whilst awaiting Ministerial authority, and every step must be taken to avoid advertising their presence in the locality affected.' The Home Office also restarted work on the emergency regulations and in September circulated a draft code for departments to consider.[40]

During the summer of 1946 the Home Office itself examined the desirability of reviving the CCR scheme – or something similar – put into abeyance in 1939. On 4 July Miss J. J. Nunn, a Principal in the Home Office who had been Secretary to each of the official conferences since 1945 and who was in the 1950s to head the Office's civil defence division, circulated a memorandum raising the question. She noted some immediate obstacles to re-establishing the CCR. Because of the 'importance attached by the Cabinet to secrecy', no arrangements at this stage could be made either with the army or Chief Constables. In addition, 'the obvious source from which this machine would recruit' had been closed by 'the War Office decision of 1939 that members of the Territorial Army were not to be enrolled'. It seemed likely that the army would continue this ban for the meantime. Miss Nunn mentioned that it was currently being recommended to the 'Police Post-War Committee' that in future every force should have a reserve of Special Constables 'amounting to at least half its regular strength'. This body might provide a solid basis for enlargement to meet emergency requirements. 'The provision of an adequate Police Force', she wrote, 'is essentially the business of the civil authorities and if they can handle it without bringing in the Army (except to deal with actual rioting) it will probably be better for both parties.' She asked her colleagues 'whether it would be possible for the police to undertake the recruitment and administration of all the men required to assist them in time of emergency.' Their reaction on the whole came down strongly against a revival of the CCR. One official remarked that in 1926 the force had 'created at least as many problems as it had solved'. But employing the Special Constabulary might also raise difficulties. An Assistant Secretary, R. S. Wells, wryly noted that the present Home Secretary had voted against the Special Constables Bill in 1923 and 'a Major C. R. Attlee' had said during the debates, 'if you start this sort of organisation . . . which is so like the White Guards, the Ku Klux Klan, the Fascisti, which are all developed on these lines, then you are heading for a revolution in which you must get violence and in which you will ruin the country altogether.' 'Fortunately', added Wells inconsequentially, 'this gloomy prophecy has not been fulfilled and quite different agencies have brought about the country's ruin.' More pertinently he stressed the problem of both recruiting and employing Special Constables in working-class areas. Some Chief Constables, for example in Glamorgan and Coventry, both industrial regions, had 'given their special constables an undertaking that they will not be asked to perform duty when the need for assistance arises out of a strike'. Wells thought they had gone too far in this respect, 'since it is precisely in times of industrial disturbance that the regular police most need help.' It was generally felt that in future the police could provide their own reinforcements. Nevertheless, a paper was prepared on the question for the STO protection sub-committee to consider. It noted that there were at present 49,500 full-time police available in England and Wales, along with 72,000 part-time Special Constables, of whom 23,000 were regularly employed. The tone of the paper did not favour re-establishing the CCR. 'Experience during the war', moreover, suggested that 'the police could, even in an emergency, cope with the enrolment, organisation and feeding of a reserve.'[41] In the event, serious civil unrest never threatened to break out in the post-war years and no special plans were made for the large-scale reinforcement of the police.

Between the wars the pace of emergency planning had generally been determined by the incidence of industrial unrest. This was equally so following 1945 and the attention given to such planning received a massive boost from the road haulage stoppage of January 1947. The government was completely unprepared for the strike, although there had been grumbling discontent in the industry for some months past. In September 1946 the TGWU submitted a claim to the Road Haulage Wages Board principally for a reduction in the working week and an increase in paid holidays from 7 to 14 days. At the end of December the Board recommended no reduction in the hours worked, 9 days' holiday and a number of small improvements in other working conditions. On 6 January, during the

21-day period allowed under Order 1305 for representations, transport drivers employed by some of the large contractors in east London came out on unofficial strike. The stoppage was immediately joined by drivers working at Smithfield meat market, and it quickly spread to a number of other large firms in the London area. On 7 January the strikers rejected a union appeal to return to work and called on the Executive to give official support to their action.

The strike was especially solid among meat drivers and the government soon began to worry about food supplies. On Thursday 9 January the Minister of Food announced that owing to the strike it would be impossible to honour all meat rations during the week. That morning the Ministry of Transport called an urgent meeting with the War Office, Food and Labour Ministries to discuss the movement of foodstuffs. Over 2,000 tons of meat were immobilised in Smithfield market and operators' yards. Even if the men went back to work over the weekend, there would probably be no meat ration at all available the following week. There would also be a considerable shortage of bacon, although butter and margarine stocks were sufficient 'to tide over' for the meantime. The 'sugar position had appeared fairly satisfactory', but picketing 'at Tate and Lyle's now put it in doubt'. It was suggested that civilian lorries might be brought in from other areas to distribute food in London, but the Transport officials believed that this would merely 'precipitate a spread of the strike'. The only alternative was military transport. Mr Keely from the Ministry of Food said that the amount of meat to be moved was between 5,000 and 6,000 tons per week. This would require at least 500 lorries. He asked what assistance the army could provide. 'Colonel Hughes replied that Army transport was at present insufficient for their own needs. They had no reserve of vehicles and even to distribute their own rations they had, for some time, had to hire civilian vehicles.' This was singularly unhelpful. Keely was clearly not satisfied and inquired pointedly what assistance the War Office could give 'if they received a Cabinet Directive to make available all military transport that could be spared.' Hughes grudgingly said he 'could give no estimate but promised to note the requirements of the Ministry of Food.' The meeting also decided to seek help from the Air Ministry and briefly considered the possibility of recruiting volunteer civilian drivers. It was generally felt, however, that using either voluntary or service drivers 'would probably only result in further difficulties in spreading the area of disaffection at the present time.' During the meeting news came that the Minister of Labour had made a press announcement emphasising the unconstitutional nature of the strike. Hoping that this might have 'a salutary effect' on the strikers, it was decided to take no positive action until the men's attitude became clear.[42]

The lorry drivers did not return to work, indeed more came out, and efforts had to be made to find substitute transport. Faced with War Office intransigence, the Ministry of Food resorted to *force majeure*. They had a strong case. Food was a highly sensitive political issue. Even when available, the post-war food rations were meagre enough, and in some cases actually smaller than during the war. The fact that most of the major strikes during the Attlee administration directly impeded food supplies goes a long way towards explaining the government's consistently tough attitude and the regular use of service labour. The Prime Minister was approached and needed little persuasion that service assistance was essential. He ordered A. V. Alexander, the Minister of Defence, that it should be provided. On the morning of Friday 10 January Alexander convened a Cabinet committee to investigate the problem. With the overnight escalation of the strike the Food Ministry's needs had appreciably increased. If the strike 'did not spread any further in London', or to the provinces, their requirements 'would be limited [*sic*] to 1,000 lorries . . . together with drivers and about 2,500 loaders.' If there were a substantial expansion of the stoppage, their requirements would be doubled. Attlee's intervention was effective. All three services found transport. By the end of the day the Admiralty had offered 250 lorries, the Air Ministry 500 and the War Office 600. They would be driven and loaded by 3,500 officers and men. But a dilemma which emerged in Alexander's committee was that of balancing the probably provocative effects of using service labour against the need to keep food supplies going. The Ministry of Labour stressed the former problem; the Ministry of Food the latter. In the end they compromised. Service transport was to be held available, but not necessarily used, from Monday and Tuesday the following week but 800 tons of meat in danger of deterioration were to be distributed from Smithfield on Monday. Over the weekend the Minister of Labour also personally made arrangements with the TGWU to ensure the delivery of meat to hospitals. Summing up the meeting, Alexander said 'it was clear from the discussion . . . that a very great deal of organisation and executive work remained to be done before the transport offered by the Services could be put to work.' He therefore asked the Ministry of Transport to form a working party with other departments to work out details and 'remain in constant session until their task was completed.'[43] Here was the government facing precisely the sort of problem the STO before the war had been designed to meet. But because post-war emergency planning had so far been limited to the secret preparation of paper plans at a high official level, the government had no organisation immediately available. Instead they had hurriedly to improvise arrangements in exactly the fashion Bevan had recommended to the Cabinet. The resulting action was inefficient, unco-ordinated and in sharp contrast to the apparently smooth running of the pre-war STO. The point was not lost on Chuter Ede, who was to take it up with the Prime Minister and the Cabinet after the strike was over.

The introduction of service labour at Smithfield had the antici-pated result. On 13 January over 2,000 meat packers and provision workers struck, but there was no disorder or interference with the troops. By this stage it was estimated that about 14,000 men were on strike in London and a number had also come out in provincial centres. The stoppage was entirely peaceful. Reports from Chief Constables to the Home Office indicated that the strikers appeared 'anxious to avoid conflict with the police in every way'. The only noteworthy incident occurred early on 13 January when the tyres of seven lorries parked at a transport cafe in Hertfordshire were let down. A police escort was provided into London and there were no further incidents. Scotland Yard inquired into the possibility of Trotskyist or Communist influence behind the strike but found nothing more damning than the distribution of Trotskyist pamphlets at a strike meeting on Sunday 12 January.[44]

George Isaacs brought the Cabinet up to date regarding the strike on Monday afternoon. He suggested that a settlement might be reached by setting up at once a 'Joint Industrial Council' for the road haulage industry and submitting the dispute to it. This the Cabinet agreed to do. They approved the arrangements made for using service labour and decided that civil employers would have to pay for this assistance at normal rates. They also agreed that a Cabinet committee should be appointed to oversee the working party already formed by Alexander. Worried by the possible exten-sion of the stoppage, one of the ministers present urged that 'it might be represented to the B.B.C. that the position was not likely to be improved by frequent announcements of fresh areas to which the strike had spread.' Greenwood undertook to do this. After the meeting Brook reminded Attlee that there was already an Industrial Emergencies Committee, which had been appointed in October 1945. Although Alexander had directed the government's initial action over the weekend, Brook doubted whether it would be wise to have the Minister of Defence preside over the committee. 'Though we try to avoid disclosing the membership of Cabinet Committees,' he noted in terms that could be repeated today, 'information does sometimes leak out; and critics could make much of the fact that the Minister of Defence should be the Chairman of what they would represent as a strike-breaking Committee.' Attlee agreed and asked Dalton, the original chairman, to convene the committee. But Dalton, possibly reluctant to take on this contentious task, replied that he was already 'pretty heavily loaded, particularly in this pre-Budget period' and suggested that perhaps Greenwood or Ede could chair the committee. Attlee gave the job to Chuter Ede.[45]

The Industrial Emergencies Committee (IEC) met for the first time on Wednesday 15 January 1947. It faced a gloomy prospect. On 14 January large numbers of London dockers had struck against the use of service labour: 20,000 men were now out in the capital and 8,000 in the provinces. There were growing shortages of supplies other than food. The Newspaper Proprietors Association reported that the national dailies had only enough newsprint to last out the current week. A note from Attlee ordered the committee to consider this as a matter of urgency. In another paper Emanuel Shinwell asked for army transport to supply coal for two London power stations. At the committee Isaacs warned that 'if no settlement was reached that day a very serious situation might arise.' The first matter discussed by the IEC was the possible recruitment of volunteer labour. Isaacs repeated his Ministry's objections to this. 'Such a move', he declared, 'would almost certainly be followed by outbreaks of industrial unrest all over the country, and the situation might deteriorate almost to the extent of a general strike.' In addition, 'if the Labour Exchanges were used to enrol volunteers, their reputation in the eyes of organised labour would be irreparably damaged.' The committee decided that the official working party should draw up a plan for recruiting volunteers, but 'on the understanding that the plan should not be put into force except on the authority of the Cabinet'. Later in the meeting Isaacs was alarmed by Cripps's bizarre suggestion that the large number of Polish ex-servicemen in the country might be used for the maintenance of essential supplies. He was 'confident that if any overt use whatever was made of Poles any possibility of ultimately settling them in this country with the co-operation of the Trade Union movement would completely disappear.'

Throughout the meeting ministers were acutely conscious that anything they might do to improve supplies generally would inflame labour opinion. They rejected the notion that road traffic should be diverted to the railways since this 'would involve the risk of opposition by railwaymen'. The committee heard from the War Office that, if they decided to instruct the army to provide the 'maximum possible amount of transport', it would be possible to mobilise over 3,000 lorries in addition to the 1,650 already promised. But Lord Pakenham, Parliamentary Under-Secretary for War, pointed out that this 'would leave the Army dependent upon civilian drivers and vehicles for a number of essential purposes, including the movement of Army food', and he warned that 'if these civilian drivers came out on strike it would be necessary to withdraw Service vehicles and personnel to take their places.' Isaacs was faced with a particular problem on the question of newsprint. The maintenance of supplies for newspapers might well stimulate trouble in the industry. 'On the other hand', he argued, showing a nice regard for public opinion, 'the newspapers in general had supported the attitude taken by the Government in dealing with the strike.' Ede was less troubled by the matter. 'Newsprint', he virtuously observed, 'could hardly be put in the same category as food and fuel, and it might be difficult to hold that the publication of newspapers was essential to the life of the community.' It was agreed, nevertheless, to offer assistance in the movement of newsprint, with the proviso that more vital supplies would take precedence. The meeting ended with an illustration of the committee's anxiety to avoid any possible conflict with the trade unions. They permitted Isaacs to give members of the TUC General Council 'a general indication of the lines on which it was proposed to deal with any development of the transport strike', not that the currently moderate TUC leadership were likely to have much influence over the TGWU rank and file.[46]

While the IEC were meeting in the Cabinet Office, the official working party gathered at the Ministry of Transport. Soon after their meeting began Sir Reginald Hill, Deputy Secretary to the Transport Ministry, arrived from the IEC and asked them to consider arrangements for the maximum mobilisation of service transport, the extent to which naval personnel could 'take over the operation of docks and cold stores machinery' and to work out a scheme for volunteer recruitment. This was required by the Home Secretary for 10 o'clock the following morning. Working late into the evening, the officials eventually reported on most of these points, although the Admiralty proved unable to answer until the afternoon when they offered 150 skilled and 500 partly skilled men for service in the docks. Regarding transport, all three services together could provide at short notice a total of 4,500 vehicles. In addition the army could find another 500 spare drivers to man privately owned lorries if available. If pushed, and at some inconvenience, the services 'could certainly find a substantially larger number of drivers than the 5,000 already planned for to man additional civilian vehicles'. The working party estimated that there were some 100,000 civilian heavy goods vehicles throughout the country and they noted that under Defence Regulation 53 the Minister of Transport had power to requisition vehicles. This power could be delegated and it was assumed that the twelve Regional Transport Commissioners would take general administrative control of their regions in an emergency. The extraordinary lengths to which departments were prepared to go in their search for emergency transport stemmed from fears that there might very well be a general transport strike. They were, however, put into immediate perspective the following morning when the Ministry of Food informed their colleagues at Transport that they already had at their disposal far more vehicles than they needed. Three options were offered for the recruitment of volunteers: Employment Exchanges, local authorities and Ministry of Transport local offices. Local authorities were sufficiently 'ubiquitous' to cover the whole country, but 'some may be of doubtful reliability'. By contrast, the Transport offices would provide only about a hundred centres which was thought insufficient. The working party favoured using the 1,200 Employment Exchanges and felt that 'unless the objections to the[ir] use . . . are insuperable, their advantages for recruitment are overwhelming.' The utilisation of volunteers would have to be organised principally by Area Road Haulage Officers in consultation with local haulage firms.[47] The odd thing about all these grandiose schemes was that no one seems to have referred to the pre-war organisation. It was as if it had never existed. Perhaps senior officials had taken the Cabinet's rubric on secrecy seriously to heart. In effect what the working party were doing was re-creating the STO *ab initio*.

Next morning Isaacs told the Cabinet that 'further extensions of the strike were thought to be imminent.' He said that 'for the moment the emergency transport arrangements were proving sufficient', but 'if the strike continued for much longer, or extended further, it would become necessary to appeal for volunteer drivers', particularly to assist in moving stocks of food 'which had accumulated at the railheads in the docks'. He declared that there were serious objections to the use of Employment Exchanges for enrolling volunteers, but observed that the IEC 'had been unable to devise any alternative method'. The Cabinet had nothing better to offer and concluded that this apparently insoluble problem 'made it even more important that means should be found of securing the early termination of the strike'. They were told that a special delegate conference of strikers was to meet at 2 p.m. that afternoon, when they would be informed that the new Joint Industrial Council was to begin meeting at 5 p.m. in an effort to reach a settlement. The Cabinet resolved that if the strike continued after this meeting the government would issue a proclamation of emergency under the 1920 Act. Not only would this enable them to take over the road haulage industry, but it would also give the government power to supersede the established procedures for settling disputes and thus intervene directly in negotiations between employers and men.[48]

At 3 p.m. the IEC met to discuss the implications of an emergency proclamation. Jowitt, the Lord Chancellor, who had been specially invited to attend, explained the legal position and the wide powers provided for under the 1920 Act. The Minister of Transport commented that he 'already possessed very considerable powers' remaining from the war and that these might be 'sufficient to enable the strike to be dealt with'. Jowitt agreed that 'in some respects it might be better to proceed under existing powers' and went on to make the extraordinary observation that although the 1920 Act prohibited 'any form of compulsory military service or industrial conscription', under the existing Defence Regulations 'it would be possible, technically, at any rate, to direct labour to particular work'. But the committee barely had time to digest this disturbing remark.

In the middle of their meeting they were informed that the strikers' conference had voted to return to work in two days' time. At 9 p.m. the Cabinet met for the second time that day and thankfully confirmed the IEC's proposals for winding down the emergency transport organisation. They agreed that 'the Government's appreciation of the work done by the troops should be conveyed to those members of the Services who had been engaged in this duty.' The following day Attlee wrote identical letters of thanks to the three service ministers. Each was accompanied by a covering note from the Cabinet Office. 'With reference to the attached letter,' it read, 'the intention is that there should not be any public statement, but C.-in-Cs. should convey thanks from the Prime Minister to the troops. In these circumstances the letter should *not* be given to the Press.'[49] As for the dispute, ironically the Joint Industrial Council was unable to reach agreement. The matter was put to a court of inquiry which, to the workers' satisfaction, on 23 January recommended the reduction in working hours sought, 9 days' paid holiday and a number of other general improvements.

A week after the strike had ended Sir Norman Brook (he was knighted in 1946) recommended to Attlee that since the IEC had never met to consider wages policy, and was unlikely to do so, its terms of reference should be changed. In future it should be 'confined to supervising the preparation of plans for maintaining supplies and services in an emergency' and should be assisted by a committee of officials which would be responsible in an emergency 'for co-ordinating the executive action of Departments'. Attlee agreed and, since the IEC would 'no doubt often need advice on points of law', he invited the Attorney-General to serve on the committee.[50] Chuter Ede had wider ideas for the IEC. In the absence of serious industrial unrest they took some time to germinate, but on 17 March he proposed to the Prime Minister that the scope of the committee might be widened to include not just emergencies caused by strikes, but also short-term emergencies arising from *any* breakdown in essential services. Having consulted Brook, on 24 March Attlee approved Ede's suggestion that the question be considered by the IEC itself.[51]

Ede had already prepared a lengthy memorandum on the subject for the IEC. The first part of his paper was devoted to a discussion of the emergency powers currently available to the government. Those remaining from the war had a number of deficiencies. The power to direct labour – which Jowitt had mentioned – was not of 'much practical use'. It would have little effect on strikers generally and would probably do no more that 'secure the services of a few waverers who would prefer to appear to be working under compulsion'. The only benefit accruing from Order 1305 was 'psychological' and even that would 'depend entirely upon the state of public opinion and the temper of the strikers'. Ede mentioned Defence Regulation 6 without qualification, but the service ministries were not so convinced of its value. In February the Home Office had circulated a draft set of emergency regulations and had inquired if they needed to retain the regulation providing for the employment of servicemen on non-military duties which had been used in 1921 and 1926. This was especially so since Regulation 6 had sufficed during the road haulage strike. The Admiralty argued that it should be kept as it was assumed that Regulation 6 would soon lapse, while the Air Ministry contended that the application of the Defence Regulation during the strike had been technically illegal since it only applied to duties with a specific military object. Ede did, however, mention the Law Officers' hesitation in 1936 regarding powers under the 1920 Act to impose duties on local authorities.[52]

In the second part of his paper Ede asserted that, even if all the powers necessary were available, an emergency organisation could not be mobilised quickly unless extensive and detailed plans had been made in advance. 'The recent road haulage strike', he remarked, 'showed that the Services alone would be unable to deal with a strike not confined to one area, and that if the strike spread beyond those limits there would be little time to improvise.' Because of the Cabinet's insistence on secrecy, senior officials had found it impossible to make any satisfactory progress in drawing up emergency schemes. Ede concluded with a most powerful plea – doubtless drafted by those same officials – for extending the official range of emergency planning:

There are thus only two alternatives. One is to make paper plans and to rely on improvisation, including arrangements for recruiting volunteers, when the emergency arises. The danger of this course is that chaos may develop before the improvised arrangements can be brought into operation, and *there may be a temptation for persons with Fascist inclinations to usurp the Government's responsibility for maintaining essential services under the pretext that the*

*Government had failed to take the necessary measures.* The other alternative is to work out in advance schemes on the regional level. The creation of a field organisation would involve instructing regional officials to work out specific plans in local consultation. Except as regards Chief Officers of Police, it need not involve consultations with people outside Government service, though limited unofficial consultations would be useful. This increases the risk that the preparations will become known, but in view of Government action and statements during the recent transport strike, such a discovery is not likely to cause much surprise, and with the strikes fresh in their minds, the public would be less inclined to condemn preparation than lack of it.

This argument had the desired effect, and on 26 March the IEC unanimously agreed that departments should be authorised to include their regional officers in the planning process. They also approved Ede's proposed expansion of the committee's terms of reference and decided that legislation should be drawn up enabling powers to be taken to impose duties on local authorities.[53]

The IEC's recommendations were favourably received in the Cabinet Office. Broadening the committee's terms of reference was a master stroke. Apart from making sound administrative sense, as Ede remarked, 'it would incidentally help to counter any suggestion, should its plans become known, that the Supply and Transport Organisation was a strike-breaking weapon.' Brook thought the time was especially propitious for this change, while 'the dislocation caused by last winter's snow and floods is still fresh in the public mind.'[54] The winter of 1946–7 had been the worst in living memory. The effect of the extreme cold, moreover, had been exacerbated by acute fuel shortages. At the end of January blizzards paralysed the national transport system. Troops were extensively used to help out in the crisis, especially to ensure coal supplies to power stations. 'At the peak period during the fuel crisis,' reported the War Office afterwards, '21,500 men, including prisoners of war . . . and 3,322 vehicles were diverted from their normal tasks.'[55] Here, indeed, was a non-contentious function for an emergency organisation. But Ede did not want the matter raised in Cabinet, evidently fearing a repetition of the fierce debate in March 1946. Yet when it was put before his colleagues on 17 April there was no dispute at all. The IEC was quietly reconstituted and instructed 'to supervise the preparation of plans for providing and maintaining in any emergency supplies and services essential to the life of the community; and in any emergency to co-ordinate action for this purpose'.[56] The 'Emergencies Committee', as it was to be known in future, has remained a standing committee of the Cabinet ever since. With its name changed and its scope widened, the STO was back in business.

# 7
# Strikers and subversives
# Spring 1947–1951

THE EMERGENCIES COMMITTEE was established in April 1947 during renewed unrest in the docks. On the same day as Sir Norman Brook circulated details of the reconstituted committee to the Cabinet, 10,000 London stevedores and lightermen came out in sympathy with dockers striking in Glasgow. The Glasgow dispute stemmed from efforts to decasualise dock labour and to slim down the swollen wartime workforce. In March the Regional Port Director had announced that he was going to dismiss 500 men: '270 . . . on the basis of poor work records, and 230 on the basis of "last in first out" '. Before the notices were issued the dockers struck. Within a week a small contingent of Royal Engineer stevedores was sent in to unload perishable food. On 14 April the Cabinet authorised the employment of additional troops to unload all types of food in order to maintain rations in the Glasgow area. By the end of the month 700 soldiers had been deployed. The spread of the strike to London was partly due to inter-union rivalry, with members of the Stevedores' and Lightermen's unions supporting action in order to embarrass the TGWU, which held a predominant position in the industry's National Joint Council. In addition, the Minister of Labour told the Cabinet that the strikes were 'symptomatic of a growing tendency to ignore the advice of responsible Union leaders'.[1]

On 30 April the Minister of Transport informed the Emergencies Committee that of the 125 ships on the Thames, 76 were idle, including 27 food ships. 'The continued immobilisation of shipping', he noted, 'is involving serious waste of shipping resources' and threatened to 'dislocate our import programmes for timber, paper and other essential materials, besides food.' When the committee met on 1 May to consider the position, they learned that the TGWU executive had recommended that the Glasgow men went back to work. This had been rejected at a mass meeting by a small majority, but the union now proposed to hold a secret ballot on the question. In London a meeting convened by the Stevedores' union had decided to return to work the following day. This, however, 'had been followed by a much smaller meeting organised by certain dissident elements, which had affirmed its intention to remain on strike'. The committee, therefore, had to consider what should be done if the stoppage continued. Sir Frank Newsam reported that the official committee had made arrangements for troops to be moved into the London docks from 2 May, working up to a maximum of approximately 7,000 men by 10 May. He observed, however, that 'this force would be no more than sufficient to hold the position for about a fortnight'. Thereafter it might be necessary to consider proclaiming a state of emergency, which, among other things, 'would enable civilian labour to be recruited'. The ministerial committee were less pessimistic than the official. In view of the likelihood of the strike ending, they ordered that the troops 'should not approach the docks until it was clear that the men did not intend to return to work'. Since the strikes in London and Glasgow were both unofficial, Chuter Ede thought that his colleagues ought to consider the government's general attitude towards such stoppages. The committee agreed that the TUC should be approached formally and informed that the government intended to prosecute the ringleaders of illegal strikes. Bevan suggested that the TUC should also be told about the establishment of the Emergency Organisation to deal with all emergencies, 'not merely industrial ones', and deviously added that the question of prosecution could most advantageously be 'raised incidentally in the course of discussions about the nature of the organisation'. If the TUC were informed about the organisation in this way, Bevan declared that he would be prepared to let his ministry's General Inspectors preside over the Regional Committees. The meeting decided that the official committee should 'make all possible progress with the establishment of the Emergency Organisation' and Chuter Ede laid down that 'when the scheme was more complete further consideration could be given by the Committee to the form in which the approach should be made to the TUC'.[2] There is, however, no evidence to suggest that the TUC were ever formally apprised of the Emergency Organisation. Both Bevan's proposal and the apparently firm intention to prosecute 'ringleaders' were quietly forgotten. During the meeting on 1 May it is clear that the ministers did not expect the dock strikes to continue. They were right. There was no need to use troops or contemplate further a state of emergency. On 2 May the London strikers resumed work, followed two days later by the dockers in Glasgow.

Aneurin Bevan never became fully reconciled to the existence of the Emergency Organisation and remained somewhat suspicious of its equivocal function. Within the revived organisation the Ministry of Health played a much less important role than it had done before the war. The central co-ordinating function taken by men such as Christopher Roundell was transferred to the Home Office. On taking office himself, Bevan's immediate reaction had been strongly critical. It was said in Whitehall in 1946 that one of the first things he did was to call for the papers of the Chief Civil Commissioner's department and have them destroyed.[3] But after two years as a minister he seemed to lose some of his earlier reforming zeal. He certainly approved widening the Emergency Organisation's scope. Nevertheless, he kept his ministry as detached as possible from it. When he permitted the ministry's Inspectorate to take charge of the regional organisation, he also arranged for them to report directly to the Home Office. Apart from anything else, Bevan was fully occupied for the first few years of the Attlee government with the particular duties of his own ministry. Although he had a prodigious capacity for work, the introduction of the National Health Service, the huge post-war house-building programme and his own lively interest in steel nationalisation can have left relatively little time or energy for a sustained campaign to widen still further the Emergency Organisation's remit.[4] In 1948 and 1949 he spasmodically attended meetings of the ministerial committee, but took little part in discussion. Perhaps familiarity bred tolerance.

In May 1947 the Secretary for War circulated a memorandum noting the army's difficulties in supplying continued assistance to the civil ministries. It could have been written by Sir Henry Wilson. Both training and administrative services had seriously been disrupted by calls on the army during the first three months of the year. Staff and resources generally were so stretched in every military department that 'the effect of an abnormal task, on however small a scale, has disproportionate and cumulative results'. Although it was recognised that 'emergencies which put the life of the nation in jeopardy must, of course, be met by all the resources at the disposal of the Government,' the War Office also begged the civil ministries to bear in mind not only that the employment of the armed forces had seriously disadvantageous effects, 'but also that the physical ability of the Army to meet these extraneous tasks is rapidly diminishing.'[5]

Any hopes the War Office may have had that calls for assistance might abate were swiftly dashed by an unofficial transport strike in the Midlands and north England. On 23 June Ness Edwards told the Emergencies Committee that some 10,000 men had stopped work in support of a wage claim and as a result many miners were having difficulty getting to work. Newsam reported that the most severely affected area was in the Nottingham, Leicester and Derby region where the National Coal Board had diverted lorries from other work to carry miners. This was only a temporary expedient and arrangements had been made for 200 military vehicles and drivers to move in on 27 June. If the strike spread in the Midlands, 'some 900 military vehicles with drivers would be required', but 'it should be understood that this was 50% of the total number of vehicles which the Military authorities would make available without major detriment to normal Service activities.' Shinwell was so concerned about the effect of the strike on coal production that he persuaded the committee to send the service lorries in on 26 June. The committee also agreed that a public statement should be issued calling on the men to return to work and emphasising the damage their action was causing to the national economy. This exhortation seems to have been effective. On the morning of 25 June the Emergencies Committee learned that many men had returned to work and military assistance would not immediately be needed. They decided, however, to keep 80 army and air force lorries in readiness in case the position did not continue to improve. On 30 June, although 6,500 men were still out in Lancashire and Northumberland, nearly all the strikers in the Midlands had resumed work. There was no further need to keep service vehicles standing by. Nevertheless, they were only released 'on the understanding that the Army and the Royal Air Force would be able, if called upon, to make available up to 100 vehicles at 36 hours' notice, and up to 900 at 3 days' notice'.[6]

For almost exactly a year after this dispute the government were not faced with any serious stoppages in 'essential' industries and the opportunity was taken to press on with detailed planning for the Emergencies Organisation. In the late spring and early summer of

1947 a number of reports were prepared for consideration by News-am's official committee. The 'labour supply' sub-committee saw no reason to adjust the procedure for using service labour first agreed in 1942. They noted, however, that 'it would be unwise for Departments to assume that military labour could in future be made available to any appreciable extent'. Regarding civilian labour, it was recommended that in a dispute affecting only one industry the industry itself, in consultation as necessary with government departments, should be responsible for recruiting and deploying voluntary labour. But in the case of a more general emergency, 'it would still be convenient' to have a national organisation 'which could either recruit labour direct or serve a very useful purpose in redistributing in accordance with the needs of the situation'. To do this the committee effectively revived the old VSC scheme, although they envisaged a more extensive local organisation. Noting that the actual use of Employment Exchanges would be 'politically and socially undesirable', they proposed that separate local enrolment centres should be established wherever Employment Exchanges already existed. These centres would be organised by local authorities and co-ordinated in each of the ten Regions in England and Wales by a 'Regional Labour Supply Committee', whose chairman would be a non-official 'of standing'. They observed that it might be an advantage in some localities to appoint sub-regional committees, including 'local personages of influence such as the Mayor and trade union officials'. Detailed guidance was given on the organisation and running of enrolment centres. A specimen registration card was drawn up and a draft poster or press announcement which read 'National Emergency: volunteers wanted for essential services only to maintain the life of the nation'. The committee also devised an elaborate system for classifying recruits which indicated the extraordinarily wide range of jobs they believed volunteers might be able to do. This covered all branches of transport, the Post Office, docks, power supplies, food distribution, sanitary services and coal-mining, within which there were three categories: underground worker, above-ground worker and winding engineman.[7] In anticipating that coalminers might volunteer to blackleg, the sub-committee demonstrated that they were not only thorough, but also optimistic.

The report on communications stressed the extent to which the maintenance of communications depended on the Post Office, which already had its own plans for moving mail by road if railway services

were interrupted and a scheme using Post Office vehicles to transport some 5,000 key telecommunications staff daily to and from
their offices. The operation of these schemes, however, was dependent on the Post Office's own staff remaining at work. The provision
of telephone and telegraph services relied heavily on public power
supplies, although all telephone exchanges had batteries containing
48 hours' supply of electricity and some of the larger ones had
standby generators. It was assumed in the event of a power strike
that 'the Government would take urgent steps to ensure the maintenance of the power supplies needed for essential services.' The
report noted that plans for special inland air mail services were
being worked out with the Ministry of Civil Aviation and the Air
Ministry, but the former particularly feared that, unless permission
was given to consult with airline companies, 'they would not be in
a position to undertake any responsibilities in an emergency for the
transport of air mail.'[8]

The publicity sub-committee recommended that the Central
Office of Information (COI) should liaise with the Post Office in the
preparation of a national emergency communications scheme. The
COI had been established in April 1946 and continued most of the
services performed by the wartime Ministry of Information. In the
opinion of the publicity committee it provided 'a vastly more efficient means of getting Government news to the Press and radio than
existed before the war'. During an emergency the COI's News
Distribution Unit would be trebled in size and extensive use would
be made of the Office's regional organisation. It was not, however,
suggested that the government should plan to set up its own newspaper. The committee urged that special attention should be paid
to security, since 'it was found in wartime that it could not be left
to the Government Departments originating news to ensure that
such news did not involve a breach of the security rules.' This
problem, and that of possible 'bogus information', which in a civil
emergency would be 'a very real risk', should be met by establishing
a special vetting body to scrutinise the issue of all information.[9]

As with publicity, the transport sub-committee supported the
modification of an existing regional network to meet emergency
needs. Under the general supervision of the Ministry of Transport
in London, local executive action would be taken by regional transport sub-committees, which would include representatives of industry, other government departments and the ministry's own

Divisional Road Haulage Officers. On the question of recruiting volunteer labour, it was argued that the railway companies, which had specialised requirements, should enrol their own volunteers. On the other hand, 'the present lack of any high degree of co-ordination in the road transport industry' made it 'undesirable that the responsibility for recruiting volunteer labour should be placed upon the industry'. Unless a general scheme of enlistment was established, this would be organised by the Ministry of Transport at special recruiting points scattered about the country. In contrast to the other committees, the 'food and essential supplies' sub-committee had very little progress to report by July 1947. It had the widest brief of all, including food, power, essential consumer goods, medical services, refuse collection, sewerage and water supplies. The various departments concerned with these matters had been directed to prepare plans on the interesting, and probably realistic, assumption that 'a National industrial emergency affecting all the main supplies and services would be unlikely to last more than fourteen days'. The departments had all begun to work out schemes, but it had soon become evident that planning could not proceed beyond a preliminary stage 'unless the ban on discussions with the trade and industry is removed, at any rate, in part'.[10]

This point, made with varying force in all the sub-committee reports, was taken up by Newsam in September 1947 when he reported progress to the ministerial committee. He strongly urged that authority now be given for consultations to take place with leading representatives of non-government organisations. The Emergencies Committee met to consider this in October. Newsam assured the ministers that these consultations 'would not extend beyond a small number of leading representatives of vital industries and services and clerks of local authorities'. Bevan observed that there might be 'some difficulty in consulting local authority officials without consulting the local authorities themselves', but he recognised that 'it might be embarrassing to consult local authorities'. No decision was taken on this at the time, but after the meeting Bevan and Ede decided that local authority officials could be consulted. It was in its way a victory for the public service freemasonry. The committee as a whole approved Newsam's request. They also discussed some general points which had arisen over the summer. Ede commented on the post-war demobilisation of the armed forces and wondered if it might impair their ability to help in the future.

Alexander reassured him that while the run-down 'would undoubt-edly make it more difficult for the Services to help, he was confident that they would do everything possible to render assistance to any future emergency.' The extensive plans made by the labour supply sub-committee were remarked on only by George Isaacs. Displaying a notable anxiety to have his cake and eat it, he said that, while the Ministry of Labour regional organisation was not to be used 'as such' for recruiting purposes, 'there would be no objection to mak-ing plans to use the services of senior regional officials' of his ministry 'to help in the recruitment of volunteer labour'.[11]

The Labour government's programme of nationalisation placed the consultation of industry in a slightly different context than had been the case before the war. Within four years of taking office most of the industries providing essential goods and services had been brought under public ownership. The only major exceptions were the food and oil industries. The first to be nationalised was civil aviation in 1946, although this was largely a formality since the industry had been dominated by the government from the early 1920s. The National Coal Board came into operation on 1 January 1947. A year later the British Transport Commission took over the railways, long distance road haulage and some passenger transport undertakings. The Commission's first chairman, Sir Cyril Hurcomb, was a veteran of emergency planning. He had spent over twenty years as a civil servant in the Ministry of Transport and in October 1919 had attended the very first meeting of the STC official sub-committee. In April 1948 electric power stations, mostly owned already by local authorities, were transferred to the new British Electricity Authority, which with twelve area boards was given full responsibility for the generation and distribution of electricity. A similar measure established the Gas Council in 1949. Within the dock industry public corporations such as the Port of London Authority and the Mersey Docks and Harbour Board had long been in existence. Railway nationalisation brought further docks into the public sector and government influence in the industry was in-creased by the creation of the National Dock Labour Board in June 1947 to administer a permanent decasualisation scheme for dock workers. These extensions of public ownership were hardly revol-utionary and little or nothing was done to 'socialise' the industries. Although a number of prominent trade unionists took office in the new concerns – Lord Citrine, for example, elevated to the peerage in 1946, left the TUC for the National Coal Board and later became Chairman of the Electricity Authority – the TUC itself declared in 1945 that the aim of nationalisation was to be 'public control of industry, rather than workers' control as such'.[12] Nevertheless, from the Emergency Organisation's point of view, the process of nationalisation must have taken the edge off possible criticisms of close consultation with industry.

The close relationship established between government and trade unions during the war for the most part continued under the Attlee administration. As had happened in the First World War the enhanced status of trade unions – and war-induced expansion in highly unionised industries such as steel and engineering – stimulated a rise in membership between 1939 and 1945. Post-war full employment confirmed this trend. In 1939 there had been 6 million trade unionists; ten years later there were over 9 million. After the Second World War there was little of the sometimes violent acrimony which had characterised industrial relations when Lloyd George had been in power, and none of the really large-scale strikes which the STO had been created to meet. Labour militancy was certainly mitigated by full employment in the post-war years, but it was also softened by a mainly moderate and amenable trade union leadership. Union co-operation was especially valuable to the government, faced as it was with a series of severe economic crises. Perhaps the most serious was the currency crisis in the summer of 1947, which indicated all too clearly the frailty of a war-weakened economy and highlighted the urgent need to earn more foreign currency, especially dollars, through an expansion of exports. One way to encourage this was to keep costs down at home. In the autumn of 1947 Dalton introduced a deflationary budget. On his way in to deliver it to Parliament he carelessly leaked some proposals to a journalist and subsequently had to resign from the government. He was succeeded by Cripps who initiated a period of national austerity during which domestic consumption was clearly subordinate to the export drive. Early in 1948 the government scored a signal success in securing TUC approval, albeit with reservations, to a measure of voluntary wage restraint. But the closeness of government and trade unions also exacerbated the frustrations of many rank-and-file trade unionists which had begun to emerge during the war. This was especially so in the dock industry, where wartime expansion, post-war attempts to reduce numbers and the introduction of the decasualisation scheme had a particularly unsettling effect on the workforce, illustrated by the strikes in 1945 and 1947. In stimulating emergency planning after the Second World War, dockers played much the same role as the miners had done after the first. They continued to be at the forefront of industrial unrest during the life of Attlee's administration. In the early summer of each year from 1948 to 1950, stoppages in the docks provoked sharp reaction from the government, which on two occasions resorted to proclaiming a state of emergency under the 1920 Act.

Over the winter of 1947–8 enough progress was made in the Emergencies Organisation for the Home Office to circulate in June a memorandum giving general guidance to the chairmen of regional committees on the preparation of local schemes. It summarised the decisions already taken and strongly stressed the need for continued secrecy. If chairmen required further information they were requested to communicate with 'F.3 Division' in the Home Office, one of the three divisions devoted to police affairs. Such communications were to be enclosed in double envelopes and sent by registered post. 'Outer envelopes', instructed the Home Office pedantically, 'should *not* be addressed "The Secretary, Emergencies Co-ordinating Committee".' The memorandum explained that regional committees would have 'the greatest possible freedom' in preparing local schemes and that the central committee's role would be confined to laying down general principles. One exception to this was the recruitment of 'alternative labour', which was not to be begun without reference to the Co-ordinating Committee. It is evident from the instructions that the Home Office had abandoned any plans to set up a special organisation for volunteer recruitment. If needed, the Ministry of Labour would recruit volunteers 'through its local Offices'.[13] The exact date of the memorandum's issue, 23 June 1948, may well have been influenced by the outbreak of renewed unrest in the London docks.

The dispute arose over the loading of 100 tons of zinc oxide. Between 27 May and 8 June eleven men refused on several occasions to handle the cargo, arguing that the established rate of pay was insufficient for such an 'obnoxious' commodity. The local Dock Labour Board, on which employers and unions were equally represented, suspended the men for a week and withdrew their attendance money for thirteen weeks. The dockers appealed, but before their appeal was heard workers throughout the London docks began to strike on their behalf. By 18 June there was an almost complete stoppage and the Co-ordinating Committee, with Ernest Bevin's approval, began making plans to use service labour for moving perishable foods. The strike was a threat both to food supplies and the authority of the established trade union leadership, who were heavily committed to the running of the new dock labour scheme. Throughout the stoppage Arthur Deakin doggedly maintained that the strike was political. But Scotland Yard found no evidence that it was fomented by Communists. On Monday 21 June, with 16,000 men out, the Emergencies Committee decided that if the stoppage continued troops should go in to move eggs and tomatoes on Wednesday. Immediate hopes for a return to work were pinned on a meeting which Deakin was calling on Tuesday morning in the Albert Hall. The meeting was only a qualified success. Two thousand strikers voted by a large majority to resume work, but three times that number attended a rival meeting in Victoria Park, Bethnal Green, and voted to stay out. At the same time as the strikers were meeting, the Cabinet gathered in No. 10. They were told that Deakin himself had agreed that, unless the men went back, 'the Government would have no alternative but to use troops to load and unload the ships.' Fearing that the strike might continue for some time, the Cabinet instructed the Co-ordinating Committee to arrange for the possible movement of non-perishable goods. Having considered the dock strike, the next item on the Cabinet agenda was, ironically, the proposed end to bread rationing on 1 July.[14]

That afternoon at the War Office a meeting of representatives from all three services, the Ministries of Food and Transport, and the Port of London Authority, began making firm plans 'for providing labour up to 5,000 men, and 900 vehicles'. Next morning the Emergencies Committee were informed that 'the situation was grave.' There was no general willingness to return to work. They decided to send in the troops. At noon 300 Guardsmen began unloading the most perishable foodstuffs at Poplar Docks. Later in the day Attlee told the House of Commons that the dispute was jeopardising the future of the dock labour scheme, which, he noted, had been established with the trade unions' agreement. The hold-up of London's food supplies, he declared, 'will inevitably cause hardship and grave inconvenience to millions of householders', and, by hindering exports, the stoppage was likely to slow down the pace of national recovery. 'I cannot believe', concluded the Prime Minister, 'that the general body of strikers have hitherto realised the true consequences of their action.'[15]

Attlee's call and continued pressure by Deakin and the TGWU executive persuaded some 2,000 dockers to return on Thursday 24 June. The original grievance, too, was softened by the result of the men's appeal, which reduced their disentitlement to attendance pay to three weeks. But the lightermen, quick to take any opportunity to embarrass their TGWU rivals, began a sympathetic strike and 1,400 men stopped work. Late on Thursday evening Attlee called a special conference of ministers to review the position. A total of 19,000 men were still out. Deakin had told the Ministry of Labour that the union leaders 'were doing their best to get the men to return to work, but he did not expect any general return before Monday, 28th June.' Brook recorded dryly in the minutes that a wild request from port employers 'for leave to recruit volunteers from the Universities and similar sources' had 'been discouraged'. It was, however, intended to send in additional servicemen after the weekend to begin unloading meat and grain, even though the police had advised that this would probably precipitate strikes in the meat markets. At this point in the meeting Bevin burst in with a singularly vigorous demand that the government should break the strike:

> There must be no sign of weakness on the part of the Government: they must show their determination to maintain the distribution of essential foodstuffs. They should not be deterred by threats that, if further troops were employed, the strike would spread to the meat markets. If the strikers got their way, the Government would be at the mercy of unofficial strikes for many years to come. Whether the strike continued for one week or five, no concessions should be made by the Government until the men had returned to work. He himself would be inclined to move in further troops by degrees over the week-end.

Bevin was certainly very sensitive on the question of dock labour. He had won his spurs in the trade union movement as the 'Dockers' KC' just after the First World War. He had initiated decasualisation in 1941 and regarded the post-war labour scheme to a very great extent as a personal triumph. With both the scheme and his beloved TGWU threatened by the strike, Bevin was in no mood to be conciliatory. But his colleagues were not so fierce and the increased introduction of troops was postponed over the weekend. It was suggested that it might be appropriate for a minister to broadcast an appeal to the dockers. The use of the BBC was becoming a regular feature of Attlee's government. Cripps, for example, employed the wireless most successfully to argue the need for austerity. But Bevin vetoed this. 'It would', he asserted, 'be inexpedient for a Minister to intervene. It would be preferable that the men should be brought back to work by their trade union leaders.'[16]

Over the weekend highly detailed plans were made for expanded service intervention. Beginning on Monday 28 June, it was intended to work up to a total of 12,000 men and 3,000 vehicles by 4 July. The army and air force were deputed to provide 'the vast bulk of the labour force and all the motor transport', while the navy, in what the Admiralty called 'Operation Zebra', supplied 'technical ratings to operate cranes, ship winches, tugs, lighters, and Dock installations etc.'. The Co-ordinating Committee's chief difficulty was that no one knew whether or not the men would go back on Monday morning. 'If the return . . . were on a considerable scale,' observed Newsam somewhat needlessly, 'it would probably be unwise for the troops to be in the docks when the strikers began to come in.' The best solution the committee could find was 'that advance parties . . . should move in their lorries to convenient places near to the dock gates and be ready to go in at a moment's notice'. It was clearly apparent that 12,000 men would be insufficient to operate the docks at anything like full capacity. Afterwards it was estimated that 'the services could never be capable of dealing with more than about one third of the daily business of the Port of London Authority.' Ness Edwards fully appreciated this and in a top secret memorandum addressed himself to the problem of finding alternative volunteer labour. Open recruitment by the government, he observed with commendable understatement, 'would create a situation of great delicacy.' In order to enable the employers themselves to engage volunteers, he proposed that the entire dock labour scheme be suspended, possibly by using the Emergency Powers Act. One advantage of this course would be to put 'the Government on the offensive against the unofficial strikers'.[17]

Monday 28 June was the worst day of the strike. At 7 a.m. 1,600 troops, including 100 naval technicians from 'Party Zebra', assembled at East Ham police station to await developments. At about 10 a.m., by which time it was evident that the dockers were not returning, the servicemen moved in and began unloading meat. The Cabinet met at 11 a.m. and were told that the strike had spread to Merseyside. They dolefully noted that there was 'a powerful organisation behind the strike and some reason to regard it as part of a general attempt to create industrial unrest'. Edwards's dramatic proposal was rejected, but it was agreed to proclaim a state of emergency. By providing powers to requisition buildings and equipment, this would enable the troops to be employed 'to the best advantage'. It had the additional benefit of giving 'a firm legal basis for the use of troops', not a consideration which had hitherto bothered the Cabinet. Effectively bereft of any constructive policy, ministers agreed that Attlee should broadcast that evening. In the afternoon, with 60 food ships affected in London and 20 in Liverpool, a state of emergency was proclaimed. During the evening the Emergencies Committee considered a draft code of regulations drawn up by the Home Office, who recommended that, since 'the temper of the strikers was good . . . there was no need at present to introduce regulations about public safety and public order or disaffection from duty'. But the ministers disagreed, notably Bevan. He argued that 'it would be prudent to have wide powers in order to deal with any trouble that might arise if relations between troops and the strikers became strained'. Regulations against sedition and disaffection were therefore included in the final draft. Attlee broadcast at 9 p.m. He made a moving personal appeal to the dockers. He understood their feelings; he had 'lived in Dockland for many years'. But he told the dockers they were 'punishing thousands of innocent people and injuring your country'. The dispute was now clearly political and fomented by 'just a small nucleus who have been instructed for political reasons to take advantage of every little disturbance that takes place to cause disruption of British economy, British trade, to undermine the Government and to destroy Britain's position'. Finally he appealed to their patriotism: 'Your clear duty to yourselves, to your fellow citizens and to your country is to return to work.'[18]

On Tuesday morning, as the Cabinet were looking in detail at the emergency regulations, news came that a mass meeting in Victoria Park had voted in favour of resuming work the following day. Ministers agreed that the change had been entirely due to the emergency proclamation and the Prime Minister's broadcast. On Wednesday the London and Liverpool dockers returned to work. No regulations were made and the state of emergency was left to lapse on 27 July. Reviewing the strike, the navy prepared extensive plans for any future operations in the docks and drew up lists of personnel required to man each of the main groups of docks on the north side of the river. But it was clearly recognised that servicemen could not immediately take over many of the highly skilled and specialised duties in the docks without at least a concentrated period of emergency training. One aspect of Operation Zebra caused considerable dissatisfaction to the navy. The accommodation provided by the army at Woolwich Barracks was 'desperately crude'. The naval party had been put up in disused stables and harness rooms, 'empty except for the fittings which betrayed their origin, for Army "biscuits" [mattresses] laid in the closest proximity on the floor and for certain unpleasant denizens whose unwelcome presence became all too apparent on the first night'. The War Office retorted that no mention had been made at the time of the existence of 'unpleasant denizens', and letters had subsequently been received at Woolwich 'almost embarrassing in their praise for all that had been done to make the sailors comfortable'.[19]

The experience of the dock strike indicated the need for non-government organisations – in that particular case the Port of London Authority – to be closely involved in emergency work. In July the Co-ordinating Committee established a new fuel and power sub-committee, and it was asserted that it could not satisfactorily draw up emergency fuel allocation schemes unless various unofficial groups, such as the Coal Board and the oil companies, were actually represented at their meetings. No one on the Emergencies Committee objected and the sub-committee appointed representatives from the Coal Board, the gas and electricity industries and the leading petroleum interests. Its report, which was completed in December 1948, laid the basis for emergency fuel and power planning ever since. Many of the recommendations were tactical. If a coal or transport strike was at all likely, coal stocks should be built up discreetly, for example by the railways, gas and electricity industries reducing services, 'if possible without assigning the reason for such action'. Even if an emergency occurred at the beginning of winter when coal stocks were at their peak, 'general restrictions of consumption (by Order) would be the only prudent policy'. Restrictions would need to be severe to be effective, 'and although some of them would be difficult to enforce legally, experience has shown that in circumstances such as those envisaged the restrictions would be observed by the mass of loyal citizens.' It was believed that an electricity strike was improbable; there had been no serious stoppage for many years and the British Electricity Authority were 'confident of maintaining good relations with their staff'. In the event of a strike, the Authority believed that the technical staff would remain loyal and they could be assisted by service men or even civilian volunteers drawn from 'the operating and testing staffs of Turbine and Boiler manufacturers and possibly from 3rd-year students at Universities and Technical Colleges'. The committee warned, however, that 'a close scrutiny of all volunteers would be desirable in order to ensure that subversive elements did not gain access into power stations with the intention of carrying out acts of sabotage.' The gas industry were similarly confident that a general stoppage was unlikely. They had the added advantage of widely dispersed installations and the workers were represented by several unions who might not be able to agree on joint action. While the services could provide some assistance in an emergency, it was not thought that skilled workers in any numbers would be available from civilian sources. The problems facing the petroleum industry were much the most manageable. Eighty per cent of oil needs were imported in a finished state and the domestic oil companies were principally concerned with distribution. In the event of a strike substitute drivers should be easy to find. Petrol rationing, which was still in force, would also enable close control to be kept on consumption. The committee did not feel that the Emergency Powers Act need be invoked at all. It was considered that the 'existing legal powers under the Defence Regulations are adequate to meet an emergency in the Fuel and Power Industries'.[20]

The fuel and power report was as timely as the British Electricity Authority's confidence was misplaced. From 1947 onwards the government became increasingly worrried about subversive activities. In a context of the developing cold war and the British Communist Party's open espousal of policies hostile to the government, wage restraint and a recovery programme largely based on United States aid under the Marshall Plan, ministers and employers tended to identify any industrial stoppage with Communist subversion. This was especially so in the power stations, where there was sporadic unrest during 1948. Several trade unions were dominated by Communist leaders. The largest of these was the Electrical Trades Union.

In December 1948 Citrine, striving to establish his new Electricity Authority on a sound basis, approached Gaitskell, who had succeeded Shinwell at Fuel and Power in October 1947, and Isaacs about the problem of lightning strikes. Taking a grave view of the matter, he urged the need to deal with them firmly. Gaitskell and Isaacs consulted Morrison, who agreed that 'unless there is a determination to stand firm against threats of unconstitutional action in this industry, there would be serious risk of continuing attempts to coerce the British Electricity Authority and the Government by means of threats to the electricity supply.' In February 1949 Isaacs asked Attlee if the matter could be raised in Cabinet. He noted that 'the danger of extremist action is greatest at certain stations where the Communist element is believed to be considerable', but reasonably added that 'trouble may develop from some real grievance'. Alexander Johnston, Deputy Secretary to the Cabinet, observed that the question was much wider than the particular problem in the electricity industry and suggested that the Cabinet might consider the general difficulty of strikes by 'workers engaged on essential activities'. There is, he wrote, 'something to be said for marking in a special way the disapproval felt towards workers who use the essential character of their work to threaten lightning strikes.'[21]

The topic came before the Cabinet in March. Isaacs reviewed the legal position. Under the Conspiracy and Protection of Property Act 1875, as extended by the Electricity (Supply) Act 1919, the British Electricity Authority were empowered to prosecute workers who had broken their contract and cut power supplies. He raised the possibility of using this power, notwithstanding the fact that there was 'no recorded instance of previous proceedings under the Act'. The Cabinet, however, recognised the effective futility of legal sanctions. It was acknowledged that 'in the last resort, the Government and public authorities would have to rely on public opinion to induce persons contemplating lightning strikes which would damage the community to realise their responsibilities.' If the trouble stemmed from Communist activity, then 'steps might have to be taken to weed them out'. The Cabinet agreed that Isaacs and Gaitskell could inform the Electricity Authority that 'the Government would support them in resisting unauthorised strikes threatening public supplies of electricity, which appeared to be fomented for political reasons or without adequate justification.' Isaacs was also asked to prepare a memorandum regarding contracts of service in

essential industries generally. Although he had mentioned the possibility of legal action, Isaacs himself was reluctant to recommend
it. After the Cabinet meeting, with Order 1305 particularly in mind,
he observed, 'the difficulty is not lack of power to take proceedings
but the impracticability of dealing in this way with large numbers.'[22]

Before Isaacs could make any progress on his memorandum, the
Ministry of Labour's attention was taken up with renewed unrest
in the docks. In Holy Week 1949 a sudden strike of 13,000 London
dockers was sparked off by the dismissal of 33 'ineffective' workers.
This was an unusual stoppage in that although 6,000 TGWU men
had come out unofficially, the executive of the National Amalgamated Stevedores and Dockers declared the strike official. It was
nevertheless illegal, since the procedure under Order 1305 had not
been followed. On 12 April the Emergencies Committee heard that
the army could provide 1,600 men for the docks within 24 hours,
but it was decided that no benefit would accrue from bringing troops
in during the Easter weekend and service intervention was postponed until Wednesday 20 April. In any case the Ministry of Food
did not regard the food position as particularly urgent over the
holiday period. Even so, within the committee there was general
agreement that 'the strike was unreasonable and unjustified, and
constituted a challenge which the Government must meet with firm
and prompt action.' The previous strike had dragged on for three
weeks before the emergency proclamation and Attlee's broadcast
had brought the men back. 'Such drastic and exceptional measures
would lose their effect if too often resorted to.' Next day the Cabinet,
having heard that the stevedores' union were 'under Communist
influence', endorsed the Emergency Committee's decisions. They
also considered the possibility of legal action. It was argued that 'the
Government could not appear to condone illegal action by a Trade
Union', yet prosecutions 'might have the effect of stiffening the
attitude of the rank and file'. Before making a final decision, the
Cabinet agreed to wait for a day or two, but instructed the Director
of Public Prosecutions to collect evidence 'so that, if the strike
continued, the way would be clear to launch prosecutions about the
time when military assistance was brought into the docks.'[23] They
were spared the necessity of having to decide whether or not to
prosecute. On 13 April the strikers decided to submit their grievance
to the established disputes procedure and there was a general return
to work from Easter Saturday onwards. The idea of prosecuting

strikers and sending troops in at the same time – both of which might be regarded as highly provocative actions – demonstrates how severely the government's tolerance was being tested by recurring disruption in the docks. Worse was to come.

For over two months from the middle of May 1949 there was an almost continual series of dock strikes stimulated, oddly enough, by a dispute in Canada. Following failure to secure improvements in an agreement with the ship owners, the Canadian Seamen's Union had gone on strike in March 1949.[24] Contrary to Canadian law, however, they extended the stoppage to include ships arriving at British destinations. The president of the Canadian Union, Harry Davis, came to Britain and persuaded dockers at a number of ports to 'black' the affected ships, for which the owners had flown in new crews from a rival union. In George Isaacs's opinion, Davis, 'a known Communist. . ., while taking great care to remain within the law, had been extremely active in stirring up trouble among British dockers.' In most of the ports the problem had been met by leaving the Canadian ships strikebound while normal work proceeded on other vessels, but on 17 May the port employers at Avonmouth refused to employ any dockers at all until one Canadian ship, the *Montreal City*, was manned and worked. Despite calls from the TGWU to unload the ship, on 19 May the Avonmouth and Bristol dockers, faced with what they regarded as a virtual lock-out, voted to strike. On 23 May Attlee convened a small ministerial meeting to assess the position. Isaacs recommended that the government should not intervene since it was hoped that Deakin would persuade the men to go back to work. This was accepted, but the Emergencies Committee were instructed to keep a watching brief and prepare for action if necessary. They were warned, however, that only limited service assistance was available and the armed forces could not deal with a complete stoppage at more than one port.[25]

On the following day the Co-ordinating Committee met under Newsam's chairmanship. They did not think that the immediate problem was very urgent. The Bristol Channel ports affected were 'not of great importance to the export trade' and the only immediate worry concerned a cargo of bananas at Avonmouth. The committee, however, prudently considered the possibility of the strike spreading to other ports. In this case 'it would be beyond the resources of the Services to work them and an appeal for volunteers would be necessary.' Precautionary plans, therefore, were being made for the use of the Emergency Powers Act. On 25 May the ministerial committee took a graver view of the stoppage. There was some support for the employers' action at Avonmouth, since, if they retreated from the attitude adopted, the dockers would claim a victory 'and they and their Communist instigators would have just what they were after – they would have established *de facto* the right to refuse to work certain ships.' On the other hand, because it had been the employers' action which had caused the stoppage and bearing in mind the need for the government to remain impartial, Isaacs was asked to inform both the employers and the TGWU that 'the national interest demanded that the port should be reopened'. Thereafter it could only be hoped, as Isaacs had told the meeting on 23 May, that Deakin could 'succeed in bringing the dockers to a more sensible frame of mind'. Looking at the wider context of the dispute, the Minister of Transport was particularly gloomy. 'The whole structure of the dock labour scheme,' he said, 'and the orderly working of the ports, were being endangered by the readiness of the dockers to take part in disputes arising outside the United Kingdom.'[26]

On Thursday 26 May, the Cabinet expressed concern about the wider aspects of the dispute. The incident at Avonmouth 'illustrated the need for a more general campaign to put the dockers and other workers in this country on their guard against this sort of Communist exploitation.' Ministers also despaired that 'counter-action on the Government's behalf should always have to be taken from a defensive position' and they mused on how the government could 'take the initiative in this struggle'. Beyond suggesting a wireless broadcast, the Cabinet had nothing much to offer. It was decided that Isaacs should press the port employers to permit the banana ship to be unloaded, if the local TGWU itself provided volunteer labour. Although Deakin had been confident that volunteers would come forward, the Emergency Committee learned later in the day that the men had refused to co-operate. They decided to move 400 troops in. Over the weekend the strike spread to Liverpool where 1,500 dockers refused to work Canadian ships which had been diverted there from Avonmouth. On Monday, with no movement on the part of the dockers, the Emergencies Committee began to get a little anxious. They agreed that the troops should move on from unloading bananas to handle other less perishable foodstuffs. They asked the Admiralty and War Office 'to find and assemble as many skilled men as possible' in readiness to load an urgent export cargo of motor cars at Liverpool. Ede reported a 'most unsatisfactory' interview with Deakin, who stoutly maintained that 'if the Government took no action the strike would collapse in two days'. Ede was not convinced. 'There was no sign', he said, 'that Mr. Deakin had any control over the strikers or even expected them to pay attention to what he said.' Disappointment was also expressed at the 'apparent ineffectiveness' of propaganda prepared by the TGWU, 'who appeared to have none of the facilities possessed by the Communists for the rapid issue of brief and intelligible statements'. On Wednesday 1 June, with over 6,000 men out in Liverpool, the Emergencies Committee postponed plans for using troops on Merseyside, lest the strike should spread further. But they decided that the 800 soldiers now at Avonmouth should begin to unload all the ships in the port, no matter what the cargo, with the exception of the *Montreal City*. Deakin had advised that if it was unloaded 'the Government might find themselves obliged . . . to unload every Canadian vessel now in a British port.' Overnight the government's resolve hardened and on Thursday the Cabinet authorised the Avonmouth troops to handle every ship according to an order of priority drawn up by the Ministries of Transport and Food. With the *Montreal City* eleventh on the list, ministers could only hope that the dispute would be settled before its turn came.[27]

As the strike entered its third week, it is apparent that the government quite simply did not know what to do. The TGWU had proved to be a broken reed. Although troops were working at Avonmouth, the Emergencies Committee first hesitated to commit further units to Liverpool for fear of being provocative and then changed their mind. On 7 June Ede told Attlee that the stoppage had intensified on Merseyside and it was not proposed to send troops in to unload perishable foodstuffs from Friday 10 June. On Thursday this was postponed until the following Monday, but the Co-ordinating Committee now asked permission for the troops at Avonmouth, who had begun unloading the *Montreal City*, also to load the ship with a cargo of cars for Canada. Apparently having consulted only Bevin, Attlee agreed that this could begin on Monday. Isaacs was appalled when he found out about the decision, which, if implemented, would mark a major departure from the established policy of using troops simply to *un*load vessels. He insisted that the matter be first considered by ministers. Attlee called a meeting late on the evening of 10 June. They were encouraged to hear that at Liverpool, where the troops had not yet been used, 500 men had returned to work. But the position at Avonmouth was 'virtually unchanged'. The Prime Minister inquired 'what had been done to bring home to the dockers the unjustified nature of their action'. The short answer was nothing. The Emergencies Committee had relied, with misplaced confidence, on the TGWU. Indeed, it almost seemed as if 'Mr. Deakin was keeping from the dockers the real issues in the case, and was also attempting to obscure the fact that the strike, though not inspired by the Communists, was being vigorously exploited by them.' The efforts of both the Ministry of Labour and the TGWU had merely been 'directed to limiting the extent of the strike in the expectation that it would collapse of itself'. This was not enough and the meeting felt that the time had come for a government statement, particularly in view of Bevin's strongly expressed opinion 'that it would be disastrous to let the Unions gain the power of deciding which ships should be unloaded and which not'. It was agreed that Isaacs should broadcast the following evening. Once again the magic of wireless worked. The Minister of Labour specifically blamed the Communists for the dispute and stressed at length the damage and suffering it had caused. Evidently he convinced the strikers. By 15 June all the men at Liverpool and Avonmouth had resumed work.[28]

Industrial unrest in mid-1949 was not confined to the docks. During the Avonmouth dispute the Emergencies Committee and the Cabinet had intermittently been troubled by a series of 'go slows' and Sunday strikes on the railways. Although it never seemed very likely that this would develop into a full-scale strike, Newsam had the Co-ordinating Committee take the precaution of considering the steps necessary in the event of a complete stoppage. It was assumed without question that there would be a proclamation of emergency, and since 'it would be quite impossible to run any appreciable part of the railway system . . . with the assistance of the Services alone', it would also 'be necessary to issue a general appeal to the country for civilian volunteers'. This would be handled through the Employment Exchanges in co-operation with the Railway Executive, who had already collected 'details of certain persons who have particular skill or experience'. In considering the expanded use which would have to be made of road transport, the committee noted that the Post Office had sufficient vehicles to run emergency mail services entirely by road, but had also expressed doubts that their staff might refuse 'to do anything outside their normal duties to assist in dealing with mail which is ordinarily carried by rail'. This raised 'an important general question of principle, viz;. are civil servants, whether industrial civil servants or not, to be allowed to refuse to undertake work on the ground that by doing so they would be taking sides in an industrial dispute?' The problem was submitted to the Cabinet for consideration. Ede noted that in 1926 the Postmaster General had given the Post Office staff associations an assurance that their members would not be asked to blackleg. The Home Secretary did not recommend that this precedent, laid down by a Conservative minister, should be followed. In his opinion the Postmaster General could either insist that postal workers performed *any* duty 'essential to the life of the community', including, for example, the transport by road of 'mails which would usually go by rail', or he could 'deal with the situation solely on a voluntary basis'. The Cabinet took a strong line and favoured Ede's first alternative. There was no question of raising the matter in advance with the staff associations, as that might 'suggest that it was for the staff to define what were properly the duties of Post Office workers in emergency conditions'. Someone craftily proposed that arrangements could occasionally be made 'for mails to be carried by road over considerable distances'. This, it was thought, might 'break down the impression that these duties in time of emergency were highly exceptional'. The Cabinet decided that 'in the event of an industrial dispute, civil servants might be expected to undertake work different from, though analogous to, that on which they were ordinarily employed, when this was necessary for the maintenance of essential services.' In his brief for the Prime Minister before the Cabinet meeting, Sir Norman Brook, a civil servant, had recommended the second, 'voluntary', alternative.[29]

Although the dockers had returned to work at Avonmouth and Liverpool, the Canadian dispute also had serious repercussions in London. Since late May two Canadian ships in the Surrey docks had been blacked, but on 27 June the port employers issued an ultimatum to their dockers similar to that of the Avonmouth employers on 17 May. It had exactly the same effect. 2,500 men struck and by 29 June both the Surrey and Royal Docks had shut down completely. 'Once again', remarked Philip Noel-Baker, 'our good-hearted dockers have been duped by Communist lies.' The government's immediate reaction was to do nothing. On 4 July the Emergencies Committee were told that only a minority of dockers had come out and that, although nearly 90 vessels were held up, there was no immediate threat to food supplies. It was asserted that 'the effect and timing of these and other industrial troubles clearly demonstrated the existence of a Communist attempt to cause industrial and financial damage', but 'at the same time, the Communist poison, if allowed to work, might prove to be its own antidote.' To send in troops 'purely for strike breaking, and for handling cargoes other than food, would . . . undoubtedly cause the trouble to spread widely.' At the same meeting Gaitskell warned the committee that there was a serious threat of an electricity strike. 'To maintain the normal output', he said, 'would require the assistance of 1,500 Servicemen in London.' The dispute concerned pay relativities. Ironically, considering ministers' views on the docks unrest, it was being threatened by TGWU members, while the Communist-led Electrical Trades Union was recommending its members to stay at work. In this case the committee's attitude to the use of troops was absolutely unequivocal. They 'agreed as a matter of principle that the use of service labour to maintain the supply of electric power was fully justified'. In the event the threat of a stoppage soon receded.[30]

On 5 July Lord Ammon, chairman of the National Dock Labour Board, government chief whip in the Lords, and a veteran trade unionist who had served in both of MacDonald's governments, wrote to Attlee stressing the danger of inaction. He felt that 'the matter should be fought to a finish.' If it was not possible to declare a state of emergency, 'then action should be taken against some of the people who are wilfully misleading the men – with particular reference to the imported agitators – not only to have them deported, but also brought to trial.' Bevin and Alexander echoed this concern and told Isaacs that troops should be sent in at once, even if there was no danger of food supplies in the docks deteriorating. As for Ammon's fulminations against 'imported agitators', the Director of Public Prosecutions reported that all the persons involved, so far as they had been traced, were British subjects and in any case nothing had come to his notice which would justify legal action. But the strong feelings of senior ministers had their effect on the Emergencies Committee. On Tuesday 6 July they decided that 'the question of foodstuffs should not be viewed too narrowly' and instructed that troops should go in the following day 'to safeguard food supplies'. They also agreed it should be put to the Cabinet that if the strike continued into the following week a state of emergency should be proclaimed. Next morning in the Cabinet the view was mildly put that 'the Act of 1920 appeared to be a somewhat heavy weapon to employ to secure the unloading of two Canadian ships', but the general feeling was that 'a continuance of the present dispute was intolerable, especially at a time of grave economic crisis when it was essential that exports should move without hindrance.' There could be 'no compromise on the issue that dockers must unload ships without discrimination'. Such action would only lead to 'endless difficulties in the future'. At this meeting it was reported that the police had little evidence that Communists were 'fomenting the various dock strikes'. The Cabinet, nevertheless, were determined to find a conspiracy and evidently felt that this report was both unsatisfactory and unrealistic. They thought it would be 'useful' if further inquiries could be made into 'the ramifications of the organisation which was causing disputes in ships and docks'.[31] The government's concern about Communist activities was rapidly turning into an obsession.

In the evening of Thursday 7 July the Emergencies Committee discussed the question of emergency powers. They appreciated that 'little more could be done under emergency powers than . . . under existing arrangements', but believed that a proclamation of emergency would have a considerable moral effect. It would not only support the 18,000 dockers still at work, but also those among the 5,000–6,000 strikers 'who were out only because of their almost pathological fear of being called blacklegs, and might well be prepared to volunteer to work in the national interest'. Regarding the timing of the proclamation, the results of a secret ballot of dockers would be published the next day. If the men voted to stay out, then the committee recommended that 'failing a full resumption of work on Monday, 11th July, His Majesty would be advised to proclaim a state of emergency on that day.' On Friday it emerged that so few men had voted in the ballot that 'the result would be inconclusive either way'. This the Emergencies Committee agreed was 'tantamount to a declaration by the dockers and stevedores of their intention to continue the dispute', and they moved on to consider a draft set of emergency regulations.[32] On 11 July, although 'some 15,000 men' were still at work, the number of strikers now exceeded

10,000. The Cabinet decided to press ahead with the emergency proclamation, which was signed by the King at 12.30 p.m. They had before them an astonishing paper by the Attorney-General, Sir Hartley Shawcross, concerning legal aspects of the emergency regulations. Shawcross proposed that a Port Emergency Committee should be appointed with full executive control over the London docks. It would, among other things, direct the Dock Labour Board to operate all provisions of the dock labour scheme, 'including the disciplinary provisions'. He added that it was doubtful whether this power would be legally enforceable:

> I do not think that matters. The men would know that the disciplinary provisions of the Scheme were not being operated, as they might otherwise think, at the whim of local Boards in whose members they had no confidence but at the insistence of the Government on the part of the community. It is, indeed, possible that other powers which the Regulations purport to give may not be strictly *intra vires* the Act. I have advised that this risk should be taken and that the Regulations should cover matters on which action is required without undue regard to the niceties of the law. In an emergency the Government may have, in matters admitting of legal doubt, to act first and argue about the doubts later, if necessary obtaining an indemnification Act.

No comment was passed on this in the Cabinet.[33] The end clearly justified the means.

Shawcross, however, was not a fool. He believed that the overriding need was for the dock labour scheme to continue to operate throughout the strike. In common with emergency planners before him, he no doubt also regarded the possibility of any legal challenge as acceptably remote. Neither was he one of the government hawks. Although he thought that unofficial strikes were 'subversive of our Trade Unions, our negotiating machinery, our industrial democracy and indeed the whole basis on which our society rests', he strongly and wisely advised Attlee against prosecuting strikers. 'Persuasion', he observed, 'is more effective than coercion.' But many dockers seem to have regarded the emergency proclamation as both coercive and provocative. It did not have the moral impact the Emergencies Committee had hoped. Two days after the proclamation the number of strikers had risen to 14,000. The Port Emergency Committee, chaired by the recently retired Sir Alexander Maxwell, started work on 13 July. At this stage 24 ships were being worked by dockers, 16 by 2,500 servicemen and 127 were idle. On 15 July the Emergencies Committee told Maxwell that a total of 20,000 troops could be put at his disposal. Maxwell thought that the use of volunteers would be less inflammatory than additional troops, but the committee advised against any appeal for civilians.[34]

In the meantime the government lapsed into inactivity again. On 18 July the Cabinet rejected a proposal by the Minister of Transport to begin an inquiry into the working of the dock labour scheme. Bevin had predictably strong views. He was mainly concerned with the effect on labour opinion if it became known that the government were reviewing the scheme. 'Grave disquiet', he asserted, 'was bound to be aroused among dock workers . . . and encouragement would be given to all those unsettling elements which wished to bring to an end the Scheme and the benefits it had conferred on dock workers generally.' They also agreed that the Ministry of Labour should cease negotiating with the unions. There were, however, renewed calls for the deportation of 'Canadian Communist agitators' and it was asked if provision for deportation should not have been included in the emergency regulations. 'Against this, it was pointed out that the enactment of legislation to enable British subjects to be deported from the United Kingdom would involve a major departure from accepted policy.' Next day Bevin had cause to be anxious. Lord Ammon decided to take matters into his own hands and, without reference to the Port Emergency Committee, issued a statement ordering all dockers to resume work on 21 July. He added that 'disregard of this order would jeopardise the very existence of the Dock Labour Scheme'. Attlee immediately issued a denial that the government were considering ending the scheme. This was followed by a rejoinder from Ammon criticising the committee's handling of the dispute and on 21 July he resigned his political office in the House of Lords.[35]

Despite Bevin's fears, Ammon's action seems to have had some beneficial effect. On 20 July the Emergencies Committee heard that the lightermen's union were recommending that their members should return to work. Still preparing for the worst, however, they learned that the number of troops available could 'with difficulty' be increased to 25,000. After this, 'in the somewhat remote contingency of a total stoppage at the docks', the number could be brought up to 'the 35,000 estimated to be necessary for working the whole of the docks', but 'only at the expense of gravely dislocating the programmes of the services'. Fortunately the Emergencies Committee did not need to resort to such extreme measures. Following intervention by the Canadian Minister of Labour, the Canadian seamen's strike committee recommended that the London dockers called off their stoppage. On 22 July a mass meeting voted to resume work. The troops were withdrawn over the weekend of 23–4 July and on 26 July the state of emergency was formally rescinded.[36]

During the dock strike specific reports on aspects of the emergencies organisation were completed by two bodies: the 'working party on air transport' and the publicity sub-committee. The air transport group, which included representatives from British European Airways (BEA), noted that there were sufficient numbers of aircraft available to transport mail, urgent foodstuffs, medical supplies and newspapers. They took into account both BEA and RAF machines, but did not include in their calculations the forty-one Viking aircraft which BEA used on its Continental services. It was thought that 'an undesirable impression' might be created abroad if BEA's foreign services 'were withdrawn for reason of national emergency'. In the event of the civil airline itself being strikebound, the RAF could handle most of the operation on its own and the working party added that the air force had gained invaluable experience running the Berlin airlift. A nice reversal of the Admiralty's old 'yeast scheme' in the 1920s was the provision for transporting a possible 50 tons of yeast per week from Liverpool to Northern Ireland. The report concluded with the observation that any airlift scheme was 'entirely dependent upon the Ministry of Fuel and Power ensuring that sufficient supplies of aviation fuel are delivered to the aerodromes'. The publicity sub-committee considered it of the highest importance that work should immediately begin with newspaper proprietors themselves on emergency plans. They specifically did not recommend, 'in any circumstances', the production of an official newspaper akin to the *British Gazette*.[37]

On 19 September George Isaacs finally got round to circulating the paper on 'contracts of service in essential industries' which he had been asked to write in March. He had nothing dramatic to offer. It was impossible effectively to enforce obligations on workers in essential industries and 'the insertion of a special provision in contracts of service which enabled an employer to sue a worker for damages would be merely declaratory and *in terrorem*'. In October the Cabinet agreed with him that 'a solution for the problem of unauthorised strikes should be sought through the development of the appropriate consultative machinery.'[38] Within two months they were reconsidering this conclusion as a result of strikes in the electric power stations. Although these disputes principally arose out of the amalgamations and reorganisation of the industry under the Electricity Authority, in late 1949 there were general signs of an increase in union dissatisfaction with the continuing policy of wage restraint. At the TUC Congress in September delegates voted in support of this policy by a majority of nearly 5½ million. But a special Congress called in January 1950 passed a somewhat complicated new proposal for 'wage stabilisation' with a majority of less than 700,000. The government were also aware that the devaluation of sterling in September 1949 was likely to put inflationary pressure on retail prices as its effect progressively worked through the economy. At the end of 1949, too, the administration had been in office for over four years and a general election was widely expected early in the New Year. In dealing with industrial unrest, therefore, the government were faced with the familiar dilemma of assessing the electoral benefits of either conciliating or coercing the trade unions. In the case of electric power, however, there was no question but that they would take a hard line.

On 2 December the Emergencies Committee met to contemplate the possibility of an unofficial strike at four London power stations. Trouble had been simmering since the summer, and, although Citrine had posted notices drawing the workers' attention to the provisions of the Conspiracy and Protection of Property Act, this seemed to have had little effect. Gaitskell told the committee that the prospect of cuts in electricity supplies 'could not at this time of year be countenanced on any grounds'. He therefore asked for immediate service assistance. On the assumption that senior technicians would not strike, 480 men would be required. One difficulty, which did not occur in the docks, was the need to keep the generators working continuously. The troops would have to move in within fifteen minutes of the strike beginning, but they would also have to take care that they avoided 'encountering the strikers as they left their work'. The committee agreed that if the stoppage took place, 'Service labour should be brought in at once to maintain electricity supplies without interruption.' The threat passed, but ten days later the Emergencies Committee was urgently summoned after the morning shift at Brimsdown power station in Enfield had walked out. This was followed later in the day by a strike at two other stations. Gaitskell again asked for troops. Citrine, who had been invited to the committee, said that the strike was 'part of an organised movement and must be met as such'. He told the committee that so long as the Electrical Power Engineers' Association stayed in, which was likely, it should be possible using troops to maintain the supply at 80 per cent of normal. This was over-optimistic and during the strike output stayed at only about 30 per cent. Parties of servicemen, consisting of naval technicians with army and RAF personnel in support, moved into the three power stations on the evening of 12 December. The next day a fourth station came out and service assistance was provided there as well. In all some 420 men were used. They remained working in the power stations until the strike ended on 17 December. The Electricity Authority supplied roughly equivalent numbers of volunteers 'drawn from their own non-manual staffs and loans from plant installation contractors'. It was afterwards explained that the low efficiency stemmed from the unfamiliarity of the servicemen with the generators and the complex coal handling equipment, but it was estimated that within a fortnight up to 75 per cent output could be achieved. The question of advance training for naval personnel was also subsequently raised. But the Admiralty observed that 'this would be impracticable to arrange without Trade Union outcry, and in any case even if once trained, the men would not be held available indefinitely.' The strike prompted the Cabinet to re-examine the problem of industrial disruption in essential industries. On 15 December it was strongly urged that the Electricity Authority should take civil proceedings against the strikers. This, it was asserted, would help to extirpate 'the political forces which were at the root of the present strike'. Gaitskell promised to discuss the question with Citrine.[39]

During the electricity strike the servicemen were employed under Defence Regulation 6, which both the Home Office and the War Office had been reviewing since September 1949. The regulation was shortly due to lapse with other wartime measures, but the civil departments had found it most convenient to use in circumstances when the Emergency Powers Act was not suitable and they were most anxious that it should continue in force. Newsam, however, argued that 'we cannot rely on extending the Defence Regulation year by year after 1950 by Motions of both Houses of Parliament and Orders in Council'. It would therefore be necessary to introduce special legislation, which was 'almost certain to arouse political controversy'. Within the War Office it was felt that the permanent enactment of Regulation 6 'in a special one-clause Bill' was 'not a specially attractive prospect' and that perhaps 'the Home Office had another Bill in view in which this clause might conveniently be included.' It was left to the Home Office to take the initiative. Eventually the regulation was continued under the Supplies and Services (Defence Purposes) Act 1951, which extended various emergency powers dating from 1939. Although no specific time limit was placed on the statute, Herbert Morrison presented it to Parliament as essentially a temporary measure, the principal purpose of which was defence and maintenance of world peace.[40] It was to be another thirteen years before Regulation 6 was finally made permanent.

Prompted by Citrine, on Christmas Eve 1949 Gaitskell wrote a lengthy minute to the Prime Minister on matters arising out of the recent electricity strike. 'There is', he observed, 'a good deal of evidence to show that this strike was deliberately fomented by "un-official" Communist elements after careful preparation. I am told that in such circles it is regarded as a rehearsal.' In these circumstances the government ought urgently to examine a number of important general questions. 'Can we', he asked, 'continue to deal with such strikes in the same way as ordinary industrial disputes?' Should strikes at power stations be 'tolerated at all'? He noted the disappointingly slow rate at which capacity had been increased after the troops had gone into the strike-bound power stations. Perhaps this was due to 'lack of trained personnel', and 'if so, what more can be done in *advance* to provide the necessary training?' Once again he raised the question of taking action against strikers, although he appreciated that the government could not in practice rely on the Conspiracy and Protection of Property Act. Adopting a point of view barely mentioned in emergency planning since Bevan had urged it on the Cabinet in October 1945, he asked if the problem should not be discussed with the TUC, 'or is this policy too dangerous and, if so, what exactly should we expect of the Unions?' Gaitskell stressed the wide general relevance of these questions. Although the Communists seemed at present to be concentrating on 'power stations as the places where strikes can effect the greatest and most immediate threat to the life of the community, similar dangers could arise as regards gas works, water supplies, disposal of sewage and possibly other public utilities'. He finally proposed that the problems could initially be considered by a group of senior civil servants.[41] Gaitskell's thought-provoking minute was a valuable corrective to the *ad hoc* fashion in which emergency planning had developed during the post-war period, despite the heart-searching in Ede's original working party and their anxiety to establish an agreed statement of principle.

Sir Edward Bridges was given the task of consulting relevant permanent secretaries and on 18 January he submitted a top secret memorandum systematically answering Gaitskell's inquiries. The civil servants thought that, while 'there can be no question of banning all strikes' at power stations, the government could not 'stand by and see the community deprived of essential services'. In the event of a stoppage in an essential service, Bridges simply recommended that the government should 'do what is practicable to ensure that the community does not suffer and that the service is carried on'. But he thought that no general statement of this policy should be made in advance. It would 'not be welcomed by the Trades Union Congress, and would give a useful pointer to anyone engaged in planning a further dispute.' His inquiries confirmed that specific training of servicemen was not feasible. He pointed out, moreover, that service labour could only deal with a limited strike. They 'could not cope with a country-wide stoppage and if one took place it would be necessary to enrol civilian volunteers through the employment exchanges.' Regarding legal sanctions, Bridges gave qualified approval to civil proceedings, but not criminal. 'We doubt', he wrote, 'whether any useful purpose would be served by informing the Trades Union Congress of the Government's intention to maintain essential services.' The TUC would 'almost certainly accept this policy, but they could hardly be expected to give open or tacit approval to it'. On the question of Communist activists, Bridges strongly opposed anything 'in the nature of a purge'. The Electricity Authority, however, might be able to rid themselves 'of known Communists where this could be done unobtrusively and in the ordinary course of engaging and re-engaging staff'.[42]

Attlee thought the matter sufficiently important for him to call a special meeting of ministers on 24 January. Much of Bridges's memorandum was accepted, but, since there was 'sufficient ground' for expecting an electricity strike in February, ministers agreed that service labour should temporarily be kept available and that there should be 'direct consultation at the technical level between the British Electricity Authority and the Service authorities'. They also thought that the long-term quality of service assistance might be improved 'by including in the Service educational programme lectures on electricity generation'. One mitigating factor was the impending general election. On 11 January Attlee had called an election for 23 February. Gaitskell thought that over the election period 'it was probable that a strike would not spread as far as had the recent strike'. But he also argued that Bridges had not taken a hard enough line on power stoppages. He 'did not share the view that there was little difference between strikes in electricity generating stations and other industrial disputes.' 'Because of their special effects and because of the way in which they were brought about', electricity strikes were 'in a class by themselves', and he thought that 'in due course the Government ought thoroughly to review the principles involved.' When the discussion moved on to the question of legal action against strikers, Bevan agreed that civil proceedings would have a much better effect than criminal. They had 'worked as an effective deterrent in the mining industry, and, unless their use was adopted wherever else they were appropriate, it would be hard to continue taking them against miners'. The meeting approved Bridges's general conclusions regarding trade union involvement in the emergency organisation, but they decided nevertheless that 'individual members of the General Council, who were opposed to the efforts of the Communists to disintegrate the trade union movement' could 'be asked to help the Government in connection with such measures as were necessary to maintain essential services.' Gaitskell, who seems to have been particularly keen on a specific prohibition of electricity strikes, was not entirely happy with the result of the meeting. 'The fundamental issue', he wrote in his diary, 'is still more unresolved. . . . When the Election is over the Government ought really to face up to the issue of Power Station strikes, and decide whether they can afford to treat them as ordinary industrial disputes. In my view they cannot.'[43]

Attlee won the election, but with a majority of only six seats.[44] The anticipated electricity stoppage did not materialise and the first major strike the government had to face was once again in the London docks. After the 1949 dispute the TGWU, striving to hold the government line and maintain union authority, had disciplined some members of the unofficial 'Port Workers' Defence Committee'. On Wednesday 19 April 1950, it was confirmed that three men should be expelled from the union. By 20 April 6,000 dockers had struck in sympathy. Over the weekend ministers and officials rehearsed the by now familiar arguments as to the advantages and disadvantages of using troops. Although Isaacs had publicly announced that the strike was 'clearly caused by Communists', the Emergencies Committee noted that because the dispute 'was not one between employers and employees but was a purely domestic matter between a union and its members', the issue 'was a particularly difficult one for the Government to take a stand on.' Yet the Cabinet, aware that the use of troops would probably exacerbate the stoppage, showed less hesitation than it had done in 1948 and 1949. Servicemen started work in the docks on Monday 24 April. Beginning with one thousand men working in the worst-hit Royal Docks, the Cabinet instructed that the numbers should quickly be built up to 20,000. Somewhat belatedly ministers also recognised what should have been apparent to any disinterested observer for some time, that 'quite apart from Communist agitation, there were unsatisfactory features in the present organisation of dock labour in the port.'[45]

The irony of the government taking its swiftest and most effective action against a docks dispute since October 1945 soon became apparent. On 26 April Ede observed that there were 'signs of a desire on the part of some of the men on strike to return to work', but that they were 'unable to do so as long as Service-men are employed in the docks'. There had, therefore, been calls for a temporary withdrawal of the troops. But Ede continued to recommend a hard line. 'While the Service forces are being built up', he wrote, 'and before the dockers realise that the docks will be worked without their help, it might be taken as a sign of weakness to make a general withdrawal of the Service-men even temporarily.' He recognised, however, that this policy was 'attended with considerable difficulty'. Next day the Cabinet confirmed their determination 'to keep the port in operation, by continuing with the building-up of the numbers of troops.' On 28 April, with 14,000 men out and 5,000 troops actually working in the docks, a mass meeting of strikers agreed to call off the stoppage and on 1 May there was a general resumption of work. It had never been a full-scale strike and a large minority of the 25,000 London dockers continued to work throughout the dispute.[46] Its early end came from a combination of labour disunity, the government's unusually quick and resolute action and the equally tough stand taken by the London Dock Labour Board who had announced on 27 April that all the strikers would be dismissed if they did not return to work. Despite the government's automatic identification of Communist subversion, the deeper causes of the dispute were put into perspective by the cool good sense of Sir John Anderson, chairman of the Port of London Authority since 1946. On 2 May he told Attlee that, while it was 'fashionable' to attribute the recurring troubles in the docks to Communism,

> It seemed to him that the real trouble was that the rank and file of the Dock labourers did not trust their leaders. They were under the impression that their official leaders were too closely associated with the employers and to some extent the Government and did not really stand up for the interests of the men. That was why the unofficial leaders commanded confidence. The Communists were, of course, not slow to take advantage of this position.[47]

The difficulties accompanying the use of troops as strikebreakers, to which the government were increasingly easily resorting, were sharply highlighted by a dispute towards the end of June 1950. At midnight on Friday 23 June all 1,500 London drivers of the wholesale Meat Transport Organisation Limited struck in support of a pay claim. At the beginning of the following week the Emergencies Committee, accepting the urgent need to maintain meat rations in London, drafted in almost 400 service lorries to distribute 'canned corned meat from buffer depots to the retail butchers'. They anticipated that from Monday 3 July troops would be required to move carcases from cold stores to Smithfield Market and possibly also from the docks to the cold stores. 'These additional measures', they told the Cabinet on 29 June, 'might have the result of extending the strike.' It was put to the Cabinet that the real reason for the stoppage was political rather than industrial, since the drivers 'had secured a substantial increase in wages in September last'. The Emergencies Committee's proposals involved the employment of 1,000 vehicles and 5,000 men, who could only be provided at very great inconvenience. The services, moreover, 'viewed with some disquiet the repeated demands which were being made upon them in connection with strikes; and there was some risk that ill-will might be created between Servicemen and strikers.' The Cabinet, however, resolved to maintain London meat supplies. The effect of their determination became apparent on 3 July when troops started work at Smithfield and the cold stores. As feared, the strike spread to these two areas and in addition some 500 wholesale provision drivers came out in sympathy. By 4 July 640 vehicles and 3,000 troops were being used to distribute meat and general provisions from warehouses and cold stores to retailers. So far the Emergencies Committee had specifically instructed the servicemen not to enter the docks, but Ede told the Cabinet on 5 July that 'by the end of the week . . . the cold stores which are not in the dock area will be practically exhausted of meat, and on Monday, 10th July, it will be necessary for Servicemen to begin work on the cold stores in the dock area.' There was a strong likelihood that this would precipitate a complete shutdown in the docks and preparations were being made for the entire London docks to be operated by 20,000 troops.[48]

On 6 July the Cabinet considered this gloomy prospect with some misgivings. 'All alternative courses . . .', they thought, 'ought . . . to be thoroughly explored in the short time available.' In a sense it was 'playing into the hands of Communist agitators to place thousands of dockers, who had no Communist sympathies and were reluctant to come out on strike, in a position in which they felt obliged to stop work.' A suggestion was made that the TGWU might be persuaded to co-operate in issuing permits to van-men collecting foodstuffs from the cold stores. 'While this might place a strain on the cohesion of the Union,' recorded the Cabinet minutes, 'it was unreasonable that the Government should assume responsibility for breaking an unofficial strike which was largely directed against the principal officers of the Union.' If this did not succeed, the Emergencies Committee were authorised to employ servicemen in the docks from 10 July. On 7 July Newsam's official committee heard that the TGWU could not assist the government, but, on the advice of the Minister of Food, they felt able to postpone the introduction of troops into the docks until 11 July. Their prudence was understandable in the face of an apparently uncontrollable escalation of the dispute. On 8 July the official committee were informed that the expanded use of troops might provoke a general road haulage strike, in which case a call for civilian volunteers would be necessary. Newsam told the committee that Sir John Anderson had telephoned him 'to point out the dangers of introducing Servicemen into the Dock area next week'. Anderson was clearly unimpressed by the government's handling of the strike and had 'questioned whether it was worth bringing the port to a standstill in order to maintain the supplies of one commodity'. He bluntly told Newsam 'that if the Government brought about a general stoppage through the introduction of servicemen, they would have against them not merely the workers but the employers.' On Monday the Cabinet were relieved to learn that the call for a road haulage stoppage had met with 'comparatively little success'. On the other hand, 'an effort was being made to induce the petroleum tanker drivers to come out on strike.' If this were successful, 'it would eventually have a paralysing effect on road transport throughout the country'. There were also rumours of possible action at Billingsgate and Covent Garden. At this 'crucial stage' it was decided that Attlee, Ede, Isaacs and Barnes should see Deakin and urge the TGWU to 'make a sustained effort to enlist the support of loyal members of the Union in combating the continuation or spread of the strike'. Much to everyone's relief this move succeeded and a settlement was reached late that evening. By the end of the week normal working had been resumed at Smithfield.[49]

The meat transport strike of June–July 1950 saw the last major use of strikebreaking troops by the Attlee government. In October 1950 68 servicemen were briefly employed in three London gas works during a stoppage of maintenance workers.[50] The fact that troops were not used again during the life of the Labour government was certainly a relief to the armed forces themselves, who from the middle of 1950 were considerably stretched by the outbreak of the Korean War. Although Newsam's official committee continued to discuss and refine emergency plans, during this period they were also concerned with the apparently grave problem of Communist-inspired unrest. In August 1950 Philip Noel-Baker, who had succeeded Gaitskell at Fuel and Power in February, reported to Attlee Lord Citrine's continued worries about possible sabotage. Citrine 'was satisfied that the Russians regarded our Power Stations as the nerve centre of British industry, and that they had made special efforts to get influence among workers in Power Stations'.[51] Attlee agreed that the matter should be taken up with the Security Service (MI5). An investigation was conducted by R. H. (later Sir Roger)

Hollis and P. A. Osborne of MI5. On 15 August they attended a meeting of the official Emergencies Committee, but the minutes do not record them as having said anything.[52] The following day, however, the Home Office reported to the Cabinet that there was little cause for concern and 'no reason to believe that any organised outbreak of sabotage was imminent'. Nevertheless, in September the Cabinet returned to the problem of 'Communist endeavours to cause industrial unrest' and discussed the possibility of legal sanctions to meet the threat. One result of this concern was a revival of prosecutions under Order 1305. In October ten leaders of the gas maintenance workers' strike were convicted of failing to comply with the Order. This was followed in February 1951 by the prosecution of seven dockers. The TUC, who had happily accepted the continuation of Order 1305 on the apparent assumption that only the provision regarding arbitration would be invoked, were so alarmed by the government's new policy that they formally requested the Minister of Labour to amend the Order. In August 1951 it was replaced by Order 1376, which retained compulsory arbitration, but omitted the prohibition of strikes and lock-outs.[53]

In the last year of Attlee's administration Sir Frank Newsam and his colleagues took the opportunity to press ahead with forward planning. In December 1950 Newsam circulated a memorandum on the question of 'broadcasting in a civil emergency'. Although the paper was mostly concerned with technical problems, such as providing electricity supplies for the BBC during a power stoppage, it also touched on 'policy control of broadcasting'. It was this latter point which most exercised the Emergencies Committee. From time to time in the late 1940s ministers had complained about the way in which the BBC had reported labour disputes. During the discussion of Newsam's memorandum it was observed that 'the Corporation had interpreted their obligation to be neutral in politics as requiring them to give facilities not only to the Government but to unofficial strikers; moreover, important Government statements had been distorted by editing.' Chuter Ede thought that 'a discreet approach to the Corporation might induce greater co-operation, or, at the worst, elucidate their attitude to disputes in which the Government were opposed by strikers acting against the national interest as interpreted by the Government.' The committee agreed and early in the New Year Newsam met Sir William Haley (Director-General of the BBC) 'informally and in secrecy' at the Home Office. Newsam raised the delicate question of whether in an emergency the BBC 'would be prepared to accept the view of the Government as to what matters should or should not be broadcast having regard to the national interest'. But Haley was determined to defend the BBC's independence. He told Newsam that the Corporation's Governors 'regarded themselves as having a direct responsibility to the public, in the discharge of which they must be guided by their views of what was in the national interest.' He was 'not in a position to give any blank cheque' to the government. In the last resort ministers had powers under the BBC Charter to exercise editorial control over broadcasts. Newsam thought 'that it would clearly be better if matters could be settled amicably rather than by the use of threat of compulsory powers'. Haley, however, would concede nothing more than a rather vague assurance that the Governors, as 'a responsible and patriotic body, possessed of discretion,' would 'always be ready to listen to the point of view of the Government'. He also noted that 'in the past alterations to Government messages had been necessary so as to make them intelligible to the public.'[54] All in all, it must have been a somewhat unsatisfactory meeting for Sir Frank Newsam.

As if to add point to Newsam's frustration, less than a week after the minutes of his meeting had been circulated there was a complaint in Cabinet concerning the BBC's coverage of a dispute. Early in February 1951 groups of dockers throughout the country stopped work in protest against a nationally agreed wage settlement. When 6,000 London dockers joined the strike on 9 February it seemed that the dispute might escalate into a full-scale stoppage. On 12 February, however, the London men decided to resume work. The same day the view was put to the Cabinet 'that the British Broadcasting Corporation in its news bulletins had tended to exaggerate the extent of the dock strike and had failed to draw attention to the number of men who had remained at work.'[55]

Intermittent dock disputes continued to trouble the official Emergencies Committee throughout 1951. In March they discussed the problem of accommodating the 27,000 troops it was estimated would be required to work the London docks in the event of a 'major stoppage'. Although 'tented accommodation' was thought adequate in the summer, it was not acceptable in winter and the Ministry of Works were invited to make a survey of suitable buildings. By October they had prepared a list of buildings which included Brixton

Roller Skating Rink, the Royal Festival Hall and Clapham Common
Deep Tube Shelter. An unofficial stoppage at Manchester docks in
May, which apparently stemmed from 'small grievances which had
been seized upon by the Communist leaders of the unofficial Port
Workers Committee', led the ministerial committee to consider,
though not approve, employing service labour. The following month
a strike of 1,500 tally clerks in London and Tilbury docks briefly
held up 19 food ships, but again it was decided not to use troops.
In October another dispute at Tilbury – this time it was the dockers
on 'go-slow' – interrupted tea shipments.[56] The Tilbury 'go-slow'
coincided with a general election campaign. Unhappy about the
strain imposed on Labour MPs by their slim Parliamentary majority,
in September Attlee called an election for 25 October. The Conservatives were returned to power with a comfortable working
majority.[57] The change of government had no apparent effect at all
on the emergencies organisation. On 29 October the official committee met to consider both the Tilbury dispute and the accommodation of servicemen in London. The new Home Secretary, Sir
David Maxwell Fyfe, who had been appointed to the post just the
previous day, took the chair for part of the meeting.[58] Churchill's
incoming Cabinet, unlike Attlee's, did not discuss the need for an
emergencies organisation; its existence was accepted without question. Emergency planning, it seemed, had finally become part of the
'seamless robe' of modern British administration.

By the end of 1951 the broad outline of the contemporary emergency machine had become well established. To a very great extent
it was a straightforward revival of the pre-war arrangements. In the
absence, however, of any national stoppages, the regional organisation and the planned involvement of local authorities largely fell
into abeyance. Wide-ranging plans to recruit civilian volunteers,
which had come to look somewhat unrealistic, also quietly slipped
into the background. But detailed emergency arrangements were
made, and continued to be revised, in close consultation with the
principal 'essential' industries. The trade unions were not admitted
to these discussions. This was one policy, at least, which the new
Conservative government was likely to share with Attlee's administration. Increasingly during the 1940s and early 1950s the government became almost obsessed with the domestic threat of
Communism. After five years in power Attlee's Cabinet, which
began its emergency planning with such careful deliberation, had

convinced itself that virtually all industrial unrest stemmed from a subversive challenge to established order. In these circumstances, detailed and systematic emergency planning seemed both necessary and desirable. Ironically, fear of revolution, or at least subversion, which had been the initial stimulant for the establishment of a strikebreaking machine after the First World War, did much to sustain the development of a similar organisation after the Second.

# 8
# Contemporary civil contingency planning
# 1951–1982

VIEWED FROM THE perspective of the jumpy, uncertain early 1980s, the two decades spanning the period 1951–70 have a definite glow about them when compared with earlier and subsequent sequences of industrial and civil disorder. Only twice in those twenty years did Cabinets need to take the formal emergency powers granted them by the 1920 statute – during the rail strike of 1955 and the seamen's dispute of 1966. With the blurring that comes from the passage of time, the Butskellite era of consensus politics is remembered as the high-water mark of Keynesian economics, of a sensibly if undynamically managed economy, with a favourable climate of world trade allowing industrial peace to be bought at the cost of slight inflation after comparatively harmonious negotiations with reasonable union leaders. Hovering over this pleasing picture is the benign image of Sir Walter Monckton, Minister of Labour in Churchill's last administration, a man in the long British tradition of legal-fixer. Monckton, who had only entered the Commons at a by-election in February 1951 at the age of sixty, confidently expected to be offered the post of Attorney-General when summoned by the new Prime Minister after the Conservative general election victory the following October. After this the Woolsack, or the post of Lord Chief Justice, beckoned within the span of a few years. Instead, Churchill greeted him with the words: 'I have the worst job in the Cabinet for you.'[1]

As with all golden eras, the reality was somewhat tarnished. Far from feeling they were at the beginning of a time of industrial peace and economic prosperity, Churchill and Monckton, like all others throughout our period whose high office required them to grapple with the immediate problems of British industrial relations, believed themselves to be on the rim of a precipice. Monckton's instructions, however, were crystal clear. He was to use his formidable skills as a conciliator ('that old oil can', as Lord Margesson called him) to buy time. 'Winston's riding orders to me', recalled Monckton, 'were that the Labour party had foretold grave industrial troubles if the Conservatives were elected, and he looked to me to do my best to preserve industrial peace. I said that I should seek to do that by trying to do justice . . . without worrying about party politics.'[2]

To a large extent, the Monckton/Churchill tactic produced the desired effect in the short term. With the frequent use of Courts of Inquiry, and the contents of his personal 'oil can', Monckton won the plaudits of both Parliamentary opponents and the TUC. Deakin, for example, said publicly in July 1953: 'I believe Sir Walter Monckton has given us a square deal and we have been able to do things that were difficult under our own people.'[3] But to the Conservative Cabinet it all seemed immensely precarious at the time, and some voiced fears of the inflationary consequences of Monckton's mollifying style. Industrial militancy in the docks and on the railways provided an ever-present warning against premature euphoria. Churchill, while leaving Monckton to get on with his job, took a particular interest in unrest in the electricity supply industry in September 1953, the railways, as they teetered on the brink of national stoppages in 1953 and 1954, and the newspaper strike which blanked out coverage of the last days of his premiership in 1955.[4]

In the autumn of 1953 minds were concentrated by trouble in the oil supply industry. In a pre-echo of what proved to be a persistent worry in Whitehall in the late 1970s, an unofficial strike of petrol tanker drivers broke out in London on 19 October. It was caused principally by the combination of a wage claim and the refusal of some men to join the dominant TGWU. By 22 October over 3,000 men were out, cutting off petrol supplies to nearly all filling stations in the London area. Bus services and private motoring all but ceased. Monckton told the Commons that the government would take steps to secure essential supplies. To complete a familiar routine, Deakin appealed to the men to go back, was ignored and on 23 October, under Defence Regulation 6, 2,000 troops were brought in to distribute fuel. Two days later 6,000 servicemen had been deployed to considerable effect. During the dispute, which lasted just over a week, they moved some 8 million gallons of fuel, bringing supplies to most garages in London and the Home Counties. On 26 October what must be a textbook case for Whitehall's contingency planners was closed when the strikers agreed to return to work and resume negotiations provided the military withdrew.[5]

The still huge railway industry was not so amenable to Sir Frank Newsam's short, sharp, shock treatment. Serious skirmishing between the three rail unions (the National Union of Railwaymen, the Amalgamated Society of Locomotive Engineers and Firemen, and the Transport Salaried Staffs Association) and the British Transport Commission in 1953–4 seemed to have ended in the first weeks of 1955 with the publication of an interim report from a Court of Inquiry under Sir John Cameron QC. But the problem of differentials intruded. The aristocrats of the industry, ASLEF's footplatemen, were not reconciled to the undermining of their position vis-à-vis the less-skilled workforce of the NUR and negotiations broke down on 19 May 1955, just six weeks after Sir Anthony Eden had succeeded Churchill as Prime Minister. From the outset Eden played a direct part alongside Monckton in working with the TUC General Council to avert a strike. Adding to the government's difficulties was a dispute in the docks, caused by the long-standing rivalry between the TGWU and the stevedores' union. On 23 May 18,000 stevedores in London, Merseyside, Manchester and Hull came out. Last-minute peacemaking with ASLEF was to no avail. At midnight on 28 May, during the Whitsun holiday weekend, over 60,000 footplatemen went on strike. Not all footplatemen belonged to ASLEF. Those in the NUR continued working, but were able to run only the most skeletal of skeleton services. About 200 special passenger trains ran on 29 May, compared with the normal weekday total of 24,000. Goods traffic halted almost entirely. That evening Eden broadcast from Chequers. He warned that the stoppage would inevitably cause 'hardship and loss', but assured his audience that 'we will do all we can to protect the nation from the worst effects of this strike. That is the Government's clear duty, and we intend to discharge it.' Food would be supplied for everyone, along with sufficient fuel for essential public services. 'The Government', he added, 'will not hesitate to obtain any further power that may be necessary for this purpose. You can help us. We will tell you how. Plans have been prepared, and will now be put into operation.'[6]

Even without a sight of Emergencies Committee papers still locked in the Cabinet Office registry, a detailed reconstruction of the planning for a rail strike initiated by Newsam and his organisation in the late 1940s is possible, thanks to a government statement issued to back up Eden's broadcast. It noted that supplies to industry would be curtailed. Postal, telegraph and telephone services would continue to operate, but, since the postal services depended very heavily on the railways, the movement of letters and parcels would be seriously affected. 'In order to keep the essential postal services going, the Service Departments are assisting the General Post Office by providing aircraft and up to 250 lorries to carry essential mails over the longer postal trunk routes.' Nevertheless, 'even with this assistance there will be some delay in the delivery of mails.' A single sentence appended to the statement reveals what must have been a strategic decision of great importance taken by ministers in the build-up to the strike: 'No Servicemen are being employed anywhere on the railways.' The breaking of the petrol tanker drivers' strike in October 1953 showed that the Churchill government had no objection in principle to employing military labour. But, as had been demonstrated in the 1940s, the use of troops often merely exacerbated an existing dispute. In May 1955 the government seemed to have been motivated by a sharp and understandable desire not to alienate the several thousand NUR men who remained at work. In June 1949, moreover, the Emergencies Co-ordinating Committee had accepted that civilian volunteers as well as service labour would be required to keep the railways running. Their employment would if anything have been even more provocative than that of troops alone. The advance of technology in locomotion and signalling may also have counted against the use of volunteer labour. This was to become an increasingly important consideration for government emergency planners. During a railways strike in the 1960s it was found that less than twenty soldiers in the entire army were able to drive railway locomotives.[7] Certainly by the 1970s the Civil Contingencies Unit harboured no illusions about the possibility of either volunteers or troops keeping British Rail in motion should the NUR or ASLEF close down the network in a national strike.

The rest of the government's statement on 29 May urged the public to be frugal in its use of fuel, light and power, the postal and telegraphic services, and, wherever possible, for those with private cars to give lifts to others. Alan Lennox-Boyd, Minister of Transport and Civil Aviation, announced that an arrangement had been concluded with the insurance companies whereby use of private cars for giving lifts (but not for hire) would be covered by an owner's existing policy, and that immediate cover should be given to owners with vehicles in mothballs who wished to use them during the emergency. Drivers would be indemnified by the government against the risk of injury or death to passengers, provided that their vehicles displayed the sign 'FREE LIFTS AT YOUR OWN RISK', and that passengers' attention had been drawn to it before boarding. The public were told that food stocks were high throughout the country, though there was a prospect of severe curbs on gas and electricity supplies. Enterprises were expected to make their own arrangements for carrying goods and people, but the Ministry of Transport undertook to 'do all that is physically possible to secure the movement of traffic necessary to maintain essential supplies and services'.

Over the next few days matters improved somewhat on the railways. On 30 May more footplatemen reported for work and it proved possible to run 1,200 passenger and 200 goods trains. The following day movements rose further to 2,000 passenger and 850 freight trains. On 31 May the government proclaimed a state of emergency under the 1920 Act. It promulgated twenty-five regulations allowing ministers, as in the past, to regulate the supply of gas and electricity, oil fuel, and the carriage of mails, while giving force to the emergency insurance arrangements for indemnifying private motorists. It took two more weeks before Monckton was able to announce success in negotiations to end the strike. The previous day the House of Commons had approved the emergency regulations. With a nice echo of past emergency arrangements, they were introduced to Parliament by the Home Secretary, Major Gwilym Lloyd George, whose father had been in power when the 1920 Act was passed. Because talks between government, TUC and ASLEF were at an advanced stage, there was little debate on the regulations, and following the end of the stoppage the emergency was revoked on 21 June.[8]

The effects of the strike proved less grave than had been feared, helped partly, no doubt, by the planning of the Whitehall Emergencies Organisation, which had come a very long way since Maxwell's meeting in the Home Office exactly ten years earlier. The main reasons for the successful containment of damage were the extensive use by industry of road and water transport, and the continued working of 11,000 NUR footplatemen, which allowed the movement of up to one-sixth of normal passenger and freight traffic.

Over the weekend of 11–12 June, for example, British Railways operated 5,901 passenger and 5,043 goods trains. Heavy industry was the worst hit, particularly the steel and engineering industries. Steel plants in the Swansea area, Barrow-in-Furness, Lincolnshire and Scotland closed down wholly or partly on 3 June, but by 5–6 June they were able to resume working. Motor manufacturers suspended overtime and some engineering firms issued precautionary notices, but few dismissals took place. The mining industry, to everyone's surprise, was scarcely affected at all. The National Coal Board announced on 9 June that not a single colliery had had to close and output was down by 'only a relatively few tons'. For his part, poor Monckton, according to his biographer, worked himself to exhaustion.[9] His conciliatory efforts, however, also succeeded in the dock dispute, although it was not eventually settled until 4 July. Yet he was without the consolation of anticipating just how golden his period as the oil-can of St James's Square would seem when glimpsed through the jaundiced eyes of later generations. Indeed, there is evidence that in the mid-1950s Newsam, whose forte according to his colleagues lay in emergency planning rather than in other areas of Home Office work, was asked to draw up a revised plan for handling the consequences of a general strike. In the aftermath of the 1955 strikes Sir Anthony Eden also considered the possibility of legislation to restrict trade union powers, but he abandoned this idea in the face of TUC advice.[10]

Though its officials had no way of knowing it, the Emergencies Organisation was about to enter a relatively tranquil decade. The government did not need to wheel out the Emergency Powers Act again until eleven years, three Prime Ministers and several TUC General Councils later when Harold Wilson found himself confronted by a National Union of Seamen in militant mood. There were, nevertheless, a few incidents of note during these years. In March 1957 Harold Macmillan, two months after having become Prime Minister, was faced with a wave of industrial unrest with threatened strikes in the shipbuilding and engineering industries, the power stations and on the railways. During the afternoon of 15 March Macmillan reviewed the government's contingency plans. 'The emergency organisation is working well,' he noted in his diary, 'the regional organisation is being re-activated; we have quite enough troops (soldiers, airmen and sailors) without bringing back any from Germany. But it will be a fierce struggle.'[11] In the event only the shipbuilders and engineers came out and emergency powers were not required. The following May there was a full-scale strike of London busmen. Since both the Underground and suburban railway services continued to run, there was no need for the government to make explicit emergency arrangements. During the fourth week of the stoppage, however, it seemed possible that oil tanker drivers might strike in sympathy. At this stage officials clearly dusted off the 1953 plans. On 30 May the Ministry of Fuel and Power advised all motorists to conserve fuel. The War Office stopped weekend leave for 6,000 troops, most of whom were drivers. Macmillan explained that these moves were merely precautionary. The tanker drivers' strike did not materialise and the crisis passed, but it was a further two weeks before the busmen returned to work.[12] Servicemen were actually employed on strikebreaking duties only once between 1955 and 1966. In 1960, during an unofficial seamen's dispute, the navy carried supplies to the Western Isles of Scotland.

The only other significant event in this decade was a change in the law. Following the bad winter of 1962–3, when troops had been extensively employed for relief work, the government of Sir Alec Douglas-Home took the little-noted and, at the time, uncontroversial step of amending the Emergency Powers Act 1920 and making permanent Defence Regulation 6. Section 1(1) of the 1920 statute enabled the government to proclaim a state of emergency if it appeared that 'any action has been taken or is immediately threatened by any persons or body of persons' which was likely to deprive the community of the essentials of life. By the Emergency Powers Act 1964[13] the reference to 'action by . . . any persons or body of persons', which clearly referred to labour stoppages, was changed and broadened to cover the actual or probable occurrence of 'events'. This, explained the Home Secretary to Parliament, was simply to enable the government to proclaim an emergency to meet disruption caused by abnormal weather, natural disasters or 'interference from abroad'. He defended in similar terms the permanent codification of Defence Regulation 6, emphasising the humanitarian work which servicemen could perform. The Bill as a whole, he declared, 'is a wise exercise in foresight. It is an insurance policy against contingencies – remote contingencies perhaps, but real ones nevertheless.' The only significant criticism levelled against the measure by the opposition was of its timing. Evidently a government cannot win when introducing emergency legislation. If they do so during a crisis, they are accused of being provocative. If in tranquil times, the opposition will deny the need for any action at all. Chuter Ede spoke briefly in the Second Reading debate. He had no real objection to the Bill provided, he said, that power to employ troops on non-military tasks was only used for the benevolent purposes outlined by the Home Secretary.[14] Ede, however, ought to have had a shrewd idea that this would not be the case. After all, he himself in 1947 had widened the remit of the emergency organisation to include natural disasters in order to make the organisation more acceptable to the public. Since 1964, proclamations of emergency have only been made to meet industrial disruption, and under the 1964 Act, without an emergency proclamation, troops have been used on a number of occasions to break strikes. One difficulty which the government did not clear up in 1964 was the apparently dubious legality of emergency powers over local authorities, which had intermittently exercised the Home Office since the mid-1930s. Perhaps at this stage they had shelved any plans to involve local authorities in the emergency machine.

The seven-week seamen's dispute of May-July 1966 will leave a vivid trace on post-war British history for two quite separate reasons. First, it helped kill Labour's 'National Plan' less than a year into its life, a blow from which the Wilson administration's economic strategy never recovered. Second, it inspired the Prime Minister to read to the Commons very thinly disguised MI5 reports about the 'tightly knit group of politically motivated men' behind the Communist Party's attempt to manipulate the dispute for its wider purposes.[15] Not even the Attlee government in the 1949 dock strike had gone so far in reproducing Security Service material for public consumption. One has to go back to Baldwin in 1927 and the so-called 'Arcos raid', when Special Branch officers broke into the Soviet trade mission in London, for such a clear example of raw intelligence data being flaunted in Parliament.

For all the high drama of the late spring and early summer of 1966, the roots of the seamen's dispute were prosaic enough. A once-docile union (which had not joined the general strike), in an industry where organising a mobile and dispersed workforce is extremely difficult, sought both flat pay increases and consolidation of a complicated system of overtime and weekend pay arrangements. The concentration on wages prompted a new dimension that was to recur in several disputes in essential industries over the next fifteen years: the government's resolve to stick to a prices and incomes policy. This played an important part in exacerbating the seamen's strike. Richard Crossman, at that stage Minister of Housing and Local Government, was absolutely convinced it made the crucial difference between settlement and strike. In his diary entry for 19 May, three days into the stoppage, he noted:

> Cabinet felt that there was no alternative but to back George Brown [First Secretary of State and Minister for Economic Affairs] and his prices and incomes policy. If it hadn't been for that the Cabinet would have been for standing aside and letting the ship-owners do what they always wanted to do. We have got to be clear with ourselves that it is we, the Labour Cabinet, who have prevented the ship-owners from surrendering to the seamen, simply because a surrender would have made nonsense of the 3½ per-cent-norm and given the men too big an increase. We are paying a very high price for George Brown and his policies.[16]

Harold Wilson had given Crossman some ground for this judgment in his television broadcast on the evening the strike began. Adopting the kind of language used by Edward Heath and James Callaghan in the mid and late 1970s during winter crises in which their own marques of incomes policy came under strain, Wilson said that 'to accept this demand would breach the dykes of our prices and incomes policy.' To abandon the policy 'would mean the end of our hopes of solving our national economic problems on a basis of maintaining full employment.' In his broadcast the Prime Minister castigated reactionary employers and a stubborn NUS. In Baldwinian terms he described the stoppage as 'a strike against the state – against the community'. Contingency plans were ready. The Royal Navy was standing by to carry supplies to isolated parts of the nation, such as Orcadia and the Hebrides. A state of emergency would be declared if it became necessary.[17]

In 1966 the Whitehall emergency organisation was the bailiwick of Sir Charles Cunningham, Permanent Secretary to the Home Office and a veteran of the contingency planning community. For many years head of the Scottish Office's home and health department, he had been present at Maxwell's meeting in June 1945 which paved the way for the rebuilding of the emergency apparatus after the war. Sir Charles retired on 30 June 1966, the day after the seamen had decided to return to work. The minister in charge of the Emergencies Committee was the up-and-coming Home Secretary, Roy Jenkins. Disappointingly for the contemporary historian, the chief 'whistleblower' of the Wilson Cabinet, Crossman, declined to serve on it during the dispute 'because I get bored sitting there under Jenkins, doing nothing'.[18] Crossman's attitude was slightly surprising, as earlier in his diary he had been expressing outrage that the Labour government was making an example of the seamen after allowing substantial pay increases for doctors, judges and civil servants. He was also worried that the strike 'may go on all through the summer, although it may involve the docks and although there may be clashes between the dockers and the armed forces.'[19]

On 23 May, the eighth day of the strike, the government reached for its powers under the 1920 Act and declared a state of emergency. Foreign vessels were continuing to enter British ports and the government were worried that congestion caused by immobilised ships would result in perishables and essential supplies rotting before they could be unloaded. Thirty-four emergency regulations were promulgated, giving ministers power to fix maximum prices of specified foodstuffs, to control ports and dock labour in order to relieve congestion, to restrict postal services, to relax restrictions on road transport, to requisition ships, vehicles and aircraft, and to prevent sabotage. RAF Transport Command stood by to move post and parcels to Northern Ireland, which had been particularly badly hit, and the navy were ready to move supplies to the Scottish Islands. The government were clearly anxious to keep the use of the services as limited as possible. Although the NUS announced that they would allow the passage of essential goods, they warned that if the Prime Minister used the navy to move strikebound ships, 'we will go to the precipice and we will go right over, and take him with us.'[20] Since the seamen did not stop work until their ships reached a British port, the stoppage developed relatively gradually and there was no need at first to employ extensive emergency action. But when the regulations came up for renewal on 22 June, the government announced the establishment of port emergency committees to act as agents for the Ministry of Transport, on the model of the London port emergency committee during the 1949 dock strike. They were given powers to keep out vessels that might add to congestion and operated in Bristol, Glasgow, Grimsby, Hull, Leith, Liverpool, London, Manchester, Middlesbrough, Southampton, Newcastle and the south Wales ports.[21] Two days earlier the Prime Minister had dropped what can only be described as his bombshell about the hidden men behind the strike.

In the Commons on 20 June Wilson did not mention the Communist Party of Great Britain by name, but the message was clear to all. Eight days later to the absolute consternation of the Security Service themselves, he named and provided considerable detail of who had met whom at a specified address, material clearly drawn from MI5 surveillance.[22] In his memoirs Sir Harold describes how he furnished Edward Heath, Leader of the Opposition, with his evidence privately, just as Harold Macmillan had done for him a few years earlier to explain why Kim Philby, the MI6 man who spied for Russia, had been allowed to escape to the Soviet Union. He recalled:

> My earlier statement led to strong denunciation from the left, and a challenge from the press and Opposition to publish my evidence. Mr. Heath asked to see me and the press were informed of his concern at my statement. He pressed me to give more facts and to produce the evidence on which I relied. I decided to make all the facts available to him on Privy Counsellor terms, and for good measure to bring to our meeting their senior people responsible for these matters, and one of the operators in the field.[23]

More than a decade later, Chapman Pincher, former defence correspondent of the *Daily Express*, who, it seems, had subsequently become privy to Sir Harold's thoughts on MI5 and similar organisations, returned to the seamen's strike in some detail:

> Wilson was provided with irrefutable evidence by MI5, including records of bugged conversations and photographs of intercepted documents, that the strike was being orchestrated by a few communists imposing their will on the others and determined to bring in the dockers and other workers so that the country could be brought to a standstill.[24]

At the time it was widely, and possibly correctly, believed that Wilson's exposure of Communist influence helped inspire a revulsion amongst rank-and-file seamen which assisted in ending the strike. The Communist party, said George Wigg, then Paymaster-General, 'threw up the sponge'. On 29 June the NUS executive voted to call off the strike after the employers had offered additional annual leave. The strike ended at midnight on 1 July; the state of emergency on 5 July. It had affected more than 900 ships and 27,000 seamen.[25] The Labour Cabinet swiftly tottered into the financial crisis of July 1966, felt obliged to deflate and, in all but name, abandon its plan for economic recovery. Three years later the government tried and failed to curb trade union power with its *In Place of Strife* proposals, settling instead for a 'solemn and binding' undertaking from the TUC to put its own house in order, which is where matters rested when Labour lost the 1970 general election.

Applying the ready-reckoner of states of emergency declared under the 1920 Act,[26] the premiership of Edward Heath stands alone. Of the twelve occasions a proclamation has been issued in the past sixty-two years, five of them occurred between 1970 and 1974. Indeed the three occupants of 10 Downing Street since Heath's departure – despite a number of near misses – have managed to avoid applying the full might of the 1920 statute, though on several occasions its less awesome 1964 twin has been used. The two decades of comparative desuetude between the disappearance of the Attlee government and the installation of the Heath administration in June 1970 left the Whitehall emergencies machinery somewhat unprepared for the difficulties that were to descend upon it in rapid succession. It took some time for a full appreciation to be made of just how far technological advances had tilted the balance of power against the government in handling industrial disputes that endangered the country's essential services. The first major stoppage which the government had to face, however, recalled the 1940s. On 14 July, less than a month after the general election, 42,000 dockers throughout the country came out on strike. Two days later the government, resolved to stand firm against inflationary wage claims, declared a state of emergency. In order to avoid the employment of service labour the strikers themselves agreed to move perishable cargoes. The stoppage ended on 3 August after a Court of Inquiry had awarded a moderate pay rise, regarded by the dockers as 'an interim measure'. In September a wave of strikes by local authority workers raised the possibility that servicemen might be needed to operate pumps in sewage stations, and soldiers were actually deployed as dustmen in the London borough of Tower Hamlets.[27]

But the new realities of trade union power were sharply brought home to the Heath administration by a 'go-slow' in the electricity supply industry during December 1970. Douglas Hurd, then political secretary to the Prime Minister, wrote in his diary for 7 December: 'Cold, and the electricity go-slow hits harder and quicker than expected.' Next day he noted: 'A bad day. It is clear that all the weeks of planning in the Civil Service have totally failed to cope with what is happening in the electricity dispute; and all the pressures are to surrender.'[28] On 12 December the government proclaimed its second state of emergency within five months, in order to take authority to regulate electricity supplies. In Parliament, the Secretary of State for Trade and Industry declared that it was quite impracticable to use troops in the power stations.[29] Faced with the apparently irresistible power of the electricity workers, the government quickly settled the dispute with a relatively generous – and inflationary – pay rise. The emergency powers were withdrawn on 17 December. Towards the end of the dispute Douglas Hurd sent a minute to the Prime Minister with a suggestion that the practical side of contingency planning be reviewed, and that something be done to improve the Emergencies Committee. His warning went unheeded. It took a more sustained and dramatic dispute to bring home to the government and people the shift in favour of union power engineered by a combination of new technology, the strength of unions enjoying a monopoly position, and the sense of its own power felt by a trade union movement that had successfully resisted the attempt to reform it by a Labour government in 1969, and was well on the way to doing the same to Heath's Industrial Relations Act.

The national miners' strike of January-February 1972, the first since 1926, marked the moment of the new awareness. It was preceded by a ten-week overtime ban at the pits which ran down coal stocks. On 9 January 1972 the strike began. For an entire month the government did nothing practical to conserve coal supplies. Anxious perhaps not to repeat the precipitate proclamations of 1970, a state of emergency was not declared until 9 February. On the next day an event occurred that has haunted contingency planners ever since. Saltley coke depot in Birmingham was closed after a six-day struggle involving, at peak moments, 800 police and 15,000 massed secondary pickets, many of whom were 'flying pickets', transported from all over the country. By the time it was closed, Saltley contained the nation's last substantial stockpile of coke for gas works and power stations.[30] Shortages of fuel, especially for power stations, had caused crippling and destructive power cuts, put industry on a two-day week and even threatened a complete shutdown. This was more than the government could tolerate. They accepted that the miners were 'a special case' and conceded pay rises well above the limits set before the dispute began. The effectiveness of the miners' secondary pickets, enabling them to control power supplies with the passive support of their trade union colleagues, meant that one union in the 1970s could do what both the Triple Alliance and the general strike had failed to do in the 1920s. It is a demon still to be exorcised in the contingency planning community.

The significance of Saltley was not lost on the principals concerned, as two commentaries made three years after the event illustrate. Brendon Sewill, in 1972 special adviser to the Chancellor of the Exchequer, wrote:

At the time many of those in positions of influence looked into the abyss and saw only a few days away the possibility of the country being plunged into a state of chaos not so very far removed from that which might prevail after a minor nuclear attack. If that sounds melodramatic I need only say that – with the prospect of the breakdown of power supplies, food supplies, sewerage, communications, effective government and law and order – it was the analogy that was being used at the time. This is the power that exists to hold the country to ransom: it was fear of that abyss which had an important effect on subsequent policy.[31]

Arthur Scargill of the National Union of Mineworkers' (NUM) Barnsley area strike committee, who had turned flying secondary pickets into a national phenomenon overnight, saw matters from a rather different perspective:

You see, we took the view that we were in a class war. We were not playing cricket on the village green, like they did in '26. We were out to defeat Heath and Heath's policies because we were fighting a government. Anyone who thinks otherwise was living in cloud-cuckoo land. We had to declare *war* on them and the only way you could declare war was to attack the vulnerable points. They were the points of *energy:* the power stations, the coke depots, the coal depots, the points of supply. And this is what we did.[32]

Conventional wisdom in Whitehall has it that the central government's handling of the 1972 miners' strike was a shambles, that the old Emergencies Organisation, as developed in the late 1940s, had rusted throughout the 1950s and 1960s, and finally fell apart when required to tackle the economic and physical consequences of Mr Scargill. This view is directly challenged by some of the excellent quality officials who were involved in it throughout the period. The 'shambles' story, they claim, was put about by the Cabinet Office, who took over responsibility for civil emergency planning in the aftermath of the 1972 crisis, in order to justify their imperialism at the expense of the Home Office. The real reason for the move, according to this school of thought, was the difficult relationship between the Prime Minister and his Home Secretary, Reginald Maudling. Heath wanted to bypass a colleague in whom he had lost confidence. From his memoirs it is clear that Maudling absorbed a lot of criticism from his own side over the Saltley *débâcle*, but the tail end of his recollection shows that, whatever his shortcomings may or may not have been, Maudling had a ripe appreciation of the limits to the use of troops in industrial disputes in the 1970s:

I remember when during the miners' strike pickets threatened to close the Birmingham Coal Depot [*sic*], and, in fact, succeeded in doing so, the then Chief Constable of Birmingham assured me that only over his dead body would they so succeed. I felt constrained to ring him the next day after it happened to enquire after his health! I am sure the decision he took was a wise one, because the number of strikers involved was so great, and feelings were running so high, that any attempt by the relatively small body of Police who could be assembled to keep the Depot open by force could have led to very grave consequences. Some of my colleagues asked me afterwards, why I had not sent in troops to support the Police, and I remember asking them one simple question: 'If they had been sent in, should they have gone in with their rifles loaded or unloaded?' Either course could have been disastrous.[33]

Heath was evidently dissatisfied with the way the Emergency Organisation had primed ministers for handling the miners' strike. That and the quantum leap in trade union power demonstrated by the massed secondary picket outside the Saltley Depot led him to commission a thoroughgoing review of the civil emergency planning machine to be carried out by Lord Jellicoe (Lord Privy Seal) and John (later Lord) Hunt, at that stage a Cabinet Office Deputy Secretary. The outcome of the review was a refashioned, streamlined emergencies organisation, the Civil Contingencies Unit (CCU), located in the Cabinet Office and having the status of a standing Cabinet committee. It has remained to this day the central government's principal mechanism for meeting the effects of stoppages in essential industries. Within Whitehall it is sometimes known by the acronym 'Cuckoo'. Shortly after it had been established, the CCU had to face a dock strike. The government's action followed that of 1970. A state of emergency was proclaimed on 3 August 1972 as a precaution against possible food shortages. The Home Secretary, Robert Carr, told the Commons that the emergency regulations were 'not directed against the dockers or their union. Their purpose is not to break the strike. It is to protect the life of the community.' Port emergency committees were set up. Arrangements were made for the RAF to airlift fuel oil to the Scottish islands, while the dockers agreed to co-operate in moving other essential supplies. The government promised that they would strive to avoid using troops. The dispute, caused by a number of grievances arising out of containerisation and working conditions generally, lasted for less than a month. A compromise settlement was reached in the third week of August and by the end of the month all the strikers had returned to work. The state of emergency was allowed to lapse on 2 September.[34]

The secretary of the CCU from 1972 until his death in 1981 was Brigadier R. J. 'Dick' Bishop. No one else in Whitehall stayed longer at the epicentre of the industrial earthquakes that disturbed Britain in the 1970s. Bishop joined the civil service after leaving the army in 1972 and was straightway put in charge of planning and running the Cabinet Office emergencies organisation. With the office's communications experts he was responsible for keeping the Cabinet Office's 'doomsday' operations centre in running order. Known in Whitehall as 'COBRA' (Cabinet Office Briefing Room), it is fitted with a large table around which CCU ministers and officials sit. A cluster of microphones drop out of the ceiling and enable the Home Secretary, who chairs the committee whenever ministers are present, to speak directly with Chief Constables and major-generals in the military districts up and down the country. Brigadier Bishop, who doubled up as Secretary of the legendary Cabinet Office mess where the nation's bureaucratic power brokers are said to swap confidences, always declined with great courtesy to speak to the press. But with his battle scars from the winter crises of 1972, 1973–4 and 1979, he became something of a friend and mentor for new recruits to the slightly alarming world of the contingency planning community. 'He's been through everything. Dick is a mine of information,' as one of them put it. He died suddenly in harness on 3 May 1981 and received a warm obituary tribute prepared by the Cabinet Secretary, Sir Robert Armstrong, who noted how Bishop had built up an organisation not simply concerned with industrial stoppages, but to meet any type of civil emergency. 'What was required was an organisation which could be brought into effective action at an hour's notice, at any time of the day or night, and stay in action, day and night if necessary, for as many hours, days or weeks as circumstances demanded.'[35] The modern development of the official contingency machine has extended further than even Chuter Ede envisaged. It should not only be prepared for industrial crises and natural disasters, but also hijackings and other terrorist threats. The CCU has close links with the civil defence structure and, as in 1939, much of the civil emergency organisation can easily be adapted to meet possible wartime requirements.

One of Brigadier Bishop's first tasks was to draw up a list of vital services and industries most vulnerable to union action. By early 1973 he had completed detailed appraisals of sixteen key industries, their capacity for disruption, their importance to the country's well-being, and the possibility of using alternative military labour in the event of strikes. Then, as now, electricity supply was top of the list. Others have moved up and down as amendments have been made in the light of experience. After the winter crisis of 1979, for example, the road haulage industry rose somewhat higher than the sixteenth place it occupied in 1972–3. Water supply, always in the top ten, was shifted in 1979 to join the docks, coal, rail and oil in the group just beneath power, as the placidity of its labour force could no longer be taken for granted. Even in the early 1970s the docility of *any* group of workers was increasingly becoming a thing of the past. In October 1973, for example, there was a firemen's strike in Glasgow, and 500 troops were deployed on strikebreaking duties under the 1964 Act.

Contingency planning since 1972 has been directed towards mitigating the consequences of industrial strength exercised in the direct, Saltley manner. The means do not exist for curbing that power in a once-and-for-all fashion and no government has yet sought to create them. When in late 1973 a re-run of the 1972 coal strike seemed certain, there was acute anxiety in Whitehall. The 1973–4 'winter crisis' arose from a number of factors.[36] On the union side there was resistance to 'Stage Three' of the government's prices and incomes policy, which depended on a complex and restrictive mixture of price controls, productivity agreements, bonus schemes and 'threshold payments' designed to keep step with the Retail Price Index. The government, for their part, were strongly determined to resist inflationary wage claims. In November 1973 both the miners and the electrical power engineers began campaigns of industrial action in support of pay demands above the limits set by Stage Three. Although stopping short of actual strikes, their action caused a sharp drop – between 20 and 25 per cent – in coal production and an almost immediate series of unpredictable power cuts. Early in December ASLEF banned Sunday, overtime and rest-day working, which restricted the movement of coal to power stations. Magnifying the effects of these domestic disputes was the sudden cutback in Middle Eastern oil supplies imposed by the Arab oil-producing countries in the aftermath of the 1973 October War. On 13 November the government proclaimed a state of emergency and the following day imposed the first in a long line of orders restricting the use of electricity. Since 1972 steps had been taken to build up strategic reserves of fuel and to provide emergency generating equipment for hospitals and other institutions. In mid-December the Prime Minister announced that, in order to conserve fuel, a three-day working week would be introduced in the New Year. With the return of the power engineers to normal working at the end of December, having received a pay settlement technically within Stage Three, the government were able to apply power cuts on a selective and systematic basis. The coal dispute, however, dragged on through January. While government, TUC, NUM, the Confederation of British Industries and the Pay Board all became involved in the search for a settlement, the Prime Minister stood firmly against the miners' claim. On 4 February the miners voted to come out on strike. Three days later Heath called a general election, apparently posing the question: 'Who governs the country?' On 9 February the miners began their strike. Last-minute attempts to settle the dispute before the election came to nothing. On 28 February 1974 a House of Commons was returned in which neither Conservative nor Labour had an absolute majority,[37] but on 4 March Harold Wilson formed his final administration. The miners returned to work on 11 March with a pay award which had been specially exempted from Stage Three.

Given its limited aims, the CCU stood up well to the test of the 1973–4 winter crisis. A prime reason was the successful efforts of the NUM to prevent ugly scenes on picket lines during the election campaign for fear of jeopardising Labour's chances at the polls. On top of that, the policy of declaring a state of emergency in plenty of time to conserve fuel supplies paid off. The difficulties of forecasting, as usual, bedevilled the planners. What would run short first, electricity or essential raw materials such as steel? Would industrial paralysis come in stages, or would the bulk of industry suddenly collapse together? To everybody's surprise production during the three-day week was maintained at 75 per cent of normal, even when working hours were cut by 40 per cent. Nevertheless, one official remembers 'it was pretty close at the end'.

The main prop of the returning Wilson government for the first eighteen months of its life was comparatively harmonious relations with the trade unions. This happy state of affairs no doubt contributed to the narrow Labour victory in the October 1974 election.[38] There were no major stoppages in Great Britain, although early in the government's life events in Northern Ireland demonstrated the vulnerability of the nation's vital infrastructure to an uncompromising withdrawal of labour. On 14 May 1974 the Ulster Workers' Council (UWC) began a 'general' strike in protest against the 'power-sharing' Executive and the proposed Council of Ireland contained in the Sunningdale Agreement of December 1973.[39] The UWC shrewdly concentrated their attention on restricting generation at the province's three power stations, although with the help of widespread intimidation they also closed down most industrial concerns. Over the fourteen days of the strike electricity output was reduced to 10 per cent of normal. With the assistance of middle management technical operators electricity supplies were maintained throughout the province, though at times there were twelve-hour power cuts. The government examined various possibilities to counter the UWC. 'Military establishments at home and abroad', recalled Harold Wilson, 'were combed for specialists of various kinds, particularly those who could help keep the power stations in operation.' Although a 'useful number' of such specialists were produced,[40] following a discreet reconnaissance of the main power station at Ballylumford by six army technicians in plain clothes, the army concluded that they could not run the station without the co-operation of the civilian control room operators, who threatened to withdraw if the army came in. The Northern Ireland Electricity Service were unable to use their own emergency reserve gas turbine generators since the fuel required for these was itself cut off by the UWC. After ten days of the strike the telephone system began to break down as the GPO's standby generators ran out of butane gas. A wild idea, recalling the London docks in 1926, to take power from a nuclear submarine moored in Belfast Lough was dismissed as impractical. The strike came to a head over the weekend of 26–7 May when the army finally took over oil depots and began distributing fuel from a number of filling stations. The UWC threatened a complete electricity stoppage. To meet the real possibility of pumping works shutting down and raw sewage spilling on to the streets, arrangements were started to organise decontamination squads. Since road haulage was at a standstill, the government also prepared plans for food distribution. On 28 May the Executive resigned and the strike was called off. The whole affair constituted a sombre lesson in the ability of the armed services to break a large-scale strike.

Localised stoppages, however, are a different matter. In March 1975 a strike of Glasgow dustmen resulted in troops once again being engaged there on strikebreaking work. Servicemen, indeed, can be used extensively where relatively unskilled work is involved. This was the case in the firemen's strike from November 1977 to January 1978. Espousing firm incomes restraint and haunted by the memory of the 1976 currency collapse, the Callaghan government resolved to resist the firemen's claim, which broke the official 10 per cent pay 'norm'. Service labour was deployed on a widespread scale. During the three-month stoppage in order to replace 32,000 strikers over 20,000 troops in all were used, assisted by 4,000 senior fire officers and large numbers of part-time firemen. Apparently to avoid provocation by crossing picket lines, the troops did not use Fire Service appliances, but hurriedly prepared 'Green Goddess' fire engines, retained in mothballs for possible civil defence needs.[41] More to the point, without a proclamation of emergency under the 1920 Act, the government had no power to requisition the Fire Service machines.

One of the more intriguing side-effects of the firemen's strike was that it led the Ministry of Defence and the Home Office to undertake the first review of emergencies legislation for more than a decade. To meet the dispute, James Callaghan, with the memory of Heath's five states of emergency in four years still green, preferred to make use of Section 2 of the 1964 Act when applying troops to break the strike. The procedure under this Section is that the military can be used in industrial disputes without Parliamentary approval if their use is authorised by a Defence Council Order (DCO), issued by order of the Defence Council and signed by two of its members, neither of whom need necessarily be a member of the political executive. An emergency proclamation can be avoided, provided the government does not need powers to requisition property or equipment, or to save energy reserves by placing industry on a three-day week. Shortly after the strike ended, the magazine *State Research* noticed that in Queen's Regulations, under the heading 'Military Aid to Civil Ministries' (the official euphemism for strike-breaking), regulation J11.004(b) read as follows:

> Where there is no proclamation and the emergency is limited and local, the Defence Council may, under the Emergency Powers Act 1964, authorise service personnel to be temporarily employed on work which the Council have approved as being urgent work of national importance.

The 'Green Goddesses', *State Research* observed, had been used on a widespread and national scale. The Ministry of Defence, avid readers of the underground press, looked into the problem. Officials discovered that the words 'limited and local' had been inserted into the Queen's Regulations in the 1960s without any thought being given to the matter. They were deleted in June 1978.[42] The ministry admitted it was embarrassed by the sharp-sighted-ness of *State Research*. Whitehall believes, however, that the 'superfluous' phrase never affected the basis of the 1964 Act, which was intended to place beyond doubt the legality of orders given to servicemen assigned to non-military duties of an emergency kind. Queen's Regulations, it was pointed out, are administrative guidelines and not a source of legal authority. That the regulation, revised or not, ignored the proclaimed intention of the 1964 Act does not seem to have bothered the Ministry of Defence. Officials also maintained that action taken under a DCO can be accounted for to Parliament by the Secretary of State for Defence who, as Chairman of the Defence Council, is answerable to the House of Commons, and that the government, therefore, had a watertight basis for using troops in industrial emergencies. A similar question of legality of orders was raised privately in Whitehall when the military came to terms with new realities after the mass picketing at Saltley. The police are responsible for clearing a way for military convoys passing in and out of picketed installations. If, however, a Chief Constable sees his men being overwhelmed, he can under common law invoke the assistance of the military present in aid of the civil power. It was not clear to senior officers in 1972 what the commander on the spot should do in such circumstances. The answer to that is now apparent. He can accede to the request of the Chief Constable immediately, without recourse to senior officers or the Defence Secretary. In practice, however, as Sir Robert Mark disclosed in his Metropolitan Police Commissioner's report for 1975, the Chief Constable would first seek permission from the Home Secretary, who in turn would consult his colleague at Defence.

In the late 1970s the CCU revised a number of detailed plans to meet specific contingencies, including an oil tanker drivers' strike, a problem which had exercised emergency planners twice in the 1950s. Towards the end of 1977 a scheme, code-named 'Operation Raglan', was worked out by which 3,000 troops manning requisitioned tankers would distribute fuel. The country would be divided into five 'Emergency Divisions', each to be supervised by one of the five main oil companies.[43] In February 1978 the code-name was changed to 'Drumstick' and in November 1981 it emerged as 'Leadburn'. During the Callaghan government's winter crisis of January-March 1979, ministers and officials reviewed a series of emergency schemes with similarly exotic titles. Operation 'Brisket' was drawn up to cope with a road haulage stoppage, 'Bittern' to meet an ambulance drivers' dispute and 'Nimrod' for trouble in the water industry. Gerald Kaufman, a junior minister at the Depart-

ment of Industry who was appointed to assist the Home Secretary
with emergency preparations, suggested that the next plan would
be called 'Loony'.[44] The 'winter of discontent', prompted by Callaghan's determination to enforce 5 per cent pay limits, contributed
substantially to Labour's loss of the May 1979 general election and
its replacement by a government under Margaret Thatcher which
is still, at the time of writing, engaged upon a 'search and destroy'
mission against the more important conventional wisdoms of post-
war British politics. A spate of bad weather tumbled into a road
haulage dispute, which, with a rash of public service disputes involving hospital workers and local authority employees, produced
general national misery, as bins went unemptied and food supplies
dwindled inconveniently, though not fatally, in the shops.

At Cabinet level the Prime Minister set up a secret *ad hoc* committee, known as 'GEN 158' and chaired by the Home Secretary.
Of the officials in the central emergency organisation only Brigadier
Bishop and Sir Clive Rose, a Deputy Secretary in the Cabinet Office
and Chairman of the CCU, regularly attended this ministerial group.
The CCU itself, with a mixture of ministers and officials, met two
or three times each day at the Cabinet Office, and its regional
network swung into operation in a manner not seen since Heath's
three-day week of early 1974. Throughout England and Wales
eleven Regional Emergencies Committees (RECs) were established.
Based on the regional economic planning boards, with officials from
the Departments of Environment, Trade, Transport, Energy, Employment and Agriculture, the RECs also included representatives
of the local authorities, the police and the military. Beyond the
RECs in any emergency there is a fallback in the home defence
system, which comprises regional seats of government, designed to
co-ordinate administration after a nuclear attack. If there is a severe
breakdown of food distribution arising from an industrial dispute,
the home defence emergency feeding depots, using strategic stockpiles of food, might be activated as a last resort. Short of such
desperate circumstances, home defence's secure telephones and tel-
exes are a useful adjunct to the often overloaded lines between RECs
and London. The RECs can exercise executive functions if the
government takes powers to limit energy consumption under the
1920 Act. In 1973-4, for example, regional offices were able to grant
permits to local companies with standby generators to work longer
hours than those prescribed by the three-day week.

The role of the RECs can be illustrated by showing how they fitted into the CCU's daily timetable during the 1979 dispute. At 8.30 each morning the regional committee chairmen would meet official representatives of the TGWU. They were not permitted to meet others, whether pickets or unofficial strikers, for fear of undermining the authority of the official union leadership. A representative of the Manpower Services Commission would attend to give the latest estimate of lay-offs resulting from the strike, based on figures from the Department of Employment's local offices. Next the chairmen would consult representatives of the Road Haulage Association and the Confederation of British Industry to gauge the general position in the region. Additional information would come from the RECs' reporting centres responsible for receiving evidence of alleged breaches of the TGWU's voluntary code on picketing. Then the full RECs would meet. By 11.30 a.m. telex reports from each region would be in the Department of Transport's emergency operations room in London. By 2.00 p.m. a summary of the national position would be with Brigadier Bishop in the Cabinet Office. An hour later he would have an agenda prepared for a full CCU meeting under the Home Secretary, Merlyn Rees, at which decisions would be taken on which definite cases of disruption to the voluntary code should be put before the TGWU. At that stage a most unusual meeting in constitutional terms would take place. Three senior civil servants from the CCU would call on the TGWU. They were Sir Clive Rose, Peter Lazarus from Transport and John Moss from Agriculture. For the TGWU, Alex Kitson would promise to do what he could. The next morning at 8.30 REC chairmen would see if Kitson had prevailed and the cycle would start again.

The RECs worked best where departmental and regional boundaries were conterminous, and where officials with experience of past winter crises knew how to avoid swamping the CCU with superfluous material. Some in the upper reaches of Whitehall preferred, in the end, to use the military network as the most reliable source of information. Soldiers have two advantages over civil servants in such circumstances: they are trained to ask direct questions ('how many ambulancemen have come out, how many army ambulances do you need to provide minimum cover?'); and they know how to grade crises. Indiscriminate use of the word 'crisis' weighed down many of the reports reaching the CCU. The major-generals in the military districts are a hidden source of strength. Most make a point of getting to know regional local authority chief executives, as well as leading trade unionists. Many of the weaknesses in the REC system arise from the difficulty of predicting danger points in advance. No two 'strike seasons' are the same. In the north-west in 1979, for example, it was believed that Merseyside would be the focus of most trouble, but Manchester docks, not Liverpool, proved to be more troublesome. The greatest difficulty of all was picketing outside the British Salt plant at Middlewich in Cheshire. However well the regional reporting system and the London organisation worked, the realities of union life often brought the emergency staff near despair. After vigorous protests to TGWU officials the Middlewich pickets might melt away, and salt, essential to the food proceesing industry, would get through, only for secondary pickets to reappear a few hours later. 'It was rather like punching a pillow,' a civil servant said at the time. During the 1979 public service workers' disputes relatively little use was made of the armed forces. To counter the effects of ambulance drivers' strikes, however, army and RAF personnel and vehicles were deployed in a number of cases. But it is significant that, both in the ambulance drivers' dispute and the seven-month social workers' strike which ended in February 1979, there was a very extensive reliance on police resources. It was a far cry from Sir John Anderson's insistence in 1926 that the Metropolitan Police should not deliver medical supplies on the grounds that such action would undermine their position of impartiality.

Among the most serious contingencies exercising CCU planners at the end of the 1970s were the possibility of stoppages in two particular industries: electricity and water. Strikes in the electricity supply industry have preoccupied emergency planners for over sixty years. In no other sector are the consequences of breakdown so swift, widespread or devastating in their effects on manufacturing industry, sewage and water pumping stations, and households. One insider has described a national power failure as 'the slippery path to hell'. Technology has moved relentlessly against the government in this area since 1945. It is over thirty years since troops were last sent into a British power station. The poor performance of the servicemen in 1950, coupled with the experience of the 1974 UWC strike, was recalled in March 1978 when members of the Electricity Council told the Department of Energy that they alone, and not the government, must implement contingency arrangements in the event of industrial trouble. The complexity of modern power stations places them far beyond the capacity of army engineers.

In the autumn of 1977 the CCU commissioned Richard Mottram of the Ministry of Defence to investigate the possibility of using troops. The conclusion was that there were not enough of them and that they were not up to it. There are about a hundred Royal Engineers, trained at Brompton Barracks, Chatham, holding a safety certificate from the Central Electricity Generating Board (CEGB), declaring them fit to control a power station. The great 2,000-megawatt coal-burning stations, the backbone of the grid, each need between 90 and 100 engineers to run them on a three-shift system. Such installations would seize up if soldiers, trained to run small power plants at army depots, were let loose on them. The tolerances on the boilers are so fine that danger of overload or even explosion is substantial if control is in unskilled hands. The Electricity Council has insisted, and the CCU accepted, that members of the 28,000-strong Electrical Power Engineers' Association (EPEA) are indispensable and irreplaceable. What Royal Engineer and Royal Electrical and Mechanical Engineer (REME) technicians could do is to help power engineers to keep more equipment going than might otherwise be the case – three rather than two 500-megawatt generators in a large coal-burner is the estimate. But such action would only be possible if EPEA men agreed to supervise the servicemen on maintenance and monitoring duties in place of striking manual workers.

The Electricity Council and the EPEA, however, are adamant that they would not welcome military assistance. The Council and the CEGB have drafted detailed contingency plans to protect the country from disaster. They are based on computer simulations of how the grid can shed its load in an orderly fashion without the danger to switching equipment, industrial appliances and household goods that an uncontrolled degradation of the system would bring. The authorities believe that with EPEA support they could sustain half of normal supplies, well above the 30 to 40 per cent range where run-down could become unstoppable, for a substantial time without manual workers' or military help. Their estimate was tested on 4 November 1977 when the 10.00 p.m. shift walked out at the four huge South Yorkshire coal-burning stations of Drax A, Ferrybridge C, Eggborough and Thorpe Marsh. Other stations in the Midlands suffered similar disruption. Engineers used to working in the control room took over, with some trepidation, such unfamiliar tasks as monitoring the pumps, fans and boilers, and even unloading coal. Most important of all, the handful of chemists at each station who maintain the critical purity of water supply for boilers stayed at work. In sustaining half of normal output until the unofficial action ended on 11 November, engineers at the stations and the National Grid Control Centre in London, with the five regional control centres, demonstrated great resource and stamina as the nation teetered closer to a three-day week than was appreciated outside the industry and the government at the time.

Power engineers are the most powerful group of workers in the country. The government has no alternative but to rely on them to keep a sense of responsibility to the public that has accompanied their power since they were granted the right to strike by Heath's Industrial Relations Act in 1971. A senior EPEA official said:

> If we decided to come out, that is it. We would beat any government. But I would not frighten people too much. There is no way that our members would come out and take on the government unless there was extreme pressure. To shut the whole system down is not a strike, it is a catastrophe. I do not think it is a power that ought to be used. It does not matter how many the army have got, if we will not let them in.
>
> If we were going to do the job of keeping the stations going we would stop anybody else. Technically, we could run a good half of the system by ourselves for a long time, almost indefinitely. However it is virtually inconceivable that we would run the system against an official strike of manual workers and it would depend on the circumstances what we would do if the action was unofficial.

If the grid did collapse, danger to public health would be the greatest worry. The water system can withstand rota power cuts of up to six hours. The Thames Water Authority, and many others, have standby generators at all their pumping stations. If those failed and mains supply became contaminated, households without power would find it very difficult to make supplies safe by boiling. Sodium hypochloride tablets are an effective disinfectant in trained hands, such as the Royal Engineers, but in untrained hands they are useless. Short of ultimate disaster, the CEGB has become increasingly diligent since the early 1970s in strengthening its hand against lesser but still worrying contingencies like a miners' strike, with secondary pickets preventing the movement of supplies into power stations. Apart from coal, power stations need other strategic supplies like chlorine for water treatment, hydrogen for cooling activators, furnace oil for starting the boilers and oxy-acetylene for maintenance staff. Two months' supply of those are kept on site. The British national grid is the strongest in the world, with more alternative routes for bringing power into conurbations than, say, the United States. If the unthinkable did happen, the damage would be enormous but the blackout would not be perpetual. Up and down the country the CEGB has placed in sheds alongside the boilers clusters of jet engines designed for Concorde and the Vulcan bomber. These gas turbines can be started from cold within two and a half minutes. Between them they can add almost 2,500 megawatts to the grid, enough to get the pumps, fans and boilers started again. Their unit cost is high, but as an insurance policy they are worth every penny.

After electricity, water supply is one of the contingency planners' most intense worries. The prospect of sewage in the streets is a politician's nightmare, and a vivid indication that the government has lost the capacity to govern. There has never been a national water strike. All the CCU has to go on is the experience of limited and local breakdowns such as the one which afflicted the Pennine division of the North West Water Authority in early 1979 when manual workers came out on unofficial strike. In January the North West Military District had 27 service water treatment teams on standby at Fulwood Barracks, Preston. Each unit consisted of a Land Rover, a driver, an electrician and a chlorine expert. A DCO had been prepared under the 1964 Act, and needed only the signature of two Council members for the operation to go ahead. But the water authorities were most reluctant to call in troops. Officials kept their talks with the military secret by meeting at a public house some distance from their Warrington headquarters. They applied great ingenuity to the task of fulfilling their twin responsibilities of treating sewage and supplying drinking water without military assistance. A number of expedients was used. Where the quality of raw water draining off the Pennines was high, treatment plants were by-passed and supply flowed directly from reservoir to household. Floculants, normally added to assist the coagulation of solids, were held back to eke out the time before filters became clogged. Supplies in the Bolton area were discoloured as a result, but health hazard was avoided and boiling recommended. Managerial staff went into treatment plants at night to carry out essential operations such as backwashing filters and applying chlorine to kill bacteria. Sewage was diverted from the Bolton treatment plant into the river. Of the 350,000 households in the Pennine division, 2,000 were affected. Of these, only 200 were totally without piped water because of bursts caused by frosts. The lesson of the north-west experience, and similar eruptions across the Pennines in Yorkshire, was that the government could 'win' a long-drawn-out battle with manual water workers provided the dispute was local and, above all, unofficial, enabling supervisory and managerial staff to keep working with easy consciences.

What genuinely frightens the planners is the unknown territory of an official national water strike. In 1979 the CCU updated its plan for dealing with such an eventuality. Unlike the electricity supply study, the widespread use of troops was contemplated. It concluded that the country could be saved from disaster in the guise of health hazard, provided supervisory staff co-operated. Without their assistance the attempt would fail. The bulk of the supervisory and managerial grades are members of the National and Local Government Officers' Association. The best guess is that most of them would stay at their posts during a national emergency, though some might take a minimalist position, confining themselves to performing their normal duties, but refusing to supervise REME servicemen ordered to work with them. The first stage of the plan requires for its implementation a proclamation of emergency under the 1920 Act, as water authority equipment would need to be requisitioned by the forces. All three services would provide personnel, with REME and Royal Navy electricians and Royal Engineer experts the most vital. The plan specifies the use of 3,000 technicians, 2,200 drivers and vehicles, and 5,000 general duties men. With control and command staff added, the total service complement would be about 15,000 men, close to the upper limit of troops available without severe disruption to NATO and Northern Ireland commitments. In addition to treatment teams of the type that stood by in Preston, four-ton army lorries with 400-gallon water tanks in the back and 200-ton trailers in tow, would be ready to move into areas where supplies became seriously contaminated. In a national emergency troops and equipment would be stretched very thinly across the country. The Cabinet would have no reserves of military labour to give assistance if other essential supplies and services were disrupted. Even if its concentration was not diverted, the planners believe that the government would have to step in very quickly to settle the dispute. If all 15,000 troops were deployed, the risks would still be very great. Probably a walk-out by supervisory staff in just one large conurbation would tip the scales against the government.

Within forty-eight hours of manual workers striking, health hazards could become a real danger. The most immediately vulnerable points are sewage treatment plants upstream of water supply intakes drawn from rivers. If the strike coincided with a period of wet weather, sewage storage tanks would fill more quickly than usual and untreated effluent would be discharged into rivers. The greatest worry is the backsiphonage of sewage and industrial waste into the mains water supply. Metallic contaminates cannot be dealt with by the simple expedient of boiling the water. It needs to be distilled to separate it from such impurities, not an operation the normal household can undertake with ease. The most common disorder resulting from contaminated water supplies would be diarrhoea. Salmonella would be another relatively widespread danger. The risk of typhoid would be about 1 in 750,000, that of cholera lower still. Yet unless the dispute was especially bitter, the worst consequences could, with luck, be avoided relatively easily. Strikers, if the experience of the north-west is a guide, would cut off supplies to industry with little compunction. But they would think very carefully before putting family and friends at risk.

Unlike, say, the miners, water workers are very evenly spread throughout the community and cannot isolate themselves from the vilification that would certainly follow if they jeopardised the health of the population. Both sides of industry are acutely aware that chlorination, the disinfection of water supply, is the breaking point. They set great store by paragraph 30.2 of the 1977 national agreement, known in the industry as the 'Green Book'. It reads:

The water service is essential to the public and it is agreed by both sides that every effort shall be made to avoid any industrial action which would prejudice public health and public safety and ensure that in the event of industrial action every effort should be made to avoid harm to the health of consumers.

The paragraph has never had to be invoked. Like electricity workers, water workers live constantly with the knowledge that their formidable industrial power is trammelled by a succession of trigger points, beyond the last of which the consequences are unthinkable. As one veteran manager of essential public services put it: 'Because they are so strong, they are also weak.'

The actual or contemplated employment of servicemen on non-military duties is a theme which runs through the entire history of emergency planning. This is for the simple reason that the armed forces are the only practical source of alternative labour the government has at its disposal in a time of acute industrial unrest. Involvement in industrial disputes is cordially disliked throughout all levels of the services. It is 'not what they joined for' and interferes with training and leave. The one bright feature of strikebreaking for them is their justified conviction that their efforts during the 1977–8 firemen's strike created a fund of public goodwill that helped to achieve better pay for the forces. At the highest levels of the Ministry of Defence the warrior politicians have a set of sophisticated reasons for their dislike. One very senior officer put it this way:

'High up in the Army it is felt that it is a very bad thing because we do not want the Services to antagonise the unions. Mind you, the fact that the Services are available to maintain essential services is a very important power in the hands of the government. It means they cannot totally be blackmailed. But if you have a major strike affecting all the essential services, then it could not just be handled by the Services. That is a good thing because it stops diehard conservatives thinking they can just bash the workers. It is not the primary purpose of the Army to provide essential services. To maintain in being a trained force capable of doing that would be a misuse of money and priorities. It would not be constitutionally improper, but it would be politically undesirable.'

Such political and constitutional fine-tuning does not extend very far down the ranks, but the visitor to a sergeants' mess can find himself surprised by the range of views, some very moderate. Here is a selection taken in 1979:

'I don't think the country will be held to ransom by the unions.

Commonsense will prevail in the end. I feel sorry for the union leaders. They get a lot of stick from the public. Yet the structure of the unions means they cannot control their members.'

'If an officer told the men to drive through or break a picket line, they would. It would be an [expletive] good scrap.'

'The services is [*sic*] a very physical type of life. I'm not saying the men would enjoy thumping civvies. They would look on it as a challenge, of getting through a line of men against them like a rugby scrum. If it was a unit that had just come back from Northern Ireland, the picket line wouldn't know what had hit them.'

'It's not the power that we have got. It's the power we deny to others. We owe an allegiance to the Queen, not to a political group. The fact that the services are there denies the excesses of out-and-out maniacs.'

At the private soldier level balance tends to disappear:

'The trade unions have got too much power. They have got the country by the balls.'

'What we need in this country is a government that will control the unions.'

'I'm pretty convinced that the services would enjoy breaking up a massed picket. It would be the same as rioting. Riot drill is something we know about. The massed riots in Northern Ireland were good fun. No other military in the world is better at breaking up riots than the British.'

Even at this level, however, elementary constitutional propriety can break through:

'The country would have to make new laws. You could not just break it up. The country would come to a halt.'

Within the Ministry of Defence the use of troops in industrial

disputes is handled by two policy divisions: Defence Secretariat 6
and Army Staff Duties 2. Their primary task is making clear to
ministers what the forces are capable of doing and what is not on.
Being the bearers of stark reality is not an enviable job. In the often
heated and hurried atmosphere of CCU meetings, ministers are
sometimes prone to suspect the military of attempting to usurp the
prerogatives of the civil power. A memorable moment during the
interminable series of CCU meetings in 1979 arose when Peter
Shore, then Secretary of State for the Environment, expressed outrage at the dead going unburied on Merseyside. The troops must
go in, he said. But the military politely inquired if there was any
other way, as there was a limit to what the men could be asked to
do. In his anguish the minister cried out, 'If only we had a skeleton
organisation for this kind of thing.' The awkward moment passed
in gales of laughter. One of the finer judgments the CCU has to
make is weighing the potential damage to the reputation of the
forces against the likely disruption of essential services if they are
not sent in. Overshadowing contingency planning at every level
today is the inescapable fact that there are not enough troops or
police, or sufficient skills in those forces, to cope with a general
strike or even a rash of public sector strikes well short of the 1926
stoppage.

## Postscript: the Thatcher administration

At the official launching of her election manifesto on 11 April 1979,
Mrs Margaret Thatcher was asked by a foreign journalist, 'Do you
think you have enough policemen, soldiers, whatever it takes, to
have a confrontation with extremists on an issue of face?' 'I don't
think we are quite on the same wavelength', came the brisk reply.
The general laughter which greeted it was led by her deputy, William Whitelaw, seated beside her. Just over three weeks later Mrs
Thatcher entered Downing Street and inherited the CCU, with its
supporting networks, whose antennae are permanently tuned to that
wavelength. Shortly after she took power, the new Prime Minister
appointed Whitelaw to be the CCU's ministerial overlord. The story
illustrates the serious way politicans treat such vital matters at election times. To the chagrin of the contingency planning community,
Mrs Thatcher adopted a relatively insouciant attitude towards their
work in her early months – part, it seemed, of her *laissez faire*

approach towards disputes unless they involved the government's own employees. It was not until October 1979, several weeks after they had received the annual 'Civil Contingencies Review', prepared by the unit in the normally slack summer months, that the Cabinet came to brood about the possibilities of a strike in the coal mines (which did not materialise) and the level of coal stocks.

The Prime Minister's attitude was somewhat baffling, as one of her earliest actions after becoming party leader in 1975 had been to commission a small group of ex-ministers and advisers to prepare for her a list of the lessons to be drawn from Heath's confrontation with the unions in the winter of 1973–4. They met under the chairmanship of Lord Carrington, who, as Secretary of State for Energy, had been at the heart of that crisis. Lord Carrington took evidence in great confidence from businessmen and former senior civil servants who had been close to events during the three-day week. The predominant theme of his report was a warning to Mrs Thatcher that it was not the political incompetence of her predecessor that lay behind the Tory trauma. Strong unions and the advanced technology operated by their members, especially in fuel and power industries, had irrevocably shifted the balance of industrial power in their favour. The former civil servants in particular strove to impress on the opposition that there was no magic formula for defeating the unions. The harsh reality encapsulated in the views of witnesses who appeared before the inquiry is said to have opened the eyes of some of the more hawkish Tories involved. The Carrington report told Mrs Thatcher that the armed forces could not be used on any large scale to break strikes as they had insufficient men for the task, and that any attempt to use them on a lavish scale would do permanent damage to the country's social and political fabric. The document, however, was not wholly pessimistic in tone. It urged that higher priority should be given to emergency planning in periods of political and industrial quiet and that the best brains in Whitehall should be devoted to it. It also placed great emphasis on projecting the government's case to the public in good time in order to counteract the defeatism that can creep in when daily life becomes uncomfortable because of industrial action. Skilled use of the 'publicity weapon' was deemed crucial to the public's will to resist.

Towards the end of 1979 the government were faced with the possibility of an oil tanker drivers' strike. Happily, as in the previous two years, the dispute did not develop into a full-scale stoppage. In order to give an idea of how the CCU works in anticipation of a serious dispute, we can reconstruct the sort of planning meeting which took place in November-December that year. The meeting would be opened by Robert Wade-Gery, who succeeded Sir Clive Rose as chairman of the CCU in April 1979, with a summary of 'Operation Drumstick' (or whatever name the planners had chosen). The scheme is intended to maintain about 25 per cent of normal petrol and oil supplies, provided a state of emergency is declared, rationing introduced and the Royal Corps of Transport requisitions oil company vehicles since the army does not have enough of its own. Discussion would then be opened to the various government departments involved. The latest intelligence on the position inside the relevant section of the TGWU would be provided by the Department of Employment. The representative from Transport would explain their rationing scheme and the priority to be given to public transport and essential users. The Department of Energy would convey the oil companies' readiness to co-operate with the government through the medium of their Oil Industries' Emergencies Committee. From the Ministry of Defence would come logistical details. In any such emergency some 5,000 drivers and 10,000 general duties men would have to be trained to handle pumps and pipes at the army's West Moors petroleum centre in Dorset. At least eighteen days' notice is required to get men back from Germany and through West Moors. Both the Home Office and the Ministry of Defence would emphasise the importance of impressing upon Chief Constables their responsibility for securing the safe passage of men and vehicles as they are driven out of company depots to army barracks and emergency distribution centres. At this point the needs of special interest groups might have been raised. Agriculture might appeal for farmers to be given preferential treatment and essential feed manufacturers to be made a 'special case'; Industry might speak up for companies requiring oil to maintain continuous production processes. In summing up, Wade-Gery would stress the need for an urgent meeting of ministers to authorise the drafting of emergency regulations and the proclamation of a state of emergency. Before ministers gathered, a handful of officials would receive a special briefing from MI5 on the origins of the strike, indicating whether a small group of extremists is manipulating the men, or whether it is a straight 'pay and conditions' affair. Invariably the evidence points to the latter, although the Security Service did see a conspiracy behind the 1966 Seamen's strike. A joint meeting of ministers and civil servants, under the Home Secretary's chairmanship, would then prepare recommendations for the full Cabinet. If the strike materialised, the CCU would meet each afternoon to collate reports from the Department of Transport's regional emergency committees and react to events until the stoppage ended.

At the time of writing Mrs Thatcher has managed to avoid the political Waterloos experienced by Heath in 1973-4 and Callaghan in 1979. She successfully weathered a protracted steel strike between January and April 1980, while the relatively slight impact of the five-week seamen's strike in 1981 demonstrated how the importance of the British merchant marine to the life of the nation had diminished since 1966. In June 1981 troops prepared to provide an emergency ambulance service after unofficial stoppages occurred in London, but Mrs Thatcher's reluctance to intervene in disputes was confirmed the following month when the government announced that RAF air traffic controllers would not replace striking civilians, although they had done just that during a similar dispute in 1977. Nevertheless, the threat of a miners' strike over pit closures in 1981, and two very near-misses with the water industry in 1980 and 1981, made the Prime Minister intimately aware of the contents and importance of the CCU and its files. All three cases involved surrender by the government at the last moment. Looking to the long term, a government green paper on possibilities for future labour legislation in January 1981 raised the notion of 'no-strike' agreements in especially vital industries. At the opening of the 1981-2 session of Parliament the government announced that legislation would be introduced to 'redress the balance of bargaining power'.[45]

In 1980 a favourite old strategy of emergency planners had new life breathed into it by ministers – the idea of using civilian volunteers to replace striking workers. When on 17 July 1980 *The Times* disclosed that the possibility was under consideration the 10 Downing Street press office took great pains to pour cold water over the notion. The story in *The Times* was based on a confidential Department of the Environment document specifying the work of its emergency planning division. It gave a very high priority to

*Tasks*. Planning for the consequences of industrial disputes.
*Objectives*. To plan for the use of volunteers in industrial disputes.

*This period: Performance Assessment.* Preliminary papers written; discussion with LA [Local Authority] associations deferred pending pay settlements.
*Next period: Planned Performance.* Discussions with LA associations to be held.

In the Commons Mrs Thatcher responded to what was clearly a planted question. A Conservative back-bencher asked if she recognised the desire of unemployed youth to serve the community by 'keeping essential services, such as hospitals, running in the event of strike action by those who have jobs?' She replied: 'I very much agree that large numbers of school leavers are anxious to give service to the community, including voluntary work. They expect to see essential services kept going. If a time were to come when those services were not kept going, young people would be the first to lend a hand.'[46] It was clear that veterans of the civil contingency planning community were most alarmed at the prospect. One seasoned figure in Whitehall warned that 'you cannot run a modern industrial society from the CCU. What you can do is buy time, give yourself a bit more room for manoeuvre. There are very few industries where volunteers would be of any help.' From the local authority side an experienced official added: 'If you introduce volunteers, or take any action that can be construed as strikebreaking, you have to look at the consequences in the aftermath. In no way do you want an escalation of the militancy of those concerned, and the moment you introduce volunteers you get it.'

The debate among ministers on the issue of volunteers rumbled on for several months, with William Whitelaw consistently throwing his substantial political weight against the idea. Among those who favoured it were Michael Heseltine (Environment), John Biffen (Chief Secretary to the Treasury) and John Nott (Trade). By autumn the ministerial 'doves' on the CCU had won one important victory. They had quashed the idea that the 70,000-strong Territorial Army should be used alongside regulars in breaking strikes. The possibility had great appeal, not least in Downing Street, as the Territorials would have more than doubled the numbers of full-timers available for substitute labour. Repeating arguments first put forward in 1921, the Defence Secretary, Francis Pym, eventually persuaded the Prime Minister that the basic military purpose of the country's reserve forces could be jeopardised, particularly as many of them belong to trade unions in civilian life, should they be used on strikebreaking duties. He also convinced her that it would be undesirable to use TA drill halls for civilian volunteers mustered in an emergency. At the beginning of November 1980 the CCU met as a purely ministerial body, with only official note-takers present. Discussion, which was fairly heated at times, concentrated on a paper prepared by Brigadier Bishop setting out the arguments for and against using civilian volunteers. The meeting proved inconclusive. But, to the relief of the contingency planning community, the civilian volunteer option played no part in the CCU's considerable build-up in December 1980–February 1981 for the national water strike which never came, even though a full set of emergency regulations was prepared in case the 1920 Act had to be invoked. The idea, however, could swiftly be revived by Thatcher Cabinet hardliners in any future clash with the unions and, provided Prime Ministerial backing was available, could result in a whole new dimension being added to the post-war management of industrial crises.

Just after the British victory in the Falklands war of April-May 1982, the government were faced with disputes involving three separate groups of railway personnel: workers on the London Underground protesting against new timetables necessitated by the Law Lords cutting down the Greater London Council's cheap fares policy; members of the NUR in a traditional pay dispute with British Rail; and the footplatemen's union, ASLEF, resisting the introduction of 'flexible rosters' which the management believed would boost productivity. At the time of writing (the second week of July), a temporary peace reigns on the Underground. The NUR executive called a national strike on British Rail, but a rank-and-file revolt levered its annual delegate conference into suspending the strike call almost immediately. A few days' grace intervened before ASLEF called its people out on official strike. During the first five days of the stoppage sufficient ASLEF members broke the strike to enable British Rail, with help from NUR drivers, to run a ten per cent passenger service overall, with particular success in the North-west and South-east of the country.

The rash of rail trouble served to blood Mr Arthur Goodall, latest of the Foreign Office diplomats to be put in charge of the CCU. He replaced Mr Wade-Gery on 1 June 1982. In his capacity as head of the Cabinet Office overseas and defence secretariat, his first days were dominated by the aftermath of the Falklands conflict. But Mr Goodall was soon sidetracked by the railway disputes. One consolation was that in 1982 life was much easier for the nation's top contingency planner than in 1955 when Sir Frank Newsam had to grapple with a national railway strike. Since the Newsam era there had been a flight of goods traffic from rail to road. In 1955 48 per cent of inland freight was moved by rail, 51 per cent by road. By 1980, rail's share had fallen to 14.3 per cent, with roads carrying 77.6 per cent. There was little prospect of Mr Goodall's CCU having to advise the Home Secretary, William Whitelaw, to declare a state of emergency under the 1920 Act, provided that the ASLEF-British Rail dispute was settled within two months, at which point coal stocks would begin to run out at the power stations.

The government did invoke the 1964 Act, however, to help the capital cope on 28 and 29 June when NUR members in both British Rail and London Transport stopped work simultaneously. In order to accommodate the vastly increased volume of cars entering the metropolitan area, free parking was provided in the London parks. Since one of the wettest Junes in living memory had left the ground soft and damp, troops were employed to lay wire netting for the cars to park on. A Defence Council Order was used to provide the necessary legal authority. One other small but important factor had changed since Newsam's day. The government no longer needed to indemnify for insurance purposes drivers who offered lifts during the strike, as local radio stations gladly reminded commuters. A section of the 1980 Transport Act, amending the 1972 Road Transport Act, legalised the practice, so long as any money paid to the driver/owner by passengers did not exceed the vehicle's running costs.

Though the willingness of some ASLEF members to rupture the traditional solidarity of their union led certain commentators to conclude that the Thatcher administration was well on the way to breaking the back of union power, by midsummer 1982 nothing had happened to change the landscape of modern civil contingency planning in the manner of events a decade earlier. As Whitehall planners passed the tenth anniversary of Saltley, no final answers had been produced to the questions raised by that seminal incident. No government had tried to amend the law, through, for example, a resuscitated Riot Act, in such a way as to prevent a repetition of that disruption. Nor had a shadow army of workers in the shape of more and better equipped troops or civilian volunteers been created. What could or should be done is the subject of the final chapter.

# 9
# Strikebreaking past and future

DURING A COMMONS' debate on the London dock strike in July 1949, Sir John Anderson, uniquely experienced in contingency planning as civil servant, Cabinet minister and employer, made two general points concerning the use of emergency powers in industrial disputes. He declared that 'the Emergency Powers Act and the regulations made thereunder are not to be regarded as in any sense a strike-breaking mechanism', and he asserted that 'an emergency organisation cannot be established on the basis of conciliation'.[1] These two points neatly encapsulate the inherent contradictions within the British government's approach to major industrial stoppages. While neither Lloyd George in 1919 nor Baldwin in 1926 might wholeheartedly have agreed, Anderson's belief that the implementation of emergency powers did not constitute 'strikebreaking' has been strongly espoused by every British government since the war. Indeed, throughout our period ministers have firmly stressed the government's over-riding responsibility to maintain the nation's essentials of life, to act as 'a trustee for the community'. In May 1919, when the threat from the Triple Alliance seemed most acute, Winston Churchill rejected the term strikebreaking in typically vivid language:

> To use soldiers or sailors, kept up at the expense of the taxpayer, in an ordinary trade dispute, to employ them as what are called blacklegs, would be a monstrous invasion of the liberty of the subject. . . . But the case is different where vital services affecting the health, life and safety of large cities or great concentrations of people are concerned. . . . Light, water, electric power, transport, the distribution of food, all these are indispensable to the existence of these mighty cities which cover our land. If any of these commodities or facilities are suddenly cut off, the State

must intervene and come to the rescue of the population whose lives are in danger, by every means in its power, including the use of military and naval forces, so as to avoid a general catastrophe.[2]

Although few succeeding politicians have had Churchill's graphic powers of expression, they have, nevertheless, similarly justified emergency action as a moral imperative. In these terms the creation of an emergency machine is seen as a positive benefit to the community, and certainly as an indispensable arm of modern government.

But Anderson's second point indicates a less agreeable characteristic of emergency planning, and even casts doubt on the validity of his first remark. His specific intention was to establish the fundamental incompatability of the official conciliation machinery in the Ministry of Labour with the government's emergency organisation. 'Conciliation and all that goes with it. . .', he argued, 'is very important, but it should not be allowed to dominate the situation.' The corollary to his observation is that emergency planning contains some element of coercion. So it does. In securing vital needs, protecting the community and mitigating the immediate consequences of a major strike, the government inevitably undermines the effectiveness of that strike. So much so that the distinction between 'maintaining essential services' and 'strikebreaking' becomes blurred. Indeed, these two functions are inseparable within the government's emergency machine. The former cannot be met without involving the latter. To assert otherwise is, to say the least, disingenuous. If, for example, a government is determined not to concede demands made by electric power workers, backed up with a widespread stoppage, the only alternative is to break the strike. Since it is no longer possible to replace skilled power workers with volunteer labour or troops, the most the CCU can do is to ration such electricity as may still be available and, perhaps, provide alternative sources of power, from auxiliary generators to stockpiles of candles. In this way the emergency organisation might be able to buy time for the government to break the strikers' will. The most extreme circumstance in which a government will be determined to break a strike is when that strike is seen as a threat to the state itself. This was most nearly the case in the years immediately after the First World War and in 1926. But even then the issue was not quite so clear cut. It never is.

None of the major strikes in Britain this century has specifically been aimed to bring down the government. But as the motives behind strikes may be mixed, so too are the responses of both government and community. The use of an emergency organisation is just one weapon in the official armoury. To a very great extent it represents a purely mechanical and functional reaction to industrial disruption. That is one reason why emergency planning fits so easily into the regulated world of the British bureaucrat. As such it can be both inflexible and unsubtle. For a civil servant to estimate the numbers of troops required to unload perishable foodstuffs in strikebound docks is a simple mathematical exercise. To apply that paper plan in practice is a very different affair. Within the wider circle of industrial relations generally the number of troops employed may matter much less than the actual decision to use them in the first place. Such decisions are usually left to the politicians. It would be wrong, however, to suggest either that civil servants have no influence in these circumstances or that, in fact, they exercise this influence thoughtlessly.

The history of the government's strikebreaking machine suggests that the actual form and detailed organisation of emergency arrangements lies almost entirely in the hands of permanent officials. Men like Roundell, Anderson, Newsam and Bishop have laboured to meet the sometimes extravagant demands of their political masters. On the whole, officials, and soldiers too, have acted as a moderating influence on the wilder notions of ministers. Certainly since 1945 they have emphasised the limits of emergency action; they have stressed what it *cannot* do. But the world of the senior civil servant is in many respects insulated from the harsh and occasionally violent realities of modern industrial relations. The winter crisis of 1972 looked very different from the soundproofed Cabinet Office Briefing Room than from Arthur Scargill's flying picket Operations Room in Barnsley. While the decision to implement emergency arrangements must be political, and take into account the particular circumstances obtaining at a given time, the very fact that contingency plans have been drawn up, largely in secret and often in a highly detailed form, may provide the politicians with a deceptively straightforward choice. The existence of confidential emergency plans can promote the dangerously seductive illusion that a social and political phenomenon as complex as an industrial dispute is susceptible to a mechanistic solution. The proclamation of an emergency, the introduction of special regulations, the sending in of troops, can all be attractive options since they satisfy abundantly the contemporary politician's over-riding need to demonstrate that 'something is being done'. If plans exist, for example, to employ substitute military labour, there is a risk that in the heat of a crisis a government may decide to implement them without fully considering the consequences. The post-war Attlee government reached a stage at which using troops became an almost automatic reaction to serious disputes. In the case of the docks, this response not only exacerbated industrial unrest, but also blinded the government to the underlying causes of the trouble.

If, as successive governments have asserted, the emergency organisation exists only to maintain 'the essentials of life', then the government's definition of 'essential services' assumes some importance. The supply of food and water can indisputably be called vital, as, for the most part, can that of fuel and power. Such is the dependence of modern Britain on the continuous supply of oil fuel and electric power, that even a localised stoppage in either of these industries can have a disproportionately damaging effect on all other sectors of the economy and the day-to-day life of the community. The widespread adoption of continuous processes in many industries has increased their reliance on a number of crucial supplies. In the late 1970s, for example, the CCU took the threat of stoppage at British Oxygen very seriously indeed because of the severely disruptive 'knock-on' effect this would have had. Since the government has an irreducible duty to maintain vital supplies and services, it follows that plans must be made to mitigate the effects of such stoppages.[3] After all, they may not result only from industrial action.

Food, water and fuel are unequivocally essential. So too are fire and ambulance services. But governments have at times also to decide whether to implement emergency arrangements in less clear-cut cases, such as public transport and communications. Much depends upon the existence of substitute services. Thus the interruption of all London's bus and tram services, along with a threatened Underground stoppage in 1924, was judged sufficient cause, to proclaim a state of emergency, while the strike of busmen alone in 1958 was not. Similarly, the postal services' stoppage between January and March 1971 did not prompt a mobilisation of the emergency machine since telecommunications remained available. With different stoppages causing varying degrees of inconvenience or suffering, it is desirable for the government to adopt a flexible response. To invoke the full majesty of the 1920 Emergency Powers Act to meet every stoppage, whether in essential or 'near-essential' industries, would be absurd. The 1964 Act fills a clear need for less Draconian powers, but the procedure by which military assistance can be made available, the Defence Council Order, is unsatisfactorily obscure. It enables the crucial decision to employ troops to be taken almost by stealth, and, unlike the 1920 Act, makes no provision for direct and formal Parliamentary scrutiny. A DCO may be a proper instrument to use in war, or times of extreme national peril. It is not a suitable mechanism to use for deploying servicemen as strikebreakers, or in the memorable phrase coined by the TGWU during the 1947 road haulage strike, as 'blacklegs in uniform'.

In certain instances the government has defined 'the essentials of life' somewhat generously. In the early days of emergency planning, and to a lesser extent in the late 1940s, a major factor in the implementation of emergency powers lay not so much in the immediate stoppage as in the government's belief that behind particular industrial disputes was a threat to the state's very existence. During the dock strikes of the 1940s, moreover, the government took a broad view of the term 'essential services'. Strikebreaking troops were sent into the docks not only to secure food supplies but also to load cargoes of general merchandise, which Attlee and Isaacs asserted were absolutely vital to the economic survival of the nation. Harold Wilson made a similar case during the 1966 seamen's strike. More recently governments have begun to argue the rather less specific point that the maintenance of a prices and incomes policy is 'essential' to the nation's well-being. Most of the 'vital' strikes of the 1970s arose from union pay claims which broke successive pay 'norms' or 'guidelines'. In such cases as the miners' action of 1973–4 and the firemen's strike of 1977–8, the government used emergency powers not merely to maintain necessary services but also in defence of a particular economic policy.[4] Whether or not this is a justifiable use of emergency powers is open to question.

The actual implementation of emergency arrangements also depends on the resources available to the government. It is clear that a strike of miners or power engineers cannot be broken by the introduction of substitute labour, either civilian or military.

Although the idea of recruiting civilian volunteers is periodically considered by ministers and officials, in the end the only practical instrument is the armed services. Calling for civilian volunteers to break strikes has always worried emergency planners for fear of dividing the country in half. Trained and disciplined pairs of hands, under tight government control, are infinitely preferable. But the introduction of troops is in itself an emotive step. It may very well escalate a dispute and will certainly throw the forces into the thick of political controversy. Servicemen themselves are always delighted to perform 'military aid to the civil community' – the Ministry of Defence's term for civil relief measures during natural disasters – but they are markedly less enthusiastic to offer 'military aid to the civil ministries' – strikebreaking.[5] Yet every government since the war has contemplated the possibility of using service labour to break strikes and, so long as no other source of organised labour exists, future governments will continue to do so. As an alternative to the armed forces, the civil defence corps, which was disbanded in 1968, might be reconstituted. There are sound strategic reasons for such a move in addition to wider considerations. For instance, the Soviet Union's ability to wage prolonged conventional war, with devastating air strikes against the United Kingdom, before 'going nuclear', has increased substantially in the last ten years. A civil defence corps, under civilian Home Office control, would be well placed, for example, to decontaminate water supplies at street and household level should a power or water strike create widespread health hazards. Locally recruited men, of the 'Dad's Army' type, well known in their neighbourhoods, could protect individuals from danger and distress without the stigma of 'strikebreaking' necessarily being attached to their actions. It would be for the police and army to handle affairs at picketed installations, not civil defence volunteers. Such a force would be a national and not a sectional asset, indispensable when the necessities of life are cut off by act of God or man.

Since the very beginning emergency planning has been conducted in what Josiah Wedgwood described in 1924 as 'an almost melodramatic air of secrecy'. Partly this illustrates no more than the congenital secrecy of British administration. But it also reflects a morbid concern that, whatever public proclamations may be made, the implementation of emergency arrangements might unhappily be misinterpreted as 'strikebreaking', and a residual fear that major industrial disputes may pose a threat to the state. Resulting from this has been the pusillanimous – and insulting – reluctance of successive governments to take the public into its confidence. From time to time ministers and officials have attempted to break down the barrier raised by this miserable lack of trust. In 1932 Sir John Anderson asserted that some degree of publicity for the STO would bring positive benefits, and his Home Office successors in November 1945 argued in similar vein. Not surprisingly, such attempts have been made by Labour ministers soon after taking office, when they still carry with them the evangelical fervour of the Opposition benches. Wedgwood is one example. Aneurin Bevan is another, but his radical proposal to conduct public discussions with a wide range of official and non-official bodies, including the TUC, barely survived his making it. The admirable ambition to lift the blanket of secrecy within which the emergency machine has been smothered has not been confined to Labour politicians. Late in 1979 Lord Jellicoe, whom Edward Heath appointed ministerial head of the CCU in 1972–3, declared that

> the Government should come clean about civil contingency planning. It is an important area about which the public ought to be reassured. I do not consider it strike-breaking. It is a matter of sensible precautions, which any government should be thinking about, to mitigate the consequences of industrial action for the benefit of society as a whole. The generalities should not be concealed. Specific contingencies are another matter.[6]

An essential requirement for a civilised system of emergency planning is a greater measure of openness. Besides, even Section 2 of the Official Secrets Act cannot disguise the fact that emergency powers have been used to break strikes. The government has no reason to be ashamed if the CCU exists solely to feed the hungry and protect the weak. But they have very good cause to be circumspect if it is also a political weapon.

The nature of contemporary contingency planning has disturbing implications. The involvement of employers (both in public and private sectors), *but not trade unions,* in preliminary planning introduces an unpleasantly sectional flavour to the whole procedure. Government claims that emergency action is designed solely to protect the community as a whole ring hollow if the organisation itself categorically excludes a major interest group – the trade unions – from the planning process. While involving organised labour in emergency planning, the government has also to recognise the acute power of particular unions, especially in the electricity, oil distribution and water industries. So great is this power that the government must consider what is called the 'code of conduct' option, as an adjunct to the present policy of relying, in the main, on managerial staff, assisted where possible by servicemen, to keep public utilities going if manual workers walk out. Removing more extreme kinds of disruption from the armoury of industrial action, on the basis of joint agreement, is, on the face of it, a sensible and desirable course. In exploring this avenue the government, however, ought not to take material advantage from the unions' self-restraint. The problem, as in all attempts formally to regulate industrial relations, lies in striking the delicate balance between the rights of workers, the obligations of employers and the greater good of the community at large. Realistically, 'no-strike' agreements would probably have to be for specified and limited periods, of say, five years at a time. They would also have to be coupled with a mutually agreed and binding arbitration procedure. Yet it must be recognised that even such self-denying ordinances, however faithfully the parties concerned may respect their own side of the bargain, cannot be expected to eliminate all strikes. This is amply illustrated by the experience of Order 1305, which raises the difficulty that the closer government, employers and established union leaders co-operate, the more likely becomes the alienation of the rank and file worker. In order to meet this difficulty, there would certainly have to be a high degree of close and continuous local participation in the making and monitoring of agreements.

When all is taken into account, the country depends on the government and the trade unions recognising that it is in nobody's interests that there should be a final showdown, a conclusive answer to the question posed by Lloyd George in 1919. Should such a 'High Noon' occur, the balance of social and institutional forces in the nation, the kind of checks and balances that preserve our liberties, could be tilted permanently in favour of one side or the other, changing the political and constitutional landscape of the country beyond recognition.

# Appendix I

[10 & 11 Geo. 5.]
*Emergency Powers Act*, 1920.  [Ch. 55.]

## CHAPTER 55.

An Act to make exceptional provision for the Protection of the Community in cases of Emergency.
[29th October 1920.]

BE IT ENACTED by the King's most Excellent Majesty, by and
with the advice and consent of the Lords Spiritual and Temporal, and Commons, in this present Parliament assembled,
and by the authority of the same, as follows: –

1. – (1) If at any time it appears to His Majesty that any
action has been taken or is immediately threatened by any
persons or body of persons of such a nature and on so extensive
a scale as to be calculated, by interfering with the supply and
distribution of food, water, fuel, or light, or with the means of
locomotion, to deprive the community, or any substantial portion of the community, of the essentials of life, His Majesty
may, by proclamation (hereinafter referred to as a proclamation
of emergency), declare that a state of emergency exists.

No such proclamation shall be in force for more than one
month, without prejudice to the issue of another proclamation
at or before the end of that period.

(2) Where a proclamation of emergency has been made, the
occasion thereof shall forthwith be communicated to Parliament, and, if Parliament is then separated by such adjournment
or prorogation as will not expire within five days, a proclamation shall be issued for the meeting of Parliament within
five days, and Parliament shall accordingly meet and sit upon

the day appointed by that proclamation, and shall continue to sit and act in like manner as if it had stood adjourned or prorogued to the same day.

**2.** – (1) Where a proclamation of emergency has been made, and so long as the proclamation is in force, it shall be lawful for His Majesty in Council, by Order, to make regulations for securing the essentials of life to the community, and those regulations may confer or impose on a Secretary of State or other Government department, or any other persons in His Majesty's service or acting on His Majesty's behalf, such powers and duties as His Majesty may deem necessary for the preservation of the peace, for securing and regulating the supply and distribution of food, water, fuel, light, and other necessities, for maintaining the means of transit or locomotion, and for any other purposes essential to the public safety and the life of the community, and may make such provisions incidental to the powers aforesaid as may appear to His Majesty to be required for making the exercise of those powers effective:

Emergency<br>regulations.

Provided that nothing in this Act shall be construed to authorise the making of any regulations imposing any form of compulsory military service or industrial conscription:

Provided also that no such regulation shall make it an offence for any person or persons to take part in a strike, or peacefully to persuade any other person or persons to take part in a strike.

(2) Any regulations so made shall be laid before Parliament as soon as may be after they are made, and shall not continue in force after the expiration of seven days from the time when they are so laid unless a resolution is passed by both Houses providing for the continuance thereof.

(3) The regulations may provide for the trial, by courts, of summary jurisdiction, of persons guilty of offences against the regulations; so, however, that the maximum penalty which may be inflicted for any offence against such regulations shall be imprisonment with or without hard labour for a term of three months, or a fine of one hundred pounds, or both such imprisonment and fine, together with the forfeiture of any goods or money in respect of which the offence has been committed: Provided that no such regulations shall alter any existing procedure in criminal cases, or confer any right to punish by fine or imprisonment without trial.

(4) The regulations so made shall have effect as if enacted in

this Act, but may be added to, altered, or revoked by resolution of both Houses of Parliament or by regulations made in like manner and subject to the like provisions as the original regulations; and regulations made under this section shall not be deemed to be statutory rules within the meaning of section one of the Rules Publication Act, 1893.

56 & 57 Vict.
c.66.

(5) The expiry or revocation of any regulations so made shall not be deemed to have affected the previous operation thereof, or the validity of any action taken thereunder, or any penalty or punishment incurred in respect of any contravention or failure to comply therewith, or any proceeding or remedy in respect of any such punishment or penalty.

Short title and application.

**3.** – (1) This Act may be cited as the Emergency Powers Act, 1920.

(2) This Act shall not apply to Ireland.

## *Emergency Powers Act 1964*    Ch. 38

# ELIZABETH II

## 1964 CHAPTER 38

An Act to amend the Emergency Powers Act 1920 and make permanent the Defence (Armed Forces) Regulations 1939.

[10th June 1964]

BE IT ENACTED by the Queen's most Excellent Majesty, by and with the advice and consent of the Lords Spiritual and Temporal, and Commons, in this present Parliament assembled, and by the authority of the same, as follows: –

Amendment of
s. 1(1) of
Emergency
Powers Act
1920.
10 & 11 Geo. 5
c.55.

**1.** In section 1(1) of the Emergency Powers Act 1920 (by virtue of which Her Majesty may by proclamation declare that a state of emergency exists if at any time it appears to Her that any action has been taken or is immediately threatened by any persons or body of persons of such a nature and on so extensive a scale as to be calculated, by interfering with the supply and distribution of food, water, fuel or light, or with the means of locomotion, to deprive the community, or any substantial portion of the community, of the essentials of life), for the words from 'any action' to 'so extensive a scale' there shall be substituted the words 'there have occurred, or are about to occur, events of such a nature'.

**2.** The Defence (Armed Forces) Reglations 1939 in the form set out in Part C of Schedule 2 to the Emergency Laws (Repeal) Act 1959 (which regulations enable the temporary employment in agricultural work or in other work, being urgent work of national importance, of members of the armed forces of the Crown to be authorised) shall become permanent.

Defence (Armed Forces) Regulations 1939 made permanent.
7 & 8 Eliz. 2 c.19.

**3.** – (1) This Act may be cited as the Emergency Powers Act 1964.

Short title and extent.

(2) Section 1 of this Act shall not extend to Northern Ireland.

# Appendix II

PROCLAMATIONS OF STATES OF EMERGENCY UNDER THE
EMERGENCY POWERS ACT 1920

| *Date of Proclamation* | *Date state of emergency ended* | *Nature of dispute* |
| --- | --- | --- |
| 31 March 1921 | 26 July 1921 | Coal miners' strike |
| 28 March 1924 | 1 April 1924 | Bus and tram strike in London |
| 30 April 1926 | 19 December 1926 | General strike and coal miners' strike |
| 28 June 1948 | 27 July 1948 | Dock strike |
| 11 July 1949 | 10 August 1949 | Dock strike |
| 31 May 1955 | 21 June 1955 | Rail strike |
| 23 May 1966 | 5 July 1966 | Seamen's strike |
| 16 July 1970 | 4 August 1970 | Dock strike |
| 12 December 1970 | 17 December 1970 | Electricity workers' strike |

| Date of Proclamation | Date state of emergency ended | Nature of dispute |
| --- | --- | --- |
| 9 February 1972 | 8 March 1972 | Coal miners' strike |
| 3 August 1972 | 2 September 1972 | Dock strike |
| 13 November 1973 | 11 March 1974 | Coal miners' and electricity power workers' dispute |

# Appendix III

CIVIL SERVICE HEADS OF THE EMERGENCY
ORGANISATION.

| | |
|---|---|
| Mr Christopher Roundell, Ministry of Health. | 1920–22 |
| Sir John Anderson, Home Office. | 1922–32 |
| Sir Russell Scott, Home Office. | 1932–38 |
| Sir Alexander Maxwell, Home Office. | 1938–47 |
| Sir Frank Newsam, Home Office. | 1947–57 |
| Sir Charles Cunningham, Home Office. | 1957–66 |
| Sir Philip Allen, Home Office. | 1966–72 |
| Sir John Hunt, Cabinet Office. | 1972–73 |
| Sir Patrick Nairne, Cabinet Office. | 1973–75 |
| Sir Clive Rose, Cabinet Office. | 1976–79 |
| Mr Robert Wade-Gery, Cabinet Office. | 1979–82 |
| Mr Arthur Goodall, Cabinet Office. | 1982– |

# Notes

## Chapter 1 War and revolution

1 There is a succinct account of pre-war industrial relations in H. Pelling, *A History of British Trade Unionism* (2nd edn, 1971), ch. 7. For a broader discussion of the period, see K. Middlemas, *Politics in Industrial Society* (1979), ch. 2.

2 V. L. Allen, *Trade Unions and the Government* (1960), pp. 148–9.

3 Details of wartime administration and control will be found in J. A. Fairlie, *British War Administration* (1919).

4 D. Lloyd George, *War Memoirs* (Odhams, n.d.), vol. I, p. 150. See also Peter K. Cline, 'Eric Geddes and the "experiment" with businessmen in government, 1915–22', in K. D. Brown, *Essays in Anti-Labour History* (1974), pp. 74–104.

5 Working days lost in industrial disputes ('ooos):
   1911  10,155
   1912  40,890
   1913   9,804
   1914   9,878
   1915   2,953
   1916   2,446
   1917   5,647
   1918   5,875

6 A phrase used in Middlemas, *Politics in Industrial Society*, p. 101.

7 Although Macready had no previous direct experience of commanding police, he had seen military service in aid of the civil power at Tonypandy in 1910 and Belfast in 1914.

8 Quoted in G. W. Reynolds and A. Judge, *The Night the Police went on Strike* (1968), p. 5.

9 Wilson diary, 24 September 1918.

10 Milner to Lloyd George, 1 June 1917, Lloyd George MSS. F/38/2/8. Milner was a member of the War Cabinet. The Milners of this world have, of course, been saying things like this since time immemorial.

11 Stephen R. Ward, 'Intelligence surveillance of British ex-servicemen, 1918–20', *Historical Journal*, vol. XVI (1973), pp. 179–88; and Trevor

Barnes, 'Special Branch and the first Labour government', *Historical Journal*, XXII (1979), pp. 941–51.

12   One issue (no. 23, Nov. 1933) of the 'Civil Security Intelligence Summary' is in the MacDonald MSS. PRO 30/69/598.

13   Aneurin Bevan, *In Place of Fear* (1952), pp. 20–1.

14   Walter Kendall, *The Revolutionary Movement in Britain* (1969), pp. 194–5.

15   George Pettee, 'Revolutionary typology and process', in C. J. Friedrich (ed.), *Revolution* (1969), pp. 18–20.

16   Report on revolutionary organisations in the UK, no. 38, 22 Jan. 1920, CAB 24/96 C.P. 491.

17   Middlemas, *Politics in Industrial Society*, p. 447.

## Chapter 2   Establishing the Supply and Transport Organisation

1   Law to Lloyd George, 28 Jan. 1919, Lloyd George MSS. F/30/3/9.

2   Lloyd George's organisation of a small executive War Cabinet, established in Dec. 1916, lasted until Nov. 1919.

3   CAB 23/9/W.C. 525. The papers of the IUC are in CAB 27/59.

4   Lloyd George to Law, 29 Jan. 1919, quoted in A. J. P. Taylor, *Beaverbrook* (Penguin, 1974), p. 174 n. 1.

5   IUC meetings, 4–17 Feb. 1919, CAB 27/59; 'A short history of the IUC', Jan. 1920, CAB 27/82, no. 1, appendix I.

6   'A short history of the IUC', Jan. 1920, CAB 27/82, no. 1, appendix I.

7   CAB 23/15 G.T. 6998; War Cabinet Meeting, 19 Mar. 1919, CAB 23/15/W.C. 546A.

8   IUC meetings, July-Aug. 1919, CAB 27/59; CAB 27/82, no. 1, appendix I. Geddes was Minister without Portfolio, Jan.-May 1919, and Minister of Transport, Aug. 1919-Nov. 1921.

9   Sir Nevil Macready, *Annals of an Active Life* (1924), vol. II, p. 411.

10   Note by Col. H. E. Braine, 27 Oct. 1919, W.O. 32/5611, no. 18A; Churchill to Lloyd George, 25 Sept. 1919, quoted in M. Gilbert, *Winston S. Churchill*, Companion Volume IV part 2 (1977), p. 881; Haig diary, 15 April 1919.

11   Lord Ironside, *Archangel 1918–19* (1953), p. 188.

12   Memo by Maj. W. W. Torr, 15 Oct. 1919, W.O. 32/5553 no. 1A.

13   Haig diary, 28 June 1919.

14   Ibid., 2 Sept. 1919.

15   W.O. 32/5611 nos 1 and 8.

16   The papers of the Strike Committee (Sept.-Oct. 1919) are in CAB 27/60–61.

17   Haig diary, 27 Sept. 1919.

18   Report on railway strike, 22 Jan. 1920, appendix III, CAB 27/82 no. 1.

19   Report on military measures during railway strike, W.O. 32/5467 no. 1A; Haig diary, 27 Sept. 1919.

20   'How to Help', CAB 27/60 S.C. 9.

21 Report on railway strike, CAB 27/82 no. 1.
22 Home Office to Chief Constables, 24 Jan. 1919, H.O. 45/11200, file 375227/1. In mid-1919 a particular appeal was made to members of West End clubs. See correspondence in M.H. 78/28.
23 Report by chairman of protection sub-committee, 28 Oct. 1919, CAB 27/77 T.S.C. 22.
24 Ibid.; Strike Committee 8th meeting, 3 Oct. 1919, CAB 27/60; protection sub-committee meeting, 5 Oct. 1919, CAB 27/61 S.C. 135.
25 Strike Committee 11th meeting, CAB 27/60.
26 'Citizen Guards', 23 Oct. 1919, CAB 24/90 G.T. 8394. By the end of the month the STC had come round to Shortt's opinion. See extract from STC minutes of 31 Oct. 1919, circulated to the Cabinet as CAB 24/92 C.P. 78.
27 The decision was finally made at a conference of ministers on 18 Nov. 1919, CAB 23/18/9(19) appendix. On 2 Dec. 1919 a circular was spent to all Chief Constables embodying Shortt's four criteria, H.O. 45/11200, file 375227/46. For the economic position see 11, 20 Aug. and 22 Oct. 1919, Finance Committee 2nd, 3rd and 11th meetings, CAB 27/71.
28 Hankey diary, 12 Oct. 1919. Sir Maurice Hankey as Secretary to the Cabinet, 1916–38, was arguably the most powerful civil servant in the country.
29 Haig diary, 'Sunday 28th Sept. to Saturday 4th Oct.' 1919.
30 11th and 12th meetings of Strike Committee, 6 and 7 Oct. 1919, CAB 27/60; War Cabinet meeting, 14 Oct. 1919, CAB 23/12/W.C. 630.
31 Cabinet meeting, 10 Dec. 1919, CAB 23/18/12(19). On 2 Feb. 1920 Churchill and Long, together with the Secretary for Scotland, were formally added to the STC, CAB 23/20/10(20) appendix I.
32 Haig to War Office, 17 Oct. 1919, W.O. 32/5467 no. 1A.
33 Ibid., 16 Oct. and 26 Nov. 1919, W.O. 32/5279 nos 1B and 13A.
34 Memo by Maj. Torr, 15 Oct. 1919, and note by Col. Braine, 12 Nov. 1919, W.O. 32/5553 nos 1A and 2A. Maj. Torr was later able to indulge his penchant for information-gathering in the War Office Directorate of Military Intelligence (European Section), 1929–32, and as Military Attaché in Washington, 1934–8, and in Madrid, 1939–46.
35 Adjutant-General to Deputy CIGS, 13 Oct. 1919, W.O. 32/5611 no. 12.
36 Intra-departmental minutes, 15–23 Oct. 1919, ibid., nos 13–15, 17A.
37 'The employment of troops in industrial disturbances', 12 Nov. 1919, CAB 24/93 C.P. 111. The final minutes for the conference on 18 Nov. show approval for only three of Wilson's proposals. See CAB 23/18/9(19) appendix. For the original decision see 'Note regarding wireless', 25 Nov. 1919, CAB 27/74 T.C. 13, and STC 2nd meeting, 8 Dec. 1919, CAB 27/73.
38 Note by Col. Braine, 5 Jan. 1920, and Home Office to War Office, 6 Jan. 1920, W.O. 32/5553 nos 11B and 11A.
39 The Directorate of Military Operations, along with those of Military

Intelligence and Staff Duties, was part of the CIGS's department in the War Office.

40  Minutes by Col. Braine and DMO, 12 and 13 Nov. 1919, W.O. 32/4812 nos 1A and 1.

41  Intra-departmental minutes, 3 Dec. 1919–17 Jan. 1920, ibid., nos 7–14; War Office to Home Office, 6 Feb. 1920, W.O. 32/5553 no. 18A.

42  'Reorganisation of Road Transport Board', 14 Aug. 1919, CAB 27/59 U.C. 22; STC sub-committee 9th meeting, 4 Dec. 1919, CAB 27/76; Draft memo. on STO, 2 June 1920, CAB 27/82 no. 3; Interim report on recruitment of volunteer labour, 10 Feb. 1920, CAB 24/97 C.P. 593; STC 4th meeting, 9 Feb. 1920, CAB 27/73; Cabinet meeting, 18 Feb. 1920, CAB 23/20/11(20).

43  STC 1st meeting, 31 Oct. 1919, CAB 27/73; note by Hankey covering memo. by Geddes, 11 Nov. 1919, M.T. 49/172, circulated to the Cabinet as CAB 24/92 C.P. 97.

44  Geddes to Hankey, 13 Nov. 1919; Hankey to Geddes, and minute by R. H. Tolerton (Geddes's private secretary), 14 and 15 Nov. 1919, M.T. 49/172.

45  Hankey to Chamberlain, 19 Nov. 1919, T. 172/1085. Chamberlain had missed the conference through illness.

46  Conference of ministers, 18 Nov. 1919, CAB 23/18/9(19) appendix.

47  Geddes to Lloyd George, 9 Dec. 1919, and minute by Parliamentary Secretary to Ministry of Transport, M.T. 49/163; Minutes of Adjutant-General's sub-committee, 18 Dec. 1919, CAB 27/77 T.S.C. 63. On 15 Jan. 1919 the STC were informed that four Irish distilleries supplied 50 per cent of British commercial yeast, STC 3rd meeting, CAB. 27/73.

48  Intra-departmental minutes, 20–21 Dec. 1919, W.O. 32/5467 nos. 23–25; Rawlinson diary and Wilson diary, both 3 Jan. 1920.

49  War Office memo., 3 Jan. 1920, W.O. 32/5467 no. 30A, circulated to the Cabinet, 7 Jan. 1920, as CAB 24/96 C.P. 472, and to the STC as CAB. 27/74 T.C. 42. In a memo, of 19 Jan. the Air Council 'associate [d] themselves generally with the view of the Army Council', CAB 24/96 C.P. 475.

50  Rawlinson diary, 14 Jan. 1920.

51  STC 3rd meeting, 15 Jan. 1920, CAB 27/73; STC memoranda, CAB 27/74 T.C. 31, 33, 40–2 and 52.

52  Wilson diary, 15 Jan. 1920.

53  Cabinet conferences, CAB 23/35/S.10 and 11, and Wilson diary, 16 and 18 Jan. 1920.

54  Wilson diary, 19 Jan. 1920; Hankey diary, 24 Jan. 1920; Hankey to Lloyd George, 17 Jan. 1920, Lloyd George MSS. F/24/2/3 (also in CAB 1/29/12); Jones to Hankey, 19 Jan. 1920, quoted in Thomas Jones, *Whitehall Diary* (1969), vol. I, p. 98.

55  Wilson diary, 22, 28 Jan., 2 and 6 Feb. 1920; Rawlinson diary, 28 Jan. and 6 Feb. 1920.

56  STC sub-committee 15th meeting, 22 Jan. 1920, CAB 27/76; minute by Neal, 28 Jan. 1920, M.T. 49/163.

57 There were 20 ministers and officials, plus 3 secretaries, at the meeting. The average age was 51. Bonar Law was the only man present over 60. Wilson was 55.

58 Wilson diary, 2 Feb. 1920; Jones, *Whitehall Diary*, vol. I, pp. 99–103; Cabinet minutes, CAB 23/20/10(20) appendix I; memo. by Geddes, 26 Jan. 1920, CAB 24/97 C.P. 501.

59 Minute by T. St Quintin Hill, 21 June 1920, and Geddes to Greenwood, 27 March 1920, M.T. 49/167; STC 7th Meeting, 27 March 1920, CAB 27/73.

## Chapter 3 The Supply and Transport Organisation in action

1 STC 3rd meeting, 15 Jan. 1920, CAB 27/73. There was a considerable amount of labour unrest in Norway from 1917 onwards. The Norwegian Labour Party, which had adopted a revolutionary programme in March 1918, won 18 seats in the October 1918 general election. The Party was represented at the inaugural congress of the Third Communist International in March 1919, and became formally aligned to the Comintern in 1920. See T. K. Derry, *History of Modern Norway* (1973), pp. 310–17.

2 Draft memo for the information of the French government, 2 June 1920 (marked 'never sent' by T. St Q. Hill 21/6/20), CAB 27/82 no. 3. France suffered a series of major strikes in 1919–20, of which the most serious occurred in May 1920 when nearly 400,000 workers came out in sympathy with a railway stoppage. See E. L. Shorter and C. Tilley, *Strikes in France* (1974), pp. 122–7.

3 Geddes to Greenwood and vice versa, 7 and 11 April 1920; Geddes to Bonar Law, 26 April 1920; Note by T. St Q. Hill, 26 April 1920, M.T. 49/167.

4 Max Beloff, 'The Whitehall factor; the role of the higher civil service, 1919–39', in G. Peele and C. Cook (eds), *The Politics of Reappraisal 1918–39* (1975), p. 210.

5 Beloff, op. cit.; H. Roseveare, *The Treasury* (1969), pp. 254ff. There are hints also that the Treasury was equally assertive in matters of social policy. See Bentley B. Gilbert, *British Social Policy 1914–39* (1970), *passim*, and M. Gilbert, *Churchill* (1976), vol. V, chs 4, 13–14.

6 Note by H. Brittain, 9 Aug. 1938, T. 163/114/2. See also Emergency arrangements (Ministry of Transport) 1924–6, T. 163/26/8; Emergency arrangements (Board of Trade) 1925–39, T. 163/118/5.

7 Administrative arrangements for the STO in Scotland were handled wholly by the Scottish Office.

8 L. S. Amery, *My Political Life* (1953), vol. II, p. 217. Roundell's only official honour was a CBE awarded in 1920.

9 Geddes to Hankey, 27 Apr. 1920, M.T. 49/167; conference of ministers, 4 May 1920, CAB 23/21/27(20) appendix II; minutes by A. Neal, 10 May 1920, and Geddes 7 May 1920, M.T. 49/167.

10 Memo by Worthington-Evans, 11 May 1920, CAB 24/105 C.P. 1253.

11   Memoranda by Shortt and McCurdy, 15 and 26 May 1920, ibid., C.P. 1294 and CAB 24/106 C.P. 1345.
12   Conference of ministers, 14 June 1920, CAB 23/21/37(20) appendix II.
13   Geddes to Worthington-Evans and vice versa, 15 and 16 June 1920; Geddes to Law, 7 July 1920; minute by Neal, 12 July 1920; Kellaway to Geddes and vice versa, 23 and 26 July 1920, M.T. 49/167.
14   Report of Macready's committee, 26 Feb. 1920, CAB 24/99 C.P. 796.
15   *Hansard,* 10 June 1920, 130 H.C. Deb. 5., col. 681.
16   Troup to Chief Constables, 2 Dec. 1919 and 3 Mar. 1920, and minute by H. B. Simpson (Assistant Secretary, Home Office), 4 Mar. 1920, H.O. 45/11200, files 375227/46, 64 and 69; Note by Troup, 25 Mar. 1920, and report of protection sub-committee, 26 Mar. 1920, CAB 27/74 T.C. 63 and 76.
17   Memo by CIGS, 25 Mar. 1920, Lloyd George MSS. F/24/2/21, also W.O. 32/5467 no. 59; Report on protection, 30 Apr. 1920, CAB 27/74 T.C. 89; Protection sub-committee report, 16 Aug. 1920, CAB 27/75 T.C. 108; Wilson diary, 26 Aug. 1920.
18   STC 3rd meeting, 15 Jan. 1920, CAB 27/73; memo by Home Office, 15 Mar. 1920, CAB 27/74 T.C. 58; STC 5th – 7th meetings, 23, 25 and 27 Mar. 1920, CAB 27/73.
19   Memo by Neal and Churchill, 15 Mar. and 16 Apr. 1920, CAB 27/74 T.C. 59 and 27/75 T.C. 87; memo by Worthington-Evans, 11 May 1920, CAB 24/105 C.P. 1253; conference of ministers, 14 June 1920, CAB 23/21/37(20) appendix II.
20   Memo by Geddes, 6 July 1920, CAB 24/108 C.P. 1575; Home Affairs Committee 69th and 70th meetings, 12 and 21 July 1920, CAB 26/2; memo by Fisher, CAB 24/109 C.P. 1659; Cabinet meeting, 4 Aug. 1920, CAB 23/22/45(20).
21   STC 10th meeting, and Finance Committee 27th meeting, 12 Aug. 1920, CAB 27/73 and 27/71.
22   Report on revolutionary organisations in the UK, week ending 20 Aug. 1920, CAB 24/111 C.P. 1805; STC 12th and 15th meetings, 18 Aug. and 23 Sept. 1920, CAB 27/73.
23   STC 11th, 13th and 15th meetings, 13 Aug., 2 and 23 Sept. 1920, CAB 27/73; STC sub-committee meetings, Aug.–Sept. 1920, CAB 27/76. Supply department: note on Voluntary Emergency Committees, 21 Aug. 1920, H.O. 45/11075 file 399004/34.
24   Wilson diary, 15 Sept. 1920.
25   STC 17th and 18th meetings, 14 and 15 Oct. 1920, CAB 27/73; Cabinet meeting, 15 Oct. 1920, CAB 23/22/56(20); Wilson diary, 15 and 16 Oct. 1920.
26   Wilson diary, 21 Oct. 1920; STC 20th meeting, 22 Oct. 1920, CAB 27/73.
27   The Commons' debates are in *Hansard,* 133 H.C. Deb. 5s., col. 1226, 1345–50, 1399–1468, 1591–1708, 1779–1892, 2117–8, and 2205; House of Lords' debate, 42 H.L. Deb. 5s., col. 97–123.
28   The 58 noes comprised 43 Labour MPs, 7 Asquithian Liberals, 5 Coalition Liberals and 3 others.

29 Reproduced in Appendix I.

30 Up to July 1982. See Appendix II.

31 Note on emergency expenditure, 12 Dec. 1921, H.O. 45/11075 file 399004/91; memo by Food Controller, 14 Dec. 1920, CAB 24/116 C.P. 2287; memo by Geddes, 7 Jan. 1921, CAB 24/118 C.P. 2432; Conference of ministers, 10 Jan. 1921, CAB 23/24/4(21) appendix I; memo by Geddes, 24 Feb. 1921, CAB 24/120 C.P. 2628; Cabinet meeting, 3 Mar. 1921, CAB 23/24/10(21); minute on emergency finance, 4 Nov. 1926, T. 163/26/8.

32 31 Mar. 1921: STC 24th meeting and sub-committee 34th meeting, CAB 27/73 and 27/76; memo on the 'Zero list', CAB 27/75 T.C. 155; Wilson diary.

33 STC 25th meeting, 1 April 1921, CAB 27/73.

34 *Hansard*, 140 H.C. Deb. 5s., col. 129–236 and 297–370. Much of the debate was spent discussing the general position, but specific emergency regulations were considered in col. 315–70.

35 General Secretary of the National Union of Railwaymen.

36 4 Apr. 1921: Wilson diary; Fisher diary; Cabinet meeting, CAB 23/25/17(21); conference of ministers, CAB 27/110; Jones, *Whitehall Diary*, I, pp. 132–7.

37 6 Apr. 1921: Wilson diary; Lloyd George to Worthington-Evans, Lloyd George MSS. F/16/3/16. See also *War Office War Book* (1927), W.O. 33/1147.

38 Useful accounts of the coal crisis will be found in Alan Bullock, *Ernest Bevin*, I (1960), pp. 150–79, Jones, *Whitehall Diary*, vol. I, pp. 131–53, and Patrick Renshaw, *The General Strike* (1975), pp. 81–96.

39 Wilson diary, 9 Apr. 1921.

40 STC 30th – 34th meetings, 12–16 Apr. 1921, CAB 27/73; conference of ministers, 14 Apr. 1921, CAB 23/25/23(21) appendix III; Amery, *My Political Life*, vol. II, p. 217; Jones, *Whitehall Diary*, vol. I, p. 153; 18 Apr. 1921, Cabinet meeting, CAB 23/25/(21).

41 Jones, *Whitehall Diary*, vol. I, p. 148.

42 Internal protection arrangements committee meetings, 7 and 8 Apr. 1921, CAB 27/110; conferences of ministers, 8, 9 and 13 Apr. 1921, CAB 23/25/22(21) appendix II; Cabinet meeting, 12 Apr. 1921, 23/25/18(21); parliamentary answers concerning the Defence Force, 28 Apr. and 2 May 1921, *Hansard*, 141 H.C. Deb. 5s., col. 371 and 660; Responses of local authorities, Lloyd George MSS. F/189/7.

43 Wilson to Sir Charles Sackville-West (Military Attaché, Paris), 14 Apr. 1921, Wilson MSS. File 12G; account of the incident at Newport from the *Hampshire Telegraph*, n.d., in the Kennedy MSS. (we are grateful to Dr A. Clayton of R.M.A., Sandhurst, for this reference); Wilson diary, 7–9 May 1921; memoranda by the Admiralty, War Office and Air Ministry, 9 Nov. 1921, 20 Jan. and 3 Mar. 1922, CAB 24/129 C.P. 3471, 24/132 C.P. 3646, and 24/134 C.P. 3806.

44 J. M. Cowper, *The King's Own* (1957), vol. III, p. 254; Lord Russell, *That Reminds Me* (1959), pp. 76–7.

45 Statement by the Prime Minister, 8 Apr. 1921, CAB 24/122 C.P. 1812;

conferences of ministers, 7 and 9 Apr. 1921, CAB 23/25/22(21) appendixes IV and IX; Jones, *Whitehall Diary*, vol. I, p. 139; Report by Amery, 12 July 1921, CAB 27/83.

46  STC 35th – 44th meetings, 22 Apr.–1 July 1921, CAB 27/73; note by STC secretary, May 1921, CAB 27/78 T.S.C. 154; Cabinet meeting, 2 June 1921, CAB 23/26/47(21).

47  Weekly Special Branch reports, 30 June and 18 Aug. 1921, CAB 24/125 C.P. 3100 and 24/127 C.P. 3252.

48  Cabinet meeting, 2 Aug. 1921, CAB 23/26/62(21); memoranda by Geddes, Amery and Baldwin, 15, 28 Sept. and 21 Oct. 1921, CAB 24/128 C.P. 3308, 3343, and 24/129 C.P. 3433.

49  Home Affairs Committee 101st and 109th meetings, 29 Nov. 1921 and 30 Mar. 1922, CAB 26/3 and 26/4; STC sub-committee 67th–69th meetings, 6 Dec. 1921–1 Mar. 1922, CAB 27/76; Report on reconstitution of STO, 3 Mar. 1922, CAB 24/134 C.P. 3800; Ministry of Health circular no. 312, 23 May 1922, T. 163/141/1.

50  Note on the Supply Department, 17 May 1922, CAB 27/78 T.S.C. 171; memo. by T. St Q. Hill, 23 June 1922, CAB 27/82.

## Chapter 4  Conservative concern and Labour caution

1  The result of the 1922 general election owed more to the idiosyncrasies of the British electoral system than shifts in public opinion. While the Conservatives won 56 per cent of the seats with 38 per cent of the votes cast, Labour won 23 per cent with 29 per cent of the votes, and the Liberals only 19 per cent of the seats in return for 29 per cent of the votes.

2  Gilbert, *Churchill*, Companion vol. IV, part 3, p. 2110.

3  Robert Blake, *The Unknown Prime Minister* (1955), p. 466.

4  Jones, *Whitehall Diary*, vol. I, pp. 218–19; Stephen Roskill, *Hankey: Man of Secrets*, (1972), vol. II, pp. 304–29; Patrick Gordon Walker, *The Cabinet* (1972), pp. 47–8; draft memo, by Hankey, 23 Oct. 1923 (*sic*, probably 1922), Hankey MSS. CAB 63/35.

5  Blake, *Unknown Prime Minister*, pp. 466–8, 476, 502; 'Review of the year', *Whitaker's Almanack 1924*.

6  Memo by Hankey, 21 Mar. (circulated 7 July) 1923, CAB 24/159 C.P. 160(23).

7  Note by Sir Warren Fisher, 1 June 1923, CAB 24/160 C.P. 260(23).

8  Anderson report, 5 July 1923, CAB 24/161 C.P. 314(23).

9  Cabinet meeting, 11 July 1923, CAB 23/46/36(23); STC meetings, 17 and 24 July, CAB 27/205; Amery diary, 17 July 1923, in *The Leo Amery Diaries* (1980), vol. I, p. 334; R. Rhodes James, *Memoirs of a Conservative* (1969), pp. 169–9.

10  K. Middlemas and J. Barnes, *Baldwin* (1969), p. 172.

11  Cabinet meeting, 31 July 1923, CAB 23/46/42(23); Amery diary, 17 July 1923, in *The Leo Amery Diaries*, vol. I, p. 334; STC meeting, 17 July 1923, CAB 27/205.

12  James, *Memoirs of a Conservative*, pp. 178–9. The STC sub-committee

met in the autumn of 1923, but its minutes do not seem to have survived. Minor revisions were made, for example, to the communications scheme. See draft report by Anderson, 6 Aug. 1925, CAB 23/ 51 C.P. 390(25); Home Office to Admiralty, 7 Dec. 1923, ADM 116/ 3180.

13  STC meeting, 17 July 1923, CAB 27/205; War Office to Home GO-CinCs, 15 Nov. 1923, W.O. 32/5314 no. 23A appendix J; a copy of *Duties in Aid of the Civil Power* is in W.O. 32/3455; War Office – Admiralty letters, Jan.-Feb 1924, ADM 116/3181; War Office to Air Ministry, 10 Jan. 1924, AIR 5/340 no 69A; 'Orders for the RAF (Home) in the event of industrial unrest', 1 Nov. 1923, ADM 116/ 2180.

14  Papers relating to the Special Constables Act, 1923, are in H.O. 45/ 20012 file 435162. Also see above, pp. 17–18.

15  Middlemas and Barnes, *Baldwin*, pp. 214, 229.

16  This result was rather more proportionally representative than Nov. 1922, although the Conservatives remained over-represented with 38 per cent of the vote winning 42 per cent of the seats. The figures for the other two parties were: Liberal, 30 per cent vote and 26 per cent seats; Labour, 31 per cent of both votes and seats.

17  David Marquand, *Ramsay MacDonald* (1977), p. 298.

18  Ibid., pp. 311–12.

19  *The Leo Amery Diaries,* vol. I, p. 371.

20  Marquand, *MacDonald*, p. 298.

21  Renshaw, *The General Strike*, pp. 99–100.

22  Josiah C. Wedgwood, *Memoirs of a Fighting Life* (1941), p. 186; Mac-Donald diary, 3 Feb. 1924, MacDonald MSS. PRO 30/69/1753. The contents of these diaries were, in Ramsay MacDonald's own words, 'meant as notes to guide and revive memory as regards happenings and must on no account be published as they are'.

23  Jones, *Whitehall diary*, vol. I, p. 267; Lord Cavan, 'Recollections Hazy by Happy' (typescript memoirs), chs 9, p. 5 and 10, p. 10, Cavan MSS. CAVN 1/3; War Office to GOCinCs, Home Commands, 26 Jan. 1924, W. 32/5314 no. 23A appendix A.

24  Memo by Lancelot Storr, 10 Dec. 1923, quoted in James, *Memoirs of a Conservative*, pp. 179–80.

25  Ibid., p. 180.

26  See distribution lists in Admiralty papers on the dock and electricians' strikes, 1924, ADM 116/3181, M. 0284/24 and M. 0517/24. These lists, of course, indicate intention rather than implementation and it is possible, though unlikely, that neither Hodges nor Ammon received the relevant documents.

27  Cabinet meeting, 23 Jan. 1924, CAB 23/47/7(24); STC bulletins in MacDonald MSS. PRO 30/69/87; Bullock, *Bevin*, vol. I, p. 236.

28  Bullock, *Bevin*, vol. I, p. 237; Cabinet meetings, 12 and 13 Feb. 1924, CAB 23/47/12(24) and 13(24); STC 1st meeting, 12 Feb. 1924, CAB 27/259.

29  M. A. Hamilton, *Arthur Henderson* (1938), pp. 238–9; memo by Wedg-

wood, CAB 27/259 E.C.(24)1; U.C. Scheme 'P', 19 Nov. 1924, and Admiralty file on 1924 dock strike, ADM 116/3494 and 3181 M.0284/24; note by Board of Trade, 13 Feb. 1924, CAB 27/259 appendix II; STC bulletin no. 2, 22 Feb. 1924, PRO 30/69/87.

30   Memo by Wedgwood, 15 Feb. 1924, CAB 27/259 E.C.(24)1.

31   STC 2nd-5th meetings, 18–20 Feb 1924, CAB 27/259; Cabinet meetings, 18 and 20 Feb. 1924, CAB 23/47/14(24) and 15(24); Draft emergency regulations 1924, H.O. 45/12640 file 453.900/4; Bullock, *Bevin,* vol. I, p. 237.

32   There is a detailed account of the strike in Bullock, *Bevin,* vol. I, pp. 237–42.

33   STC 6th meeting, 24 Mar. 1924, and memo by Wedgwood, 21 Mar. 1924, CAB 27/259. The memo was circulated to the Cabinet as CAB 24/166 C.P. 211(24).

34   26 Mar. 1924; Cabinet meeting, CAB 23/47/22(24); STC 7th meeting, CAB 27/259; Admiralty to CinCs, Plymouth, Portsmouth and Chatham, ADM 116/3181 M.0517/24.

35   Cabinet meeting, 27 Mar. 1924, CAB 23/47/23(24); *Hansard,* 171 H.C. Deb. 5s., cols 1680–84.

36   28 Mar. 1924: Admiralty to CinCs, ADM 116/3181 M.0517/24; STC 8th meeting, CAB 27/259; memo by A. L. Dixon, 1 April 1924, H.O. 45/12640 file 453.900/7.

37   Bullock, *Bevin,* vol. I, p. 241.

38   Home Office circular, 20 Aug. 1924, H.O. 45/12640 file 453.900/4.

39   Renshaw, *The General Strike,* pp. 102, 117.

40   Marquand, *MacDonald,* p. 302.

41   Ibid., pp. 364–5.

42   Ibid., p. 374.

43   Kenneth Lyon to Derby, 20 Nov. 1924, Derby MSS. DER (17)/29/7. Lyon was private secretary to successive Secretaries for War, 1921–4.

44   Memo by Home Secretary, 19 Nov. 1924, CAB 24/168 C.P. 496(24); Cabinet meetings, 26 Nov. and 3 Dec. 1924, CAB 23/49/64 and 65(24); James, *Memoirs of a Conservative,* p. 180.

45   James, op. cit., p. 230.

46   'Duties in aid of the civil power' (draft memo), 7 Nov. 1924, and War Office minutes, 19 June 1925–4 June 1926, W.O. 32/5314, nos. 1A, 13A, 24–36.

47   'Duties in aid of the civil power', 6 July 1925, ibid., no 23A.

48   STC 2nd meeting, 12 Feb. 1925, CAB 27/260.

49   STC 3rd-5th meetings, 4, 14 and 27 May 1925, ibid.

50   There are accounts of this crisis in Renshaw, *The General Strike,* pp. 117–27; Middlemas and Barnes, *Baldwin,* pp. 378–90; and Bullock, *Bevin,* vol. I, pp. 260–78.

51   STC 6th meeting, 15 July 1925, CAB 27/260; Home Office action in H.O. 45/12640 file 453.900/10; memo by Joynson-Hicks, 14 July 1925, CAB 24/174 C.P. 356(25); Ministry of Health action in M.H. 78/22; Cabinet meeting, 29 July 1925, CAB 23/50/41(25).

52   Cabinet meeting, 30 July 1925, CAB 23/50/42(25); Jones, *Whitehall*

*Diary*, vol. I, p. 325; Middlemas and Barnes, *Baldwin*, pp. 384–8; STC 7th meeting, 31 July 1925, CAB 27/260.

53 Baldwin quoted in G. M. Young, *Stanley Baldwin* (1952), p. 99; Cunliffe-Lister quoted in Jones, *Whitehall Diary*, vol. I, p. 325.

54 Memo by Ashley, 6 Aug. 1925, CAB 27/261 S.T. (24)8; Middlemas and Barnes, *Baldwin*, p. 388; Amery, *My Political Life*, vol. II, p. 482.

55 Cabinet meeting, 5 Aug. 1925, CAB 23/50/43(25).

56 Draft report by Anderson, 6 Aug. 1925, CAB 24/174 C.P. 390(25).

57 STC 8th meeting, 7 Aug. 1925, CAB 27/260; J. W. Wheeler-Bennett, *John Anderson* (1962), p. 102; Cabinet meetings, 7 and 13 Aug. 1925, CAB 23/50/44(25) and 45(25).

58 Joynson-Hicks to Baldwin, 25 Aug. 1925, Baldwin MSS., vol. 9, ff. 257–9.

59 The correspondence is in H.O. 45/13364, part I, file 447.130/38.

60 Cabinet meeting, 7 Oct. 1925, CAB 23/51/47(25); Home Office papers on the OMS, including notes of an interview between representatives of the government and the OMS, 7 Dec. 1925, H.O. 45/12336; papers by Minister of Labour and Home Secretary, 2 Nov. and 7 Dec. 1925, CAB 27/261 S.T. (24) 17 and 18; STC 9th meeting, 30 Oct. 1925, CAB 27/260; memo by Minister of Labour, 6 Nov. 1925, CAB 24/175 C.P. 462(25); *Hansard*, 19 Nov. 1925, 188 H.C. Deb. 5s., col. 553–5.

61 STC sub-committee meeting, 1 Oct. 1925, T. 163/141/1; STC 9th meeting, 30 Oct. 1925, CAB 27/260; Cabinet meeting, 18 Nov. 1925, CAB 23/51/53(25); the text of 'Circular 636' is in CAB 24/175 C.P. 441(25); report by Home Secretary, 22 Feb. 1926, CAB 24/178 C.P. 81(26).

62 Reports by Home Secretary, 6 Oct. 1925 and 22 Feb. 1926, CAB 24/176 C.P. 416(25) and 24/178 C.P. 81(26).

63 Chief Civil Commissioner: Sir W. Mitchell-Thomson (Postmaster-General). Divisional Commissioners: Eastern, Sir Philip Sassoon (Under-Secretary for Air); London and Home Counties, W. Cope (Government Whip); Midland, Hon. G. F. Stanley (Parliamentary Secretary, Ministry of Pensions); North-Eastern, D. H. Hacking (Parliamentary Secretary, Ministry of Transport) and Sir H. Kingley-Wood (Parliamentary Secretary, Ministry of Health); North Midland, H. Douglas King (Financial Secretary, War Office); North-Western, C. Hennessy (Government Whip); South Midland, Earl Winterton (Under-Secretary, India Office); South Wales, The Earl of Clarendon (Under-Secretary, Dominions Office); South-Western, Earl Stanhope (Civil Lord, Admiralty). Baldwin MSS., vol. 22, D.3.4. There was a separate divisional arrangement for Scotland under the supervision of the Scottish Office.

64 Board of Trade – Treasury letters, Oct. 1925, T. 163/118/5; Treasury to Home Office, 23 and 26 Oct. 1925, T. 163/26/4 and 163/141/1; minute by Beresford, 3 Dec. 1925, T. 163/26/5.

65 Report by Home Secretary, 22 Feb. 1926, CAB 24/178 C.P. 81(26); 'Volunteer drivers to be sworn in as Special Constables', 12–22 Feb. 1926, H.O. 45/13364 part I, file 447.130/58A.

66 STC standing sub-committee meeting, 17 Feb. 1926, T. 163/141/2.
67 Report by Home Secretary, 22 Feb. 1926, CAB 24/178 C.P. 81(26).

## Chapter 5 The general strike and after

1 *Report of the Royal Commission on the Coal Industry (1925)*. 1926, Cmd 2600.
2 The description of the pre-strike period is generally drawn from the following useful accounts: Renshaw, *The General Strike*, pp. 134–65; Bullock, *Bevin*, vol. I, pp. 289–315; Middlemas and Barnes, *Baldwin*, pp. 393–410; and Jones, *Whitehall Diary*, vol. II, pp. 7–36, 48–51.
3 Lord Citrine, *Men and Work* (1964), pp. 145–53.
4 Jones, *Whitehall Diary*, vol. II, pp. 17–18.
5 Bevin, quoted in Ralph Desmarais, 'The Supply and Transport Committee, 1919–26' (Ph.D. thesis, University of Wisconsin, 1970), p. 213. Chapters V and VI of this thesis contain much interesting material drawn from Labour movement archives.
6 STC 10th meeting, 27 Apr. 1926, CAB 27/260; Notes on STC meeting Baldwin MSS. vol. 22, ff. 2–4; Cabinet meeting, 14 Apr. 1926, CAB 23/52/15(26).
7 Cabinet meeting, 28 Apr. 1926, CAB 23/52/19(26); STC 11th meeting, 29 Apr. 1926, CAB 27/260; James, *Memoirs of a Conservative*, p. 252.
8 Mitchell-Thomson to Baldwin, 29 Apr. 1926, Baldwin MSS, vol. 22, ff. 5–6.
9 Cabinet meeting, 30 Apr. 1926, CAB 23/52/20(26).
10 Ministry of Labour report on General Strike, LAB 27/9. The emergency proclamation and regulations were not actually published in the *London Gazette* until about noon on 1 May.
11 'TUC orders for a General Strike as issued on Saturday, May 1st 1926', 9 May 1926, Hankey MSS. CAB 63/38 no. 9; Citrine to Baldwin, 1 May 1926, CAB 23/52/21(26) appendix II; Citrine, *Men and Work*, p. 157.
12 STC 12th and 13th meetings, 1 May 1926, CAB 27/260; 3 May 1926, *Hansard*, 195 H.C. Deb. 5s., col. 123, 71–2.
13 Cabinet meetings, 2 May 1926, CAB 23/52/21(26) and 22(26).
14 STC 14th meeting, 2 May 1926, CAB 27/260; R. P. Hastings, 'Birmingham', in J. Skelly (ed.), *The General Strike 1926* (1976), p. 210.
15 Cabinet meeting, 2 May 1926, CAB 23/52/23(26); *The Leo Amery Diaries*, vol. I, pp. 450–2.
16 STC 15th meeting, 3 May 1926, CAB 27/260; London District report on General Strike, 18 Nov. 1926, W.O. 32/3455 no. 1A.
17 Ministry of Labour report, LAB. 27/9; Renshaw, *General Strike*, p. 175; Hastings, 'Birmingham', in Skelly, *General Strike*, p. 216; Margaret Morris, *The General Strike* (1976), pp. 62–3.
18 Renshaw, *General Strike*, p. 182; STC Information Bulletins nos 1A and 7, 3 and 9 May 1926, CAB 27/331.
19 London District report, W.O. 32/3455 no. 1A; C. R. Attlee, *As It Happened* (1954), pp. 56–7; STC 17th, 24th and 26th meetings, 5, 12

and 13 May 1926, CAB 27/260; Ministry of Labour report, LAB 27/9; Ministry of Transport report, M.T. 45/249; Drage diary, 10 May 1926, Drage MSS. PP/MCR/99; Summary of Naval service in the General Strike, ADM 116/3494; P. Carter, 'The West of Scotland', and I. MacDougall, 'Edinburgh', in Skelly, *General Strike*, pp. 132, 146.

20 STC 18th and 23rd meetings, 6 and 11 May 1926, CAB 27/260; J. H. Porter, 'Devon and the General Strike', in *International Review of Social History*, vol. XXIII (1978), p. 338; Earl Winterton, *Orders of the Day* (1953), p. 138; memo on Cambridge University volunteers in the General Strike, probably by Sir Joseph Larmor, Baldwin MSS. vol. 22, ff. 88–9.

21 Summary of Naval service, ADM 116/3494; War Office War Book, 1927, pp. 66–9, W.O. 33/1147; H. Francis, 'South Wales', and Hastings, 'Birmingham', in Skelly, *General Strike*, pp. 235 and 218; London District report, W.O. 32/3455 no. 1A; Special Constabulary recruiting, 11 May 1926, H.O. 45/13364, file 447.130/68.

22 London District report, W.O. 32/3455 no. 1A.

23 There is a detailed account of this in Renshaw, *General Strike*, chapters 21 and 22. The principal documentary source is J. C. C. Davidson's report, 24 June 1926, H.O. 45/12431, file 493.234/18, much of which is quoted in James, *Memoirs of a Conservative*, pp. 233–50.

24 Jones, *Whitehall Diary*, vol. II, p. 44.

25 Middlemas and Barnes, *Baldwin*, p. 412.

26 Cabinet meetings, 6 and 8 May, CAB 23/52/24(26) and 27(26); STC 15th meeting, 3 May 1926, CAB 27/260; London District report, W.O. 32/3455 no. 1A.

27 Jones, *Whitehall Diary*, vol. II, p. 38; Cabinet meeting, 7 May 1926, CAB 23/52/25(26). The Postmaster-General's letter to the staff associations is quoted in CAB 129/35 C.P. (49) 143.

28 Cabinet meetings, 7–8 May 1926, CAB 23/52/25(26) and 27(26); *The Leo Amery Diaries*, vol. I, p. 453.

29 CAB 23/52/25(26); Wheeler-Bennett, *Anderson*, p. 106; Churchill to Worthington-Evans, in Gilbert, *Churchill*, Companion vol. V, part I, pp. 709–10.

30 Cabinet committee on the CCR, 1926, CAB 27/323; Lord Ismay, *Memoirs* (1960), p. 57; Cabinet meeting, 7 May 1926, CAB 23/52/26(26); War Office War Book, 1927, pp. 68–9, W.O. 33/1147.

31 London District report, W.O. 32/3455 no. 1A; STC 20th meeting, 8 May 1926, CAB 27/260; Morris, *General Strike*, pp. 74–5. Basil Liddell Hart claimed that it was his idea to use gas if necessary, Liddell Hart, *Memoirs*, (1965), vol. I, p. 143.

32 STC 22nd meeting, 10 May 1926, CAB 27/260; James, *Memoirs of a Conservative*, p. 251; London district report, W.O. 32/3455 no. 1A; Bullock, *Bevin*, vol. I. pp. 323–4; Jones, *Whitehall Diary*, vol. II, p. 53; Renshaw, *General Strike*, chapter 24 discusses the end of the strike.

33 Wheeler-Bennett, *Anderson*, p. 106; James, *Memoirs of a Conservative*, p. 252.

34 Harold Nicolson, *King George V* (1952), p. 418. The announcement,

published in the *British Gazette* on 8 May, had been issued to the services the previous day. See Admiralty circular, 7 May 1926, ADM 1/8697.

35   Jones, *Whitehall Diary*, vol. II, pp. 44–7; *The Leo Amery Diaries*, vol. I, pp. 453–4; Cabinet meeting, 10 May 1926, CAB 23/52/28(26).

36   Bullock, *Bevin*, vol. I, pp. 327–40; Cabinet meeting, 12 May 1926, CAB 23/52/30(26); STC 25th-29th meetings, 12–17 May 1926, CAB 27/260; London District report, W.O. 32/3455 no 1A; Circular telegram to Civil Commissioners, 17 May 1926, Baldwin MSS. vol. 23, f. 54; Instructions for disbandment of CCR, 14 May 1926, T. 163/26/4.

37   STC 31st and 32nd meetings, CAB 27/260. In April 1926 over 5½ million tons of coal had been exported. See *Mines Department Statistical Summary*, 1927, Cmd 2927.

38   Future of the OMS, 17 May-30 June 1926, H.O. 45/12336, file 484.910/20; Chief Commissioner's report, T. 163/26/8.

39   Report by Lt. Col. E. F. Strange, 24 May 1926, Baldwin MSS., vol. 22, ff. 92–106.

40   Ministry of Labour report, by C. W. K. MacMullan, LAB 27/9. MacMullan was a successful playwright under the name of C. K. Munro.

41   Middlemas and Barnes, *Baldwin*, pp. 444–52; Churchill to Baldwin, 10 Jan. 1927, in Gilbert, *Churchill*, companion vol. V, part I, p. 912; Bullock, *Bevin*, vol. I, p. 378; Alan Anderson, 'The Labour Laws and the Cabinet Legislation Committee', in *Bulletin of the Society for the Study of Labour History* no. 23 (Autumn 1971), pp. 37–54.

42   Gilbert, *Churchill*, V, p. 234; Note on Emergency Services Vote, Mar. 1928, POWE 10/73; Treasury – Board of Trade correspondence, Aug. 1926-Apr. 1927, T. 163/118/5; STC finance sub-committee minute no. 1, 7 May 1926, T. 163/141/2.

43   Metropolitan Police reports on Special Constabulary, MEPO 2/3135, file 22/C.G.S./286/D; Chief Civil Commissioner's report, T. 163/26/8.

44   London District report, W.O. 32/3455 no. 1A.

45   AG to Secretary of State, 5 Nov. 1926, and memo by Col. Dobbie, 28 Jan. 1927, W.O. 32/3456 nos 5A and 1A.

46   War Office to Home Office, 30 Jul. 1927, ibid., no. 26A.

47   War Office minutes and correspondence, Feb.-Aug. 1927, W.O. 32/3513; Cabinet meeting, 16 Nov. 1927, CAB 23/55/56(27).

48   Papers concerning the CCR scheme, Feb. 1928-Nov. 1932, W.O. 32/3513.

49   STC standing sub-committee meeting, 26 July 1926; STC general purposes committee 1st meeting, 22 Sept. 1926; minute by J. B. Beresford, 4 Nov. 1926, T. 163/26/8.

50   Minutes by J. Rae (establishment officer) and A. E. Watson, 8 and 10 Nov. 1926, ibid.

51   STC general purposes committee 2nd meeting, 1 Dec. 1926, and Treasury minutes, Dec. 1926, ibid.; STC 33rd meeting, 24 Mar. 1927, CAB 27/260; Returns of expenditure, 10 May and 18 Dec. 1928, T. 163/118/6.

52 Interim report of general purposes committee, 12 Jan. 1927, CAB 27/
   261 S.T. (24) 24; STC 33rd meeting, 24 Mar. 1927, CAB 27/260.
53 STC 34th meeting, 27 July 1927, CAB 27/260.
54 2nd interim report of general purposes committee, 27 May 1929, CAB
   27/261 S.T. (24) 28.
55 Conservative, 260 seats; Liberal, 59; Labour, 287; others, 9.
56 V. L. Allen, *Trade Unions and the Government* (1960), pp. 241–4.
57 Ibid., pp. 248–9. See also *Report from Standing Committee 'C'*, 3 Mar.
   1931, House of Commons Papers, 1931 (67).
58 Viscount Swinton, *I Remember* (1948), p. 47. Extensive searches, concentrated especially in the Home Office and Ministry of Health papers,
   have failed to unearth the records of the STO's central secretariat,
   which might have thrown some light on this period.
59 Instructions for the preparation of civil emergency schemes, 30 Mar.
   1930, W.O. 33/1216; memo on London Electric Power Scheme, 5 May
   1931, and note by Civil Assistant, Admiralty Operations Division, 27
   May 1931, ADM 116/3494.
60 Minute by H. W. Naish, 5 Mar. 1928. In the event, the Public
   Accounts Committee made only sporadic enquiries concerning emergency expenditure. See *First and Second Reports from the Select Committee of Public Accounts*, 1 Mar. and 10 July 1928, House of Commons
   Papers, 1928 (35 and 99).
61 There is a good account of this period in R. Skidelsky, *Politicians and
   the Slump* (1967), especially chapters 13 and 14.
62 Hankey diary, 20 Sept. 1931, Hankey MSS. HNKY 1/7; memo by Sir
   John Anderson, 15 Dec. 1931, CAB 27/477 S.T. (31) 2; Cabinet
   meeting, 9 Sept. 1931, CAB 23/68/55(31).
63 See Ministry of Transport minutes, Sept.-Oct. 1931, M.T. 45/249.
64 National Government, 554 (Conservative, 469; Liberal, 33; National
   Liberal, 35; National Labour, 13); Independent Liberal, 4; Labour,
   52; others, 5.
65 National Government, 429 (Conservative, 386; National, 2; National
   Liberal, 33; National Labour, 8); Liberal, 21; Labour, 154; others, 5.
66 Memo by Anderson, 15 Dec. 1931, circulated 7 Jan. 1932, and STC
   meeting, 15 Jan. 1932, CAB 27/477 S.T. (31) 2 and S.T. (31) 1st
   meeting; memo by Home Secretary, 16 Jan. 1932, CAB 24/227 C.P.
   26(32); Cabinet meeting, 26 Jan. 1932, CAB 23/70/8(32); Ministry of
   Transport to Treasury, 28 Nov. 1932, T. 163/114/1.
67 Civil Commissioners and their districts, 17 Dec. 1932, CAB 27/477
   S.T. (31) 4. The 'odd man out' was Dr J. H. Morris-Jones, Liberal
   National MP for Denbigh. He became an Assistant Government Whip
   in 1932.
68 Board of Trade to Treasury, 23 Feb. 1938, T. 163/118/5; Treasury to
   Ministry of Health, 5 May 1934, T. 163/118/6; memo on STO prepared
   in Home Office, 15 June 1945, T. 221/19; memo by Home Secretary,
   24 Feb. 1936, CAB 24/477 S.T. (31) 9.
69 STC meeting, 4 Mar. 1936, CAB 27/477 S.T. (31) 3rd meeting.

70 War Office minutes and correspondence, Jan. 1937-May 1939, W.O. 32/3513.

71 R. J. Hammond, *Food* (1951), vol. I, pp. 11, 37; memo by Hankey and Fisher, 23 May 1938 and memo on modifications necessary in the Civil Emergency Organisation, 26 July 1938, CAB 3/7, papers 287-A and 293-A; CID 326th and 331st meetings, 2 June and 27 July 1938, CAB 2/7.

72 In Feb. 1938 Anderson, standing on an Independent National ticket, was elected an MP for the Scottish Universities. Later the same year he was appointed Lord Privy Seal, with special responsibility for civil defence.

## Chapter 6 Mr Attlee faces the dilemma

1 Introduction to D. N. Chester (ed.), *Lessons of the British War Economy* (1951), p. 2.

2 The account of wartime labour affairs which follows is, unless otherwise noted, drawn from: W. K. Hancock and M. M. Gowing, *British War Economy* (1949); H. M. D. Parker, *Manpower* (1957); and Eric Wigham, *Strikes and the Government* (1976).

3 War Office minute, 15 Dec. 1949, W.O. 32/13300 no. 2. For Regulation 6, see *Manual of Military Law* (9th edn, 1968), part II, section V, para. 27.

4 Bevin did not become an MP until June 1940, when he was elected unopposed for Central Wandsworth.

5 Bullock, *Bevin* (1967), vol. II, p. 15.

6 Parker, *Manpower*, p. 456.

7 Ibid., p. 457.

8 'Legal proceedings against strikers under Order 1305', LAB 10/998. The first prosecution was on 13 Feb. 1941; the last on 6 Jan. 1945.

9 'Facts to be faced in the present state of industrial relations', c. Sept. 1943, LAB 10/281.

10 'Unofficial strike at Clydesbridge Works, Nov. 1939', and 'Dock Labour: stoppages of work in Newcastle district, Jan.-July 1942', LAB 10/103 and 10/184.

11 Bullock, *Bevin*, vol. II, p. 269; minutes by Harold Emmerson (Chief Industrial Commissioner), 28 Sept. and 23 Nov. 1943, and Ministry of Labour press release, 18 Apr. 1944, LAB 10/281: '1945: Review of emergency regulations', LAB 10/548.

12 Maxwell to Sir Edward Bridges (and others), 4 June 1945, and memo on the STO, 15 June 1945, T. 221/19.

13 Minutes of meeting held at the Home Office, 19 June 1945, T. 221/19.

14 Conservative and National, 210 seats; Liberal, 12; Labour, 393; others, 25.

15 Hugh Dalton, *High Tide and After* (1962), p. 297; Lord Butler, *The Art of the Possible* (Penguin, 1973), p. 95; Ede diary, 17 Mar. 1946, Ede MSS. 390/2/11. Some notes in the Attlee Papers suggest that the

Prime Minister originally considered appointing Ede Minister of Labour. See MS, Attlee dep. 18.

16  *Hansard*, 15 Aug. 1945, cols 55–7.
17  Circular Home Office letter and draft memo, 2 Aug. 1945, T. 221/19; Ede to Attlee, 22 Aug. 1945, PREM 8/673.
18  Note by Brook, 31 Aug. 1945, PREM 8/673.
19  Lord Moran, *Winston Churchill* (1966), p. 758. A severe judgment of Brook, who had the misfortune of being educated at a direct grant grammar school, and not at Eton.
20  Minutes by Attlee, and Leslie Rowan (PM's principal private secretary) to R. J. P. Hewison (Ede's private secretary), 3 Sept., 8 and 11 Oct. 1945, PREM 8/673. The ministers nominated for the new committee were, respectively, Ede, Alfred Barnes, Sir Ben Smith, Bevan, Isaacs, Sir Stafford Cripps and Joseph Westwood.
21  Cabinet meeting, 9 Oct. 1945, CAB 128/1/39(45); *The Times*, 24 and 31 Jul., 1 and 2 Aug. 1945.
22  *The Times*, 10 Oct. 1945.
23  *The Times*, 9 and 13 Oct. 1945; Susan Barnes, *Behind the Image* (1974), pp. 224–5; George Thayer, *The British Political Fringe* (1965), pp. 128–30.
24  Cabinet meeting, 15 Oct. 1945, CAB 128/1/41(45).
25  We are indebted to the labour journalist, Mr Peter Paterson, for this story.
26  Cabinet meeting, 26 Oct. 1945, CAB 128/1/46(45); memo by Alfred Barnes, 25 Oct. 1945, CAB 129/3 C.P.(45) 248.
27  C.P.(45) 248.
28  Cabinet meeting, 26 Oct. 1945, CAB 128/1/46(45).
29  Note by Brook, 26 Oct. 1945, PREM 8/673.
30  Circular note by Miss J. J. Nunn, 29 Oct. 1945, and minutes of meeting in the Home Office, 10 Nov. 1945, T. 221/19.
31  Quotation from The King's Diary, 27 Nov. 1945, in J. W. Wheeler-Bennett, *King George VI* (1958), p. 652.
32  Admiralty correspondence, Jan.-Mar. 1946, ADM 1/21476.
33  Draft memo by Home Secretary, Nov. 1945, T. 221/19; final version, GEN 116/1, 22 Jan. 1946, PREM 8/673.
34  Committee GEN 116 1st meeting, 29 Jan. 1946, PREM 8/673.
35  Draft statement of principle, 8 Feb. 1946, and GEN 116 2nd meeting, 13 Feb. 1940, PREM 8/673.
36  Note by Brook, 7 Mar. 1946, PREM 8/673.
37  Cabinet meeting, 8 Mar. 1946, PREM 8/673, and CAB 128/7/22(46).
38  It received the Royal Assent on 22 May 1946.
39  Private information.
40  Note of Home Office conference, 17 May 1946, and Treasury correspondence, Sept.-Oct. 1946, T. 221/19; memo by Minister of Labour, 9 Sept. 1946, S. & T. (L.S.) App. I to Report, T. 221/20; Admiralty correspondence, Sept.-Oct. 1946, ADM 1/21476.
41  Home Office papers on CCR, July-Sept. 1946, H.O. 45/20536 file 658.780/11.

42   Minute by C. A. Birtchnell, and minutes of meeting in Ministry of Transport, 9 Jan. 1947, M.T. 33/404.
43   Committee Gen 165 1st (and only) meeting, 10 Jan. 1947, CAB 130/16; note on emergency transport arrangements, and minutes of inter-departmental meeting, 10 Jan. 1947, M.T. 33/404.
44   'Transport strike 1947: police reports', H.O. 45/23174.
45   Cabinet meeting, 13 Jan. 1947, CAB 128/9/5(47); note by Brook, 13 Jan. 1947, PREM 8/672; Attlee to Dalton and vice versa, 13 and 15 Jan. 1947, PREM 8/673. Dalton in any case felt strongly that too much time was generally wasted in Cabinet committees. See Dalton diary, 1 Aug. 1946 and 17 Jan. 1947, Dalton MSS. I/34 f.35 and I/35 f.2.
46   Papers by Attlee and Shinwell, IEC (47) 1 and 3, and IEC (47) 1st meeting, 15 Jan. 1947, CAB 134/353.
47   Minutes of official committee and progress report, 15/16 Jan. 1947, and note by C. J. Macdonald, 16 Jan. 1947, M.T. 33/404.
48   Cabinet meeting, 16 Jan. 1947, CAB 128/9/7(47).
49   IEC(47) 2nd meeting, CAB 134/353; Cabinet meeting, 16 Jan. 1947, CAB 128/9/8(47); Attlee to service ministers, 17 Jan. 1947, PREM 8/672.
50   Minutes by Brook and Attlee, 23 and 27 Jan. 1947, PREM 8/673; Cabinet memo by Brook, 29 Jan. 1947, CAB 129/16 C.P.(47) 45.
51   Ede to Attlee and vice versa, note by Brook, March 1947, PREM 8/673.
52   Memo by Home Secretary, IEC(47) 5, 19 Mar. 1947, CAB 134/353; Admiralty correspondence, Feb.-Mar. 1947, ADM 1/21476.
53   IEC(47) 5, and IEC(47) 3rd meeting, 26 Mar. 1947, CAB 134/353.
54   Prime Ministerial minutes, April 1947, PREM 8/673.
55   Memo by Secretary for War, EC(47) 3, 20 May 1947, CAB 134/175.
56   Cabinet meeting, 17 April 1947, CAB 128/9/37(47); note by Brook, 28 Apr. 1947, CAB 129/18 C.P.(47) 138. The new committee comprised: Home Secretary (chairman), Secretary of State for Scotland, Attorney-General, and the Ministers of Defence, Labour and National Service, Fuel and Power, Health, Transport, and Food.

## Chapter 7   Strikers and subversives

1   Memo by Minister of Transport, 30 April 1947, CAB 134/175 EC(47)1; Cabinet meetings, 14 and 29 April, CAB 128/9/36(47) and 41(47).
2   CAB 134/175 EC (47)1; Emergencies Committee (EC) 1st meeting, 1 May 1947, CAB 134/175.
3   Private information; only a few thin files survive in the Ministry of Health papers concerning emergency arrangements. They are all pre-war and relate only to internal Ministry matters.
4   Note by Home Secretary, 13 May 1947, CAB 134/175 EC(47)2; for Bevan in office see Michael Foot, *Aneurin Bevan*, vol. II *1945–60* (1973), *passim*.
5   Memo by Secretary for War, 20 May 1947, CAB 134/175 EC(47)3.
6   EC(47) 2nd – 4th meetings, 23, 25 and 30 June 1947, CAB 134/175.

7   T. 221/20 reports of sub-committees: Labour supply, May 1947.

8   Ibid., Communications, 13 June 1947.

9   Ibid., Publicity, 22 June 1947.

10  Ibid., Transport, June 1947, and Food and essential supplies, 7 July 1947.

11  Report by Newsam, 20 Sept. 1947, EC(47)4, and EC(47) 5th meeting, CAB 134/175.

12  Henry Pelling, *A History of British Trade Unionism* (2nd edn, 1971), p. 222.

13  Home Office circular letter, 23 June 1948, enclosing memo for Regional Chairmen, T. 221/20.

14  Ness Edwards to Attlee, 18 June 1948, PREM 8/1086; Report on service assistance, 6 July 1948, ADM 1/20963; EC(48) 1st meeting, 21 June 1948, CAB 134/175; Cabinet meeting, 22 June 1948, CAB 128/13/41(48).

15  Admiralty report on dock strike, 12 July 1948, ADM 1/21121; EC(48) 2nd meeting, 23 June 1948, CAB 134/175; *Hansard*, 23 June 1948, 452 H.C. Deb. 5s. col. 1364–5.

16  Meeting of ministers, 24 June 1948, CAB 130/38 GEN 240/1st meeting. Bevin's strong line was fully supported by Deakin, see Cabinet meeting, 25 June 1948, CAB 128/13/43(48).

17  Admiralty report, 12 July 1948, ADM 1/21121; minute by Newsam, 25 June 1948, PREM 8/1086; memo by Ness Edwards, 27 June 1948, CAB 129/28 C.P. (48) 168.

18  28 June 1948; Cabinet meeting, CAB 128/13/44(48); Ministry of Food report and text of P.M.'s broadcast, PREM 8/1086; *Hansard*, 452 H.C. Deb. 5s. col. 1840; EC(48) 3rd meeting, CAB 134/175.

19  Cabinet meeting, 29 June 1948, CAB 128/13/45(48); Admiralty report, 12 July 1948, Admiralty to War Office and vice versa, 28 Oct. and 1 Dec. 1948, ADM 1/21121.

20  EC memoranda, 21 Sept. and 4 Oct. 1948, CAB 134/175 EC(48) 2 and 3; Fuel and Power sub-committee report, 31 Dec. 1948, T. 221/20.

21  Pelling, *British Trade Unionism*, pp. 227–8; Isaacs to Morrison and vice versa, 30 Dec. 1948 and 6 Jan. 1949, CAB 124/1194: Isaacs to Attlee, 28 Feb. 1949, and minute by A. Johnston, 18 March 1949, PREM 8/1082.

22  Draft statement by Isaacs, Feb. 1949, and Isaacs to Attlee, 28 March 1949, PREM 8/1082; Cabinet meeting, 21 March 1949, CAB 128/15/21(49).

23  EC(49) 1st meeting, 12 April 1949, CAB 134/176; Cabinet meeting, 13 April 1949, CAB 128/15/27(49).

24  There is a detailed account of the background to the strike enclosed with a memo by the Secretary for Commonwealth Relations, 10 June 1949, CAB 130/46 GEN 291/2.

25  Meeting of ministers, 23 May 1949, CAB 130/46 GEN 291/1.

26  Report by Newsam, EC(49)1 and EC(49) 2nd meeting, 25 May 1949, CAB 134/176.

27  Cabinet meetings, 26 and 30 May, 2 June 1949, CAB 128/15/38(49)–40(49); EC(49) 3rd-6th meetings, 26 May-1 June 1949, CAB 134/176.

28  Prime Ministerial minutes, 7–13 June 1949, PREM 8/1081; meeting of ministers, 10 June 1949, CAB 130/146 GEN 291/2; *The Times*, 13–16 June 1949.

29  Memo by Newsam, 18 June 1949, CAB 134/176 EC(49)4; memo by Ede, 23 June 1949, CAB 129/35 C.P.(49) 143; Cabinet meeting, 30 June 1949, CAB 128/15/43(49); note by Brook, 29 June 1949, CAB 21/2245.

30  Memo by Noel-Baker, 4 July 1949, CAB 130/46 GEN 291/4; EC(49) 8th and 9th meetings, 4 and 6 July 1949, CAB 134/176.

31  Ammon to Attlee and Ede to Attlee, 5 July 1949, PREM 8/1081; EC(49) 9th meeting, 6 July 1949, CAB 134/176.

32  EC(49 10th and 11th meetings, 7 and 8 July 1949, CAB 134/176.

33  Cabinet meeting, 11 July 1949, CAB 128/16/45(49); memo by Shawcross, CAB 129/35 C.P.(49) 148.

34  Shawcross to Attlee, 13 July 1949, and memo by J. Nunn, 21 July 1949, PREM 8/1081; EC(49) 13th meeting, 15 July 1949, CAB 134/176.

35  Cabinet meetings, 18 and 21 July 1949, CAB 128/16/46(49) and 47(49); Prime Ministerial minutes and correspondence, July 1949, PREM 8/1081.

36  EC(49) 14th and 15th meetings, 20 and 22 July 1949, CAB 134/176; *The Times*, 23 July 1949. Sir Alan Lascelles (private secretary to The King) to Attlee, 26 July 1949, PREM 8/1081.

37  Reports of working party on air transport, 2 July 1949, and Publicity sub-committee, 30 June 1949, T. 221/20.

38  Memo by Isaacs, 19 Sept. 1949, CAB 129/36 C.P.(49) 192; Cabinet meeting, 18 Oct. 1949, CAB 128/16/59(49).

39  Electricity strikes, 1949, LAB 10/856; EC(49) 16th and 17th meetings, 2 and 12 December 1949, CAB 134/176; Note by Home Office, 13 Dec. 1949, PREM 8/1290; Notes on meeting at Ministry of Fuel and Power, 23 Jan. 1950, POWE 10/462; Cabinet meeting, 15 Dec. 1949, CAB 128/16/72(49).

40  War Office file on employment of service personnel on civil duties, Sept. 1949 – June 1950, W.O. 32/13300; *Hansard*, 21 Feb. 1951, 484 H.C. Deb. 5s., col. 1301.

41  Gaitskell to Attlee, 24 Dec. 1949, PREM 8/1290.

42  Bridges to Attlee, 18 Jan. 1949, PREM 8/1290.

43  Meeting of ministers, 24 Jan. 1950, CAB 130/58 GEN 314/1; Gaitskell diary, 27 Jan. 1950, quoted in Philip M. Williams, *Hugh Gaitskell* (1979), p. 172.

44  Conservative and National, 298; Liberal, 9; Labour, 315; Others, 3.

45  EC(Official)(50) 2nd-4th meetings, 20–25 April 1950, CAB 134/178; EC(50) 1st meeting, 20 April 1950, PREM 8/1287; Cabinet meetings, 20–25 April 1950, CAB 128/17/22(50)-25(50).

46  Memo by Ede, 26 April 1950, CAB 129/39 C.P.(50) 84; Cabinet meetings, 2 Apr. and 1 May 1950, CAB 128/17/26(50) and 27(50).

47 Minute for Attlee, 2 May 1950, PREM 8/1289.
48 EC(O)(50) 9th-13th meetings, 26 June-4 Jul. 1950, CAB 134/178; Cabinet meetings, 29 June–4 Jul. 1950, CAB 128/18/41(50) to 43(50); memo by Ede, 5 July 1950, CAB 129/41 C.P.(50) 158.
49 Cabinet meetings, 6 and 10 July 1950, CAB 128/18/43(50) and 44(50); EC(O)(50) 14th-19th meetings, 7–13 Jul. 1950, CAB 134/178.
50 EC(O)(50) 22nd-24th meetings, 2–6 Oct. 1950, CAB 134/178.
51 Noel-Baker to Attlee, 3 Aug. 1950, PREM 8/1275.
52 EC(O)(50) 19th meeting, CAB 134/178.
53 Cabinet meetings, 16 Aug. and 14 Sept. 1950, CAB 128/18/54(50) and 58(50); Wigham, *Strikes and the Government*, pp. 104–5.
54 EC(M)(50) 9th meeting, 11 Dec. 1950, and note of informal meeting, 19 Jan. 1951 (circulated 7 Feb.) EC(M)(51)1, CAB 134/177.
55 Cabinet meeting, 12 Feb. 1951, CAB 128/19/13(51).
56 EC(O)(51) 7th-13th meetings, Mar.-Oct. 1951, CAB 134/179; memorandum on accommodation of servicemen in London, 26 Oct. 1951, CAB 134/179, EC(O)(51)5; EC(M)(51) meeting, 21 May 1951, CAB 134/177.
57 Conservative and National, 321; Liberal, 6; Labour, 295; Others, 1.
58 EC(O)(51) 14th meeting, 29 October 1951, CAB 134/179.

## Chapter 8 Contemporary civil contingency planning

1 Lord Birkenhead, *Walter Monckton* (1969), p. 274.
2 Anthony Seldon, *Churchill's Indian Summer* (1981), p. 203.
3 Ibid., p. 202.
4 Ibid., p. 199.
5 *The Times*, 21–4 and 26–8 Oct. 1953.
6 Ibid., 30 May 1955; see 31 May-15 June for details of the railway strike.
7 Robert Fisk, *The Point of No Return* (1975), p. 87.
8 *Hansard*, 13 and 21 June 1955, col. 276–90 and 1150.
9 Birkenhead, *Monckton*, p, 303.
10 Seldon, *Churchill's Indian Summer*, p. 123; David Carlton, *Anthony Eden* (1981), p. 346.
11 Harold Macmillan, *Riding the Storm 1956–1959* (1971), p. 346.
12 Allen, *Strikes and the Government*, pp. 201–12.
13 See appendix I.
14 *Hansard*, 20 Feb. 1964, col. 1409–45. The bill received the Royal Assent on 10 June.
15 Ibid., 20 June 1966, col. 38–54.
16 Richard Crossman, *The Diaries of a Cabinet Minister* (1975), vol. I, p. 524.
17 *The Times*, 17 May 1966; Harold Wilson, *The Labour Government 1964–70* (Penguin edn, 1971), pp. 299–300.
18 Crossman, *Diaries*, vol. I, p. 534.
19 Ibid., p. 524.
20 Wilson, *The Labour Government*, p. 300; Geoffrey Marshall, 'The

armed forces and industrial disputes in the United Kingdom', *Armed Forces and Society* (1979), p. 275.

21  *Hansard*, 22 June 1966, col. 584–90.
22  Ibid., 28 June 1966, col. 1612–27.
23  Wilson, *The Labour Government*, p. 311.
24  Chapman Pincher, *Inside Story* (1978), p. 137.
25  Lord Wigg, *George Wigg* (1972), p. 332; *The Times*, 30 June 1966.
26  See appendix II.
27  Denis Barnes and Eileen Reid, *Strikes and the Government* (1980), pp. 145–6.
28  Douglas Hurd, *An End to Promises* (1979), p. 99.
29  Marshall, 'Armed forces', p. 276.
30  There is a detailed account of the Saltley affair in Richard Clutterbuck, *Britain in Agony* (Penguin rev. edn 1980), ch. 4.
31  Ralph Harris and Brendon Sewill, *British Economic Policy, 1970–74: Two Views* (1975), p. 50.
32  Quoted, with original italics, from an interview with Scargill in *New Left Review*, no. 92 July-Aug. 1975, p. 13.
33  Reginald Maudling, *Memoirs* (1978), pp. 160–1.
34  Barnes and Reid, *Strikes and the Government*, pp. 161–2: *Hansard*, 8 Aug. 1972, col. 1580–1655.
35  *The Times*, 9 May 1981.
36  There are accounts of this period in Barnes and Reid, *Strikes and the Government*, pp. 174–88, and Clutterbuck, *Britain in Agony*, chs 6–9.
37  Conservative, 297 seats; Liberal, 14; Labour, 301; others, 23.
38  Conservative, 277; Liberal, 13; Labour, 319; others, 26.
39  There is an excellent, detailed account of the UWC strike in Fisk, *The Point of No Return*.
40  Harold Wilson, *Final Term: the Labour Government of 1974–1976* (1979), pp. 75–6.
41  Marshall, 'Armed forces', pp. 276–7.
42  *State Research Bulletin*, vol. 3 no. 14 (Oct.-Nov. 1979), p. 16.
43  Ibid., p. 21.
44  Joel Barnett, *Inside the Treasury* (1982), p. 171.
45  *Trade Union Immunities*, 1981 Cmnd 8128; *The Times*, 5 Nov. 1981.
46  *Hansard*, 17 July 1980, col. 1750.

## Chapter 9  Strikebreaking past and future

1  *Hansard*, 26 July 1949, col. 2264.
2  Quoted from *The Times*, 30 May 1919, in K. G. J. C. Knowles, *Strikes* (1952), p. 135.
3  The obligations of both government and trade unions are discussed in L. J. Macfarlane, *The Right to Strike* (1981), especially ch. 6.
4  This point is made in C. J. Whelan, 'Military intervention in industrial disputes', *Industrial Law Journal*, vol. 8 (1979), pp. 222–34.
5  A book written by a serving officer and published in 1972 (Lt.-Col. J. C. M. Baynes, *The Soldier in Modern Society*) discusses 'aid to the civil

community', but does not mention 'aid to the civil ministries' in any shape or form.

6 *The Times*, 23 Nov. 1979.

# Bibliography

A  *Primary sources*

1  Official records at the Public Record Office, Kew. Coded as in references

| ADM | Admiralty |
| AIR | Air Ministry |
| CAB | Cabinet Office |
| H.O. | Home Office |
| LAB | Ministry of Labour |
| MEPO | Metropolitan Police |
| M.H. | Ministry of Health |
| M.T. | Ministry of Transport |
| POWE | Ministry of Fuel and Power |
| PREM | Prime Minister's Private Office |
| T. | Treasury |
| W.O. | War Office |

2  *Private papers*

Attlee Papers, at the Bodleian Library, Oxford.
Baldwin Papers, at Cambridge University Library.
Cavan Papers, at Churchill College, Cambridge.
Dalton Papers, including Dalton diary, at the British Library of Political and Economic Science, London.
Derby Papers, at Liverpool City Library.
Drage Papers (microfilm), including General Strike diary, at the Imperial War Museum.
Ede Papers, including Ede diary, at Surrey Record Office, Kingston upon Thames.
Fisher Papers, including Fisher diary, at the Bodleian Library, Oxford.
Haig Papers, including Haig diary, at the National Library of Scotland, Edinburgh.

Hankey Papers: collections at Churchill College, Cambridge (including Hankey diary), and the Public Record Office.

Kennedy Papers, copies made available courtesy of Dr A. Clayton, Royal Military Academy, Sandhurst.

Lloyd George Papers, at the House of Lords Record Office.

MacDonald Papers, including MacDonald diary, at the Public Record Office.

Rawlinson Papers, including Rawlinson diary, at the National Army Museum.

Wilson Papers, including Wilson diary (microfilm), at the Imperial War Museum.


B   *Secondary sources*

Allen, V. L., *Trade Unions and the Government*, Longmans, 1960.

Amery, L. S., *My Political Life*, vol. II, Hutchinson, 1953.

Amery, L. S., *The Leo Amery Diaries* (ed. J. Barnes and D. Nicholson), vol. I, Hutchinson, 1980.

Anderson, Alan, 'The Labour Laws and the Cabinet Legislation Committee', *Bulletin of the Society for the Study of Labour History*, no. 23 (Autumn 1971), pp. 37–54.

Attlee, C. R., *As it Happened*, Heinemann, 1954.

Barnes, Denis, and Reid, Eileen, *Strikes and the Government*, Heinemann Educational Books, 1980.

Barnes, Susan, *Behind the Image*, Cape, 1974.

Barnes, Trevor, 'Special Branch and the first Labour Government', *Historical Journal*, vol. 22 (1979), pp. 941–51.

Barnett, Joel, *Inside the Treasury*, Andre Deutsch, 1982.

Baynes, J. C. M., *The Soldier in Modern Society*, Eyre Methuen, 1972.

Beloff, Max, 'The Whitehall factor: the role of the higher civil service, 1919–1939', in Peele, G., and Cook, C. (eds), *The Politics of Reappraisal 1918–39*, Macmillan, 1975, pp. 209–31.

Bevan, Aneurin, *In Place of Fear*, Heinemann, 1952.

Birkenhead, Lord, *Walter Monckton*, Weidenfeld & Nicolson, 1969.

Blake, Robert, *The Unknown Prime Minister*, Eyre & Spottiswoode, 1955.

Bullock, Alan, *Ernest Bevin*, 2 vols, Heinemann, 1960 and 1967.

Butler, Lord, *The Art of the Possible*, Penguin, 1973.

Carlton, David, *Anthony Eden*, Allen Lane, 1981.

Carter, P., 'The West of Scotland', in Skelly, *The General Strike*, pp. 111-39.

Chester, D. N. (ed.), *Lessons of the British War Economy*, Cambridge University Press, 1951.

Citrine, Lord, *Men and Work*, Hutchinson, 1964.

Cline, Peter K., 'Eric Geddes and the "experiment" with businessmen in government, 1915–22', in Brown, K. D. (ed.), *Essays in Anti-Labour History*, Macmillan, 1974.

Clutterbuck, Richard, *Britain in Agony*, rev. edn, Penguin, 1980.

Cowper, J. M., *The King's Own*, vol. III, privately printed, 1957.

Crossman, Richard, *The Diaries of a Cabinet Minister*, vol. I, Hamish Hamilton and Cape, 1975.

Dalton, Hugh, *High Tide and After*, Muller, 1962.

Derry, T. K., *A History of Modern Norway, 1814–1972*, Clarendon Press, 1973.

Desmarais, Ralph H., 'The Supply and Transport Committee, 1919–26', unpublished Ph.D. thesis, University of Wisconsin, 1970.

Desmarais, Ralph H., 'Lloyd George and the development of the British Government's strikebreaking organisation', *International Review of Social History*, vol. 20 (1975), pp. 1–15.

Desmarais, Ralph H., 'The British Government's strikebreaking organisation and Black Friday', *Journal of Contemporary History*, vol. 6 (1971), pp. 112–27.

Desmarais, Ralph H., 'Strikebreaking and the Labour Government of 1924', *Journal of Contemporary History*, vol. 8 (1973), pp. 165–75.

Fairlie, J. A., *British War Administration*, New York, Oxford University Press, 1919.

Fisk, Robert, *The Point of No Return*, Deutsch and Times Books, 1975.

Foot, Michael, *Aneurin Bevan*, vol. II, Davis-Poynter, 1973.

Francis, H., 'South Wales', in Skelly, *The General Strike*, pp. 232–60.

Gilbert, Bentley B., *British Social Policy 1914–39*, Batsford, 1970.

Gilbert, Martin, *Winston S. Churchill*, vols IV and V, Heinemann, 1975 and 1976; Companion Volume IV (Parts 1–3), 1977, and Companion Volume V (Part 1), 1979.

Gordon Walker, Patrick, *The Cabinet*, rev. edn, Fontana, 1972.

Hamilton, M. A., *Arthur Henderson*, Heinemann, 1938.

Hammond, R. J., *Food: vol. I, The Growth of Policy*, HMSO and Longmans, 1951.

Hancock, W. K., and Gowing, M. M., *British War Economy*, HMSO, 1949.

Harris, Ralph, and Sewill, Brendon, *British Economic Policy 1970–74: Two Views*, Institute of Economic Affairs, 1975.

Hastings, R. P., 'Birmingham', in Skelly, *The General Strike*, pp. 208–31.

Hurd, Douglas, *An End to Promises*, Collins, 1979.

Ironside, Lord, *Archangel 1918–19*, Constable, 1953.

Ismay, Lord, *Memoirs*, Heinemann, 1960.

Jones, Thomas, *Whitehall Diary* (ed. Keith Middlemas), vols I and II, Oxford University Press, 1969.

Kendall, Walter, *The Revolutionary Movement in Britain*, Weidenfeld & Nicolson, 1969.

Knowles, K. G. J. C., *Strikes*, Blackwell, 1952.

Liddell Hart, B. H., *Memoirs*, vol. I, Cassell, 1965.

Lloyd George, David, *War Memoirs*, Odhams edn, n.d.

Lloyd, T. O., *Empire to Welfare State*, 2nd edn, Oxford University Press, 1979.

MacDougall, I., 'Edinburgh', in Skelly, *The General Strike*, pp. 140–59.

Macfarlane, L. J., *The Right to Strike*, Penguin, 1981.

Macmillan, Harold, *Riding the Storm 1956–1959*, Macmillan, 1971.

Macready, Sir Nevil, *Annals of an Active Life*, vol. II, Hutchinson, 1924.

Marquand, David, *Ramsay MacDonald*, Cape, 1977.

Marshall, Geoffrey, 'The armed forces and industrial disputes in the United Kingdom', *Armed Forces and Society*, vol. 5 (1979), pp. 270–80.

Maudling, Reginald, *Memoirs*, Sidgwick & Jackson, 1978.

Middlemas, Keith, *Politics in Industrial Society*, Deutsch, 1979.

Middlemas, Keith, and Barnes, J., *Baldwin*, Macmillan, 1969.

Moran, Lord, *Winston Churchill: the Struggle for Survival 1940–1965*, Constable, 1960.

Morris, Margaret, *The General Strike*, Penguin, 1976.

Nicolson, Harold, *King George V*, Constable, 1952.

Parker, H. M. D., *Manpower*, HMSO and Longmans, 1957.

Pelling, Henry, *A History of British Trade Unionism*, 2nd edn, Penguin, 1971.

Pettee, George, 'Revolutionary typology and process', in Friedrich, C. J. (ed.), *Revolution*, New York, Atherton Press, 1969.

Pincher, Chapman, *Inside Story*, Sidgwick & Jackson, 1978.

Pollard, Sidney, *The Development of the British Economy, 1914–1961*, 2nd edn, Edward Arnold, 1969.

Porter, J. H., 'Devon and the General Strike, 1926', *International Review of Social History*, vol. 23 (1978), pp. 333–56.

Renshaw, Patrick, *The General Strike*, Eyre Methuen, 1975.

Reynolds, G. W., and Judge, A., *The Night the Police went on Strike*, Weidenfeld & Nicolson, 1968.

Rhodes James, Robert, *Memoirs of a Conservative*, Weidenfeld & Nicolson, 1969.

Roseveare, H., *The Treasury*, Allen Lane, 1969.

Roskill, Stephen, *Hankey: Man of Secrets*, vol. II, Collins, 1972.

Russell, Lord, *That Reminds Me*, Cassell, 1959.

Seldon, Anthony, *Churchill's Indian Summer*, Hodder & Stoughton, 1981.

Shorter, E. L., and Tilley, C., *Strikes in France*, Cambridge University Press, 1974.

Skelly, Jeffrey (ed.), *The General Strike 1926*, Lawrence & Wishart, 1976.

Skidelsky, R., *Politicians and the Slump*, Macmillan, 1967.

Swinton, Viscount, *I Remember*, Hutchinson, 1948.

Taylor, A. J. P., *Beaverbrook*, Penguin, 1974.

Taylor, A. J. P., *English History 1914–1945*, Penguin edn, 1970.

Thayer, George, *The British Political Fringe*, Blond, 1965.

Ward, Stephen R., 'Intelligence surveillance of British ex-servicemen, 1918–20', *Historical Journal*, vol. 16 (1973), pp. 179–88.

Wedgwood, Josiah C., *Memoirs of a Fighting Life*, Hutchinson, 1941.

Wheeler-Bennett, J. W., *King George VI*, Macmillan, 1958.

Wheeler-Bennett, J. W., *John Anderson*, Macmillan, 1962.

Whelan, C. J., 'Military intervention in industrial disputes', *Industrial Law Journal*, vol. 18 (1979), pp. 222–34.

Wigham, Eric, *Strikes and the Government*, Macmillan, 1976.

Williams, Philip M., *Hugh Gaitskell*, Cape, 1979.

Wilson, Harold, *Final Term: the Labour Government 1974–1976*, Weidenfeld & Nicolson/Michael Joseph, 1979.

Wilson, Harold, *The Labour Government 1964-70*, Penguin, 1971.
Winterton, Earl, *Orders of the Day*, Cassell, 1953.
Young, G. M., *Stanley Baldwin*, Hart-Davis, 1952.

## C   *Principal works of reference used*

Butler, David, and Sloman, Anne, *British Political Facts 1900–1979*, 5th edn, Macmillan, 1980.
Craig, F. W. S., *British Parliamentary Election Statistics 1918–1968*, Political Reference Publications, 1968.
*Dictionary of National Biography.*
*Who's Who.*
*Whitaker's Almanack.*

# Index